Egyptian Archaeology

Edited by

Willeke Wendrich

WILEY-BLACKWELL

A John Wiley & Sons, Ltd., Publication

Blackwell Publishing was acquired by John Wiley & Sons in February 2007. Blackwell's publishing
program has been merged with Wiley's global Scientific, Technical, and Medical business to form
Wiley-Blackwell.

Registered Office
John Wiley & Sons Ltd, The Atrium, Southern Gate, Chichester, West Sussex, PO19 8SQ,
United Kingdom

Editorial Offices
350 Main Street, Malden, MA 02148-5020, USA
9600 Garsington Road, Oxford, OX4 2DQ, UK
The Atrium, Southern Gate, Chichester, West Sussex, PO19 8SQ, UK

For details of our global editorial offices, for customer services, and for information about how to
apply for permission to reuse the copyright material in this book please see our website at
www.wiley.com/wiley-blackwell.

Library of Congress Cataloging-in-Publication Data

Egyptian archaeology / edited by Willeke Wendrich.
    p. cm. – (Blackwell studies in global archaeology)
  Includes bibliographical references and index.
  ISBN 978-1-4051-4987-7 (hardcover : alk. paper) – ISBN 978-1-4051-4988-4 (pbk. : alk.
paper) 1. Egypt–Civilization–To 332 B.C. 2. Egypt–Antiquities. 3. Excavations
(Archaeology)–Egypt. I. Wendrich, Willeke.
  DT61.E3335 2010
  932–dc22

                                                                        2009035903

A catalogue record for this book is available from the British Library.

Set in 10/12.5pt Plantin by Toppan Best-set Premedia Limited

01   2010

Contents

List of Tables and Figures

Tables

Figures

Notes on Contributors

Wolfram Grajetzki (Honorary Research Associate of the Institute of Archaeology, UCL, Ph.D. Humboldt University Berlin, Germany, 1998, on the highest state officials in Middle Kingdom Ancient Egypt, published Berlin 2000) was involved in several excavations in Egypt and Pakistan; from 1993 to 2000 he took part in a database project in Berlin, collecting Ancient Egyptian coffins and sarcophagi, from 2000 to 2003 he worked on the online teaching resource "Digital Egypt for Universities" (UCL, London). He is currently a publisher and is the author of several books (e.g. *Burial Customs in Ancient Egypt*, 2003; *The Middle Kingdom of Ancient Egypt*, 2006).

Fekri A. Hassan (Ph.D. Southern Methodist University, 1973) is Emeritus Petrie Professor of Archaeology, Institute of Archaeology, University College London. His research focuses on the management of Egyptian heritage, climate change and Nile floods, origins and dynamics of Egyptian civilization, and archaeological theory. He directed fieldwork at Siwa, Baharia, Naqada, and Kafr Hassan Dawood. He edited the *African Archaeological Review* and is currently co-directing a geoarchaeological project in Middle Egypt and involved in the development of cultural heritage educational programs.

Stan Hendrickx (Ph.D. Katholieke Universiteit Leuven, Belgium, 1989) is Lecturer in Art History at the Department of Fine Arts and Architecture of the Provinciale Hogeschool Limburg (Hasselt, Belgium). Since 1977, he has participated in excavations and surveys at Elkab, Adaïma, Mahgar Dendera, Deir el-Bersha, Hierakonpolis, on the Abu Ballas Trail, in the Khufu region, and at Kom Ombo–Aswan. Besides ceramology, his research focuses on the Predynastic period up to the end of the Old Kingdom. He edits the *Analytical Bibliography of the Prehistory and the Early Dynastic Period of Egypt and Northern Sudan*, updated yearly in *Archéo-Nil*.

Dirk Huyge (Ph.D. Katholieke Universiteit Leuven, Belgium, 1995) is Curator of the Egyptian Collection at the Royal Museums of Art and History in Brussels (Belgium). Initially specializing in the Late Palaeolithic and Mesolithic of Northwest Europe and Northeast Africa, he has developed a keen interest in Egyptian archaeology and early iconography. He began working in Egypt for the Committee for Belgian Excavations in Egypt in 1978, when he was engaged in the excavations of a Late Predynastic and Early Dynastic cemetery in Elkab (Upper Egypt). He currently directs the fieldwork at Elkab and is also in charge of rock art surveys at el-Hosh and Qurta, both in Upper Egypt. From 2001 till 2006, he co-directed an excavation project on Easter Island (Chile), with Nicolas Cauwe. He is a fellow member of the Belgian Royal Academy for Overseas Sciences.

David Jeffreys (Ph.D. London, 1999) is Senior Lecturer in Egyptian Archaeology at University College London Institute of Archaeology, and Field Director of the Egypt Exploration Society's Survey of Memphis. He has worked in the UK and the Near East (Syria, Jordan, Egypt) since 1970. He has published extensively on Memphis, and on aspects of fieldwork, excavation and survey, and more recently on landscape archaeology. Current research (with Dr. Judith Bunbury, University of Cambridge) centers on climate change, the behavior of the Nile, and the human response from the late fourth millennium onwards.

E. Christiana Köhler (Ph.D. Heidelberg/Germany, 1993) teaches Egyptology and Egyptian Archaeology at Macquarie University in Sydney. She has been working on excavations in Europe, the Middle East, and Egypt for almost thirty years. Her main areas of research are Prehistoric and Early Dynastic Egypt as well as Egyptian archaeology and society. Currently, she is directing excavations in the large Early Dynastic necropolis at Helwan in order to investigate the chronology, material culture, and social development pertinent to Egypt's first capital city, Memphis.

Mark Lehner (Ph.D. Yale University, 1990) heads Ancient Egypt Research Associates, a non-profit research organization that he cofounded in 1985, and is a research associate at the Oriental Institute, University of Chicago. He has worked at Giza since 1978 and produced the first detailed map of the Sphinx and a survey control network and grid over the Giza Plateau. In 1988 he launched an interdisciplinary survey and excavation project at the city of the pyramid builders, which is ongoing. Since 1995 his team has taught a field school for inspectors of the Egyptian Supreme Council of Antiquities that is integrated within the excavations. Lehner is author of *The Complete Pyramids* (1997).

Janet Richards (Ph.D. University of Pennsylvania, 1992) is Associate Professor of Egyptology and Associate Curator for Dynastic Egypt at the University of Michigan in the Department of Near Eastern Studies and the Kelsey Museum of Archaeology. She has directed a large-scale excavation and survey project in the Middle Cemetery at Abydos since 1995. She is the co-editor of *Order, Legitimacy,* *and Wealth in Ancient States* (2000) and author of *Society and Death in Ancient Egypt: Mortuary Landscapes of the Middle Kingdom* (2005).

Thomas Schneider (Ph.D. Basel, 1996) is Associate Professor of Egyptology and Near Eastern Studies in the Department of Classical, Near Eastern, and Religious Studies of the University of British Columbia, Vancouver. He was a research professor of the Swiss National Science Foundation at the Institute of Egyptology of the University of Basel, and Professor of Egyptology at Swansea University, Wales. His main interests are in Egyptian history and philology and cultural relations in the Ancient Near East. He is the founding editor of the *Journal of Egyptian History* and the Editor-in-Chief of the series "Culture and History of the Ancient Near East."

John H. Taylor (Ph.D. Birmingham University, UK, 1985) is Assistant Keeper in the Department of Ancient Egypt and Sudan, The British Museum, London. He has carried out studies on various aspects of Egyptian funerary practices, in particular the iconography of coffins and the investigation of mummies; his research interests also encompass Egyptian history and culture in the Third Intermediate Period, the technology of bronze casting, and the history of Egyptology. He has participated in fieldwork at Luxor and Amarna and has served on the committees of the Egypt Exploration Society, the Society for Libyan Studies, and the Association for the Study of Travel in Egypt and the Near East.

Josef Wegner (Ph.D. University of Pennsylvania, 1996) is Associate Professor of Egyptian Archaeology in the Department of Near Eastern Languages and Civilizations at the University of Pennsylvania, and Associate Curator of the Egyptian Section, Penn Museum of Archaeology and Anthropology. He specializes in the archaeology of Egypt's Middle Kingdom. Since 1994 he has directed excavations on the complex of Senwosret III at South Abydos as part of the combined Penn–Yale Institute of Fine Arts Expedition to Abydos. He also works in association with David Silverman and Jennifer Wegner on the Penn Museum's excavations at the Teti pyramid cemetery at Saqqara.

Willeke Wendrich (Ph.D. Leiden University, The Netherlands, 1999) is a professor of Egyptian Archaeology at the University of California, Los Angeles, associated with the Department of Near Eastern Languages and Cultures and the Cotsen Institute of Archaeology. She co-directed the Berenike excavations with Steven E. Sidebotham from 1994 to 2002. From 2003 onwards she has co-directed a large survey, excavation, and site preservation project in the Fayum, with René Cappers. She directed a survey project in the Yemeni highlands and participated in the Catal Hoyük excavations in Turkey. She is the Editor-in-Chief of the online *UCLA Encyclopedia of Egyptology* (UEE).

T. G. Wilfong (Ph.D. University of Chicago, 1994) is Associate Professor of Egyptology in the Department of Near Eastern Studies, University of Michigan, and Associate Curator for Greco-Roman Egypt at the Kelsey Museum of

Archaeology. He has published and lectured extensively on a variety of topics relating to the social and economic history of Greco-Roman and Late Antique Egypt, and has curated a number of exhibitions on related themes. He is currently working on the permanent installation of Greco-Roman Egyptian material for the Kelsey Museum's new exhibition wing.

Penelope Wilson (Ph.D. Liverpool University, UK, 1991) is Lecturer in Egyptian Archaeology in the Department of Archaeology, Durham University (UK). She has been Field Director of the Sais Mission for the Egypt Exploration Society (EES) and Durham University from 1997 to the present and is an active member of the Delta Survey Project of the EES. She was formerly the Assistant Keeper in the Department of Antiquities, Fitzwilliam Museum, Cambridge (UK) from 1992 to 1999 and has worked on many field projects throughout Egypt since 1983. Her research interests include religious life in Egypt, settlement archaeology, and Ptolemaic hieroglyphic texts.

Series Editors' Preface

This series was conceived as a collection of books designed to cover central areas of undergraduate archaeological teaching. Each volume in the series, edited by experts in the area, includes newly commissioned articles written by archaeologists actively engaged in research. By commissioning new articles, the series combines one of the best features for readers, the presentation of multiple approaches to archaeology, with the virtues of a text conceived from the beginning as intended for a specific audience. While the model reader for the series is conceived of as an upper-division undergraduate, the inclusion in the volumes of researchers actively engaged in work today will also make these volumes valuable for more advanced researchers who want a rapid introduction to contemporary issues in specific sub-fields of global archaeology.

Each volume in the series will include an extensive introduction by the volume editor that will set the scene in terms of thematic or geographic focus. Individual volumes, and the series as a whole, exemplify a wide range of approaches in contemporary archaeology. The volumes uniformly engage with issues of contemporary interest, interweaving social, political, and ethical themes. We contend that it is no longer tenable to teach the archaeology of vast swaths of the globe without acknowledging the political implications of working in foreign countries and the responsibilities archaeologists incur by writing and presenting other people's pasts. The volumes in this series will not sacrifice theoretical sophistication for accessibility. We are committed to the idea that usable teaching texts need not lack ambition.

Blackwell Studies in Global Archaeology aims to immerse readers in fundamental archaeological ideas and concepts, but also to illuminate more advanced concepts, exposing readers to some of the most exciting contemporary developments in the field.

Lynn Meskell and Rosemary A. Joyce

Note on Transliteration and Transcription

Ancient Egyptian is written in different scripts: hieroglyphs, used in the early manuscripts and monumental inscribed texts; hieratic, a cursive script mostly used in manuscripts; Demotic, which is both a language phase and a further developed cursive script; and Coptic, the latest phase of Egyptian written in the Greek alphabet with the addition of several signs for consonants that do not exist in Greek.

Hieroglyphic and hieratic texts can be written in two major forms in our Latin script: either as transliteration or as transcription. Similar to Arabic, the ancient Egyptian writing system mostly represents the consonants rather than the vowels of a word. The transliteration represents these consonants, using additional symbols for sounds that are not known in the European languages, while the transcription tries to convey the pronunciation of a word in normal Latin script. This is the difference between writing the same word as ꜥnḫ (transcription) or *ankh* (transliteration). For this volume, single terms, or terms that are quite generally known, are rendered in transcription (*ankh*), while more complex titles, terms, and sentences are given in transliteration (ꜥnḫ), following Allen's transcription conventions (Allen 2000).

REFERENCE

Allen, James Paul. 2000. Middle Egyptian: An Introduction to the Language and Culture of Hieroglyphs. Cambridge: Cambridge University Press.

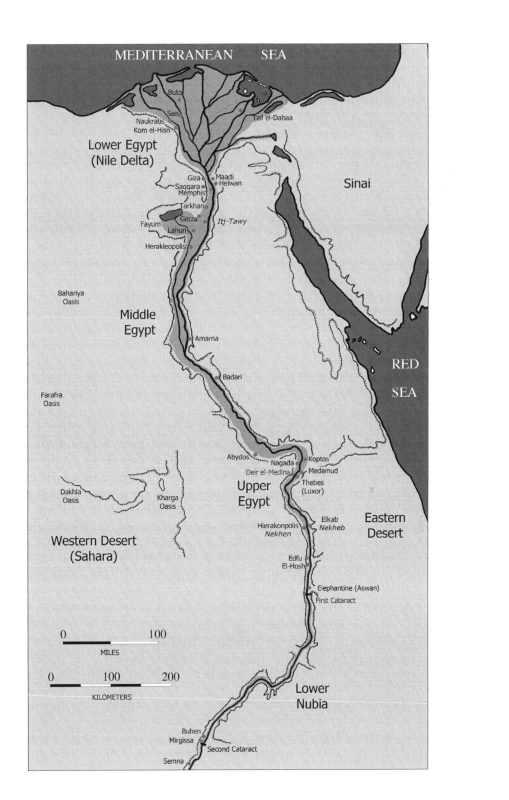

1

Egyptian Archaeology

From Text to Context

Willeke Wendrich

The Egyptian archaeological record, with its almost intact temples, vividly decorated tombs, relatively undisturbed desert sites, and incredible preservation of organic materials, makes for an embarrassment of riches. The effect of this was that until recently Egyptian archaeologists felt that this wealth of information simply spoke for itself. Wood, papyrus, textiles, basketry, leather, zooarchaeological and archaeobotanical remains were recovered without difficulty. The uniqueness of their preservation was often not even recognized and exploited, because these organic materials represented only a fraction of an impressive material culture, and an equally impressive textual record. No need was felt for an approach that would explicate research questions, and provide a theoretical framework to enhance our knowledge. Consequently, very few publications on Egyptian archaeology specifically mention method or theory. In the 1960s and 1970s, while much of world archaeology was participating in, or at least aware of, the debates, Egyptian archaeology was ancillary to Egyptology (Andrén 1998:37–38). In both scholarly and popular publications one encounters unspecified claims phrased as "archaeology has shown that … ." The misunderstanding here is, of course, that archaeology is not capable of "showing" something. It is the careful weighing of information, and the explication of how data are collected and taken to relate to the research question and theoretical context, which contributes to our knowledge. This naïve take on what archaeology is, and how it relates to our (re)construction of the past, was an effect of Egyptology's focus on textual sources, while archaeology's task was to provide illustrations or support for the texts.

Even today some Egyptologists question how archaeological theory would improve our understanding of the ancient Egyptian culture, while the question should of course be turned around: how flawed is our understanding *without* theory? Every archaeologist works from assumptions, concepts, and a knowledge base which has been built up during years of training, experience, growing insights, and perceptions, both related and unrelated to the academic world. Theory is the explication – in the sense of rendering explicit – the mutual agreement and sharing of these concepts, in order to not only record, but also interpret remnants of the past.

Theory enables us to observe more than the obvious and allows us to go beyond the anecdotal, based on unsystematic examples, without a methodical incorporation of the ancient and modern context. At the same time theory prevents simplified, naïve conclusions, and by explicating our assumptions and methods, we render our work open to criticism.

In fact every archaeologist uses theory, but often this is an implicit or even subconscious process. Phenomena are explained and "facts" are seen in the light of particular ideas, or discourses, which are all-encompassing to the point that they are never questioned. Several examples from the late nineteenth- and early twentieth-century work of Petrie, Reisner, and Caton Thompson serve to illustrate this.

Sir William Matthew Flinders Petrie (1853–1942) was ahead of his time in his interest in the material culture of daily life, and his meticulous excavation and recording methods. He excavated sites dating to the Predynastic and the Greco-Roman periods, and anything in between. His explanations of the cultural development of ancient Egypt, however, followed the trends of the time. Based on Darwin's theory, archaeologists developed an evolutionary approach, which made a developmental distinction between races and cultures. Famous Egyptologists such as Lepsius, Reisner, and also Petrie were strongly influenced by this deterministic evolutionary approach. Lepsius divided the population of Africa into distinct, separately evolved Hamitic and Negroid populations, which translated into a division into Negroids and Caucasians, with the former being considered an "inert" race, while the cultural impetus came from the latter (Trigger 2006:202). Based on this division, Petrie claimed that the pyramids could not have been built by people stemming from the African Neolithic. He, and others, surmised a "Dynastic Race," a distinct group which migrated from the Near East, and replaced the Predynastic population of Egypt. This explanation of cultural change was based on two concurrent theoretical premises: first that the ancient African "inert" race was not capable of rapid improvement, and secondly that cultural changes were the effect of migration, rather than local developments. Many others adhered to similar theories, and as recently as the 1960s the transition from Predynastic to Dynastic Egypt was characterized as follows: "Authorities are divided in their opinions as to the reason for this sudden cultural advance, but it would seem probable that the principal cause was the incursion of a new people into the Nile Valley" (Emery 1961:38). Reisner's writings are blatantly racist:

> The social mingling of the three races, the Egyptian, the Nubian, and the negro in one community, would naturally be supposed to have a marked cultural effect on the community. The most obvious result in all such cases is of course the production of offspring of mixed blood who do not inherit the mental qualities of the highest race, in this case the Egyptian. (Reisner 1923:556)

The explicit judgment of ethnic groups goes hand in hand with implicit suppositions about gender, when he continues the previous statement with: "But a portion of the offspring will perpetuate the qualities, physical and mental, of the male parent, and thus the highest race will not necessarily disappear, even after some generations" (Reisner 1923:556).

Others, who did not adhere to racist theories, nevertheless were children of their time and the then current paradigm. Gertrude Caton Thompson (1888–1985) started working with Petrie in 1921. She had received archaeological training in London, after having experienced the joy and excitement of prehistoric archaeology at a Neolithic excavation in France during two holiday periods. In Egypt she was one of the few archaeologists concentrating on survey work and the study of lithic assemblages, and consequently she discovered the late Neolithic settlement of Hammamiya. In 1923 she started working in the Fayum, excavating several Neolithic sites located in the desert north of Lake Qarun, and recording activity areas at two different elevations, related to a series of ancient lake level variations. She worked together with the geologist Elinor Gardner, who meticulously plotted the ancient shore lines and the elevations at which the cultural remains were found. It was clear that the lake level, at present at 44 m below sea level, had been 46–56 m higher in the past. Shore lines were found at around 2–4 and 10–12 m above sea level. Caton Thompson surmised that this enormous ancient lake had gradually diminished in size. She remarked as noteworthy that the oldest culture, the Fayum A, found at the highest level, was more advanced than the Fayum B culture, which was found in relation to the 2–4 m shore line and thus had to be later in date. Her explanation of cultural change by population movements and replacements, rather than internal developments, was typical for the time (Trigger 2006:207). This presupposition led her to suggest that the primitive Fayum B people overran, or conquered, the more advanced Fayum A population, destroying the more advanced knowledge of the Fayum A in their wake (Caton Thompson and Gardner 1934; Wendrich 2008). Later research by Wendorf and Schild (1976) established that the lake level changes were much more complicated than suggested by Caton Thompson and Gardner, and, supported by radiocarbon dates, they recognized that the "primitive" Fayum B culture actually appeared to be almost 800 years older than the Neolithic, pottery-producing Fayum A culture. Caton Thompson was an excellent archaeologist, whose fieldwork, methods, and publications were ahead of her time. She recorded the observations on the ground precisely, but failed to account for her premises by implicitly accepting two theories: first that the lake diminished in size over time, and second that changes in the material culture implied an influx of a different cultural group. The use of theory gave her observations a greater explanatory power, but resulted in incorrect conclusions.

In 1929 Caton Thompson was faced with an extreme example of irrational archaeological explanation, based on racist theory. She was asked to research the stone monuments of Greater Zimbabwe, an archaeological and political minefield. Based on similar arguments as outlined above, it had been maintained that the impressive stone monuments of Greater Zimbabwe must have been built by a non-African population. This fitted the need of the white population to negate the occurrence of a local ancient civilization. It was suggested, based on no archaeological information whatsoever, that the stone structures had been built by King Salomo, or the Queen of Sheba, in any case a "race" that had crossed the Red Sea from the Arabian Peninsula to Africa. Level-headed Caton Thompson studied the stratigraphy and published a report which unequivocally stated that the Greater Zimbabwe monuments had been built by a local Bantu population, and were a few centuries, rather than a few millennia, old (Caton Thompson 1931, 1983; Wendrich 2008).

In these examples theory functions as the overarching principle, the main ideas which lead to a particular explanation or interpretation of the data, and at the same time determine the method used and type of data collected. Studying the development of Egyptian archaeology shows that we can discern two main aspects which dictate changes in approach over time: the relation between theory and data, and the shift in research questions and interests.

Although Herodotus' characterization of Egypt as the gift of the river (Book II, 5) is often quoted, a much later standard work that not only enhanced, but radically changed the understanding of the Nile as central to Egyptian civilization was Karl Butzer's *Early Hydraulic Civilization in Egypt* (1976). In his introduction, Butzer explicitly states that he has taken an ecological perspective and he defines the purpose of his study to be an examination of "the emergence of a floodplain civilization in the Egyptian Nile Valley, viewed as a test case of man–land relationships" (1976:2). The book highlights environmental parameters, technological developments, and settlement patterns. This was a new approach to Egyptian archaeology, dominated by publications of excavated sites, richly illustrated, but often merely descriptive. Discussions of broader archaeological issues were rare. A successful attempt to incorporate archaeology into an overview of Egyptian history, while emphasizing the social and economic aspects, rather than the "traditional" historical narrative that concentrates on the king, chronology, and religion, was *Ancient Egypt: A Social History* (Trigger et al. 1983). This book meticulously referenced the archaeological reports on which the authors' descriptions were based. Their purpose was to stress a continuous development through time, an approach contrary to a tendency among Egyptologists to admire ancient Egypt, but despise the contemporary country and its inhabitants. In his seminal work *Ancient Egypt: Anatomy of a Civilization*, Kemp (2006) goes further, and attempts to tease out the ancient Egyptian attitudes and ways of thinking. His emphasis is on material culture, on the meaning it carries, and on how in ancient Egypt material, textual, and visual culture were continually reinterpreted. Kemp characterizes his efforts as the creation of an imaginary world, a marquee in the wind, pegged to the ground through the use of references to the extensive Egyptological literature (2006:3). His is a mildly relativist approach, allowing for multiple alternative explanations or narrations, but based on an enormous amount of archaeological material and a deep knowledge of the literature. In fact, his approach is well in keeping with the ancient Egyptian attitude to reality, which encompassed a firm belief in order, defined differently in various contexts or periods, and an enormous flexibility in allowing non-harmonized parallel truths.

Relativism is often criticized as leading to unsubstantiated speculation, with as a main argument that interpretations based on speculation "become conduits through which all sorts of unexamined prejudices and personal biases are introduced into archaeology. They ignore the alternative course of remaining silent regarding matters that are unknowable" (Trigger 2006:518). Reflecting Wittgenstein's seventh position ("Wovon man nicht sprechen kann, darüber muß man schweigen", in Ogden's translation: "What we cannot speak about we must pass over in silence" [Biletzki and Matar 2009]), Trigger criticized the construction of insufficiently supported interpretations. Wittgenstein's position, however, focused not on archaeology, but on belief systems dealing, for instance, with ideas about, and beliefs in, the afterlife. It is a reaction against both unfounded theories on supernatural phenomena and the scientific optimism of the late nineteenth century that everything will be explained by rational scientific means. One can, however, certainly speak about all aspects related to archaeology that could potentially be known. Not the personal biases of researchers are a threat to scholarship, but the presentation of those biases as an objective account. Archaeology from an explicit and methodical bias, on the other hand, has proven to provide important insights. The development and increased acceptance of gender theory has clarified that certain points of view have been systematically excluded from the archaeological interpretation (Wilfong, this volume). In the early days, when gender theory was not an accepted approach, groups of scholars and the approach itself have been actively and sometimes viciously attacked as non-scientific. A similar argument can be made for the discussion around multivocality. Granting a voice to individuals or groups whose participation has been actively prevented enables an open debate on personal or political interests, which are always an integral part of archaeology (Meskell 1998; Reid 2002; Wendrich in press). The local population, New Age devotees, school children, and tourists have their own perspectives and interests (see my Epilogue to the volume). This is not the same, however, as accepting every opinion as equally valid in a scholarly or scientific context and debate. Instead archaeologists who give serious attention to multivocality recognize that academic endeavors are one among several ways of considering ancient remains, and are not isolated, but firmly embedded in society. For archaeological work that takes place outside the country of origin of the researcher, and Egyptology is an excellent example, archeologists are embedded in their academic surrounding, their home, and their host societies.

In Egypt the integration of scientific research methods has developed in the last century. A shift in focus from architecture to stratigraphy marks this development most clearly. Multi-disciplinary excavation and survey projects which use sound stratigraphical excavation methods, and scientific study of context, soil, objects, animal bones, human bones, and botanical materials, have become the standard. The publications, however, for the most part have been descriptive. It is not until quite recently that publications have explicitly stated that the excavation of a cemetery has as its objective the understanding of social stratification or the gender-related division of labor (Wilfong, this volume).

The reinterpretation of materials and assemblages that were excavated over a century ago, and are often part of badly provenanced museum collections, has shown real promise as well. Good examples are David Wengrow's overview of prehistoric and Predynastic Egypt (2006), and Lynn Meskell's work on Deir el-Medina (1999, 2002, 2004). The Greco-Roman period (332 BCE–395 CE), much like the Late Period (Wilson, this volume) long considered as "un-Egyptian" and an age of decline "after the pharaohs," has recently been reflected on in a number of thought-provoking publications. An increased interest in cultural diversity, the problematic issue of ethnicity, and the expression of identity in the material culture has resulted in several recent books which advocate a new approach to the archaeological materials, but also a new understanding of ancient textual accounts

(Johnson 1992; Riggs 2005; Vasunia 2001; see also Grajetzki and my chapter on "identity and personhood" in this volume). These tend to gravitate towards the Greco-Roman period because of the fascinating Egyptian–Hellenistic interaction. This is a relatively recent period, and many excavations of cemeteries, temples, and settlement sites have yielded Greco-Roman material overlying the remains of earlier periods. Yet most of the contributors to this volume only refer to the Greco-Roman period in passing. This was an explicit editorial choice because this period displays enormous breaks in tradition. Where change in the earlier periods was always couched to resemble a continuation of age-old traditions, developments in the Greco-Roman period merely pay lip service to such conventions.

Stressing the role of archaeology in understanding ancient Egypt is of urgent importance to correct several biases which are the result of the overwhelming presence of the textual and visual record on the walls of temples and tombs, as well as in scholarship. The idea that Egyptian Pharaonic culture suddenly "emerged," a perception that gave rise to the racist theories outlined above, is untenable when studying the archaeology rather than the written sources (Hendrickx et al., this volume). The development of writing should be put in the context of increased craft specialization, economic changes, and state formation (Köhler, this volume). The official textual sources are colored by the state ideology, they represent only the upper levels of Egyptian society, and they operate in a different time frame than the archaeological record. The image that comes to the fore from the textual sources is a well-balanced, homogeneous, society that is characterized by continuity of thought, habits, and interhuman relations. Egyptologists have taken this imagery at face value and tried to find explanations for such a level of stagnation by suggesting that there is a relation between the cognitive structure of Egypt's ancient inhabitants and its geographical location and natural circumstances (e.g. Grimal 1992:17). The explanation of Egypt's perceived homogeneous and unique character has thus often been sought in its landscape, or topographic circumstances. The Egyptian natural borders are the steep rocky Eastern Desert, rich in copper and turquoise in the Sinai, gold in the south, and hard decorative stones in the center; then the impenetrable Western desert, dotted with a few oases, but a landscape exactly as one imagines the Sahara – a bare, arid limestone plateau with large sandy dunes; and finally the marshes in the northern Delta, which forced the people to live on *geziras* or turtlebacks, islands of Pleistocene sands embedded in a thick layer of fluvial deposits and surrounded by water during the months of the Nile inundation. Even the topographical organization was dictated by the Nile: the dead were buried at the dry top of the islands; the living stayed as close as they could near the water, so that the remains of their settlements gradually were buried under the yearly addition of a thick layer of Nile silt. Egypt's southern border was protected by the First Cataract, rapids in the Nile which formed because the river had to find its way through a threshold of hard pink granite, rather than the Nubian sandstone in the south, or the limestone north of Esna. Even though the inhabitants of Elephantine were well aware that the Nile arrived at the First Cataract from further south, the turbulent waters were considered the source of the Nile. The inundation provided temporal regularity, which was expressed in the three seasons of four months each: *Akhet,* the inundation, from August through November, which each year brought not only water to the parched land, but also a thick layer of fertile black Nile silt; *Peret* the growing season from December through March; and *Shemu*, the period of drought when the ground cracked open and aired through, from April through July. Thus pointing at the natural circumstances, Pharaonic Egypt has been represented as an isolated country, a self-sufficient kingdom that looked inwards, was never faced with a complete occupation by foreigners, and therefore had no need to change in reaction to external factors.

How realistic is this image of an isolated, calm, and orderly life, protected by impenetrable borders and regulated by the Nile inundation? It was the ideal, certainly, but probably one that reflected a situation that was strived for, rather than one that was commonly present. The seemingly impenetrable mountainous Eastern Desert has been an access route from the Neolithic period onward: the desert track to the Red Sea where we have evidence for shipping from at least the Middle Kingdom onwards. The Sahara was a fully inhabited region in the late Holocene (Hendrickx et al., this volume), and after gradual desiccation it still was a regularly traveled region to and from the Oases, but also along ancient tracks to the plains and Nuba mountains in the south. The Nile branches in the Delta were convenient inroads for ships from the Mediterranean, which could pass the marshy region along well-traveled channels to inland harbor towns, such as Buto, Avaris, and Tanis. The regions of Wawat (Lower Nubia) and Kush (Upper Nubia) to the south of the First Cataract were involved in a constant cultural exchange with Egypt, and in many periods of its history Egypt tried successfully to have direct political control over extensive areas that were the source for important prestige goods such as gold, ostrich feathers, elephant tusks, leopard skins, and ebony.

The tension between ideal and reality found an expression in Egypt's religion. Apart from an emphasis on the afterlife (Taylor, this volume), the most important concept is that of *maat*, which stands for order or justice and is visualized as a feather, or a goddess with a feather on her head. It is the king's duty to uphold *maat* and to abhor and subdue *isfet*, social chaos. *Maat* encompasses more, however, than the opposite of *isfet*. It is the cosmic order, the very fabric of which earthly life and the afterlife are integral parts (Richards, this volume). The cosmic order can only be maintained by a constant renewal and re-creation. To the modern reader this forms a potential tension field, between stability and renewal, continuity and change. The emphasis on rebirth and rejuvenation is, however, focused not on change, but on the repeated re-creation of an existing state of affairs. It represents a sense of time depth, in which generation follows upon generation. Through Egyptian history one can follow the traces of ancient Egyptians being fascinated and in awe of that time depth of their own culture. In the New Kingdom period, around 1350 BCE, a visitor left a graffito on a wall of one of the chapels of the 3rd-Dynasty complex of Djoser, dated to approximately 2650 BCE, to express his admiration for the great accomplishments of previous generations (Firth et al. 1935; Fischer-Elfert 2003). A good illustration that ancient history was of importance and carried the weight of authority is the Memphite theology, found on a stela dated to the rule of Shabaka (c. 690–664 BCE) which literally claims to be a copy of an old worm-eaten papyrus (Lichtheim 1980:5). The deep sense of the importance of forebears and of tradition translated into a creative reinterpretation of what went before. Presented as being rooted in age-old wisdom, upon closer inspection many traditions appear to show a definite development from, or even complete breach with, the past (Kemp 2006:160; Wegner, this volume).

Likewise, the writing of historical accounts, or more precisely the composition of annals, was an ideological endeavor which had a very specific purpose. It was the task of the king to uphold *maat*, maintain order in Egypt and actively fight chaos, represented by the foreign lands surrounding Egypt. The king of Egypt had to be victorious in order to ensure that order. Perhaps the best example of what we would consider a falsification of history is the account of the Battle of Qadesh between Egypt and the Hittites during the reign of Ramesses II (c. 1279–1213). Presented as a victory on several temple walls, comparison with contemporary Hittite sources reveals that this battle ended in a stale-mate at best (Kitchen 1982). The location of these battle scenes, on the pylons and outside walls of the temples of Karnak, Luxor, and the Ramesseum (Yurco 1999), is highly relevant in the interpretation of these texts: the temple as sacred space is surrounded by scenes that ward off the chaos. The ideology of kingship as the institution and person that upholds *maat* lies at the root of ancient Egyptian representations of foreigners, lands outside the Egyptian borders, and accounts of the past (O'Connor 2003, Wegner, this volume).

Materiality, and thus archaeology, does not represent a more "objective" approach to understanding ancient Egyptian society. Just as texts and images, the material remains convey messages that should be understood in their context, and we should take into consideration which parties are involved in the tacit communication. Unlike texts and wall paintings, archaeology gives us the opportunity to study the material traces of all levels of society, without mediation of the upper classes in representing the lower classes, such as is the case in "scenes of daily life" in tomb paintings. By understanding the material record in its temporal, regional, and social context, we are beginning to tease out the variation, idiosyncracies, conflicts, and changes within Egyptian society, in contrast to the stable, seemingly unchanging flow of its official history.

The State of Archaeology in Egypt

Egyptian archaeology has gone through a number of rapid changes in the last few decades, and many of these are related to a growing awareness of the importance of archaeology as an independent discipline, with theories, methods, and subject matter that differ fundamentally from the traditional Egyptological approach. The criticism of the myth of Eternal Egypt is accompanied by a recognition that archaeologists in Egypt cannot work in a vacuum, removed from archaeological debates elsewhere in the world. The discourse has changed, and so has the emphasis and reliance on textual evidence. The study of segments of society that are underrepresented in textual evidence, and therefore in much of the previous research, is actively pursued, as is the archaeology of temporal and regional variations. This volume is representative of those changing discourses. As a counterbalance against the long-lived emphasis on ancient Egypt as an unchanging monolithic culture, each chapter has a main focus on a specific period and theme.

The chapters have been arranged in chronological order, from prehistory (Hendrickx et al., Chapter 2) to the present (Hassan, Chapter 14), but they do not represent a historical narrative or "evolutionary development." Broadly speaking each chapter focuses on a particular topic, covering the major themes in Egyptian archaeology today. These themes have been set in a specific temporal context, which enables the authors to present well-argued case studies based on recent or ongoing field projects. In some cases a deliberate choice is made to focus a theme in a period which has not been subject to such a study before. A good example is the section on villages. Settlement archaeology has been underrepresented, compared with the massive amounts of work published on tombs and temples. Most recent literature on village life has concentrated on Deir el-Medina, a village with a very specific group of inhabitants and a high level of literacy (McDowell 1999; Meskell 1999, 2002, 2004). An exception is Szpakowska's work on Middle Kingdom Kahun (2008). Chapter 5 (Lehner) considers villages in the Old Kingdom period, and relates the economic and political power of villages to that of the central authority.

The book develops a focus on temporal, spatial, human, and multiple contexts. The first three chapters have in common that they concentrate on very early periods of Egyptian history, from prehistory through early state formation. In traditional text-focused Egyptology the early expressions of religious thought and political organization were often interpreted from much later textual sources. Because it is challenging to construct an underlying belief system through the interpretation of shapes, color, human interventions, and spatial distribution of objects and buildings, Egyptology has found it extremely tempting to use later religious expressions to explain such early cultic phenomena. The continuous development of Egyptian culture should prevent us from using quite explicit versions of Egyptian mythology (mostly dated to the Greco-Roman period and 4000 years younger) to interpret much earlier cultural expressions. Thus Chapters 2, 3, and 4 ("Worship without Writing"; "Theories of State Formation"; and "Kingship and Legitimation") concentrate on the importance of interpreting these themes within their temporal context. If a comparison with later sources needs to be made, then the authors do so explicitly and with the notion that it is problematic. The essay in Chapter 2, by Stan Hendrickx, Dirk Huyge, and myself, discusses non-textual religious expression and explicates the grounds on which meaning is ascribed to technological changes, burial customs, visual culture, and the built environment. To discuss this in the context of the Late Palaeolithic, Neolithic, and Predynastic periods, for which textual sources are simply not available, gives a particular urgency to this approach. It can be argued that using the same methods to study religious practice from later periods will provide a very different level of understanding than focusing mostly on textual sources. Intellectual and spiritual explanations of the conditions of life and death are expressed in cultic sites such as found at Nabta Playa, Heliopolis, Elephantine, and Hierakonpolis. The formative period of complex society and state formation gives Christiana Köhler reason to criticize the traditional narrative of the unification of the two lands (Chapter 3). Represented in official textual or visual accounts such as the Narmer Palette, and repeated in royal titulary and iconography, the mythical representation of the birth of the Egyptian nation state has long been taken at face value. The essay outlines the importance of taking both functional and regional context into account: interpretation is inevitably skewed by a bias in the archaeological database, which has a wealth of funerary materials from the south of Egypt, but a dearth of reliable information on settlements, and on the archaeology of the Delta. Early kingship has been considered analogous with the position of the king of 1000 years later, based on a comparison of the iconography. This same emphasis of the proper temporal context permeates Janet Richards' discussion of the need and forms of legitimation of kingship in the Old Kingdom period (Chapter 4). Through the study of grand architectural projects, grave-good analysis, and the identification of elite goods and trade, the essay corrects the long-held characterization that Old Kingdom kingship was absolutist, a divine power far removed from the non-elite layers of Egyptian society. The change in emphasis is illustrated with two case studies, the first concentrating on legitimation through the content and distribution of private tomb biographies, and the second analyzing the development of the landscape at Abydos.

The second premise, referring to spatial context, is found mostly in Chapters 5 ("Villages and the Old Kingdom"), 6 ("Regionality, Cultural and Cultic Landscapes"), and 7 ("Tradition and Innovation: The Middle Kingdom"). In these chapters, regionality and the relative geographical position of land, landowners, and workers is put in an economic and ideological perspective. The location and in particular the economic power of villages as counterbalance to a putative absolutist and centralized state organization is laid out in Chapter 5, in which Mark Lehner points out how the dearth of written material from settlement contexts brings to the fore how many of our ideas about the Old Kingdom are based on the well-advertised state apparatus, while there are some apparent discrepancies between the ideal of statehood and the daily realities of life in a village in Egypt during that time. By combining the archaeological data with information on land holdings and taxes, Lehner sketches a coherent image of the complexity of the village, and the limited power of the central authority. This concurs with the consideration of culture, cult, and landscape, the subject of Chapter 6, written by David Jeffreys. The chapter emphasizes the role of the nomes, or provinces, in the context of the First Intermediate Period, a time when the provincial centers rose to increased independence. The geography of the nomes differed markedly, and Jeffreys therefore includes the specific location within the Egyptian landscape in relation to regional differences, regional persistence as well as the cultic and symbolic significance of the landscape. Josef Wegner considers the Middle Kingdom developments as basis for an analysis of the establishment and reinvention of tradition in ancient Egypt. He demonstrates how the "classical" period of Egyptian history is firmly rooted in the Old Kingdom and in its turn forms the foundation for the development of the New Kingdom by highlighting examples of innovations, such as the establishment of a new capital city, the emergence of a middle class, and changes in burial customs, firmly presented as traditions.

Four chapters concentrate on what could be called the "human context," aspects of identity, defined by ethnicity, class, gender, age, and concepts of personhood. In Chapter 8, "Foreigners in Egypt: Archaeological Evidence and Cultural

Context," Thomas Schneider discusses the Egyptian attitude towards foreign individuals, countries, and influences. He argues that the concepts of "being foreign," ethnicity, and acculturation should be defined in order to understand the complexity of this subject. Archaeology is vital to balance the negative imagery of state propaganda and, in contrast to this negative discourse, provides evidence for the integration of foreigners in Egypt. The chapter gives a diachronic overview of evidence for the position of foreigners in the formal, royal inscriptions and iconography, as well as the sparse indications of actual foreigners living in Egypt who were able, and chose, to express their identity. The case study, excavations in Tell el-Dabaa, centers on the Second Intermediate Period and the insights that this archaeological case study has yielded for the rewriting of the history of the Hyksos "invasion." Previously the Hyksos were thought to be foreign hordes who conquered Egypt by force, but from the archaeology the Eastern Delta appears as a region which has known a long-lived cultural exchange, and several generations of inhabitants with a Syro-Palestinian background. The cultural identity of these inhabitants was expressed in material remains ranging from burials to weapons, and use-ware ceramics. The texts that vilify the Hyksos most fervently were written approximately five decades after Egypt had be "re-conquered" by rulers of the Theban house which would form the 18th Dynasty. In its historical context, the claims of the disputed King/Queen Hatshepsut take on a very different meaning. In Chapter 9, "Gender in Egypt," T. G. Wilfong provides a diachronic overview of the presentation and role of gender in different Egyptian sources with emphasis on the New Kingdom. The discussion of "women" and "men," as well as more complex gender categories, is based on his integration of archaeological, visual, and textual sources. The most accessible archaeological material is available in burials, where grave goods and tomb architecture can be connected to a sexed body. Settlement archaeology, for instance at Amarna, provides insights into the relation between domestic space and gender. Chapter 10, "Class in Egypt: Position and Possessions," is a critical discussion of the use of the term "elite." This is coupled with the question of how pervasive the concept of class was in ancient Egypt. Wolfgang Grajetzki illustrates how social stratification can be defined archaeologically, with mostly examples dated to the New Kingdom period. The role of the king, and that of the high-level state officials as intermediaries between the next level of society and the pharaoh at the very top, is correlated to archaeological evidence from cemeteries and settlements. In Chapter 11, "Identity and Personhood," I present a diachronic overview of how Egyptians understood themselves as a person or individual within society. The main focus is on New Kingdom evidence, and includes a brief overview of how aspects of identity feature in the large historical narrative of the New Kingdom. To understand identity and personhood the discussion explores the importance of the name as identifier both in life and after death, as well as the supernatural aspects of personhood. These relate directly to the socially negotiated identity markers which provide a material expression of ethnicity, age, health, wealth, and class.

The fourth section of the book stresses the complex multiple contexts for a period which in traditional Egyptology has often been considered to fall outside Pharaonic Egyptian history. By contributing change to foreign rule, the Late Period, as noted above, has been characterized as "un-Egyptian." Especially the pharaohs of the 25th Dynasty have suffered this fate, while several of the changes they introduced were adopted by later generations, and considered "truly Egyptian" in the Greco-Roman period. The roots of such misrepresentations lie in the disregard of development and change over time, manifest in the fact that few Egyptologists feel the need to define "real" Egyptian culture. In Chapter 12, "Changes in the Afterlife," John Taylor considers whether the beliefs of the Libyan ruling elite in the Delta should be considered as inspiration for or cause of a minimization of investment in burials during the Third Intermediate Period. By providing a diachronic analysis of funerary aspects such as the location, architecture, decoration, and equipment of burials, the contrast in investment becomes apparent, but the world of ideas behind the rituals does not appear to change significantly. Penelope Wilson uses the concept of the "two lands," an organizing notion during most periods of Egyptian history, in relation to archaeological and other evidence for the multitude of Delta states and the loss of integrity during the Third Intermediate and Late Periods (Chapter 13, "Consolidation, Innovation, and Renaissance"). Through the discussion of major settlement sites such as Sais and Naukratis, she considers the tendency towards restoration and archaizing apparent in these periods. Often dismissed as a period of decline, she suggests that, depending on one's perspective, the Late Period could be considered one of renaissance, "dynamically interwoven with the paradigm of past ideologies." In Chapter 14 ("Egypt in the Memory of the World") Fekri Hassan gives an analysis of the fascination that ancient Egypt has held for Europe. The essay deconstructs how Egypt has survived and has been reconstituted in the memory of the world. Hassan quotes the classical authors and the biblical tradition, where Egypt is praised for its (secret) wisdom or vilified as a land of paganism, or as the abode of Pharaoh, the quintessential enemy of the Jewish people. Egypt remains at the forefront of intense interest, starting with Islamic scholars in the medieval period, and early travelers from the seventeenth century onwards, towards modern-day commercialism.

The conclusion (Chapter 15, "Epilogue: Eternal Egypt Deconstructed") draws together the common theme of these chapters: the deconstruction of "Eternal Egypt," through a change in emphasis from text to context. This is based on archaeological interpretation, in which text and iconography are imbedded as sources with their own purpose, audience, and ideology. These fifteen chapters thus provide an overview of recent trends in and developments of Egyptian archaeology. In different ways each chapter illustrates not "what we know," but "how we know," by explicitly presenting and weighing the evidence. This inevitably also brings to the fore where our knowledge is lacking. Such an approach allows us to integrate the complex interdisciplinary information needed to piece together different histories, with particular explicitly formulated perspectives. While each chapter concentrates on a methodological theme, the gradual chronological shift, from prehistory to the present, provides a framework that allows the reader to situate these accounts within the traditional timeline of Egyptian history, and contrasts the archaeologically contextualized chapters with the traditional Egyptological narrative. Bringing archaeology to the fore, *Egyptian Archaeology* stimulates the study of major themes within a specific historical and archaeological context.

REFERENCES

Andrén, A. 1998 Between Artifacts and Texts: Historical Archaeology in Global Perspective. New York: Plenum Press.

Biletzki, A., and A. Matar 2009 Ludwig Wittgenstein. *In* Stanford Encyclopedia of Philosophy (Summer). E. N. Zalta, ed. http://plato.stanford.edu/archives/sum2009/entries/Wittgenstein/.

Butzer, K. W. 1976 Early Hydraulic Civilization in Egypt: A Study in Cultural Ecology. Chicago: University of Chicago Press.

Caton Thompson, G. 1931 The Zimbabwe Culture: Ruins and Reactions. Oxford: Clarendon Press.

Caton Thompson, G. 1983 Mixed Memoirs. Gateshead: Paradigm Press.

Caton Thompson, G., and E. W. Gardner 1934 The Desert Fayum. 2 vols. London: The Royal Anthropological Institute of Great Britain and Ireland.

Emery, W. B. 1961 Archaic Egypt. London: Penguin Books.

Firth, C. M., J. E. Quibell, and J. P. Lauer 1935 Excavations at Saqqara: The Step Pyramid. Cairo: Institut français d'archéologie orientale.

Fischer-Elfert, H.-W. 2003 Representations of the Past in Old Kingdom Literature. *In* "Never Had the Like Occurred": Egypt's View of Its Past. J. Tait, ed. Pp. 119–137. London: UCL Press.

Grimal, N.-C. 1992 A History of Ancient Egypt. Oxford, Cambridge, MA: Blackwell.

Johnson, J. H., ed. 1992 Life in a Multi-cultural Society: Egypt from Cambyses to Constantine and Beyond. Vol. 51. Chicago: Oriental Institute of the University of Chicago.

Kemp, B. J. 2006 Ancient Egypt, Anatomy of a Civilization. 2nd edition. London, New York: Routledge.

Kitchen, K. A. 1982 Pharaoh Triumphant: The Life and Times of Ramesses II. Warminster: Aris and Phillips.

Lichtheim, M. 1980 Ancient Egyptian Literature: A Book of Readings. Vol. III: The Late Period. 3 vols. Berkeley: University of California Press.

McDowell, A. G. 1999 Village Life in Ancient Egypt: Laundry Lists and Love Songs. Oxford, New York: Oxford University Press.

Meskell, L. 1998 Archaeology under Fire: Nationalism, Politics and Heritage in the Eastern Mediterranean and Middle East. London: Routledge.

Meskell, L. 1999 Archaeologies of Social Life: Age, Sex, Class *et cetera* in Ancient Egypt. Oxford, Malden, MA: Blackwell.

Meskell, L. 2002 Private Life in New Kingdom Egypt. Princeton: Princeton University Press.

Meskell, L. 2004 Object Worlds in Ancient Egypt. Oxford, New York: Berg.

O'Connor, D. 2003 Egypt's Views of "Others." *In* "Never Had the Like Occurred": Egypt's View of Its Past. J. Tait, ed. Pp. 155–185. London: UCL Press.

Reid, D. M. 2002 Whose Pharaohs? Archaeology, Museums, and Egyptian National Identity from Napoleon to World War I. Berkeley: University of California Press.

Reisner, G. A. 1923 Excavations at Kerma, Parts IV–V. Vol. 6. Cambridge, MA: Peabody Museum of Harvard University.

Riggs, C. 2005 The Beautiful Burial in Roman Egypt: Art, Identity, and Funerary Religion. Oxford, New York: Oxford University Press.

Szpakowska, K. M. 2008 Daily Life in Ancient Egypt: Recreating Lahun. Malden, MA: Blackwell.

Trigger, B. G. 2006 A History of Archaeological Thought. Cambridge: Cambridge University Press.

Trigger, B. G., B. J. Kemp, D. O'Connor, and A. B. Lloyd 1983 Ancient Egypt: A Social
    History. Cambridge, New York: Cambridge University Press.
Vasunia, P. 2001 The Gift of the Nile: Hellenizing Egypt from Aeschylus to Alexander.
    Berkeley, Los Angeles: University of California Press.
Wendorf, F., and R. Schild 1976 Prehistory of the Nile Valley. New York: Academic Press.
Wendrich, W. 2008 Gertrude Caton Thompson (1888–1985): Famous Footsteps to Fill.
    Archéo-Nil 17:89–106.
Wendrich, W. in press. From Practical Knowledge to Empowered Communication: Field
    Schools of the Supreme Council of Antiquities in Egypt. *In* Filtering the Past, Building
    the Future: Archaeology, Tradition and Politics in the Middle East. R. Boytner, L.
    Schwarz-Dodd, and B. J. Parker, eds. Tucson: University of Arizona Press.
Wengrow, D. 2006 The Archaeology of Early Egypt: Social Transformations in North-
    East Africa, 10,000 to 2,650 BC. Cambridge, New York: Cambridge University Press.
Yurco, F. J. 1999 Representational Evidence, New Kingdom Temples. *In* Encyclopedia
    of the Archaeology of Ancient Egypt. K. Bard and S. B. Shubert, eds. Pp. 671–674.
    London: Routledge.

2
Worship without Writing

Stan Hendrickx, Dirk Huyge, and Willeke Wendrich

Religious thought in Egypt was rich and various, as glimpsed from the visual and textual record on temple and tomb walls. Most of the theology and religious world image, however, is implicit and only alluded to through references to the rich mythology. In the Greco-Roman period, texts are more explicit about the meaning of these oblique citations, and scholars have been tempted to use these explications as guides to interpret very early religious expressions. As outlined in the previous chapter, such an approach is problematic and has led to the myth of the never-changing Egyptian culture. Prehistoric archaeology has been at the forefront of interpreting material culture as an expression of mental processes, moving away from explanation by analogy to later phenomena, and considering human expression through visual and material culture in its own temporal and spatial context. With its emphasis on human cognition, intellectual expression, and individual agency, cognitive archaeology has made great strides in understanding human culture as more than behavioral patterns based on environmental factors (Coimbra and Dimitriadis 2008; Mithen 1996, 1997, 2006, 2007; Renfrew 2007; Renfrew and Scarre 1998; Renfrew and Zubrow 1994).

The emphasis on written sources has made the study of Egyptian prehistory an endeavor that was mostly separated from traditional Egyptology. Only recently have some histories of Egypt started with a summary of the Palaeolithic and Neolithic cultures (e.g. Bard 2008; Grimal 1988, 1992; Hendrickx and Vermeersch 2000). In addition several excellent syntheses have been published (Bard 1994; Ciałowicz 2001; Midant-Reynes 2000; Wengrow 2006; Wilkinson 1999). To understand the religious and intellectual life of that period, the types of evidence available, and the body of theory that enables us to go beyond the merely descriptive, this chapter presents eight brief case studies, clustered in four themes in which sections of the vast material culture from Egypt's earliest periods are considered in the light of symbolic expression. These examples, presented within the context of time and space, highlight the importance of (1) technology (lithics, ceramics, and domestication); (2) the erection of dedicated structures (shrines) as part of the built environment; (3) burial customs; and (4) visual culture (depictions on pottery, rock art, and statuettes).

Table 2.1 summarizes the geographical distribution, approximate dates, and relations between the prehistoric Egyptian cultures featured in this chapter. It also indicates in which of the thematic studies they are mentioned.

Table 2.1 Geographical distribution, approximate dates, and relations between the different prehistoric Egyptian cultural assemblages. For a complete overview, including the Lower Egyptian sites, see Ciałowicz 2001; Midant-Reynes 2000; or Wilkinson 1999

Term/Site	Age (cal BCE)	Region	Tech.	Built env.	Burial	Visual culture
Lower Palaeolithic	700,000–250,000 BCE		✓			
Middle Palaeolithic	250,000–50,000 BCE					
Upper Palaeolithic	50,000–10,000 BCE					
Nazlet Khater 4		Nile Valley	✓			
Qurta		Nile Valley, Kom Ombo Plain	✓			✓
Epipalaeolithic	10,000–6500 BCE					
El-Hosh	8000–7000	Upper Egypt	✓	✓		✓
Elkabian	7000–6700	Upper Egypt, Eastern Desert	✓			
Djara	7700–7000	Western Desert, near Nile Valley	✓			✓
Qarunian	7000–6500	Fayum (= Fayum B)	✓			
Early Neolithic	8500–6000 BCE					
Nabta/Bir Kiseiba	7000–6700	Western Desert, Sahara	✓	✓		
El-Jerar	6500–6100	Western Desert, Sahara	✓	✓		
Middle Neolithic	6000–5200 BCE					
Djara	6000–5300	Western Desert, near Nile Valley	✓			✓
Late Neolithic	5200–3800 BCE					
Fayumian	5200–4200	Fayum (= Fayum A, Moerian)	✓	✓		
Moerian	4500–3800	Fayum, Qasr el-Sagha area	✓			
Merimde Level I (Urschicht)	6000	Western Nile Delta, probably to be dated around 5000 BCE	✓	✓		✓

Table 2.1 *Continued.*

Term/Site	Age (cal BCE)	Region	Tech.	Built env.	Burial	Visual culture
Merimde Level II (*Mittleren M. kultur*)	5500–4500	Western Nile Delta, probably to be dated 4500–4000	✓	✓		✓
Merimde Level III-IV (*Jüngeren M. kultur*)	4600–4000	Western Nile Delta, probably to be dated 4600–3800	✓	✓		✓
Nabta/Bir Kiseiba	4500–3600	Western Desert, Sahara	✓	✓	✓	
Predynastic	5300–3000 BCE					
Tasian		Nile Valley in Upper Egypt, Eastern and Western Desert	✓	✓	✓	✓
Badarian		Nile Valley, desert fringes	✓	✓	✓	✓
Naqada I		Nile Valley, Upper Egypt	✓	✓	✓	✓
Naqada II		Nile Valley, Upper Egypt	✓	✓	✓	✓
Naqada III		Nile Valley, Upper Egypt and Delta	✓	✓	✓	✓

Technology

The 700,000 years that humans have roamed the Nile Valley and its adjacent steppes have been marked by technological achievements. The analysis of stone tool development, such as the Lower Palaeolithic hand axes, not only provides information on selection and use of raw materials, but is also the basis for a reconstruction of human cognitive development (Wynn 2002). The investment of time and energy, as well as knowledge and pursuit of high-quality materials, are reflected by the subterranean chert mining during the Upper Palaeolithic (Vermeersch et al. 2002).

Stone tool technology during the Epipalaeolithic was characterized by a microlithic flint industry, found in the Nile Valley only at Elkab (Vermeersch 1978). Hardly any other human occupation has been attested in the Upper Egyptian Nile Valley between 11,000 and 5000 cal BCE, with sites covered up by later alluvial deposits. Remains in the Eastern Desert at the Tree Shelter site indicate that the Elkabians should be viewed as nomadic hunters, with wintertime fishing and hunting in the Nile Valley and exploitation of the desert during the period of inundation in the late summer (Vermeersch 2008; Vermeersch et al. 2002). In the Fayum, the Epipalaeolithic Qarunian culture dates to around 7000 cal BCE and also has a microlithic industry (Caton Thompson and Gardner 1934 used the term Fayum B; Wendorf and Schild 1976).

Compared to the Nile Valley, far more information is available for the Western Desert, where people returned around 8500 cal BCE, after a long interval since the Middle Palaeolithic. The reoccupation of the steppe landscape west of the Nile was enabled by the Holocene wet phase. The annual rainfall in the early Holocene was only about 100–200 mm, all of which probably fell during a brief summer season, and therefore seasonal contact with the Nile Valley was fundamental. This is confirmed by the fact that microlithic industries of the so-called Early Neolithic in the Western Desert (c. 8500–6100 cal BCE) correspond very well to the general technological context of the Epipalaeolithic Qarunian and Elkabian. The impressive amount of information available for the Western Desert in combination with the almost complete absence of sites in the Nile Valley results in a distorted picture. The Nile Valley is to be considered not as a boundary but rather as an occupation area linking the Eastern and Western Deserts. The climatic optima, and wettest phases during the Holocene, were reached during the el-Nabta (c. 7050/7000–6700 cal BCE) and el-Jerar (c. 6500–6100 cal BCE) Early Neolithic. After 4900 cal BCE and especially from 4400 cal BCE onwards, the desert became less and less inhabitable because of the onset of the arid climate that continues up to the present day.

The lithic technology shows the contacts between what are at present desert areas and the Nile Valley. The ceramic technology, however, displays more idiosyncratic developments, presumably linked to a differentiation of meaning. Our recognition that raw material modification, especially through pyrotechnology, has cognitive and social meaning beyond the materials and objects themselves (Dobres and Hoffman 1994; Lemonnier 1993) has important consequences for the interpretation of ceramics, even the undecorated seemingly "functional" types, such as the crude undecorated Fayum Neolithic pottery (Caton Thompson and Gardner 1934). The pottery from the Early and Middle Neolithic in what is now the Western Desert is the only "Neolithic" element attested with certainty in these cultures, which has led to the suggestion of using the term "Ceramic" instead of "Neolithic" for these pottery-producing cultures (Kuper 1995:125). The ceramics were all decorated, and consisted exclusively of deep bowls, which show no traces of cooking fires (Close 1995). They are well made, and point to an independent African invention of the pyrotechnical process. Presumably these bowls held a special meaning, attested by decoration over the entire surface of the vessel, consisting primarily of lines and points, often created by comb or cord impressions. The shape and general appearance of the vessels resembles basketry. From the late Neolithic period very fine, well-made coiled and decorated baskets have been preserved (Caton Thompson and Gardner 1934; Wendrich and Cappers 2005), which clearly represent a well-developed basketry technology at that time. From the Early and Middle Neolithic such materials are not known, but it seems likely that leather bags and baskets were used for storage, and possibly also cooking through indirect heating. Ostrich eggshells used as water containers were far more common than pottery vessels in the Western Desert at that time. The modification of properties from clay to ceramics, and the decoration that evokes basketry, suggest that the vessels were used for storage or serving in social or religious settings, perhaps related to the specific period of intensive plant gathering.

During the final Neolithic period in the Nabta–Bir Kiseiba area the wells had to be dug very deep, indicating increasing problems with the water supply. The pottery was characterized by smoothed and burnished surfaces, and occasionally by rippled ware. Another remarkable element was the occurrence of black-topped pottery, already from the Late Neolithic onwards (Nelson 2002:18). Black-topped and rippled pottery were characteristics of the later Tasian and Badarian in the Nile Valley, but the black-topped ware of the Western Desert was not produced in the same way as the more recent examples from the Nile Valley, and the term "desert black-topped" has therefore been proposed (Riemer and Kindermann 2008). During the Final Neolithic, traces of burning show that, contrary to the Early and Middle Neolithic, the ceramic vessels were also used for cooking.

The earliest Predynastic culture of Upper Egypt was identified at Deir Tasa, in Middle Egypt (Brunton 1937). In recent years the region of the Tasian culture has been expanded through finds in the Eastern (Friedman and Hobbs 2002; Vermeersch et al. 2005) and Western Desert (Darnell 2002; Kobusiewicz et al. 2004). The Tasian thus provides the earliest Predynastic evidence in the Nile Valley for the much older nomadic interaction between the Nile Valley and the deserts. Apart from the black-topped pottery, the Tasian is characterized by a tulip-shaped ("caliciform") type of beakers with incised decoration (Math 2006). These elaborately decorated beakers with small rounded base, top-heavy flaring shape, and large aperture seem unlikely to have been used for storage. They seem only suited for drinking, but would have to be held in the hand, and their content seems rather much for an individual person. Because of the particular shape and decoration, a social and perhaps ritual function of group drinking where the vessel would travel from hand to hand seems likely and would be comparable to the slightly later ritual known from the Naqada II temple at Hierakonpolis (see below). The relation between Tasian and Badarian cultures is not yet clear, but part of the ceramics in Badari consist of the characteristic rippled pottery, which probably developed from burnished and smudged pottery, present at late Saharan Neolithic sites, and from Merimda in the north to the Khartoum Neolithic sites in the south. Rippled pottery may thus have been a marker of a Saharan tradition.

The Naqada I pottery consisted mainly of black-topped ware and Nile silt vessels with white cross-line decorations (see below). Starting during Naqada IIB, a marked change in the ceramic production occurred. Nile silt was partially replaced by marl clay, which can be fired at a higher temperature. At the same time, the white cross-lined pottery was replaced by ceramics, made from marl clay and painted with purple-black. Not only were the representations on this decorated ware far more standardized than those on white cross-lined pottery (Graff 2002:771–772), but their general characteristics were also different (Wengrow 2006:102–104).

The technology of domestication has deeply influenced societies worldwide, but it is apparent that the adoption and adaptation of this knowledge complex differ markedly. In Egypt the Fayum Neolithic culture incorporated the Levantine suite of domesticates of wheat, barley, sheep/goat, cattle, and pig, in a low-level food-producing society which largely depended on fishing (Holdaway et al. in press). A very similar use of domesticates was found in the lowest stratum at Merimde, at the western edge of the Nile Delta (Eiwanger 1984). The economy of the Badari culture was primarily based on agriculture and livestock breeding. However,

fishing certainly was very important too, and may have been the principal economic activity during certain periods of the year. Hunting, on the contrary, was
apparently only of marginal importance. Social stratification seems to have been
limited, although the burials show that the society was not egalitarian (Anderson
1992; see also Köhler, this volume).

In the Western Desert, agriculture has not been attested and the domestication
of cattle is debated (Gautier 2001; critique by Grigson 2000:47–49; see also
Wengrow 2006:48–49), but there too cattle was by no means the main source of
protein. Domesticated cattle has been attested with certainty in the Western
Desert from the sixth millennium BCE onwards.The Late Neolithic tumuli burials
of both articulated and disarticulated remains of cattle, among which a young
cow, that have been found at Nabta Playa illustrate the sociological and religious
importance of bovines around 5400 cal BCE, at the beginning of the Late Neolithic
period (Applegate et al. 2001; Wendorf et al. 1997). The special treatment of
bovines should not be considered a direct continuation of Late Palaeolithic beliefs,
but a ritual that foreshadows the large number of animal burials known from the
Early Dynastic period (Flores 2003).

Built Environment: Settlements and Shrines

Recognizing sacred places, either in the landscape or in a built environment, is
notoriously difficult. Rock art (see below) is often related to important and potentially sacred landscape elements, while built shrines are hard to discern from other
buildings, and attempts to formulate criteria are still suffering from ambiguity
(e.g. Renfrew et al. 1985; revised by Pilafidis-Williams 1998). For the Neolithic it
is clear that the developments in Egypt are very different from the Levant. The
nomadic existence which lasted through the late Neolithic required either temporary or transportable dwellings. At site E-75-6 at Nabta Playa (el-Nabta Early
Neolithic), three or four rows of huts have been discovered, probably each representing a different shore line of an important lake (Królik and Schild 2001). Even
though during the dry season subsurface water could be reached by wells, this
was not a permanent settlement. Bell-shaped storage pits, presumably for wild
plant foods, could only be used during the dry season and their contents must
have been consumed during spring, before the site was seasonally abandoned. For
the el-Jerar Early Neolithic, seasonal occupation is well documented at the type
site E-99-1, with round to oval huts, measuring between 2.5 and 5 m in diameter
and many storage pits. They were flooded yearly by the lake, but frequently rebuilt.
Both early Neolithic sites were occupied during the wettest period of the Holocene.
Recent work in the Fayum, where until 2004 no trace of dwellings had been found,
has recovered clay floors, clean and dirty areas around multiple hearths, and a
few braces of post holes, which indicate that in a relatively short time span of 250
years the sites of Kom K and Kom W were occupied intensively. Nearby grain
storage pits, lined with basketry, were covered with salt-hardened lids and contained domesticated wheat and barley (Wendrich and Cappers forthcoming).

Settlement remains at Merimde from level I (*Urschicht*) were scant (Eiwanger
1984). Most probably there was an interruption of occupation at Merimde between

the levels I and II. The excavator considered the latter (*Mittleren Merimdekultur*) as related to the Saharo-Sudanese cultures (Eiwanger 1988). During this period, there was a denser occupation of the site, with simple oval dwellings of wood and wickerwork, and with well-developed hearths, storage jars sunk in the clay floors, and large clay-coated baskets in accessory pits serving as granaries. At Badari most attention went out to the cemetery sites and forty poorly documented settlement sites are known, which had mudbrick remains. Not surprisingly, no sanctuary-type structure has been identified at any of these sites, because the remains were ephemeral, seriously damaged, or badly recorded. The only indication for ritual use in Nabta is related to the cemetery (see below).

The situation is quite different at Hierakonpolis, where the only religious center known for the Naqada II period has been discovered. It is the earliest of its kind in Egypt (Friedman 1996, 2003). It consisted of a large oval courtyard in front of a shrine, which has not yet been fully excavated. The massive façade of the shrine consisted of huge wood pillars, possibly cedar logs imported from the Lebanon. The temple was used for about five centuries and underwent at least three major renovations during that period. The debris from ceremonial activities was collected in rubbish pits just outside the enclosure wall and provides unique information on religious practices. Fragments of hundreds of jars, of a kind only found at Hierakonpolis, can be divided into two types: polished, brown to black, small egg-shaped jars and matte red bottles (Friedman 2003; Hendrickx and Friedman 2003). These vessels were probably produced specifically for use in the temple, and Friedman suggested that the vessels symbolize respectively the dry red land prior to inundation and the shiny, wet and black land after the inundation. The same duality could be suggested for the large amounts of wild animal bones found in the rubbish pits: aquatic species such as crocodile, hippopotamus, and soft-shelled turtles, but also desert animals such as gazelle, barbary sheep, and hare (Linseele and Van Neer 2003). Hunted animals were overrepresented in comparison to Predynastic settlement sites, a phenomenon that could suggest that hunting and consuming game during festivals was a religious act. Control of wild animals symbolized human control over chaos, represented by the red desert and its creatures. The fish fauna was exceptional also, because of the large size of the Nile perch, some of which were at least 1.5 m long. Furthermore, elements of the skull and fins were rare, indicating that specially selected and prepared fish were served during the religious festivities in the temple area. Both the fish and wild animal remains indicate that fishing and hunting took place during the low water season (Linseele and Van Neer 2003). The red and black vessels, as well as the specific food types, would have been used during religious festivals in the time before the arrival of the annual Nile flood, a potentially chaotic period that required religious control.

Burial

Religious belief systems are often related to notions of an afterlife and reflected in burial customs. The efforts to provide the deceased with grave goods, tombs, or grave markers are the material manifestation of such beliefs, as well as the social structure of the society of the living. Until recently, a funerary interpretation of megalithic monuments seemed unlikely for the Nabta area because of the absence of cemeteries, but a Final Neolithic cemetery, dating to about 4500 cal BCE, has recently found at Gebel Ramlah, only some 30 km from the contemporaneous megalithic sites at Nabta Playa (Kobusiewicz et al. 2004). The Gebel Ramlah cemetery is connected with a settlement area, and obviously similar cemeteries would also have existed in the Nabta area. The presence of "tulip-shaped" beakers at Gebel Ramlah links the cemetery to the Tasian culture known from the Nile Valley and both the Eastern and Western Desert. Nile shells and Red Sea shells confirm the wide-ranging contacts of this nomadic population, while the difference in number and time-investment of the grave goods can be considered proof of social complexity and/or stratification, although its extent remains to be defined. The cemetery was considered by the excavators as the long-term burial ground of an extended family, among other things because of the occurrence of multiple burials. Primary individual burials are in contracted position on the right side, oriented west, facing south. One of the multiple burials contained the disarticulated skeletons of five adults, which indicates that at the moment of burial the bones probably were devoid of soft tissue. The other multiple graves seem originally to have been primary burials, disturbed when additional burials took place. This can be taken as an indication for people dying far away from the cemetery, their skeletons being brought back for burial. It illustrates the importance given to family ties, and presumably also reflected ideas about the afterlife. Special care was taken to restore elements of disarticulated skeletons, as is shown by replacing teeth, be it often in wrong sockets or even in one of the orbits or the nasal aperture (Irish et al. 2003, 2005), and the way in which the bracelets of a female were kept in their original position by the deceased's own ulna and radius (Kobusiewicz et al. 2004:572, fig. 6.3). The importance given to teeth may also be shown by a possible imitation in shell of a maxillary incisor (Irish et al. 2004). Some skeletons were at least partially covered with red ochre, illustrating another element of the funerary rites. The manipulation of bodies or skeletons was obviously very important and the associated rituals would not necessarily have been limited to the burial pit itself, but may well have taken place at megalithic monuments similar to those of Nabta.

For the Fayum Epipalaeolithic and Neolithic cultures no burials have been found, and in general the Western Desert shows a dearth of funerary remains (Kobusiewicz et al. 2004), which may be an argument in favor of a partial nomadic existence. In contrast, at Merimde Benisalame, at the edge of the Western Nile Delta, contracted burials were located among the dwellings of layer 2 (middle Merimde, *Mittleren Merimdekultur*) and were interpreted as related to Saharo-Sudanese cultures (Eiwanger 1988). During this period the occupation of the site consisted of simple oval dwellings of wood and wickerwork, with well-developed hearths, storage jars sunk in the clay floors, and large clay-coated baskets in accessory pits serving as granaries.

The Badari culture was originally identified in the region of Badari [Qaw el-Kebir, Hammamiya (Brunton and Caton Thompson 1928), Mostagedda (Brunton 1937), and Matmar (Brunton 1948)], where a number of small cemeteries, containing in total about 600 tombs, and forty poorly documented settlement sites are known. For a long time, the Badarian was thought to be restricted to this area. However, characteristic Badarian finds have also been recorded further to the south [Mahgar Dendera (Hendrickx et al. 2001), Armant (Myers and Fairman 1931:228–229), Elkab (Vermeersch 1978), and Hierakonpolis (Hoffman 1986)]. Several animal burials occurred in Badarian cemeteries, among them bovines and caprids. These burials showed no obvious pattern, nor were they related to individual tombs. The habit of individual animal burials continued in the Naqada period, and must have had a ritual meaning which did not seem directly related to the human burials. Possibly the burial of animals was related to religious festivals, which could refer to funerary ideology apart from the death of individuals.

There was no obvious break between the end of the Badari culture and the beginning of the Naqada period. The Naqada culture, consisting of three stages (Hendrickx 2006), is mainly known through its cemeteries, which by the Naqada III period were found all over Egypt and Nubia. Although about 15,000 tombs have been excavated, published evidence is only available for about 3000 of these. Most cemeteries of the Naqada culture were used over several centuries, during which they expanded horizontally, in a seemingly unpremeditated manner. This resulted in cemeteries consisting of "patches" of contemporaneous tombs, which have been considered to reflect kinship and/or social groups (Delrue 2001; Savage 1997). The number of grave goods and the investment spent in building the tombs in general increased over time, presumably reflecting improving agricultural techniques and therefore also living conditions. But concurrently the differentiation between the large majority of the tombs and a few exceptionally rich ones also increased. All in all, society was becoming more complex, with the development of local and regional elites, the latter at least from the very beginning of the Naqada II period onwards. The pottery found in the tombs was also present in the settlements and was not specially made for funerary purposes. Most cemetery pottery had been used prior to the interment. However, settlement ceramics showed a greater variety, since quite a number of types belonging to rough "utility wares" were not or hardly represented in the cemeteries. This seems to indicate a vision of the afterlife which presupposes the ready availability of consumption goods, rather than as a replication of daily life, in which tasks such as food production and processing were required.

The burials in Hierakonpolis, dated to early Naqada II (c. 3600 BCE) and III periods, show many features which provide information on religious or ritual activities and beliefs. Several tombs in the early Naqada II "working-class" cemetery HK43 (Friedman 2006; Friedman et al. 1999) contained individuals with fractures of the braincase most probably due to massive blows by mace heads (Potter and Powell 2003). In the same cemetery, 21 out of 470 individuals were found with cut marks on the neck vertebrae, indicating that their throats had been cut, or in some cases that they had been decapitated (Dougherty and Friedman 2008), a phenomenon also attested at other cemeteries, for example at Adaïma (Crubézy and Midant-Reynes 2005). There was no age or gender grouping: men and women were found ranging from 16 to about 65 years of age, among whom were five young men who had also been scalped. Because of the standard position of the cut marks and the absence of defensive injuries, violent crime and regular warfare can be excluded as causes. It is, however, impossible to decide whether throat cutting (as capital punishment or human sacrifice) was the actual cause of death or if it was part of a post-mortem ritual involving dismemberment and re-creation. The same cemetery also provided evidence for the early development of artificial mummification. A number of burials from HK43 had been (partly) wrapped in linen, with separate clumps of resin-soaked cloth used to pad body parts, especially around the face and the hands, before the actual wrapping took place. Occasionally, some of the internal organs had been wrapped in linen as well. All of this shows a growing concern with the preservation of the body, especially those parts most strongly connected to digestion.

Visual Culture

Visual culture, a term that has recently been theorized in art history as comprising the cultural expression of meaning through, among others, decoration, drawings, paintings, and statuettes, is an important means to understand religious and other cognitive principles of ancient cultures. The archaeological study of visual culture is especially of importance for cultures that do not express abstract thought in writing. Skeates (2005) stresses the importance of a contextual approach to the archaeological analysis of visual culture. Rather than studying visual culture as symbols or signifiers, the temporal, spatial, and depositional elements of archaeological artifacts should be an integral part of their interpretation. Such a contextual study includes not only objects, but also the settlements, burials, monuments, and landscapes in which they once functioned, as well as changes and reinterpretations or re-use over time (Stevens 2007). The study of portable objects and art forms such as rock art therefore concentrates on understanding their function and meaning in visual communication.

In Egypt, the study of rock art has provided important information on the earliest inhabitants of the Nile Valley and the deserts beyond. Abu Tanqura Bahari 11, a rock art site near Edfu in the Western Desert, was discovered in 2004, and is characterized by naturalistic images of bovids which are quite different from the stylized cattle representations in "classical" Predynastic iconography of the fourth millennium BCE (Huyge 2005). They are comparable to bovid images discovered in 1962–1963 on the opposite bank of the Nile, about 10 km south, near the village of Qurta along the northern edge of the Kom Ombo Plain (Smith 1985). In addition to bovids, gazelle, hippopotami, birds, fish, a number of monstrous creatures, and several stylized anthropomorphs are represented. Both localities, together with a third site in the Wadi Abu Subeira near Aswan, are part of a larger rock art complex along the Upper Egyptian Nile, a North African "Lascaux," the importance of which has never been properly appreciated (Figure 2.1). The significant relation between landscape, placement, and meaning of rock art is well attested, and provides information beyond general associations (Ouzman 1998). The Kom Ombo Plain is a broad section of the Nile Valley which is constricted to the north and south of this region, and as such would have provided sustenance for large herds of wild cattle with rich grazing and easy access to the water. Apart from interpretations of the drawings as visual representation of the mindscape, the cognitive, or "learned," landscape (Rockman and Steele 2003), or simply as

Figure 2.1 Upper or Late Palaeolithic rock art: main panel at Qurta, with a total length of about 4 m, showing wild cattle (aurochs or *Bos primigenius*), but also including a stylized anthropomorph with outstretched arms (after Huyge and Claes 2008).

markers of excellent hunting areas, the depictions could be considered expressions of sympathetic magic, mythological or cosmological world ordering. Based on patination, style, and context a date of approximately 15,000–14,000 BCE has tentatively been proposed, which would make it Egypt's earliest art and one of the oldest graphic traditions on the African continent (Huyge 2008, 2009; Huyge et al. 2007; Huyge and Claes 2008).

The context of the Upper or Late Palaeolithic rock art is very different from that of what presumably are Epipalaeolithic visual markers. Tentatively dated to the Epipalaeolithic period are a number of rock art sites at el-Hosh, characterized by representations of sophisticated labyrinthine fish fences (Huyge 2005; Huyge et al. 1998) to channel and barricade fish into a confined space. These frequently appear in clusters (Figure 2.2) and are often associated with abstract and figurative motifs, including circles, ladder-shaped drawings, human figures, footprints, and crocodiles. Direct dating attempts on samples of the dark patinated deposits from within the petroglyphs have provided a minimum-age estimate for this rock art of 5600 cal BCE (Huyge et al. 2001) and the estimation is that the el-Hosh designs are about 10,000 to 9000 years old. Rather than interpreting these as mere practical guides on how to build a fish trap, it is conceivable that the area of el-Hosh was the location of a seasonal congregation at the time of the inundation to perform concerted fishing activities, and, quite possibly, associated ceremonies and rituals. The closest parallels for the Nilotic el-Hosh representations can be found in the Eastern Desert, in particular in the vicinity of the Wadi Hammamat, which seems to indicate that the makers of the el-Hosh rock art led a nomadic existence, consistent with other cultural remains recovered from Elkab in the Nile Valley and the Tree Shelter site in Wadi Sodmein in the Eastern Desert (Vermeersch 1978, 2008; Vermeersch et al. 2002).

Figure 2.2 Epipalaeolithic rock art: typical labyrinthine fish fences and associated scenery from el-Hosh. The animal figures located in the upper right corner are more recent in age than the rest of the panel (after Huyge et al. 2001).

Portable art, such as clay or stone figurines, can be locally made and used, but are also potential trade goods. The earliest examples of sculpture in Egypt are figurines found in level I (*Urschicht*) at Merimde Benisalame (Eiwanger 1984). Remarkable is the presence of a number of clay figurines, among which are an anthropomorphic figure and fragments of bovids. Their meaning is difficult to ascertain as they are quite isolated finds which almost certainly had no influence on the development of Predynastic representations in Upper Egypt.

In the Predynastic period figurines occur much more frequently. Individuals with raised arms occur besides victory scenes, the best known being the figurines found in a limited number of Naqada I-II tombs (Ucko 1968). Most of the known examples are female, but this could be due to the hazards of preservation. The figurines are stylized in a most particular manner, with bird heads and cone-shaped legs. Furthermore, the position of the arms allows comparison with bovine horns in general and two flint bull heads in particular (Hendrickx 2002:283–284). These deliberate deviations from reality allow the combination of human, avid, and bovine characteristics but also the derivation of almost abstract symbols, the most widespread being that of two curves on top of two triangular extensions referring respectively to bovine horns/human arms and bovine ears/female breasts (Hendrickx in press). The link with bovines is confirmed by a comparison with the emblem of the cow-goddess Bat, the earliest example of which has been found at the Hierakonpolis elite cemetery HK6 and dated to Naqada IIA–B (Hendrickx 2005), but which also figures prominently on the Narmer Palette (see below).

Besides figurines with raised arms, there are also a number of male figurines in which the arms do not play an important role but for which the most notable element are large penis sheaths. Two large gold foil figurines found in 2006 at Tell el-Farkha illustrate the importance of such representations (Dębowska-Ludwin 2008). Penis sheaths occur already for the dominating persons on white cross-lined pottery, while the penis sheath(?) of the prisoners has a different shape and phallic symbolism is also important on the Narmer Palette (see below).

White cross-lined pottery represents the earliest ceramics with figurative decoration in Egypt. The decoration of white cross-lined ware does not appear to have been designed with the material features of the vessels in mind, and sometimes the adaptation of the composition was rather clumsy (Wengrow 2006:102–103). A particularly obvious example is the position of the hunter, oblique to his dogs, on the well-known plate from Moscow (Museum of Fine Arts 2947, Houlihan 1996:75–76). On this plate, the viewer can observe the entire scene at a glance, which is, however, not the case for jars, where the decoration extends around the body. But as the decoration is not symmetrical or repetitive, the starting point for viewing had to be selected by the past artisan and viewer. It would seem the scenes were transferred from compositions on flat surfaces to the vessels. It is therefore to be supposed that the limited number of figurative scenes on white cross-lined pottery bears testimony to a broader spectrum of visual representations, presumably on perishable materials, that has not been preserved. An exception is the unique painted linen shroud from Gebelein (Donadoni Roveri and Tiradritti 1998:168–169).

The most interesting white cross-lined vessels were a small group of five jars decorated with scenes including human representations (Hendrickx in press). The three jars for which the provenance is known have been discovered in cemetery U at Abydos, one in tomb U-239 (Dreyer et al. 1998:111–114, Abb 12.1, 13), the two others in tomb U-415 (Dreyer et al. 2003:80–84, Abb. 5, 6.a). The common theme among these vessels was their decoration referring to interpersonal violence and victory (Dreyer et al. 1998:111–112; Dreyer et al. 2003:80–82; Hendrickx 2004; Midant-Reynes 2003:326–330). Fundamental to this interpretation is the presence of prisoners, represented with their arms bound at the back and in some cases "attached" to larger figures, considered as the victors. Apart from their relatively large size, these latter figures are occasionally characterized by the presence of mace heads, while other elements which distinguish them from the prisoners include feathers or branches worn on the head and animal tails hung from the belt (see below). Furthermore, some of the victors are also characterized by the upraised position of the arms, a particular attitude that, in the past, has been interpreted as dancing (Baumgartel 1955:64–65) and occasionally still is (Garfinkel 2003:233–267), despite the obvious presence of prisoners. Instead, the raised arms are to be considered a symbol of power, referencing bull horns (Hendrickx 2002:283–284; Hendrickx in press).

Besides these victory scenes, two types of hunting scenes occurred regularly: hunting of crocodile and/or hippopotamus (Hendrickx and Depraetere 2004) and hunting desert animals, often with dogs (Hendrickx 2006). In the archaeological society of fourth-millennium Egypt, hunting crocodile or hippopotamus, and the economic importance of hunting in general, was marginal. After the initial phase of the Naqada culture, hunting represented less than 2 percent of the food procurement (see also Huyge 2002:192; Vermeersch et al. 2004:269). These scenes are therefore to be considered symbolic rather than reflecting reality. Hunting was probably part of the elite way of life, allowing a more varied diet, but, perhaps even more importantly, giving opportunity for weapon practice. Dogs obviously played an important role in hunting and are to be considered part of elite culture and symbolism. The hunting of hippopotamus probably symbolically represented the control over elements of chaos by positive forces, an idea that continued into Dynastic times (Hendrickx and Depraetere 2004:814–815; Säve-Söderbergh 1953).

Starting with the Naqada IIB, the white cross-lined pottery was replaced by decorated ware, made from marl clay and decorated in purple-black. Not only were the representations on decorated ware far more standardized than those on white cross-lined pottery (Graff 2007:771–772), but their general characteristics were also different (Wengrow 2006:102–104). Two types of decoration can be distinguished. The first one is non-figurative, and a number of those vases seem to imitate stone vessels. The second type is figurative and far more interesting and complex. The iconographic elements were limited in number, and most of them have been identified beyond doubt (e.g. water, boats, birds, trees, gazelle/antelope). Obviously, the decorated ware referred to a religious-intellectual world, but the way in which the different iconographic elements were combined has been widely discussed. Only recently has a breakthrough in their interpretation been made by identifying the individual elements of the decoration and analyzing their occurrences (Graff 2002, 2003, 2007). Frequently occurring combinations of signs indicate that the decorated ware of this period can be considered an intellectual stage preceding the development of writing.

Figurative representations on pottery became very exceptional from the beginning of the Naqada III period onwards, but they are attested on, for example, decorated ivories, palettes, and mace heads. The decorated ivories, mainly knife handles, are generally accepted to date to the very end of the Naqada II and the beginning of the Naqada III period (Dreyer 1999). Most of them, such as the well-known Abu Zeidan knife handle (Churcher 1984), show animals in regularly organized rows. The animals were exclusively wild and among them were even hybrid representations (Huyge 2004). The structured meaning of the animals is demonstrated by the repeated combination of elephants on snakes or the insertion of a giraffe as a second type of animal in a row of large birds of which only the first one had a serpent under its beak. At the end of some rows, individual animals, especially dogs, were depicted. These seem to have derived from the earlier hunting scenes on white cross-lined pottery and occasionally this theme also occurred on decorated ware (Hendrickx 2006). The style of representation had, however, changed over time, replacing the earlier, more anecdotal, and to some extent realistic hunting scenes by highly symbolic representations. These were only meaningful within the context of a complex iconography. The sole remaining anecdotal element on the decorated ivories was the raised front leg of the dogs or their "leaping" position, which had parallels in the hunting scenes.

Another rich source of iconographic information were the decorated palettes, most of them probably dating to the end of the Naqada II and the early Naqada III period. The Hunters' Palette (Spencer 1980:79, no. 575) was certainly among the oldest examples. On it a chaotic group of desert animals is surrounded by hunters, presumably expressing the fundamental topic of order over chaos. Most remarkably, the hunters have tails attached to their belts which are reminiscent of the tails worn by some of the dominating males on the white cross-lined vessels. In addition these can be identified as tails of the African hunting dog or *Lycaon pictus*. These animals are co-operative hunters, hunting in packs led by the alpha male. The selected prey is chased over distances of several kilometers while gradually being surrounded. The hunting organization of the *Lycaon pictus* must have impressed Predynastic hunters, who compared it with their own methods and perhaps identified themselves at least partially with the animals. This must have inspired the composition of the hunters on the edges of the Hunters' Palette, encircling the chaotic animal world in the middle. On a number of other palettes, the presence of large-size *Lycaon pictus* in a so-called heraldic position had already been recognized for a long time (Asselberghs 1961; Fischer 1958). This composition reflected that of the Hunters' Palette.

A number of iconographic elements *Lycaon pictus*, and the visual language of the decorated jars, disappeared before the start of the 1st Dynasty. Other scenes or iconographic details, however, continued. The "ruler" holding a mace head was first employed on white cross-lined pottery, approached a formal style in the Hierakonpolis "Painted Tomb," and was fully developed on the Narmer Palette. Scenes with prisoners relating to military power and control did not occur on the decorated ware. This, however, does not necessarily mean that such representations fell out of use. A contemporary example was the image of a ruler figure smiting his enemies from the "Painted Tomb" at Hierakonpolis. The victory scenes on white cross-lined pottery have been considered as part of a visual repertoire which occurred in other material forms, and the use of these scenes probably continued during the Naqada IIC–D period on objects other than pots. Indirect evidence of this is to be found in the reoccurrence of victory scenes on Naqada III objects such as the Narmer Palette. Phallic symbolism, well known from the white cross-lined pottery, referring to male fertility, dominance, and power, is obviously illustrated on the Narmer Palette by two rows of decapitated and castrated prisoners whose severed heads are positioned between the legs, with the penis on top (Davies and Friedman 2002).

The origins and development of formal iconography, as defined by Kemp (2006), were intimately linked to the emergence of kingship. Although some formal elements can be traced over an extended period, the definitive establishment of the principles that were fundamental for Early Dynastic art must have happened over a relatively short period. Accepting that formal art was largely established by the time of Narmer, we can see that even a highly important royal symbol such as the *serekh* has not yet taken its classic form during the time of Irj-Hor, only two reigns before Narmer (Jiménez-Serrano 2003).

The development of and control over a formal iconography and its syntax was probably of fundamental importance for the elite, who had every reason to stimulate a strictly uniform iconographic language, confirming their own privileged position. The development of the script was an essential part of this, opening up entirely new possibilities, far beyond those of "worship without writing."

ACKNOWLEDGMENTS

The authors would like to thank Veerle Linseele for discussing the problem of early cattle domestication.

REFERENCES

Anderson, W. 1992 Badarian Burials: Evidence of Social Inequality in Middle Egypt during the Early Predynastic Era. Journal of the American Research Centre in Egypt 29:51–66.

Applegate, A., A. Gautier, and S. Duncan 2001 The North Tumuli of the Nabta Late Neolithic Ceremonial Complex. *In* Holocene Settlement of the Egyptian Sahara. Vol. 1. The Archaeology of Nabta Playa. F. Wendorf and R. Schild, eds. Pp. 468–488. New York: Kluwer Academic/Plenum Publishers.

Asselberghs, H. 1961 Chaos en beheersing: Documenten uit Aeneolithisch Egypte. Leiden: Brill.

Bard, K. A. 1994 From Farmers to Pharaohs: Mortuary Evidence for the Rise of Complex Society in Egypt. Sheffield: Sheffield Academic Press.

Bard, K. A. 2008 An Introduction to the Archaeology of Ancient Egypt. Malden, MA: Blackwell.

Baumgartel, E. J. 1955 The Cultures of Prehistoric Egypt I. 2nd rev. ed. London: Oxford University Press for Griffith Institute.

Brunton, G. 1937 Mostagedda and the Tasian Culture. London: Bernard Quaritch.

Brunton, G. 1948 Matmar. London: Bernard Quaritch.

Brunton, G., and G. Caton Thompson 1928 The Badarian Civilisation and Prehistoric Remains Near Badari. Vol. 46. London: Bernard Quaritch.

Caton Thompson, G., and E. W. Gardner 1934 The Desert Fayum. 2 vols. London: The Royal Anthropological Institute of Great Britain and Ireland.

Churcher, C. S. 1984 Zoological Study of the Ivory Knife Handle from Abu Zaidan. *In* Predynastic and Archaic Egypt in the Brooklyn Museum. W. Needler, ed. Pp. 152–169. Brooklyn: The Brooklyn Museum.

Ciałowicz, K. M. 2001 La naissance d'un royaume. L'Égypte dès la période prédynastique à la fin de la 1ère dynastie. Kraków: Uniwersytet Jagielloński Instytut Archeologii.

Close, A. E. 1995 Few and Far Between: Early Ceramics in North Africa. *In* The Emergence of Pottery: Technology and Innovation in Ancient Societies. W. K. Barnett and J. W. Hoopes, eds. Pp. 23–37. Washington, D.C.: Smithsonian Institution Press

Coimbra, F., and G. Dimitriadis 2008 Cognitive Archaeology as Symbolic Archaeology. Oxford: Archaeopress.

Crubézy, É., and B. Midant-Reynes 2005 Les sacrifices humains à l'époque prédynastique: L'apport de la nécropole d'Adaïma. *In* Le sacrifice humain en Égypte ancienne et ailleurs. J.-P. Albert and B. Midant-Reynes, eds. Pp. 58–81. Études d'égyptologie, Vol. 6. Paris: Éditions Soleb.

Darnell, D. 2002 Gravel of the Desert and Broken Pots in the Road: Ceramic Evidence from the Routes between the Nile and Kharga Oasis. *In* Egypt and Nubia: Gifts of the Desert. R. F. Friedman, ed. Pp. 156–177. London: British Museum Press.

Davies, W. V., and R. F. Friedman 2002 The Narmer Palette: An Overlooked Detail. *In* Egyptian Museum Collections around the World. Vol. 1. M. Eldamaty and M. Trad, eds. Pp. 243–246. Cairo: Supreme Council of Antiquities.

Dębowska-Ludwin, J. 2008 Burial Custom and Political Status of Local Societies: A View from Tell el-Farkha. *In* Egypt at Its Origins 2. Orientalia Lovaniensia Analecta 172. B. Midant-Reynes, Y. Tristant, J. Rowland, and S. Hendrickx, eds. Pp. 1107–1117. Leuven: Peeters.

Delrue, P. 2001 The Predynastic Cemetery N7000 at Naga ed-Dêr: A Re-evaluation. *In* Social Aspects of Funerary Culture in the Egyptian Old and Middle Kingdoms. H. Willems, ed. Pp. 21–66. Leuven: Peeters.

Dobres, M.-A., and C. R. Hoffman 1994 Social Agency and the Dynamics of Prehistoric Technology. Journal of Archaeological Method and Theory 1(3):211–258.

Donadoni Roveri, A. M., and F. Tiradritti 1998 Kemet, alle sorgenti del tempo. Milan: Electa.

Dougherty, S. P., and R. F. Friedman 2008 Sacred or Mundane: Scalping and Decapitation at Predynastic Hierakonpolis. *In* Egypt at Its Origins 2. Proceedings of the International Conference "Origin of the State. Predynastic and Early Dynastic Egypt," Toulouse, 5–8 September 2005. B. Midant-Reynes, Y. Tristant, J. Rowland, and S. Hendrickx, eds. OLA 172, pp. 311–388. Leuven: Peeters.

Dreyer, G. 1999 Motive und Datierung der dekorierten prädynastischen Messergriffe. *In* L'art de l'Ancien Empire égyptien. C. Ziegler, ed. Pp. 195–226. Paris: La documentation Française.

Dreyer, G., with R. Hartmann, U. Hartung, T. Hikade, H. Köpp, C. Lacher, V. Müller, A. Nerlich, and A. Zink 2003 Umm el-Qaab: Nachuntersuchungen im frühzeitlichen Königsfriedhof 13./14./15. Vorbericht. Mitteilungen des Deutschen Archäologischen Instituts, Abteilung Kairo 59:67–138.

Dreyer, G., U. Hartung, T. Hikade, E. C. Köhler, V. Müller, and F. Pumpenmeier 1998 Umm el-Qaab: Nachuntersuchungen im frühzeitlichen Königsfriedhof 9./10. Vorbericht. Mitteilungen des Deutschen Archäologischen Instituts, Abteilung Kairo 54:77–167.

Eiwanger, J. 1984 Merimde-Benisalâme I: Die Funde der Urschicht. Mainz am Rhein: Philipp von Zabern.

Eiwanger, J. 1988 Merimde-Benisalâme II: Die Funde der mittleren Merimdekultur. Mainz am Rhein: Philipp von Zabern.

Fischer, H. G. 1958 A Fragment of Late Predynastic Egyptian Relief from the Eastern Delta. Artibus Asiae 21:64–88.

Flores, D. V. 2003 Funerary Sacrifice of Animals in the Egyptian Predynastic Period. Oxford: Archaeopress.

Friedman, R. F. 1996 The Ceremonial Centre at Hierakonpolis Locality HK 29A. *In* Aspects of Early Egypt. J. Spencer, ed. Pp. 16–35. London: British Museum Press.

Friedman, R. F. 2003 Return to the Temple: Excavations at HK29A. Nekhen News 15:4–5.

Friedman, R. F. 2006 The Friends of Nekhen. Ancient Egypt 6(5):45–51.

Friedman, R. F., and J. J. Hobbs 2002 A "Tasian" Tomb in Egypt's Eastern Desert. *In* Egypt and Nubia: Gifts of the Desert. R. F. Friedman, ed. Pp. 178–191. London: British Museum Press.

Friedman, R. F., with A. Maish, A. Gamal-Eldin Fahmy, J. C. Darnell, and E. D. Johnson 1999 Preliminary Report on Field Work at Hierakonpolis: 1996–1998. Journal of the American Research Centre in Egypt 36:1–35.

Garfinkel, Y. 2003 Dancing at the Dawn of Agriculture. Austin: University of Texas Press.

Gautier, A. 2001 The Early to Late Neolithic Archeofaunas from Nabta and Bir Kiseiba. *In* Holocene Settlement of the Egyptian Sahara. Vol. 1. The Archaeology of Nabta Playa. F. Wendorf and R. Schild, eds. Pp. 609–635. New York: Kluwer Academic/Plenum Publishers.

Graff, G. 2002 Approche de l'iconographie nagadienne: Les peintures sur vases Nagada I–Nagada II. Problèmes de lecture et essais d'interprétation, Université de Paris IV.

Graff, G. 2003 Les vases naqadiens comportant des représentations d'addax. Cahiers Caribéens d'Égyptologie 5:35–57.

Graff, G. 2007 Les peintures sur vases Nagada I–Nagada II: Nouvelle approche sémiologique. In Egypt at Its Origins: Studies in Memory of Barbara Adams. Proceedings of the International Conference "Origin of the State: Predynastic and Early Dynastic Egypt," Kraków, 28 August–1 September 2002. S. Hendrickx, R. F. Friedman, K. M. Ciałowicz, and M. Chłodnicki, eds. Pp. 765–777. OLA, Vol. 138. Leuven: Peeters.

Grigson, C. 2000 Bos africanus (Brehm)? Notes on the Archaeozoology of the Native Cattle of Africa. In The Origins and Development of African Lifestock: Archaeology, Genetics, Linguistics and Ethnography. R. M. Blench and K. C. MacDonald, eds. Pp. 38–60. London: University College London Press.

Grimal, N.-C. 1988 Histoire de l'Egypte ancienne. Paris: Fayard.

Grimal, N.-C. 1992 A History of Ancient Egypt. Oxford, Cambridge, MA: Blackwell.

Hendrickx, S. 2002 Bovines in Egyptian Predynastic and Early Dynastic Iconography. In Droughts, Food and Culture: Ecological Change and Food Security in Africa's Later Prehistory. F. A. Hassan, ed. Pp. 275–318. New York: Kluwer Academic/Plenum Publishers.

Hendrickx, S. 2004 Des images au service du pouvoir. Le Monde de la Bible 162: 36–41.

Hendrickx, S. 2005 The Earliest Example of Pharaonic Iconography. Nekhen News 17:14–15.

Hendrickx, S. 2006 Predynastic–Early Dynastic. In Ancient Egyptian Chronology. E. Hornung, R. Krauss, and D. A. Warburton, eds. Pp. 52–93. Handbook of Oriental Studies. Section 1 The Near and Middle East, Vol. 83. Leiden: Brill.

Hendrickx, S. 2006. The Dog, the Lycaon pictus and Order over Chaos in Predynastic Egypt. In Archaeology of Early Northeastern Africa (Studies in African Archaeology, Vol. 9). K. Kröper, M. Chłodnicki, and M. Kobusiewicz, eds. Pp. 723–749. Poznań: Poznań Archaeological Museum.

Hendrickx, S. in press. Visual Representation and State Development in Egypt. In Grenzbereiche der Schrift. S. J. Seidlmayer, ed. Berichte und Abhandlungen der Berlin-Brandenburgischen Akademie der Wissenschaften. Berlin: Berlin-Brandenburgischen Akademie.

Hendrickx, S., and D. Depraetere 2004 A Theriomorphic Predynastic Stone Jar and Hippopotamus Symbolism. In Egypt at Its Origins: Studies in Memory of Barbara Adams. Proceedings of the International Conference "Origin of the State: Predynastic and Early Dynastic Egypt," Kraków, 28 August–1 September 2002. S. Hendrickx, R. F. Friedman, K. M. Ciałowicz, and M. Chłodnicki, eds. OLA, Vol. 138. Leuven: Peeters.

Hendrickx, S., and R. F. Friedman 2003 Chaos and Order: A Predynastic "Ostracon" from HK29A. Nekhen News 15:8–9.

Hendrickx, S., B. Midant-Reynes, and W. Van Neer 2001 Mahgar Dendera 2 (Haute Egypte), un site d'occupation Badarien. Vol. 3. Leuven: Leuven University Press.

Hendrickx, S., and P. M. Vermeersch 2000 Prehistory: From the Palaeolithic to the Badarian Culture (c. 700,000 to 4000 BC). In The Oxford History of Ancient Egypt. I. Shaw, ed. Pp. 16–40. Oxford: Oxford University Press.

Hoffman, M. A. 1986 A Preliminary Report on 1984 Excavations at Hierakonpolis. Newsletter of the American Research Centre in Egypt 132:3–14.

Holdaway, S., Wendrich, W., and R. Phillipps in press. Variability in Low Level Food Production Societies as a Response to Resource Uncertainty. Antiquity.

Houlihan, P. F. 1996 The Animal World of the Pharaohs. Cairo: The American University in Cairo Press.

Huyge, D. 2002 Cosmology, Ideology and Personal Religious Practice in Ancient Egyptian Rock Art. *In* Egypt and Nubia: Gifts of the Desert. R. F. Friedman, ed. Pp. 192–206. London: British Museum Press.

Huyge, D. 2004 A Double-powerful Device for Regeneration: The Abu Zaidan Knife Handle Reconsidered. *In* Egypt at Its Origins: Studies in Memory of Barbara Adams. Proceedings of the International Conference "Origin of the State. Predynastic and Early Dynastic Egypt," Kraków, 28 August–1 September 2002. S. Hendrickx, R. F. Friedman, K. M. Ciałowicz, and M. Chłodnicki, eds. Pp. 823–836. OLA, Vol. 138. Leuven: Peeters.

Huyge, D. 2005 The Fish Hunters of el-Hosh: Rock Art Research and Archaeological Investigations in Upper Egypt (1998–2004). Bulletin des Séances de l'Academie Royale des Sciences d'Outre-Mer 51:231–249.

Huyge, D. 2008 Côa in Africa: Late Pleistocene Rock Art along the Egyptian Nile. International Newsletter on Rock Art 51:1–7.

Huyge, D. 2009 Late Palaeolithic and Epipalaeolithic Rock Art in Egypt: Qurta and El-Hosh. Archéo-Nil 19:106–118.

Huyge, D., M. Aubert, H. Barnard, W. Claes, J. C. Darnell, M. De Dapper, E. Figari, S. Ikram, A. Lebrun-Nélis, and I. Therasse 2007 "Lascaux along the Nile": Late Pleistocene Rock Art in Egypt. Antiquity 81(313, Project Gallery). http://antiquity.ac.uk/ProjGall/huyge/index.html.

Huyge, D., and W. Claes 2008 "Ice Age" Art along the Nile. Egyptian Archaeology 33:25–28.

Huyge, D., M. De Dapper, D. Depraetere, M. Ismail, E, Marchi, R. Mommaerts, I. Regulski, and A. Watchman 1998 Hilltops, Silts, and Petroglyphs: The Fish Hunters of El-Hosh (Upper Egypt). Bulletin des Musées royaux d'Art et d'Histoire 69:97–113.

Huyge, D., A. Watchman, M. De Dapper, and E. Marchi 2001 Dating Egypt's Oldest "Art": AMS 14C Age Determinations of Rock Varnishes Covering Petroglyphs at El-Hosh (Upper Egypt). Antiquity 75:68–72.

Irish, J. D., P. Bobrowski, M. Kobusiewicz, J. Kabaciński, and R. Schild 2004 An Artificial Human Tooth from the Neolithic Cemetery at Gebel Ramlah, Egypt. Dental Anthropology 17:28–31.

Irish, J. D., Kobusiewicz, J. Kabaciński, and R. Schild 2005 Two additional Egyptian Neolithic Burials Exhibiting Unusual Mortuary Treatment of Teeth. International Journal of Osteoarchaeology 15:136–139.

Irish, J. D., M. Kobusiewicz, R. Schild, and F. Wendorf 2003 Neolithic Tooth Replacement in Two Disturbed Burials from Southern Egypt. Journal of Archaeological Science 30:281–285.

Jiménez-Serrano, A. 2003 Chronology and Local Traditions: The Representation of Power and the Royal Name in the Late Predynastic Period. Archéo-Nil 13:93–142.

Kemp, B. J. 2006 Ancient Egypt, Anatomy of a Civilization. London, New York: Routledge.

Kobusiewicz, M., with J. Kabaciński, R. Schild, J. D. Irish, and F. Wendorf 2004 Discovery of the First Neolithic Cemetery in Egypt's Western Desert. Antiquity 78:566–578.

Królik, H., and R. Schild 2001 Site E-75-6: An El Nabta and Al Jerar Village. *In* Holocene Settlement of the Egyptian Sahara. Volume 1. The Archaeology of Nabta Playa. F. Wendorf and R. Schild, eds. Pp. 111–146. New York: Kluwer Academic/Plenum Publishers.

Kuper, R. 1995 Prehistoric Research in the Southern Libyan Desert: A Brief Account and Some Conclusions of the B.O.S. Project. Cahiers de Recherches de l'Institut de Papyrologie et d'Égyptologie de Lille 17:123–140.

Lemonnier, P. 1993 Introduction. *In* Technological Choices: Transformation in Material Cultures since the Neolithic. P. Lemonnier, ed. Pp. 1–35. London: Routledge.

Linseele, V., and W. Van Neer 2003 Gourmets or Priests? Fauna from the Predynastic Temple. Nekhen News 15:6–7.

Math, N. C. 2006 Die Tulpenbecher und ihre Verwandten. *In* Timelines: Studies in Honour of Manfred Bietak. Vol. II. E. Czerny, I. Hein, H. Hunger, D. Melman, and A. Schwab, eds. Pp. 45–54. Leuven: Peeters.

Midant-Reynes, B. 2000 The Prehistory of Egypt : From the First Egyptians to the First Pharaohs. Oxford, Malden, MA: Blackwell.

Midant-Reynes, B. 2003 Aux origines de l'Egypte: Du Néolithique à l'émergence de l'État. Paris: Fayard.

Mithen, S. J. 1996 The Prehistory of the Mind: The Cognitive Origins of Art, Religion and Science. London: Thames & Hudson.

Mithen, S. J. 1997 Cognitive Archaeology, Evolutionary Psychology and Cultural Transmission, with Particular Reference to Religious Ideas. Archeological Papers of the American Anthropological Association 7(1):67–74. http://dx.doi.org/10.1525/ap3a.1997.7.1.67.

Mithen, S. J. 2006 The Singing Neanderthals: The Origins of Music, Language, Mind, and bBdy. Cambridge, MA: Harvard University Press.

Mithen, S. J., ed. 2007 Creativity in Human Evolution and Prehistory. London: Routledge.

Myers, O. H., and H. W. Fairman 1931 Excavations at Armant 1929–1931. Journal of Egyptian Archaeology 17:223–232.

Nelson, K. 2002 Ceramic Types of the Nabta-Kiseiba Area. *In* Holocene Settlement of the Egyptian Sahara. Volume 2. The Pottery of Nabta Playa. K. Nelson, ed. Pp. 9–20. New York: Kluwer Academic/Plenum Publishers.

Ouzman, S. 1998 Towards a Mindscape of Landscape: Rock-art as Expression of World-understanding. *In* The Archaeology of Rock-art. C. Chippindale and P. S. C. Taçon, eds. Pp. 30–41. Cambridge, New York: Cambridge University Press.

Pilafidis-Williams, K. 1998 The Sanctuary of Aphaia on Aigina in the Bronze Age. Munich: Deutsches Archäologisches Institut.

Potter, W. E., and J. F. Powell 2003 Big Headaches in the Predynastic: Cranial Trauma at HK43. Nekhen News 15:26–27.

Renfrew, C. 2007 Prehistory: The Making of the Human Mind. London: Weidenfeld & Nicolson.

Renfrew, C., P. A. Mountjoy, and C. Macfarlane 1985 The Archaeology of Cult: The Sanctuary at Phylakopi. London: British School of Archaeology at Athens/Thames and Hudson.

Renfrew, C., and C. Scarre 1998 Cognition and Material Culture: The Archaeology of Symbolic Storage. Cambridge: McDonald Institute for Archaeological Research.

Renfrew, C., and E. B. W. Zubrow 1994 The Ancient Mind: Elements of Cognitive Archaeology. Cambridge, New York: Cambridge University Press.

Riemer, H., and K. Kindermann 2008 Contacts between the Oasis and the Nile: A Résumé of the Abu Muhariq Plateau Survey 1995–2002. In Proceedings of the International Conference "Origin of the State: Predynastic and Early Dynastic Egypt," Toulouse, 5–8 September 2005. *In* Egypt at its Origins 2. B. Midant-Reynes, Y. Tristant, J. Rowland, and S. Hendrickx, eds. Orientalia Lovaniensia Analecta Vol. 172 Leuven: Peeters.

Rockman, M., and J. Steele 2003 Colonization of Unfamiliar Landscapes: The Archaeology of Adaptation. London, New York: Routledge.

Savage, S. H. 1997 Descent Group Competition and Economic Strategies in Predynastic Egypt. Journal of Anthropological Archaeology 16:226–268.

Säve-Söderbergh, T. 1953 On Egyptian Representations of Hippopotamus Hunting as a Religious Motive. Lund: C. W. K. Gleerup.

Skeates, R. 2005 Visual Culture and Archaeology: Art and Social Life in Prehistoric South-East Italy. London: Duckworth.

Smith, P. E. L. 1985 An Enigmatic Frieze from Upper Egypt: A Problem in Nilotic Rock Art. *In* Studi di paletnologia in onore di Salvatore M. Puglisi. M. Liverani, A. Palmieri, and R. Peroni, eds. Pp. 359–368. Rome: Università degli Studi di Roma "La Sapienza."

Spencer, A. J. 1980 Catalogue of Egyptian Antiquities in the British Museum. V. Early Dynastic Objects. London: British Museum Press.

Stevens, F. 2007 Identifying the Body: Representing Self. Art, Ornamentation and the Body in Later Prehistoric Europe. *In* Material Identities. J. R. Sofaer, ed. Pp. 82–98. Oxford, Malden, MA: Blackwell.

Ucko, P. J. 1968 Anthropomorphic Figures of Predynastic Egypt and Neolithic Crete with Comparative Material from the Prehistoric Near East and Mainland Greece. London: Andrew Szmidla.

Vermeersch, P. M. 1978 Elkab II. L'Elkabien, Epipaléolithique de la Vallée du Nil Egyptien. Leuven: Universitaire Pers Leuven.

Vermeersch, P. M. ed. 2008 A Holocene Prehistoric Sequence in the Egyptian Red Sea Area: The Tree Shelter. Egyptian Prehistory Monographs 7. Leuven: Leuven University Press.

Vermeersch, P. M., E. Paulissen, and T. Vanderbeken 2002 Nazlet Khater 4, an Upper Palaeolithic Underground Chert Mine. *In* Palaeolithic Quarrying Sites in Upper and Middle Egypt, Egyptian Prehistory Monographs (Leuven) 4. P. M. Vermeersch, ed. Pp. 211–272.

Vermeersch, P. M., W. Van Neer, and S. Hendrickx 2004 El Abadiya 2, a Naqada I Site near Danfiq, Upper Egypt. *In* Egypt at Its Origins: Studies in Memory of Barbara Adams. Proceedings of the International Conference "Origin of the State: Predynastic and Early Dynastic Egypt," Kraków, 28 August–1 September 2002. S. Hendrickx, R. F. Friedman, K. M. Ciałowicz, and M. Chłodnicki, eds. Pp. 213–276. OLA, Vol. 138. Leuven: Peeters.

Vermeersch, P. M., P. Van Peer, J. Moeyersons, and W. Van Neer 2002 The Tree Shelter, a Holocene Site in the Red Sea Mountains. Archéo-Nil 12:123–137.

Vermeersch, P. M., P. Van Peer, V. Rots, L. Van Kerckhoven, and W. Van Neer 2005 The Middle Holocene Shell Mound of El Gouna on the Red Sea (Egypt). Journal of Field Archaeology 30:435–442.

Wendorf, F., and R. Schild 1976. Prehistory of the Nile Valley. New York, San Franciso, London: Academic Press.

Wendorf, F., with R. Schild, A. Applegate, and A. Gautier 1997 Tumuli, Cattle Burials and Society in the Eastern Sahara. *In* Dynamics of Populations, Movements and Responses to Climatic Change in Africa. B. E. Barich and M. C. Gatto, eds. Pp. 90–104. Rome: Bonsignori Editore.

Wendrich, W., and R. Cappers 2005 Egypt's Earliest Granaries: Evidence from the Fayum. Egyptian Archaeology 27:12–15.

Wendrich, W., and R. Cappers, eds. forthcoming. The Fayum Desert. Volume I. Survey and Excavation of the Prehistoric Remains.

Wengrow, D. 2006 The Archaeology of Early Egypt: Social Transformations in North-East Africa, 10,000 to 2,650 BC. Cambridge, New York: Cambridge University Press.

Wilkinson, T. A. H. 1999 Early Dynastic Egypt. London: Routledge.

Wynn, T. 2002 Archaeology and Cognitive Evolution. Behavioral and Brain Sciences 25:389–438.

3
Theories of State Formation

E. Christiana Köhler

The history of research into state formation in ancient Egypt goes almost as far back as the history of Egyptology, and numerous attempts have been made to explain the transition from Palaeolithic hunters and gatherers to the state system of the Old Kingdom. To bridge the gap between these two chronologically, but, more importantly, socially, politically, and economically disparate modes of ancient human existence inescapably means to consider a wide range of archaeological data and to take into account social evolutionary theory in order to determine when and to explain how and why this change occurred.

Early scholarship relied heavily on insights and answers provided by the ancient Egyptians from different periods, such as Manetho's account of the history of the pharaohs, king lists, religious and mythological texts, as well as art representations which potentially relate to the emergence of kingship and the state in Egypt. The underlying tenor of this ancient tradition is that before Menes, the first king of Egypt and himself a southerner, conquered the north, founded the capital Memphis, and in doing so unified the country under his rule, Egypt was divided into two or more kingdoms. This basic historical narrative was the backbone of research during the twentieth century, when archaeological evidence was gradually added to the historical inquiry into what was then generally referred to as the "unification of Egypt." Early scholarship therefore very much focused on the search for the historical Menes and on aspects of warfare and conquest as represented on the monuments of the period, such as the Narmer Palette. The second half of the twentieth century brought forward a discourse on the validity of these early sources which was later expanded when the slowly emerging archaeological evidence from northern Egypt was progressively taken into consideration (Kaiser 1956, 1957, 1964, 1990, 1995; Köhler 1995, 1996, 1998; Kroeper and Wildung 1985; Seeher 1991; Von der Way 1991).

This discussion was later fueled by the introduction of modern archaeological and anthropological theory, which led to the conclusion that the "unification of Egypt" was in essence a process of state formation and the emergence of complex society in Egypt which could be investigated on a much broader social, political, and economic basis and in comparison with other cultures. In this tradition, numerous theoretical approaches were added to the spectrum of the scholarly inquiry, including both conflict as well as integration theories, such as Carneiro's geographic circumscription theory (Bard and Carneiro 1989; Carneiro 1970, 1981), Wittfogel's "oriental despotism" (Atzler 1981; Wittfogel 1957), Renfrew's "multiplier effect" (Hoffman 1979; Renfrew 1972), game theory (Kemp 2006), and many others. In this context, conflict theories have been a recurring and popular theme considering that many of the ancient Egyptian sources feature early rulers in association with warfare (e.g. Campagno 2004; Hendrickx and Friedman 2003; Kahl 2003; Kaiser 1956, 1957, 1964, 1990, 1995).

However, many of these approaches, be they historical, theoretical, or archaeological, have only ever been partly successful, which has many reasons. One of these is the limited quantity of archaeological evidence covering all aspects of material culture as well as the different regions of Egypt. The overrepresentation of mortuary data in southern Egypt still restricts the scope of the various attempts at modern statistical approaches, which only ever succeed in explaining social or economic development in this region (e.g. Bard 1994; Wilkinson 1996), but cannot account for changes outside the sphere of funerary customs or in other parts of Egypt. Therefore, the debate has only very recently become more viable and productive, because the abundance of theories is gradually being complemented by archaeological evidence from the more intensive and more systematic exploration of the north and modern re-evaluation of existing evidence in the south. The current discussion has also benefited from an enhancement in the theory of social evolutionary inquiry and from a sound review of previous theories and models of state formation (see the summary in Yoffee 2005).

In addition, what many Egyptologists have often not recognized, and this applies to scholars dealing with both the formation and the collapse of the Egyptian state, was that the historical narrative as suggested by ancient sources was ultimately the result of the ancient Egyptians' *idea* of the state, namely that a unified territorial state under one king was the only possibility, a god-given law to maintain order and the object of royal intervention. Unwittingly, many Egyptologists therefore also failed to see that the formation of the state in Egypt preceded the time when this ideology was created and that state formation in Egypt needs to be clearly separated from the concept of the "unification of the two lands" and its associated ideologies.

As will be outlined in the following, the emergence of the state and of complex society in Egypt was a far more complicated process than the historical narrative of the ancient Egyptian tradition or any of the theories offered so far could ever account for. It was a multi-linear process that took place over a long period (see Table 3.1), in different parts of Egypt, with different causes and agents and at different times, and that only eventually resulted in the world's first territorial state. For this reason, this chapter will not reiterate, criticize, or test existing theories of state formation in Egypt, but instead will focus on the relevant archaeological evidence and how it can be contextualized and interpreted based on archaeological theory.

Table 3.1   Chronological table of the cultures in the Egyptian Nile Valley

Absolute date in years BCE	General cultural-historical phase			Relative chronology
2650–2100		Old Kingdom		
2700	Early		Early Dynastic	Naqada IIIC–D
3100	Bronze		(Dynasties 1–2)	
3300	Age		Protodynastic	Naqada IIIA–B
3600		Late Chalcolithic		Naqada IIC/D–IIIA
3900		Early Chalcolithic		Naqada IB/C–IIB
				Naqada IA/B
4500		Late Neolithic		Badarian
				El-Omari
				Merimde Benisalame
5100		Early Neolithic		Fayum A
7000		Epipalaeolithic		
10,000		Palaeolithic		
500,000				

The Evidence

Modern social evolutionary theory distinguishes between non-state and state
systems on the basis of a range of criteria that usually involve the varying degree
of complexity, be it economically, socially (both vertically and horizontally), or
politically. These divergent degrees of complexity can be measured archaeologically by investigating a range of interdependent areas or "subsystems," which, at
a certain level of development and in combination, help to distinguish a state from
a non-state system. These are, for example, specialized craft production and
political economy, long-distance trade, social complexity, bureaucracy and centralization, as well as a well-defined state ideology (Bard 1994; Earle 1997;
Hoffman 1979; Johnson and Earle 1987; Renfrew 1972; Sahlins 1972; Trigger
2003; Wilkinson 1996).

Economy, specialized craft production and trade

The ecology of the Nile Valley, with its annual inundation and rich fertile soils,
provided a relatively secure environment to allow for the development of a subsistence economy from the early Neolithic period that was based primarily on a
combination of agriculture and animal husbandry, supplemented by fishing,
fowling, and to a much lesser extent hunting, and that normally did not require
much control or management. Only during those periods when the floods were
either too high or too low and thus threatening the success of the crops was some
form of managerial activity required of the villagers in order to engage in hydraulic
works and to direct water flow. For most of the time, however, the families would
have produced their own goods to meet household needs or to accumulate limited
surplus for emergencies. This "domestic mode of production" provided a relatively

stable subsistence environment for a steady growth in population. Over time, this subsistence economy was gradually intensified, and in the Chalcolithic it developed into a wealth- and staple-financed economy, which encouraged the introduction of craft specialization and which served the accumulation of surplus for the emerging elites (Earle 1997; Johnson and Earle 1987:11–13; Sahlins 1972).

Among the earliest evidence for specialized craft production is pottery manufacture in southern Egypt (Friedman 1994). With the early Chalcolithic period the primary household industries became progressively more standardized, and as demand increased in areas with higher population density the potters had the opportunity and economic viability to establish full-time industries, initially supplying the local markets at the early commercial centers and to a lesser extent also the peripheral areas in their surroundings, where such ceramic wares appear with less frequency. Over time, these workshops achieved an increasingly wide regional and interregional distribution, reaching as far north as Maadi, where small quantities of these southern wares have also been found (Rizkana and Seeher 1987:29–31). During the same time period numerous other industries, such as the manufacture of flint tools and stone vessels, developed in the regional centers, where the workshops had the required supply networks and the demand for their products. At this early stage already, the emerging elites in the early centers played an important role in supporting these industries. For example, the so-called fish-tail and rhomboidal flint knives were manufactured by highly skilled flint knappers who seemed to have catered for a rather exclusive market along the Nile Valley. Given their relative scarcity, their extremely fine quality, and limited function, these knives were obviously luxury items for consumption by the elites (Hikade 2003).

Access to resources, demand, and expertise are significant factors in determining whether or not an industry could operate on a specialized and full-time basis. This is especially evident in the context of metallurgy. The significance lies in the technological requirements of mining and smelting copper ore and of casting the objects into the desired shape, a process which demands the appropriate amount and quality of fuel, infrastructure, and, importantly, the skills and expertise which can only be warranted in the context of a specialized craft industry (Costin 1991; Golden 2002). The earliest evidence for the different stages of this process comes from early Chalcolithic Maadi, where copper ore as well as cast copper ingots and utensils were found (Rizkana and Seeher 1989:13–18; Seeher 1991).

The craft industries in the various parts of Egypt further developed during the late Chalcolithic as the regional centers became more densely populated and as the elites took an increasing interest in their success and economic viability. The elites benefited by gaining access to the interregional exchange networks and thus to prestige goods, which served their desire to publicly display their position and to validate their status (Bard 1987, 1994; Hoffmann 1979). Some potters' workshops expanded or altered their production output by specializing in the manufacture of marl clay ceramic vessels of the decorated and wavy-handled classes which followed the established trade routes along the Nile Valley and traveled even beyond, for example into the southern Levant (Oren and Yekutiely 1992). It is very possible that these vessels were primarily manufactured as containers for valuable commodities, such as oils, which in turn may have also been produced by specialized industries. Such combined and attached industries are particularly well documented in the Early Dynastic period. There is evidence from early inscriptions that both the king and wealthy private individuals had estates in different parts of the country that not only manufactured commodities from agricultural produce, such as bread, beer, wine, oil, and textiles, but also a range of other associated goods such as pottery and stone vessels, perhaps primarily for mortuary needs (Wilkinson 1999:109–111). Further, there is explicit archaeological evidence for specialized industries which were attached to religious and/or administrative institutions. For example, in Buto a stone vessel workshop was found in association with a building complex whose size and architectural complexity suggest either a religious or an administrative function (Von der Way 1997:147).

As with most cultures where society can be traced over a considerable period of time and across different stages of social development, specialized craft production in early Egypt must be seen not in isolation but in a complex interplay between the social organization, the emerging elites and the state, interregional trade, and a centralized political economy (Brumfiel and Earle 1987; Costin 1991; Earle 1997).

The elites had a strong interest in sponsoring and controlling the economy and the various craft industries within their polities, especially in order to partake in inter-polity exchange and interregional trade to acquire prestige goods and to procure raw materials that were not locally available (Earle and Ericson 1977; Renfrew & Cherry 1986; Sabloff & Lamberg-Karlovsky 1975). A range of goods were imported from outside the Nile Valley proper: copper ore and ingots, cedar wood, oils and resins, wine and containers from the Levant, precious stones such as lapis lazuli from northern Mesopotamia, other luxury goods such as gold, silver, turquoise, and other semi-precious stones from the Sinai and Eastern Desert, incense, exotic animal skins, elephant ivory from Nubia and Africa, and obsidian from Anatolia or Abyssinia (Hartung 1998; Hendrickx and Bavay 2002).

Initially, the trade routes would have been traveled by independent donkey caravans and merchants who supplied goods that came into their possession as a result of direct, indirect, or down-the-line trade (Levy and van den Brink 2002). With the emergence of the regional commercial centers, located at the intersection of trade routes, where the craft industries acquired their raw materials and exchanged their products, and with the vested interest of the elites, these merchants would have found the necessary demand and economic platform. Evidence of the presence of foreign traders can be seen, for example, in the unusual subterranean structures at Maadi, whose architecture is unknown in Egypt and clearly derived from a Levantine tradition. Especially noteworthy here is a large semi-subterranean stone building that may have been used for some form of specialized central storage (Hartung et al. 2003).

The elites, and later also the state, took increasing control over this interregional trade and started to organize their own trading expeditions. There is inscriptional evidence from Dynasty 1 suggesting that ships were sent across the Mediterranean to the Levantine littoral in order to procure cedar wood (e.g. for the large-scale construction projects of the royal tombs and of temples) as well as a range of other goods such as resin, oils, and their containers (Wilkinson

1999:161). These imported commodities were subsequently distributed within the royal court to officials presumably in return for their services to the government, who then incorporated them in their tomb assemblages. Interestingly, however, imported goods are not exclusive to the tombs of the highest elites in the Early Dynastic period at Saqqara, but can occasionally also be found in the tombs of lower-class Egyptians, such as in the large necropolis at Helwan (Hendrickx and Bavay 2002). Although it is uncertain how these prestige items came into their possession, the evidence on the whole does indicate a well-established long-distance trade network at the beginning of the historical era in Egypt. This trade network became part of the overall economic system of the centralized government that collected taxes on a regular basis, and redistributed this government income to state officials, the royal treasury, and the operating administrative apparatus for production and storage (Wilkinson 1999: 126).

Bureaucracy and administration

Administration in Egypt is one of the key areas of research whose object reflects on the organization of the government and the complexity of the centralized economy as well as of society. Its evidence almost entirely rests upon textual evidence that contains information about the titles and hierarchy of officials, their responsibilities and administrative units, and the nature of the bureaucratic transactions involved. Therefore, at the most basic level, administration deals with the recording of bureaucratic processes in the form of written records.

The earliest evidence for such bureaucratic processes relates to the recording and controlling of access to goods, evident in the form of cylinder seals and clay sealings of the late Chalcolithic period (Hartung 1998). This evidence suggests that certain commodities were produced, packed, and stored under the control of a person or an institution whose interest it was to monitor access to this commodity. It is therefore conceivable that such control was exerted by the elites, who not only had a strong interest in supporting and controlling the craft industries, markets, and trade, but who also needed to accumulate revenue for economic and political leverage (Earle 1997; Johnson and Earle 1987). It is also not by coincidence that this earliest evidence comes from two of the known regional commercial centers in southern Egypt: Abydos and Naqada. Especially at Naqada South, there is evidence for a large building complex associated with significant quantities of clay sealings that would document the existence of the infrastructure and personnel to store and administer large quantities of goods (Barocas et al. 1989; Kemp 1977). However, this late Chalcolithic administration still operated without a writing system as the seals carried largely pictographic and geometric signs that hardly bear any relation to the later hieroglyphic writing system. Such evidence only comes from the early stages of Naqada III or the Protodynastic period.

The earliest evidence for phonetic hieroglyphic writing currently comes from cemetery U at Abydos, where the relatively recent discovery of tomb U-j, dating Naqada IIIA, contributed most significant results (Dreyer 1998). The evidence primarily comes in the form of commodity labels, which were originally attached to goods, such as oils and textiles, and which denote their quantity or their

provenance. This would indicate that the owner of this tomb received commodities from different parts of Egypt, where they were manufactured and either
recorded by an authority at the point of production or when they arrived at the
tomb owner's storage. There were also ink inscriptions on ceramic vessels which
show a variety of specific signs in combination with a plant sign, which the excavator has identified as the estate names of early rulers. From then on, hieroglyphic
writing developed quickly as a means of administrative control. While the realm
of writing remained largely in the context of state administration and religion,
private individuals also occasionally employed it for the purpose of administration
of their own estates, for funerary inscriptions, or simply to denote ownership of
certain goods.

On the whole however, early hieroglyphic writing was deeply embedded within
the administration of the centralized bureaucracy, which would have been operated on a continuous basis with clearly defined administrative units and personnel.
Of major concern to the central administration was the collection of revenue in
the form of taxes and surplus gained from the various craft industries, their quan-
tification, the regular recording of storage inventories, and the documentation of
expenses. In this context, one of the most important early titles was that of royal
seal bearer that appears in the written form early in Dynasty 1, but that may be
evident already earlier in the form of royal seals, such as one from Helwan dating
back as far as Naqada IIIA/B (Köhler 1999). Other inscriptional evidence clearly
indicates that by the Early Dynastic period there was a structured administrative
hierarchy with defined institutions and specifically allocated personnel. These
personnel appear to have had a high social status, which may have been the result
of kinship relations with the ruler, and therefore ascribed, or may have been
attained through special professional competence, ability, and skills.

Social complexity

It is today understood that one of the key factors to be considered in the formation
of the state is the organization and complexity of society. In spite of the many
criticisms that social evolutionary theory has received over the past several decades,
I consider Egypt as one area of research where an evolution and integration of
society from a less complex to a more complex structure, both horizontally and
vertically, can be observed over time that eventually resulted in the Old Kingdom
state. It should be pointed out that I do not intend to contribute to archaeological
theory, but instead aim to engage in a "mining-and-bridging exercise" (Yoffee
2005:182) by exploring several models or theories that I consider helpful and that
assist in interpreting archaeological evidence. I also acknowledge the difficulty in
applying certain classification systems, be it Service's band, tribe, chiefdom, and
state (1962), or Fried's egalitarian, ranked, and stratified (1960). While some of
the categories might lend themselves better to the classification of a society than
others and while the lines between them are often difficult to draw, these criteria
nevertheless can be applied in conjunction quite effectively to the different stages
in the development of society as it can be observed in early Egyptian
civilization.

The simplest or least complex form of social differentiation in Egypt can be placed in the Palaeolithic, when we can safely assume that population density was so low that the largest social unit would have comprised a nuclear family of mobile hunters and gatherers. This stage of social development is best classified under the terms of band or egalitarian society. When early Neolithic farmers became fully sedentary in villages such as at Merimde Benisalame, we can observe the first evidence for larger communities living permanently in one place and thus forming social units greater than the family unit, and for increasing social segmentation. The latter is possibly indicated by specialized activities, such as flint knapping, pottery manufacture, or basketry, which are, however, at this stage not subsistence activities. The economy is largely based on reciprocal exchange. Unequal distribution of wealth is often an indicator of social inequality and, for example, observable among the late Neolithic Badarian burials. Here, a small number of the graves (8 percent) display greater material wealth than the vast majority (92 percent), thus suggesting an early form of social distinction and a two-tiered or ranked society (Anderson 1992). Such ranking often reflects differential access to resources, but can also be found in tribal societies that accommodate age-grade associations, such as village elders who hold a certain esteem within their community and oversee ritual activities. It is possible that there is evidence for such an individual from the Neolithic site of el-Omari, where the burial of an adult male, A35, displays unusual features that cannot be matched by any other grave at this site (Debono and Mortensen 1990:67). Although his grave is no different by means of size or number of grave goods, it is marked on the surface by rows of posts, forming either a fence or a hut. Further, unlike any other on the site, his grave contained a c. 30 cm-long wooden staff, which was located in front of his body. As it does not appear to have served any practical purpose, it is possible that this staff was a marker of social distinction.

The next important step in the social development of early Egypt is indicated by the introduction of specialized, full-time craft industries, a redistributive or political economy, and centralization, which are all intertwined with the organization of society. Although this form of society could still be classified as ranked, the difference lies in the access, control, and distribution of resources that are now in the hands of high-status persons or elites. These criteria would thus enable us to term this form of society a chiefdom society, although the concept of the "chiefdom" as a universally applicable term has received sound criticism over the years. Many archaeologists nevertheless persist in using it, often "for lack of a better word" and because of the need to insert a term that reflects less complexity than a state and more complexity than a ranked society (see the summary in Yoffee 2005). There are a number of criteria that are often applied to chiefdoms and that can be ascertained from archaeological evidence in different parts of Egypt, such as Hierakonpolis, Naqada, Abydos, and probably also Maadi, Girza, and the Nile Delta. Especially in the south, where there is an abundance of well-documented mortuary data (e.g. Bard 1994; Wilkinson 1996), there is evidence for clearly distinguished elites whose graves are larger and architecturally more elaborate than normal, richly endowed with large quantities of grave goods such as pottery and stone vessels containing food and drink, tools and weapons, ornaments and personal belongings, many of which were imported. The elites and their kin literally distanced themselves from the commoners in separate burial grounds, such as cemetery T at Naqada, cemetery U at Abydos, and Locality 6 at Hierakonpolis.

From here the pace at which social development proceeds increases rapidly. Towards the very end of the Chalcolithic and thereafter, there is evidence for a further rise in social inequality and diversity at various sites in Egypt and the beginning of social stratification which takes Egyptian society well beyond the chiefdom level. The difference lies in the distinction between a ranked or two-tiered society, comprising of elites and commoners, and a multi-tiered or stratified society with several distinct social ranks or classes. An indication for the latter is, for example, given, when economic control and administration are no longer in the hands of the ruling elites alone, but are delegated to qualified individuals who are not necessarily kin members of the elite – Fried's organization of power "on a supra-kin basis" (1960:728). The population size of the polities of stratified societies is usually substantial, including a primary center where the power resides and secondary or even tertiary centers, depending on the size of the territory (Nissen 1988). While the hinterland produced the agricultural revenue, the centers accommodated, to a varying extent, the infrastructure and delegated personnel of the central administration, including storage and production facilities, officials, craftsmen, artisans, and workers, which directly implies a far more complex social organization than a chiefdom society could accommodate. Therefore, the process of state formation has now arrived at a crucial stage that for the first time allows us to speak of a state system. However, it must be noted that this process has taken place at a regional level first and initially does not have any effect on the political organization of Egypt as one polity. While we may now speak of Egyptian civilization under Norman Yoffee's terms (2005:17), this is not yet an Egyptian state. Instead, we are dealing with several regional states, "micro states" (Yoffee 2005), "proto-kingdoms" (Kemp 2006), or "proto-states" (Campagno 2002) that were headed by powerful monarchs, who had almost unlimited resources at their disposal and who shared a common material culture and ideology. A good example is the evidence from the elite cemetery U at Abydos and especially tomb U-j, which was occupied by one of the best-documented early rulers of the time. The tomb is subdivided into twelve mudbrick chambers within a large pit covering an area of more than $60\,m^2$, which makes it the largest tomb of the period (Dreyer 1998). Although U-j was plundered, there was still significant evidence left that allowed the excavator to conclude that its owner truly was a monarch. It contained several hundred wine jars imported from Syria–Palestine, thus suggesting not only a well-established infrastructure and long-distance trade contacts, but also a significant amount of wealth required for their acquisition. It also contained large quantities of exquisite artifacts of obsidian and ivory manufactured by skilled artisans and craftsmen, an ivory *heka* scepter, symbolizing rulership, and, above all, numerous commodity labels and inscribed pottery vessels that demonstrate the existence of an administrative apparatus. The society in this person's polity was clearly stratified: it was headed by a powerful and wealthy ruler, probably surrounded by a small circle of family members who oversaw the government with him, and assisted by a small number of officials running the central administration and economy on his behalf. The bulk of society that formed part of this Abydene monarch's polity was made up of artisans, craftsmen, farmers, and laborers.

There is some evidence that as a result of inter-polity competition during the Protodynastic period the territory of Naqada was gradually integrated into the polity of either Abydos or Hierakonpolis and that these two subsequently competed for access to local resources, a share in the interregional and long-distance trade networks, and ultimately dominion in southern Egypt for about 150–200 years until the beginning of Dynasty 1. Parallel to these processes in southern Egypt, there is also evidence in northern Egypt, though less tangible and well documented, pertaining to the independent formation of regional polities, which also display the necessary criteria for the stratification of society, whose complexity further increases as we approach the Early Dynastic period. Particularly significant is the wider region around Memphis, which later became the capital of the territorial state of unified Egypt. The region experiences a distinct growth in population during the Protodynastic period which is indicated by the increase in the number of cemetery sites in early Naqada III (Mortensen 1991). Of special interest are the sites of Tarkhan, Helwan, and Saqqara, which provide relevant information for the increasing stratification and nature of society.

Tarkhan is a relatively large cemetery with some 1300 graves dating between Naqada IIIA and IIIC. The detailed publication of this site, which was excavated by Petrie early in the twentieth century, allows for statistical analyses such as those conducted by Ellis (1996) and Wilkinson (1996). These revealed that there is a high degree of social distinction among the graves, measured by grave size and wealth, and that this social inequality increased from Naqada IIIA onwards, but reversed in Naqada IIIC (Ellis 1996:156–157). Some of the early tombs, dating to Naqada IIIA–B, were very large and well equipped with grave goods, such as tomb 315, which is unusually large, exceeding $6\,m^3$, and which also contained a ceramic vessel with the name of a local ruler. This could possibly indicate that the owners of such large early tombs were high-status persons (Wilkinson 1996:72) and members of the elite who benefited from the distribution of centrally produced commodities within this ruler's polity.

Of similar significance is the necropolis of Helwan, which allows for the observation of a number of equally relevant processes. The site is located on the low desert ridges along the east side of the Nile Valley and contains over 10,000 tombs, most of which presumably date to the Early Dynastic period (e.g. Saad 1969). Its earliest occupation as a cemetery goes back at least to Naqada IIIA, and at this point in time already with evidence for elite burials. For example, tomb 563.H.11 measures almost $8\,m^3$ and is thus one of the largest in the region; it also contained numerous pottery and stone vessels, jewelry, and apparently had a superstructure made of mudbrick (Köhler 2004:307). Considering its size and equipment it is equivalent with the contemporary elite tombs at Tarkhan, and we can conclude that Helwan also served as an elite cemetery within a distinct polity at the beginning of the Protodynastic period. As time progresses the site becomes densely occupied by members of different classes of early Egyptian society. The highest-ranking occupants are identified by their names and titles in inscriptions, especially on forty or so funerary reliefs, naming sons and daughters of the king, officials, priests, and craftsmen. Many of the largest tombs are elaborately built employing architectural features and construction methods that rival those of the kings and the highest-ranking elites. Importantly, though, the necropolis also contains the thousands of burials of un-named commoners, probably lower-ranking bureaucrats and priests, craft workers, farmers, and unskilled laborers who lived in the nearby city of Memphis and its surroundings.

With the beginning of Dynasty 1 the cemetery of the upper-class elite appears to have shifted to the opposite side of the valley with its steep desert plateau at Saqqara. Here, several dozen monumental niched mastaba tombs lined the escarpment overlooking the city. They were so richly endowed with grave goods that their early excavator, Walter Emery, initially mistook them for royal burials (e.g. Emery 1961). Indeed, they did contain numerous royal inscriptions on commodities which clearly indicate that their owners had close connections to the court, but, importantly, also often provide the personal name of these tombs' occupants and detail their position at the court. For example, Merka was the owner of tomb 3505 and lived during the reign of king Qa'a of late Dynasty 1. He was a royal kinsman, indicated by the title *jrj p't*, and held numerous important administrative and religious offices which are inscribed on his funerary stela. Another interesting individual was Hemaka from the time of King Den, for whom there is no indication that he may have been a member of the royal family, which means that his status was possibly not ascribed, but who held some of the highest administrative offices of his time, such as controller and administrator of several royal foundations and especially royal seal bearer.

In comparison with the contemporary tombs at Helwan and the many other cemeteries of the Memphite region, the tombs at Saqqara stand out by their sheer size, wealth, and the illustrious identities of their occupants. Given the high status of these individuals, it is possible to conclude that the Saqqara tombs housed members of the royal family as well as of the aristocracy of the Early Dynastic period.

In conclusion, it is now possible to describe Egypt of Dynasty 1 as a highly stratified, complex society that can best be portrayed with the metaphor of the social pyramid, comprising the king at its top, followed by the members of the royal family, the aristocracy, and high officials, thus forming the upper class. The middle section of the pyramid is made up of lower-ranking officials and priests, scribes, and other full-time specialists and craft workers. Finally, the base of the social pyramid, and thus the vast majority of the population, is formed by commoners such as farmers, servants, and unskilled laborers. This form of Early Dynastic society, whose foundations were laid in the different regions during the Protodynastic period, however, is also the result of the significant political and economic changes that took place when Egypt gradually transformed into a territorial state, which requires further attention.

Centralization and urbanism

It has already been noted previously that the development of specialized craft production, interregional trade, and intensified political economy go hand in hand with the growth of population in certain parts of Egypt, where the right ecological conditions existed, such as proximity to resources and sufficient agricultural hinterland as well as the intersection of trade routes connecting the Nile

Valley with lateral areas in the eastern and western deserts and beyond. Such favorable conditions were given in various places along the southern Nile Valley, near the Fayum, at the apex of the Nile Delta, and on the river branches near the Mediterranean coast, where, indeed, early centers emerged (Bard 1987; Hoffman et al. 1986). These centers primarily accommodated the infrastructure and personnel for specialized industries, the markets for trade and exchange, centralized storage facilities for the accumulation and redistribution of surplus controlled by the elites, and later their administration. For a large part these centers were inhabited by the non-agriculturally productive members of society, that is, the elites, their retainers and personnel, bureaucrats, craft workers, and their families. In contrast, the areas surrounding the centers up and down the floodplain comprised smaller villages and hamlets that were inhabited by farmers who supplied the agricultural produce for each polity. It has been observed that the size of the various polities at the end of the Chalcolithic period increased in territory and with it in population. As neighboring smaller polities were gradually integrated into a larger regional polity, the former centers assume a secondary and tertiary role whereas the center of the prevailing polity maintains its primacy and assumes a more and more urban character. Thus, the polities become increasingly diverse and horizontally differentiated as they incorporate a range of social groups. The social and economic diversity was probably greatest in the primary center and declined in an outwards direction, which explains why the villages in the periphery or province, when observed in isolation, often appear to be less complex (Nissen 1988).

During the Protodynastic period there existed a number of independent regional states with well-populated primary centers along the stretch of the Nile Valley, most notably Hierakonpolis, Abydos, Tarkhan, possibly in the Memphite region, and in various places in the Nile Delta. What happened next is a most difficult process whose details are still ill understood. It appears as if in the course of their peer–polity competition, either through warfare and coercion, economic force, or consensual and voluntary alliance, at the beginning of Dynasty 1 the Abydene polity assumes supremacy first in the south and later also in the north. But instead of maintaining its capital in the core territory at Abydos, the primary center of the now territorial state of Egypt is moved north to Memphis, where the already existing commercial center is turned into the capital of an entirely new and highly diverse polity (for possible reasons, see Campagno 2002:57; Yoffee 2005:37). This process cannot be considered the result of a gradual development involving the afore-described natural growth of a polity; it is a move that radically changes the political and economic organization as well as the face and nature of this polity. It should therefore be considered a genuinely distinct process and the creation of a new form of state system, the territorial state of Egypt, which is, at this point in time, unparalleled in world history.

The area where the new capital was to be located was not unknown to the Abydene rulers as their Protodynastic predecessors of Dynasty 0 had already maintained relatively close relations with it. This is indicated by a number of objects inscribed with their names and found, for example, at Helwan, such as ceramic vessels or the afore-mentioned royal cylinder seal. The seal is very significant as it probably indicates that an individual who resided and was buried at

Memphis undertook economic transactions on behalf of a ruler who was based at a distance of several hundred kilometers south at Abydos. One could argue that maybe the primary center was already founded by the Dynasty 0 rulers, except that they were not the only ones with whom the inhabitants of early Memphis had contacts. To the contrary, it appears as if this area maintained close relations also with a variety of other Protodynastic states in the north and the south and that the Abydene Dynasty 0 was not necessarily more dominant than the others (Köhler 2004).

The effects of the move of the primary center to Memphis can be gleaned from the trend that was observed earlier at sites such as Tarkhan, located at a distance of c. 40 km south of Memphis. In the Protodynastic period, Tarkhan was probably part of a monarchy that was headed by a certain Horus Crocodile, whose name was found on a ceramic vessel from the cemetery (Dreyer 1993). It was noted that social inequality at Tarkhan first increased during early Naqada III and then decreased, together with the number of graves, in Naqada IIIC. This was just at the time when things started to change in Memphis, resulting in a situation at Tarkhan where the vast majority of commoners were opposed by a very small number of very wealthy individuals buried in large mastaba tombs. It is possible that this development reflects an overall process of concentration in the new primary center. Tarkhan, which was an independent polity in the Protodynastic period, gradually declines in size and diversity whereas the reverse is true of the cemeteries in the direct vicinity of Memphis. While Memphis becomes the primary center of the new territorial state, Tarkhan is possibly turned into a secondary center in the periphery of Memphis and administered by members of an elite who act on behalf of the central government in the capital. It is possible that the decline of the middle section of the social pyramid at Tarkhan can be explained with the characteristic gravitational forces that primary centers tend to have, with the creation of a central government and all its new institutions, infrastructure, and new offices necessitating more personnel and providing better economic opportunities, and thus social mobility, for able workers and specialists.

In the Early Dynastic period, Memphis is an urban center with a highly diverse population, socially and economically, comprising all layers of the social pyramid and many different social groups. Although there is no specific archaeological evidence from the city itself, as it is covered by impenetrable deposits of alluvial silts and may also have been partially washed away by the changing river bed of the Nile, its surrounding cemeteries allow us to reconstruct its former appearance (Jeffreys and Tavares 1994). It housed the central government and administration, including storage facilities for the collection of the state revenue, the king's palace and court, major temples with associated economic institutions, the infrastructure and industries for the manufacture of goods, as well as a variety of domestic quarters where the majority of inhabitants lived. In its direct vicinity, there were probably numerous smaller villages surrounded by agricultural land, and at a greater distance, in the location of the former regional centers, there were secondary and tertiary centers that locally collected, stored, and administered taxes and goods on behalf of the central government. Some of the old centers in the periphery and in the provinces may have laid the foundations for the administrative district or nome capitals of the early Old Kingdom, although the evidence is inconclusive (Trigger 2003:104). The political and economic integration of the provinces was one of the main challenges of the new centralized government at Memphis. This process would have required significant reform, reorganization, and modification of the administrative system and logistics of the old regional states throughout the Early Dynastic and early Old Kingdom periods. It also required measures to assure loyalty from the descendants and kin of the old regional rulers, as well as means to express the king's overarching dominion over the now highly diverse state of Egypt.

Kingship and state ideology

While the nature and ideology of kingship in Pharaonic Egypt are well-understood concepts, its origins and development in early Egypt are still a matter of ongoing discussion (Baines 1995). As the political organization changed and the polities became larger and socially as well as ethnically more diverse over time, the role of the ruler would have equally changed in response. Especially since the social relations between ruler and subjects became increasingly distant, it was necessary for the monarch to establish a means of justifying and validating his supreme role over a population that no longer only included members of his own kin group.

Over time, an ideology was created that, on the one hand, pictured the king as a benevolent ruler whose responsibility it was to maintain order and prosperity and to protect his territory from outside forces. On the other hand, the king also needed to assure his subjects' loyalty and obedience, especially in the case of those parts of the population and members of the elite whose allegiance was originally within their own kin groups and polities prior to political integration. This ideology has its origins in the iconography of the early Chalcolithic, when a broad but central motif was introduced which conveys the idea of the strong man or leader. This motif, which can be found, for example, on ceramic vessels from late Naqada I, cosmetic palettes, knife handles, as well as part of the wall painting in tomb 100 at Hierakonpolis, is expressed in the form of representations that show a domineering man taming or killing dangerous animals, such as hippopotami or lions (Kemp 2006). It also merges with the so-called subjugation motif, when the strong man subjects one or several human enemies to acts of violence. The subjugation motif is also known from the early Chalcolithic period, and in its early expression appears to oppose the leader to a rather generic form of enemy. Over time, however, the identity of the enemy is gradually transformed into a more specific form and projected onto outsiders whose iconography corresponds to that of a non-Nile Valley inhabitant or the "foreigner," as is aptly expressed on the Narmer Palette (see a summary in Köhler 2002). This transformation of the enemy into a clearly defined non-Egyptian ethnic can only be the result of the gradual political integration of the Nile Valley into one polity and the definition of Egypt's physical and ideological boundaries. The motif thus fulfils the king's need to validate his role as a strong leader and as the protector of his subjects from outside forces.

Another means of ideological legitimation was achieved through the king's association with supernatural powers or deities and his engagement in religious rituals. This concept is first expressed in different forms during the Protodynastic period, in particular in the ruler's direct association with the falcon god Horus in the early royal titulature, and in the foundation and sponsorship of sanctuaries to deities such as Min at Koptos and Horus at Hierakonpolis.

Quite intriguing is the observation that the origin of the Horus name can currently not be traced to one location or polity as it simultaneously appears in slight variations during early Naqada III in different parts of the Nile Valley. It is employed by a whole range of Protodynastic rulers, a phenomenon which can be explained by peer competition and the exchange of religious beliefs and cultural values between neighboring regional polities (Campagno 2002:52; Trigger 2003:101) and within early Egyptian civilization. During Naqada IIIB–C, the Horus name becomes increasingly standardized, consisting of the *serekh*, which is a representation of the palace with the name of the ruler inscribed, and surmounted by the falcon god Horus. Through his association with the god, the ruler was able to claim divine legitimation and support for his political acts, an ideology that was further elaborated by representations that show the ruler in the act of subjugating his enemies involving the god, as for example on the Narmer Palette. This concept became a powerful tool in Pharaonic state ideology and decorum that remained practically unchanged for the thousands of years to follow.

Conclusion

Owing to intensive research over the past century, including archaeological investigation and theoretical discussion, modern scholarship is now in the position to draw a more precise, though nonetheless complex, picture of the formation of the Pharaonic state of Egypt. Although many of the details are still under investigation and although there is no scholarly consensus on any of the points discussed above, it is possible to summarize the process in very broad terms as follows. There were a number of interdependent factors that contributed to the development of society from an egalitarian family-level group of Palaeolithic hunter-gatherers to the socially more complex tribal or ranked society in the Neolithic and an economically more complex society that can best be termed "chiefdom" during the Chalcolithic period. At the end of the Chalcolithic, during which we see increasing horizontal integration across Egypt as reflected in the material culture and ideologies, we witness the simultaneous formation of several regional states or "proto-states" in different parts of the Nile Valley which basically completes the development towards statehood and complex society. However, a secondary political process of state formation took place when at the beginning of Dynasty 1 the Abydene polity successfully expanded its territory and eventually achieved dominion over southern and northern Egypt, thus integrating several polities into one territorial state with Memphis as the new single Egyptian polity's primary center or capital. This latter process, now, allows us to speak of a politically unified Egyptian civilization that was the result of a long and gradual process of social, economic, and political developments that cannot be reduced to a single historical narrative or theory.

ACKNOWLEDGMENTS

I am grateful to Marcelo Campagno for his helpful suggestions and insightful comments on this chapter and to Natalie Barlow for assisting in editing it.

REFERENCES

Anderson, W. 1992 Badarian Burials: Evidence for Social Inequality in Middle Egypt during the Early Predynastic Era. Journal of the American Research Center in Egypt 29:51–80.

Atzler, M. 1981 Untersuchungen zur Herausbildung von Herrschaftsformen in Ägypten. Hildesheimer Ägyptologische Beiträge. Vol. 16. Hildesheim: Gerstenberg Verlag.

Baines, J. 1995 Origins of Egyptian Kingship. In Ancient Egyptian Kingship. D. O'Connor and D. P. Silverman, eds. Pp. 95–156. Leiden: Brill.

Bard, K. A. 1987 The Geography of Excavated Predynastic Sites and the Rise of Complex Society in Egypt. Journal of the American Research Center in Egypt 24:81–93.

Bard, K. A. 1994 From Farmers to Pharaohs: Mortuary Evidence for the Rise of Complex Society in Egypt. Sheffield: Sheffield Academic Press.

Bard, K. A., and R. L. Carneiro 1989 Patterns of Predynastic Settlement Location, Social Evolution and the Circumscription Theory. Cahiers de la Recherche de l'Institut de Papyrologie et d'Egyptologie de Lille 11:15–23.

Barocas, C., R. Fattovich, and M. Tosi 1989 The Oriental Institute of Naples Expedition to Petrie's South Town (Upper Egypt), 1977–1983: An Interim Report. In Late Prehistory of the Nile Basin and the Sahara. L. Krzyzaniak and M. Kobusievicz, eds. Pp. 297–315. Poznań: Poznańska Drukarnia Naukowa.

Brumfiel, E., and T. K. Earle, eds. 1987 Specialization, Exchange, and Complex Societies. Cambridge: Cambridge University Press.

Campagno, M. 2002 On the Predynastic "Proto-States" of Upper Egypt. Göttinger Miszellen 188:49–60.

Campagno, M. 2004 In the Beginning was the War: Conflict and the Emergence of the Egyptian State. In Egypt at Its Origins: Studies in Memory of Barbara Adams. Proceedings of the International Conference "Origin of the State: Predynastic and Early Dynastic Egypt," Kraków, 28 August–1 September 2002. S. Hendrickx, R. F. Friedman, K. M. Ciałowicz, and M. Chłodnicki, eds. Pp. 689–703. OLA, Vol. 138. Leuven: Peeters.

Carneiro, R. L. 1970 A Theory of the Origin of the State. Science 1169: 733–738.

Carneiro, R. L. 1981 The Chiefdom: Precursor of the State. In The Transition to Statehood in the New World. G. D. Jones and R. R. Kautz, eds. Pp. 37–79. Cambridge: Cambridge University Press.

Costin, C. L. 1991 Craft Specialization: Issues in Defining, Documenting, and Exploring the Organization of Production. In Archaeological Method and Theory. M. Schiffer, ed. Pp. 1–56. Tuscon: University of Arizona Press.

Debono, F., and B. Mortensen 1990 El-Omari. Mainz: Phillip von Zabern.

Dreyer, G. 1993 Horus Krokodil, ein Gegenkönig der Dynastie 0. In Followers of Horus. R. Friedman and B. Adams, eds. Pp. 259–263. Oxford: Oxbow.

Dreyer, G. 1998 Umm el-Qaab I: Das prädynastische Königsgrab U-j und seine frühen Schriftzeugnisse. Mainz: Phillip von Zabern.

Earle, T. K. 1997. How Chiefs Come to Power: The Political Economy in Prehistory. Stanford: Stanford University Press.

Earle, T. K., and J. E. Ericson, eds. 1977 Exchange Systems in Prehistory. New York: Academic Press.

Ellis, C. 1996 Expressions of Social Status: A Statistical Approach to the Late Predynastic/Early Dynastic Cemeteries of Kafr Tarkhan. *In* Interregional Contacts in the Later Prehistory of Northeastern Africa. L. Krzyzaniak, K. Kröper and M. Kobusiewicz, eds. Pp. 151–164. Poznań: Poznańska Drukarnia Naukowa.

Emery, W. B. 1961 Archaic Egypt. Edinburgh: Penguin.

Fried, M. H. 1960 On the Evolution of Social Stratification and the State. *In* Culture in History. S. Diamond, ed. Pp. 713–731. New York: Columbia University Press.

Friedman, R. 1994 Predynastic Settlement Ceramics of Upper Egypt: A Comparative Study of the Ceramics of Hemamieh, Nagada and Hierakonpolis. Ph.D dissertation, University of California Berkeley.

Golden, J. 2002 The Origins of the Metals Trade in the Eastern Mediterranean: Social Organisation of Production in the Early Copper Industries. *In* Egypt and the Levant. T. E. Levy and E. C. M. van den Brink, eds. Pp. 225–238. London, New York: Leicester University Press.

Hartung, U. 1998 Zur Entwicklung des Handels und zum Beginn wirtschaftlicher Administration im prädynastischen Ägypten. Studien zur Altägyptischen Kultur 26:35–50.

Hartung, U., M. Abd el-Gelil, A. von den Driesch, G. Fares, R. Hartmann, T. Hikade, and C. Ihde 2003 Vorbericht über neue Untersuchungen in der prädynastischen Siedlung von Maadi. Mitteilungen des Deutschen Archäologischen Instituts, Abteilung Kairo 59:149–198.

Hendrickx, S., and L. Bavay 2002 The Relative Chronological Position of Egyptian Predynastic and Early Dynastic Tombs with Objects Imported from the Near East and the Nature of Interregional Contacts. *In* Egypt and the Levant. T. E. Levy and E. C. M. van den Brink, eds. Pp. 58–80. London, New York: Leicester University Press.

Hendrickx, S., and R. F. Friedman 2003 Gebel Tjauti Rock Inscription 1 and the Relationship between Abydos and Hierakonpolis during the Early Naqada III Period. Göttinger Miszellen 196:95–110.

Hikade, T. 2003 Getting the Ritual Right: Fishtail Knives in Predynastic Egypt. *In* Egypt – Temple of the Whole World. Studies in Honour of Jan Assmann. S. Meyer, ed. Pp. 137–152. New York: Brill.

Hoffman, M. 1979 Egypt before the Pharaohs. Austin: University of Texas Press.

Hoffman, M., H. Hamroush, and R. O. Allen 1986 A Model of Urban Development for the Hierakonpolis Region from Predynastic through Old Kingdom Times. Journal of the American Research Center in Egypt 23: 175–188.

Jeffreys, D. G., and A. Tavares 1994 The Landscape of Early Dynastic Memphis. Mitteilungen des Deutschen Archäologischen Instituts, Abteilung Kairo 50:143–173.

Johnson, A. W., and T. K. Earle, 1987 The Evolution of Human Societies: From Foraging Group to Agrarian State. Stanford: Stanford University Press.

Kahl, J. 2003 Das Schlagen des Feindes von Hu: Gebel Tjauti Felsinschrift 1. Göttinger Miszellen 192:47–54.

Kaiser, W. 1956 Stand und Probleme der ägyptischen Vorgeschichtsforschung. Zeitschrift für ägyptische Sprache 81:87–109.

Kaiser, W. 1957 Zur inneren Chronologie der Naqadakultur. Archaeologia Geographica 6:69–77.

Kaiser, W. 1964 Einige Bemerkungen zur ägyptischen Frühzeit. Zeitschrift für Ägyptische Sprache 91:86–125.

Kaiser, W. 1990. Zur Entstehung des gesamtägyptischen Staates. Mitteilunges des Deutschen Archäologischen Instituts Kairo 46:287–299.

Kaiser, W. 1995. Trial and Error. Göttinger Miszellen 149:5–14.

Kemp, B. 1977 The Early Development of Towns in Egypt. Antiquity 51:185–200.

Kemp, B. 2006 Ancient Egypt, Anatomy of a Civilization. 2nd edition. London: Routledge.

Köhler, E. C. 1995 The State of Research on Late Predynastic Egypt: New Evidence for the Development of the Pharaonic State? Göttinger Miszellen 147:79–92.

Köhler, E. C. 1996 Evidence for Interregional Contacts between Late Prehistoric Lower and Upper Egypt – a View from Buto. *In* Interregional Contacts in the Later Prehistory of Northeastern Africa. L. Krzyzaniak, K. Kröper, and M. Kobusiewicz, eds. Pp. 215–226. Poznań: Poznańska Drukarnia Naukowa.

Köhler, E. C. 1998 Buto III. Die Keramik von der späten Vorgeschichte bis zum frühen Alten Reich (Schicht III bis VI). Mainz: Phillip von Zabern.

Köhler, E. C. 1999 Re-assessment of a Cylinder Seal from Helwan. Göttinger Miszellen 169:49–56.

Köhler, E. C. 2002 History or Ideology? New Reflections on the Narmer Palette and the Nature of Foreign Relations in Predynastic Egypt. *In* Egypt and the Levant. T. E. Levy, and E. C. M. van den Brink, eds. Pp. 499–513. London, New York: Leicester University Press.

Köhler, E. C. 2004 On the Origins of Memphis: The New Excavations in the Early Dynastic Necropolis at Helwan. *In* Egypt at Its Origins: Studies in Memory of Barbara Adams. Proceedings of the International Conference "Origin of the State: Predynastic and Early Dynastic Egypt," Kraków, 28 August–1 September 2002. S. Hendrickx, R. F. Friedman, K. M. Ciałowicz, and M. Chłodnicki, eds. Pp. 295–315. OLA, Vol. 138. Leuven: Peeters.

Kroeper, K., and D. Wildung 1985 Minshat Abu Omar. Munich: Lipp.

Levy, T. E. and E. C. M. van den Brink 2002. Interaction Models, Egypt and the Levantine Periphery. *In* Egypt and the Levant. T. E. Levy and E. C. M. van den Brink, eds. Pp. 3–38. London, New York: Leicester University Press.

Mortensen, B. 1991 Change in the Settlement Pattern and Population in the Beginning of the Historical Period. Ägypten und Levante 2:11–37.

Nissen, H. G. 1988 The Early History of the Ancient Near East. Chicago: University of Chicago Press.

Oren, E. D., and Y. Yekutiely 1992 Taur Ikhbeineh: Earliest Evidence for Egyptian Interconnections. *In* The Nile Delta in Transition. E. C. M. van den Brink, ed. Pp. 361–384. Tel Aviv: E. C. M. van den Brink.

Renfrew, C. 1972 The Emergence of Civilisation: The Cyclades and the Aegean in the Third Millennium BC. London: Methuen.

Renfrew, C., and J. Cherry, 1986 Peer Polity Interaction and Socio-political Change. Cambridge: Cambridge University Press.

Rizkana, I., and J. Seeher 1987 Maadi I: The Pottery of the Predynastic Settlement. Mainz: Phillip von Zabern.

Rizkana, I., and J. Seeher 1989 Maadi III: The Non-lithic Small Finds and the Structural Remains of the Predynastic Settlement. Mainz: Phillip von Zabern.

Saad, Z. Y. 1969. The Excavations at Helwan: Art and Civilization of the 1st and 2nd Egyptian Dynasties. Norman, OK: University of Oklahoma Press.

Sabloff, J., and C. C. Lamberg-Karlovsky, eds. 1975 Ancient Civilization and Trade. Albuquerque: University of New Mexico Press.

Sahlins, M. D. 1972 Stone Age Economics. Chicago: Aldine.

Seeher, J. 1991 Gedanken zur Rolle Unterägyptens bei der Herausbildung des Pharaonenreiches. Mitteilungen des Deutschen Archäologischen Instituts, Abteilung Kairo 47:313–318.

Service, E. R., 1962 Primitive Social Organization: An Evolutionary Perspective. New York: Random House.

Trigger, B. G. 2003 Understanding Early Civilizations. Cambridge: Cambridge University Press.

Von der Way, T. 1991 Die Grabungen in Buto und die Reichseinigung. Mitteilungen des Deutschen Archäologischen Instituts, Abteilung Kairo 47:419–424.

Von der Way, T. 1997. Tell el-Fara'in – Buto I. Mainz: Phillip von Zabern.

Wilkinson, T. A. 1996 State Formation in Egypt. Oxford: Basingstoke Press.

Wilkinson, T. A. 1999 Early Dynastic Egypt. London, New York: Routledge.

Wittfogel, K. 1957 Oriental Despotism: A Comparative Study of Total Power. New Haven: Yale University Press.

Yoffee, N. 2005 Myths of the Archaic State: Evolution of the Earliest Cities, States and Civilizations. Cambridge: Cambridge University Press.

FURTHER READING

Campagno, M. 2000 Kinship and the Emergence of the State in Egypt. Bulletin of the Australian Centre for Egyptology 11:35–47.

Hendrickx, S., and R. F. Friedman 2003 Gebel Tjauti Rock Inscription 1 and the Relationship between Abydos and Hierakonpolis during the Early Naqada III Period. Göttinger Miszellen 196:95–109.

Hendrickx, S., and E. C. M. van den Brink 2002 Inventory of Predynastic and Early Dynastic Cemetery and Settlement Sites in the Egyptian Nile Valley. In Egypt and the Levant. T. E. Levy and E. C. M. van den Brink, eds. Pp. 346–399. London, New York: Leicester University Press.

Köhler, E. C. 2008 The Interaction between and the Roles of Upper and Lower Egypt in the Formation of the Egyptian State – Another Review. In Egypt at Its Origins 2: Proceedings of the International Conference "Origin of the State: Predynastic and Early Dynastic Egypt," Toulouse, 5–8 September 2005. B. Midant-Reynes and Y. Tristant, eds. Pp. 515–543. Leuven: Peeters.

Levy, T. E., and E. C. M. van den Brink, eds. 2002 Egypt and the Levant. London, New York: Leicester University Press.

Midant-Reynes, B. 2003 Aux origines de l'Égypte. Paris: Fayard.

Savage, S. H., 2001 Some Recent Trends in the Archaeology of Predynastic Egypt. Journal of Archaeological Research 9(2):101–155.

Siegemund, R. H. 1999 A Critical Review of Theories about the Origin of the Ancient Egyptian State. Ph.D dissertation, University of California Los Angeles.

Takamiya, I. H. 2004 Development of Specialization in the Nile Valley during the 4th Millennium BC. In Egypt at its Origins: Studies in Memory of Barbara Adams. Proceedings of the International Conference "Origin of the State: Predynastic and Early Dynastic Egypt," Kraków, 28 August–1 September 2002. S. Hendrickx, R. F. Friedman, K. M. Ciałowicz, and M. Chłodnicki, eds. Pp. 1027–1039. OLA, Vol. 138. Leuven: Peeters.

Wengrow, D. 2006 The Archaeology of Early Egypt: Social Transformations in North-East Africa 10,000–2650 BC. Cambridge: Cambridge University Press.

4

Kingship and Legitimation

Janet Richards

An essential feature of complex societies and civilizations is that, far more than other societal forms, they embody complex behaviors in lasting artifactual form (whether in architecture or in elaborate manufactured objects), extending memory and empowering new forms of communication. (Baines 1997:127)

The nature of political authority in the ancient Egyptian Old Kingdom (c. 2575–2150 BCE) has often been characterized as absolutist. This scholarly and popular impression derives from the degree of economic control implied by the scale of royal pyramid complexes in the 4th Dynasty (c. 2575–2450 BCE), and from the form and distribution of representations of, and references to, the king. These latter are comparatively sparse set against the scope of data from succeeding periods of centralized authority such as the Middle and New Kingdoms, yet communicate (it is inferred) the serene perfection and sometimes dangerous power befitting a divinity, and a concomitant and profound remoteness from his subjects, especially his non-elite subjects.

Yet, as Baines has pointed out, kingship during the Old Kingdom was socially and symbolically a continuation of an ideology that had been in place and evolving already for more than half a millennium (Baines 1997:127), and would persist in essentials and despite both internal and external conflict for two millennia more. The phenomenal long-term success of this ideology must have rested to a significant degree on political practices reproducing and communicating authority, and legitimating this power to the population over which authority was held. For ancient states a key vehicle through which authority was constituted is what Smith has termed political landscapes – "broad sets of spatial practices critical to the formation, operation, and overthrow of geopolitical orders, of polities, of regimes, of institutions" (Smith 2003:5). In his model, the concept of landscape comprises "the physical contours of the created environment, the aesthetics of built form, and the imaginative reflections of spatial representations," encouraging "a perceptual dimension of space in which built forms elicit affective responses that galvanize memories and emotions central to the experience of political belonging" (Smith 2003:8; and cf. De Marrais et al. 1996). His multivalent definition enfolds ascending levels of communication such as artifactual or monumental form, textual content, visual impact, and spatial layout and distribution, and provides a good fit for integrating these into the study of ancient Egypt.

The concept of political landscapes provides a useful lens through which to consider both the institution of kingship in ancient Egypt (perhaps *the* central institution culturally [O'Connor and Silverman 1995:XVII]) and legitimation (the processes by which elites manipulate central cultural symbols to foster acceptance of a given political and social order [Baines 1995]). Legitimating discourse can be especially apparent in times of political change, as elites modify themes rationalizing power; this chapter will focus on the later Old Kingdom, when kings seem to have been experimenting with different ways to inscribe authority throughout Egypt, perhaps in response to a perceived need to tighten central control over peripheral regions.

The King through Time

The role of the king in ancient Egypt was central to all aspects of life: cosmology, society, politics, and economy. Both human and divine in nature, the king was the mediator between the "cattle of the gods" (=the Egyptians) and the gods themselves, and conversely the representative of the gods in the terrestrial realm. His authority was vested in his divinity: in life, he was associated with the falcon god Horus, son of the mythical first king of Egypt; after death, he was simultaneously Osiris, king of the afterlife world, and a transfigured being entitled to ride in the boat of the sun god Ra during its daily circuit.

The king's principal task was the maintenance of *maat* (cosmic order), which ensured the continued functioning of the universe. In pursuit of this overarching goal, kingship entailed upholding legal justice as chief governor and judge on earth; assuring agricultural bounty and therefore economic prosperity as the chief (and in some periods, it is argued, the only) landholder; and repelling *isfet* (chaos), which perpetually threatened the cosmos in the form of either internal problems or external enemies, as supreme political ruler and warlord (O'Connor and Silverman 1995). Finally, as chief priest, the king was charged with maintaining the essential cults of gods' temples and of the dead – failure to pacify the gods could incur their displeasure and affect balance in the universe, which could in turn result in environmental consequences, especially irregular inundations. Too low an inundation could mean drought and famine; too high an inundation could be equally disastrous, and such phenomena were perceived to be directly linked to divine action or retribution.

Representations of the king engaged in cultic, ceremonial, agricultural, and warlike activity (both domestic and foreign) exist from the earliest times of centralized authority in Egypt, with the Early Dynastic Narmer Palette (c. 3100 BCE) incorporating all of these themes; and these core notions of authority seem to have remained remarkably stable throughout the Dynastic period. What varied were the aspects of kingship stressed in a given period, in response to social, political, and economic shifts over time. We can track these shifts through visual and written sources: the iconography and style of royal statuary and relief (Figure 4.1); royal and non-royal official inscriptions in tombs and temples; and literary tropes (see in particular Parkinson 2002). Another and equally fruitful route into these transformations is close analysis of the spatial patterning of archaeological phenomena, yielding information on qualitative differences in royal building initiatives, on the implications of the remains of non-royal activity, and on the construction and reworking of landscapes where these activities played out, providing the setting in which symbolically laden messages about cosmic and social order could be communicated to a variety of audiences.

Thus in the 12th Dynasty of the Middle Kingdom, scholars have suggested that one ideological emphasis was on the humanity of the king and his role as shepherd of his subjects, based upon a new "reality" in portrayals of the royal visage (seen at its most exaggerated in representations of Senwosret III). These emphases also occurred in certain tropes of the newly flowering literary tradition in reference to the burdens of kingship and the fallibility of the semi-divine beings holding that office (Parkinson 2002). An intensification of the king's responsibilities to the gods may be evident in the sharp increase of effort expended on the building of gods' temples in stone as well as the traditional emphasis on durable royal mortuary complexes (Franke 1995). And finally, a trend towards the creation or extension of non-mortuary conceptual landscapes, exemplified by the new political center at Itj-Tawy as much as by the string of fortresses in Lower Nubia and private votive arenas at Elephantine and Abydos, suggests a heightened concern with communicating and legitimating the ideology of rule to audiences beyond the inner elites of the central government (Richards 2000, and see Wegner, this volume).

Military ferocity as one facet of the ongoing battle against chaos crystallized as an evolving feature of kingship in the 12th Dynasty in inscriptions and architecture (e.g. Parkinson 1991:43–46). But beginning with the 18th Dynasty of the New Kingdom – an era initiated by the reconquest of Egypt from the Hyksos (see Harvey, this volume) – the militaristic aspects of kingship ideology were especially pronounced. As the Egyptian empire expanded further into Nubia and southwest Asia, motifs of the king smiting foreign enemies were increasingly prevalent on the exterior of temples, on artifacts, and in royal inscriptions. The renovation and creation of built environments as settings within which to communicate power and politics took place on an unprecedented scale, such as Amenhotep III's extensive reworking of the east and west banks of Thebes (Kozloff and Bryan 1992), and his son Akhenaten's establishment of the sprawling cityscape at Amarna (Kemp 2006). The messages they conveyed now addressed international as well as domestic audiences and also took on textual and portable form (commemorative scarabs, diplomatic letters) in addition to monumental and spatial practices. Side by side with imperial might, these landscapes, texts, and visual markers returned to a stress on the divinity of the king, even as his responsibility to the gods was also materialized by the scope of building activities in the realm of gods' temples. This New Kingdom brand of royal divinity, however, was paradoxically flavored with elements of the personal, real or constructed, exemplified by vignettes of fabulous expeditions, marriage and family, hunting prowess, and military wiles.

(a)

(b)

Figure 4.1 The iconography of kingship: emphases over time:
(a) Menkaure triad, 4th Dynasty, Giza. Copyright © Egyptian Museum, Cairo.
(b) Head of Senwosret III, 12th Dynasty. Copyright © Egyptian Museum, Cairo.
(c) Battle Scene, 19th Dynasty, Karnak temple. Photo: The author.

(c)

Figure 4.1 *Continued.*

We have far more archaeological data on the Middle and New Kingdoms than the Old Kingdom; and it also seems to be the case that the character of written culture was both more varied and more widely accessible in these periods. With regard to notions of kingship during the Old Kingdom, if we accept that points of visual and written contact between ruler and masses ruled were simply fewer during the third millennium BCE, and acknowledge moreover that our archaeological evidence for this time is more scarce than for later periods, how then can we adequately formulate which aspects of kingship were stressed in comparison to these later periods? Is our impression that the king's divinity and remoteness were emphasized to a greater degree simply a factor of our limited visual, written, and spatial data? If it is correct, can we move to identify the ways in which such absolute power was legitimized to different audiences, apparently successfully given the length of centralized power during the Early Dynastic and Old Kingdom periods? And finally, if it is not correct, what aspects of kingship did elites of the later Old Kingdom stress?

Kings in Their Own Place(s) and Voice

Archaeological evidence for royal activity in the third millennium BCE in general and the 5th and 6th Dynasties in particular (c. 2450–2175 BCE) (Figure 4.2) is sparse compared to the second and first millennia BCE and comes mainly from funerary and cult contexts. Rulers continued to deploy the pyramid as a central

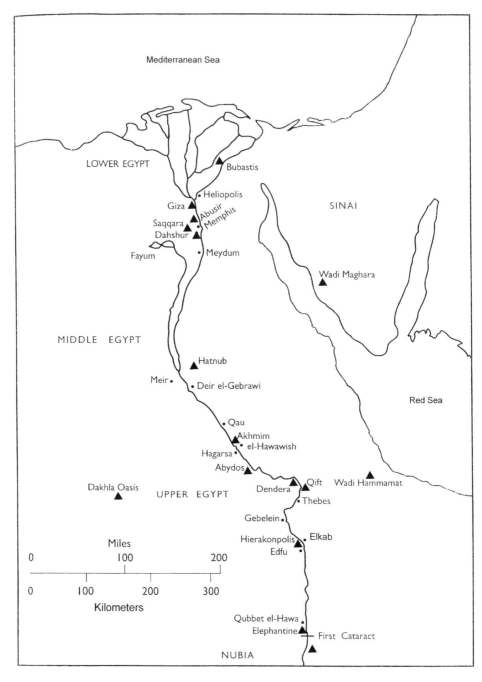

Figure 4.2 The expression of power throughout Egypt: evidence for royal activity in the 5th and 6th Dynasties. Map: Margaret Lourie (after Strudwick 2005:xxxiii).

symbol of power, permanence, and rebirth, although on a far smaller scale than their ancestors of the 4th Dynasty. Ten mortuary complexes dominated by these relatively modest architectural statements were carefully situated within the pre-existing Memphite political landscape at Abusir, Saqqara (Figure 4.3), and South Saqqara, radiating out from the monument of Djoser and bracketed at a greater distance to south and north by the 4th-Dynasty pyramid sites of Dahshur and Giza (see Dobrev 2007 on the axial relationships among the Saqqara and Dahshur pyramids). Their 5th- and 6th-Dynasty royal owners invoked therefore the symbolic power and legitimation of these previously established sacred places in establishing their individual monuments of eternity, and simultaneously signaled visually the strength and continuation of authority to audiences at the political center.

In the 5th Dynasty, several rulers also erected a series of solar temples just north of Abusir near their pyramid complexes, expressing in architectural form the heightened association of the sun god Ra with kingship ideology; only two survive, at the modern site of Abu Ghurab (see Krejči and Magdolen 2007 for a summary of research on these temples). These may also be examples of an emerging emphasis by kings on the building or renovation of gods' temples alongside that of royal mortuary landscapes, which previously constituted the vast majority

Figure 4.3 Monumentality and permanence: late Old Kingdom pyramids at Saqqara. Foreground: Courtiers' cemetery. Background: Pyramids from left to right: Teti (6th Dyn.) and Userkaf (5th Dyn.). Behind Userkaf: Djoser Step Pyramid (3rd Dyn.). Photo: Salima Ikram. Used with permission.

of stone-built construction; stressing in this way both the divinity of the king and his priestly responsibilities. In earlier scholarship on the later Old Kingdom, this shift in the deployment of labor and material resources and the concomitant decrease in size of pyramids had been cited as a consequence of economic decline; more recently scholars have viewed these phenomena as the results of deliberate choices being made regarding the appropriate contexts of kingly display (e.g. Strudwick 2005:8).

These particular political landscapes of the later Old Kingdom, while perhaps demonstrating an adjustment to the character and extent of materialization strategies of kingship ideology, remained largely focused on the political center through much of the 5th Dynasty. We can see significant changes at the end of the 5th Dynasty, however. One change relates to the character and spatial distribution of cult constructions in the 6th Dynasty (c. 2325–2175 BCE). Kings ceased building sun temples, but began to dedicate resources to the construction and/or renovation of gods' temples in more peripheral areas – at major cult centers in the provinces and the oases. There is archaeological and/or textual evidence for such activity at Bubastis in the Delta; at Akhmim, Abydos, Dendera, Koptos, and Hierakonpolis in Upper Egypt; at Elephantine on the southern frontier; and at Balat in Dakhleh Oasis, suggesting the steady development of an Egypt-wide political landscape with theological as well as administrative nodes throughout the country. There is also evidence for royal inscriptions in the Eastern Desert and the area south of the First Cataract in connection with expeditions to quarry the necessary materials for royal building projects.

Although in many cases the Old Kingdom cult installations in these areas do not survive (having been built probably mostly of mudbrick), monumental inscriptions originally erected in them provide glimpses of royal activity in these peripheral areas. The series of royal decrees from the 6th to the 8th Dynasty at ancient Koptos (modern Quft), preserved through the ancient Egyptian practice of recycling building materials in sacred contexts (they were incorporated into a Late Period wall), record actions regarding both provincial gods' temple establishments and their related estates:

> (With respect to) the overseer of priests and inspector of priests in Koptos of the Koptite nome; all the dependents of the possessions of the estate of Min; the functionaries of the entourage and daily service of Min; the workmen and builders of this temple who are there (in service).
>
> My majesty does not permit that they be set to the royal corvée (or the like), in cattle pastures or donkey pastures, in with other animals, in the administration of the guards, or in any duty or any tax imposition ... Their exemption within Koptos is renewed today by the command of the king. ... (Excerpt from Decree of Pepy II [Koptos B, trans. Strudwick 2005:108])

They also provide information on royal *ka* chapels established in or near these temples:

> The soul chapel of the royal mother Iput, in Koptos in the Koptite nome.
>
> I have ordered the exemption of this soul chapel [and its priests?], dependents, cattle, and goats [and there are no grounds for suit against it. With regard to] any

emissary who shall travel upstream on any mission, my majesty does not permit him to burden the soul chapel in any way. (Excerpt from Decree of Pepy I [Koptos A, trans. Strudwick 2005:105–106])

These texts reveal a continuing interest in provincial temples and the local deities to whom they were dedicated on a scale not recorded before the 6th Dynasty.

A second change in the overall structure of political landscapes in the later Old Kingdom, in contrast to the 3rd and 4th Dynasties, is that high governmental office seems to have moved away from royal relatives to a professional bureaucracy (Baud 2005), with more of these high officials of the central government building tombs in the provinces in the 6th Dynasty (especially after the reign of Teti; on the elite cemetery surrounding his pyramid see Kanawati 2003). As Nigel Strudwick comments, the new incidence of high officials' tombs in the provinces "may indicate not so much a shift to decentralization but rather an attempt to govern and exploit these regions more effectively, as some of these officials came from the Memphite region" (Strudwick 2005:9; contra Kanawati 1992). He further disputes that this new prominence of provincial officials contributed to the decline of central authority, hypothesizing that "it was not until the center itself became weak that there is some truth to this" (Strudwick 2005:10). This strategic situation of tombs of the central elite – in particular viziers and governors of Upper Egypt – in cemeteries of the periphery may have served ideological as well as administrative goals, acting as another avenue of broadcasting and legitimating kingship notions, a concept we will revisit below.

Alongside these shifts in the extent and nature of political landscapes in the materialization of royal ideology there were also transformations in symbolic components of these landscapes, relating to iconographic conventions, and to the appearance of what might be designated literature in royal mortuary inscriptions. Three-dimensional representations of the king, in contrast to the impression of remote and divine perfection fostered by 4th-Dynasty royal statues (see again Figure 4.1), seem in the 6th Dynasty to reveal a "new emphasis on expressiveness and action" (Romano 1998:236). This trend is exemplified by the kneeling statue of Pepy I (Hill 1999:cat. 170) (Figure 4.4), the statue of King Merenre (Hill 1999:cat. 171) in the form of a sphinx making offerings (=fulfilling cultic responsibilities) and the representation of the child king Pepy II on the lap of his mother and regent (Lilyquist 1999) (=stressing divinity by emulating the Isis–Horus relationship but simultaneously hinting at the vulnerability of the king as a child).

In nearly the same time frame, at the end of the 5th Dynasty, the earliest continuous ancient Egyptian literary texts appear, seemingly out of nowhere: the Pyramid Texts, a comprehensive collection of spells against dangers in the afterlife, intended to provide the deceased king with the magical tools needed to navigate safely the transition to afterlife. These texts first occur in the pyramid of Unis, the last king of the 5th Dynasty, at Saqqara; and along with spells for specific episodes of transformation and for warding off danger, they provide statements of kingship ideology. In contrast to recording official actions of the king as in the Koptos decrees, these reveal notions of the inherent nature of the king and his relationship to the gods:

Figure 4.4 A "new attitude": kneeling statue of Pepy I. Copyright © 2004–2009 The Brooklyn Museum. Used under the terms and conditions of a Creative Commons License.

> ... for Unis' nobility is in the sky and his power is in the Akhet, like Atum, his father who bore him ... for Unis' kas are about him, his guardian forces under his feet, his gods atop him, his uraei on his brow. ... Unis is lord of offering, who ties on the leash (of the sacrificial animal), who makes his own presentation of offerings. ... (Allen 2005:51)

The foregoing discussion reflects what we as archaeologists can read as the implications of shifts in form and in the spatial distribution of archaeological and textual phenomena generated by the king and the central authority structure. Given the patterns discussed above, it appears that the real shift in ideological emphasis occurred not between what we see as the "earlier" and "later" phases of the Old Kingdom (i.e. 3rd–4th Dynasties versus 5th Dynasty onwards), but *within* the later Old Kingdom and specifically between the 5th and 6th Dynasties. Did the ancient Egyptians themselves perceive such a shift? Apparently so – the Turin canon, a king-list written in the New Kingdom, shows an indigenous, royal, later second-millennium attitude towards the ancient past, with a distinct break between the 5th and 6th Dynasties, often understood by Egyptologists as a change in family (Malek 2000:113; Strudwick 2005:9). Yet unlike earlier bloodline shifts, the end of the 5th Dynasty was treated as a major summary point, totaling the number of years of kings of Egypt from the beginning, before moving on to a list of 6th-Dynasty kings (Gardiner 1959). Is Strudwick correct that nonetheless "the Old Kingdom continued apparently much as before" (Strudwick 2005:9)?

To answer this question, we must return to our earlier discussion: what were the thematic emphases within kingship ideology in the later Old Kingdom, and do they represent a change from earlier motifs; how broadly were these notions disseminated to the population under central authority; and what were the vehicles of this materialization given both the severely restricted access to royal and cultic precincts, and the generally low literacy rates in this time period?

In addressing these points, in the remainder of this chapter we will move to an exploration of two case studies of elite production that reinforced notions of sovereignty and supplemented royal venues for such materialization. These examples of communication and legitimation, which involve both the traditional center at Memphis and more peripheral areas in the provinces, are: the transformation of the private tomb biography in the 5th and 6th Dynasties, a central symbolic component of elite mortuary monuments (case study 1); and the reworking and development of the political and religious landscape at Abydos in the 6th Dynasty (case study 2).

Case Study 1: Kingship and Legitimation through the Content and Distribution of Private Tomb Biographies

Prior to the 5th Dynasty, hieroglyphic inscriptions in elite tombs were mostly limited to citations of the names and titles of tomb owners and lists of offerings, with only a couple of exceptions: the lengthy presentation of legal issues in the tomb of Metjen of the early 4th-Dynasty at Saqqara, and the late 4th-Dynasty narrative of Debehen in his tomb at Giza describing the construction of his tomb. Kloth has dated the latter to the mid-5th Dynasty, arguing that it may actually have been set up by Debehen's son (Kloth 2002:38–39; Strudwick 2005:43, 271). Either way, it is one of the first examples of what have been called "event-based" biographies: inscriptions which describe experiences relating to the individual owner, in contrast to "ideal" biographies dominated by standard phrases describing essential actions and abstract qualities befitting an "ideal" personality.

If we consider the timing and spatial distribution not only of event-based biographies as a whole in the 5th and 6th Dynasties, but of different categories within that genre, an interesting pattern emerges (Figure 4.5). In the 5th Dynasty, the genre is dominated by the recounting of isolated episodes during which the tomb owner interacted directly with the king; of details regarding his relationship to the king; or of rewards from the king, usually in the form of costly equipment for his tomb. These biographies are clustered mostly at the political center, in the cemeteries of Giza and Saqqara (Baines 1997, 1999; Kloth 2002; Strudwick 2005:46). The following excerpts provide an impression of the kinds of incidents described, and the behavior and mood of the king during these incidents:

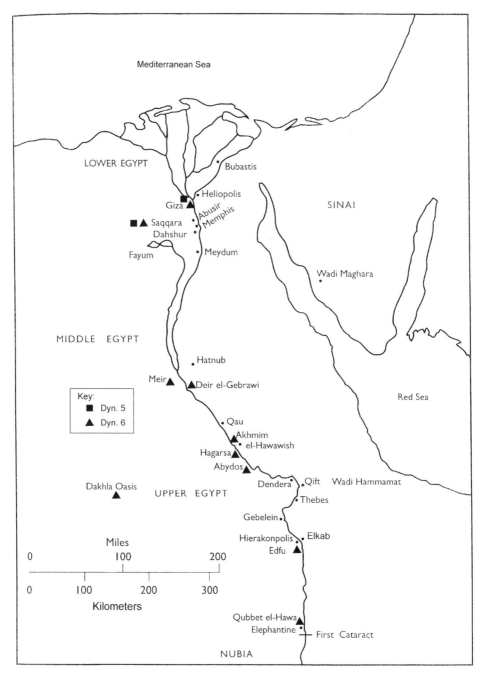

Figure 4.5 Legitimation in the periphery I: distribution of "event-based" and career/commission elite tomb biographies in the 5th and 6th Dynasties. Map: Margaret Lourie (after Strudwick 2005:xxxiii).

With regard to this tomb of mine, it was the king of Upper and Lower Egypt, Menkaure ... who gave me its place, while he happened to be on the way to the pyramid plateau to inspect the work being done on the pyramid of Menkaure. ... he arranged for 50 craftsmen to do the work on it daily. ... His majesty commanded that they were not to be taken for any work-duty, other than carrying out work on it (the tomb) to his satisfaction. ... His majesty decided to pay a visit to the work which had been assigned. ... (Debehen, Giza, late 4th or mid-5th Dynasty [trans. Strudwick 2005:271–272])

... when (King) Neferirkare was inspecting its perfection. ... Now then he went forth upon them ... he fell. His majesty had people support him ... an emergency treatment (?) [was brought to him]. ... They said to his majesty that he had lost consciousness ... [then his majesty] prayed to Re on the *she* structure (palace or temple precinct). ... (Washptah, Saqqara, 5th Dynasty, reign of Neferirkare [trans. Strudwick 2005:318–319])

The king of Upper and Lower Egypt, Neferirkare, appeared as the king of Lower Egypt on the day of taking the prow-rope of the god's boat. Now the sem priest Rewer was at the feet of his majesty. ... The ames scepter which his majesty was holding blocked the way of the sem priest Rewer. ... His majesty said: "it is the desire of my majesty that he be very well, and that no blow be struck against him." ... His majesty then commanded that it be placed in writing on his tomb of the necropolis, and his majesty had a document about it made for him, written in the presence of the king himself. ... (Rewer, Giza, 5th Dynasty [trans. Baines 1999:23–24; 1997:138–140])

Strudwick sees a turning point at the end of the 5th Dynasty during the reign of Izezi. In the biography of Senedjemib Inti at Giza, the author did not just describe interactions with the king, but went a step further and included the text of royal letters to him:

(I have spent) five years, four months, and three days now under Izezi. ... Izezi gave me a necklace of malachite (?) (perhaps) through the greatness of favor of his majesty when he was in the document office. ... His majesty had it tied upon my neck ... and his majesty saw to it that I was anointed with unguent. ...

His majesty made for me a decree which his majesty wrote with his own hand in order to favor me for everything which I had done nobly, perfectly, and excellently. ...

(First letter quoted:) ... my majesty has seen this letter of yours which you wrote to let my majesty know everything which you have done in relation to the setting out and the inscriptions/decoration of the *meret* temple of Izezi. ... Have I been correctly informed? Do not let it be said that it is a case of (just) gratifying Izezi! Let my majesty know the truth about it immediately!

(Third letter quoted:) My majesty has seen this ground plan which you have had brought for consideration in the court council for the precinct of the broad court of the palace "it belongs to the Sed festival of Izezi." Now you say to my majesty that you have planned it as 1,000 cubits long and 440 cubits wide, in accordance with what was said to you in the court council. How (well) you know how to say what Izezi desires above all else! ... O Senedjemib the elder, I do love you and it is known that I love you. (Excerpts from the biography of Senedjemib Inti at Giza, reign of Izezi, 5th Dynasty [trans. Strudwick 2005:311–313])

These biographies depict the king taking part in ceremonial activities; making regular inspection tours of monumental building projects; issuing decrees regarding resources; interceding with the gods; and displaying emotion – compassion, concern, excitement, and love. In other words, the biographies provide a vehicle to demonstrate that the king is himself going about his responsibilities as king; and they also touch on the personality of the king in a way that demonstrates his humanity as well as his divinity. Senedjemib Inti's biography introduces perhaps a further dimension: a more sustained relationship with the king in its account of a kind of dialogue between ruler and official regarding building projects. One message of this biography might be the addition to kingship ideology of the king as a professional – the king as administrator working closely with his top officials.

As of the early 6th Dynasty, new categories of the event biography began to dominate: "career" biographies, in which individual officials detailed their steady rise through the ranks of the government and the associated tasks they performed; and "commission" biographies, describing activities undertaken on behalf of the king(s) served (see the useful charts in Kloth [2002:285] and Strudwick [2005:46]). In contrast to 5th-Dynasty biographies, these were mostly situated in peripheral areas (Figure 4.5). The two longest and best-known examples of these new types are those of a governor of Upper Egypt Harkhuf at Aswan (Figure 4.6) and a governor of Upper Egypt Weni at Abydos; both were placed in public areas of their tombs, have in common detailed descriptions of tasks and expeditions undertaken on behalf of the king, including in foreign lands, and include excerpts from actual royal documents.

Figure 4.6 The spatial context of biographies: view to Qubbet el-Hawa tombs at Aswan. Photo: The author.

The format of Weni's text evokes that of a royal decree (Figure 4.7) and includes moreover an excerpt from the decree of Merenre by which he was made Governor of Upper Egypt (Richards 2002):

> I was a fillet-bearing youth under the majesty of King Teti, my office being that of custodian of the storehouse, when I became inspector of tenants of the palace. ... When I had become overseer of the robing room under the majesty of King Pepi, his majesty gave me the rank of companion and inspector of priests of his pyramid town.
>
> ... His majesty made me senior warden of Nekhen, his heart being filled with me beyond any other servant of his. I heard cases alone with the chief judge and vizier, concerning all kinds of secrets. ... When there was a secret charge in the royal harem against Queen Weret-Yamtes, his majesty made me go in to hear it alone. No chief judge and vizier, no official was there, only I alone. ... When his majesty took action against the Asiatic Sand-Dwellers, his majesty made an army of many tens of thousands from all of Upper Egypt. ... His majesty sent me to lead this army five times, to attack the land of the Sand-Dwellers as often as they rebelled. ...
>
> ... When I was Chamberlain of the palace and sandal-bearer, King Merenre, my lord who lives forever, made me Count and Governor of Upper Egypt. ... I governed Upper Egypt for him in peace, so that no one attacked his fellow. I did every task. I counted everything that is countable for the residence in this Upper Egypt two times, and every service that is countable for the residence in this Upper Egypt two times. ... His majesty sent me to dig five canals in Upper Egypt, and to build three barges and four tow-boats of acacia wood of Wawat. Then the foreign chiefs of Irtjet, Wawat, Iam, and Medja cut the timber for them. I did it all in one year. Floated, they were loaded with very large granite blocks for the pyramid "Merenre-appears-in-splendor." (Excerpts from the biography of Weni, Abydos, reign of Merenre, 6th Dynasty [trans. Lichtheim 1975:18–22])

Harkhuf's biography was set up on the façade of his tomb at Aswan during the reign of Pepy II in the 6th Dynasty. He describes his commissions involving exploration, diplomacy, and the collection of tribute from foreign rulers, records

Figure 4.7 "Decree" format of Weni the Elder's biographical stela (CG 1435, Egyptian Museum, Cairo). Graphic by Andrew Wilburn.

solicitous actions by the palace following his long journey, and even reproduces a letter from the boy king Pepy II expressing excitement at the prospect of a dancing pygmy for his court:

> The majesty of (King) Merenre, my lord, sent me ... to Iam to open up the way to this foreign land. I made the trip in seven months, and I brought back all sorts of perfect and luxury items of tribute. ... I went out from the Thinite nome upon the oasis road, and I found that the ruler of Iam had gone away to the land of the Tjemehu. ... I followed him to the land of the Tjemehu. I satisfied him so that he might praise all the gods for the sovereign.
>
> When I had satisfied that ruler of Iam, [I came down through] south of Irtjet, Setjau and Wawat; with three hundred donkeys loaded with incense, ebony, heknu oil, shesat, panther skins, elephant tusks, throw sticks, and all sorts of wonderful products. ...
>
> Now when this servant had traveled north to the Residence ... overseer of the two cool rooms Khuni was sent to greet me with ships laden with date-wine, cakes, bread, and beer.
>
> [King's letter:] The king's own seal, year of the second occasion, third month of the Akhet season, day 15: Note has been taken of the content of this letter of yours. ... What you have said in this letter of yours is that you have brought back all sorts of great and wonderful tribute ... what you have also said in this letter of yours is that you have brought back a pygmy who dances for the god from the land of the Horizon dwellers. ... Come north to the Residence straight away! Cast (everything else) aside, bring with you this pygmy who is in your charge. ... My majesty wants to see this pygmy more than the tribute of Sinai or of Punt. ... Orders have been taken to (every) chief of a new settlement ... to command that supplies be taken which are in his charge from every estate storeroom and from every temple; I make no exemption therefrom. (Trans. Strudwick 2005:330–333)

Again, in both instances references are made to incidents or aspects of the king that touch on his humanity – the scandal in Pepy I's harem mentioned by Weni, the excited anticipation of the youthful Pepy II over the dancing pygmy. These textual glimpses of the humanity of the king foreshadow more fully developed literary treatments of this trope in the 12th Dynasty.

The biography of Sabni at Aswan also evokes an emotional response from the king; his letter praising Sabni for retrieving his father's body from Wawat: "I shall do for you all excellent things as a repayment for this great deed ... in bringing back your father from this foreign land" (Strudwick 2005:337).

In contrast to the biographies of the 5th Dynasty, these biographies also reveal royal agency in the activities of the king's officials going about his business both domestically and in foreign lands; and subtly broadcast therefore that through them, the king was attentive to his cosmic roles, continually pacifying the gods, upholding *maat*, and ensuring prosperity in the land (building temples, digging canals, seeing to economic arrangements, ensuring burial in Egypt); and repelling chaos (upholding justice, "domesticating" foreign lands through travel, and defeating hostile actions by foreigners). In this way, private biographies not only commemorated their owners through verbal portraits, but on another level they also materialized kingship ideology and inscribed the strength of that authority throughout a Nile Valley-wide landscape, most especially during the 6th Dynasty (see Petrucci 1998 on the political purposes of the biographical genre). It is worth noting that these particular political tools were deployed in a time frame during which more formal statements of this ideology in the king's "voice" crystallized in the Pyramid Texts (in the mortuary realm), in royal building programs and decrees at gods' temples (the cultic realm), and in synchrony with the "break" in the flow of history seemingly presented by the Turin canon.

It cannot be coincidence that one of the most detailed of these biographies – Weni's, produced in the format of a royal decree – was put in place at the site of Abydos at a time when the entire landscape there was undergoing a dramatic and purposeful transformation. This leads us to a second case study in which we explore the manipulation of the broader context in which this particular inscription was erected, drawing in this instance on data from recent excavations.

Case Study 2: Development of a Multivocal Political Landscape at Abydos

Within the same time frame of the turn from the 5th to the 6th Dynasties, the central government undertook a substantial reworking of the regional landscape at Abydos (ancient *ȝbḏw*) in both town/temple and cemetery components, transforming the latter from a primarily royal precinct to a broader stage for political display, and intensifying royal attention to the former through the establishment of royal *ka* chapels near the temple of Khentyimentyw, until then the chief deity of Abydos. Part and parcel of the physical transformation of Abydos was a religious shift, aspects of which were the ultimate ascendancy of the god Osiris over Khentyimentyw as the "Lord of Abydos," the initiation of a national ceremonial cult, and the broadening of access to Osirian afterlife.

As in the north with the location of their mortuary complexes, 5th- and 6th-Dynasty kings were working with a pre-existing historical and ideological landscape (Figure 4.8). Their Early Dynastic ancestors built their own tombs near the opening of a wadi in the great bay of cliffs that define the Abydos low desert landscape, with associated monumental mudbrick enclosures and other installations nearer the floodplain and the ancient town and temple. In the town, a series of cult structures dedicated to Khentyimentyw were in use from the Early Dynastic period onwards (O'Connor 1999), with some slight evidence for activity continuing through the 3rd and 4th Dynasties (see Hawass 1985 on a small statue of 4th-Dynasty Khufu found in this area).

During the 5th Dynasty there seems to have been an increase in the attention paid by the central authority to the temple complex at Abydos. Petrie's excavations there in 1902 (Petrie 1902) yielded textual and artifactual evidence for five different kings of the 5th Dynasty, including a decree of Neferirkare exempting personnel of the Abydos temple from corvée labor (Brovarski 1994a:99). He also discovered a series of large mudbrick chapels within a series of enclosure walls dating generally to the Old Kingdom, which were most likely royal *ka* chapels (Brovarski 1994b:15–20; O'Connor 1999:90–93). One of these has been securely attributed to Pepy II of the 6th Dynasty, who set up a decree regarding his own

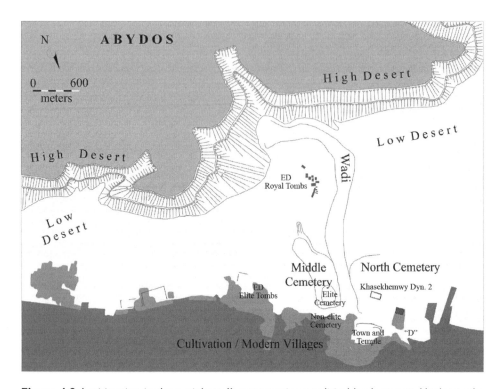

Figure 4.8 Legitimation in the periphery II: constructing a political landscape at Abydos in the Old Kingdom. Areas of Dyn. 5–6 royal and non-royal activity included the town/temple area and elite and non-elite cemeteries in Middle Cemetery area; the North Cemetery and Dyn. 1–2 royal tombs continued to be restricted areas. Map by Margaret Lourie. (Base map used with permission of Matthew D. Adams).

cult and the cults of royal relatives, referring to their statues as being "in the temple of Khentyimentyw" (Brovarski 1994b:16). The excavations of Petrie and later on of the Pennsylvania–Yale Institute of Fine Arts/New York University Expedition have further demonstrated that in the Old Kingdom a dense zone of occupation surrounded this cult area (Adams 2005:52). Excavations in the early twentieth century and within the last decade in the non-royal cemeteries of the later Old Kingdom at Abydos have confirmed the impression that the population grew dramatically at this time.

The vast area between the town and the cliffs of the Libyan desert was kept sacrosanct for a period of nearly 800 years following the construction of the first royal tombs near the cliffs (Richards 1999:93). The last Early Dynastic royal installation in what is now called the North Cemetery was that of King Khasekhemwy of the 2nd Dynasty. After his reign the royal burial ground moved to Saqqara, but the exclusivity of the Abydos low desert landscape was maintained and during those next four centuries there was neither mortuary nor cultic activity on the low desert plateau. Instead, the local population buried their dead on a ridge off the plateau, effectively outside the restricted zone (Richards 2002). But suddenly, either at the very end of the 5th Dynasty or more likely the beginning of the 6th, the central government made a decision to lift restrictions on use of this sacred space. Excavations and surveys conducted over the last decade have allowed us to pinpoint the historical moment at which this decision was made, and to delineate the multi-stage development of a political landscape that followed.

In 1999 and 2001, University of Michigan teams rediscovered and excavated the original context of Weni's biography cited above, a massive mudbrick mastaba tomb in the Middle Cemetery at Abydos whose location had been lost since the discovery of that inscription in 1860 (Richards 2002). Measuring $30\,m^2$ and preserved to a height of $5\,m$, it was situated at the summit of a low desert hill across the wadi from the enclosure of Khasekhemwy and was apparently the focus of a contemporary large and orderly city of the dead, with other large complexes nearby and a field of small subsidiary mastabas lying to its south and southwest. One piece of evidence connected to Weni's tomb was a fragment of a massive limestone pillar, depicting him making offerings to his father, a Vizier Iuu, suggesting that his father's burial also lay nearby. Two seasons of magnetic survey in 2002 and 2004 revealed both the probable location of that tomb, and the great extent and spatial organization of the surrounding cemetery field (Herbich and Richards 2006). The excavation season in 2007 has provided us with insight into key stages of the diachronic development of the cemetery, and evidence for the in-process shift from Khentyimentyw to Osiris as the primary deity of Abydos (Richards 2007a, 2007b) (Figure 4.9).

The first elite monument constructed on the blank slate of the Middle Cemetery was the square mastaba tomb of the Vizier Iuu (Figure 4.10). Massively built of mudbrick with limestone elements, its battered outer walls measure $26.3\,m$ long on each side, $5\,m$ thick, and in places are preserved to a height of $3\,m$; the original height of the mastaba was probably at least $2\,m$ more. It stood right at the edge of the low desert escarpment; to residents in the ancient town, it would have constituted a striking visual echo of the Khasekhemwy enclosure across the wadi (Figure 4.11). Its design and construction were clearly a locus of experimentation and a co-operative effort between royal and less skilled regional workforces: the lower courses of brick in the structure were expertly laid and extremely solid, while the top half was more shoddily constructed, making it easier for later generations to mine the structure for mudbricks to use in buildings.

The chapel on the exterior of the eastern wall was simply built and mostly undecorated, but there remained *in situ* the lower half of a massive limestone false door, $2\,m$ wide, produced in two pieces which were mortared together in place (visible in Figure 4.10). The high quality of the relief indicates that it is almost certainly the product of a royal workshop. The remaining portion bears eight representations of the Vizier Iuu receiving offerings from various relatives, including his son Weni; another band of decoration at the very bottom of the door depicts another series of smaller figures, presumably either more relatives (perhaps grandchildren) or persons associated with Iuu's estate. The full range of Iuu's governmental responsibilities is not preserved here because of the missing top half of the false door. But his title as chief judge and vizier and the cartouche name of Pepy (I) situate him hierarchically (at the top of civil administration under the king) and historically (at or near the beginning of the 6th Dynasty).

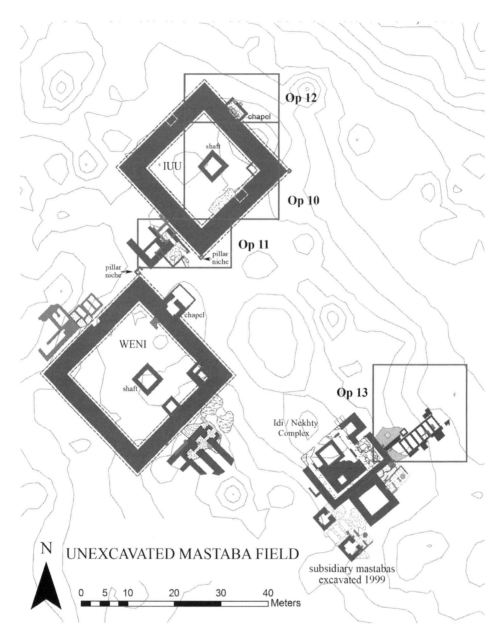

Figure 4.9 Abydos Middle Cemetery map, 2007. Map: Geoffrey Compton and Margaret Lourie.

Iuu's stone-lined burial chamber (Figure 4.12) lay at the bottom of a 10 m deep mudbrick shaft in the mastaba's interior. Beautifully preserved, its decorations are of painted low relief, depicting offerings punctuated with inscriptions painted in blue; an inscribed limestone lintel surmounts the entrance to the chamber; and a massive limestone sarcophagus rests on the floor. What is especially interesting in terms of the early 6th-Dynasty political project at Abydos is that in the ensemble

Figure 4.10 View of mastaba of Iuu with remains of false door *in situ*. Note heavily robbed brick walls of mastaba. Photo: R. James Cook, Abydos Middle Cemetery Project.

Figure 4.11 View to the mudbrick funerary enclosure of Khasekhemwy (2nd Dyn.) from the tomb of the vizier Iuu. Photo: R. James Cook, for the Abydos Middle Cemetery Project.

Figure 4.12 View into burial chamber of Iuu. Lintel in foreground demonstrates the primacy of Osiris at Abydos. Photo: Matthew D. Adams for the Abydos Middle Cemetery Project.

of inscriptions from east and west walls, sarcophagus lid, and lintel there are references to both Khentyimentyw and Osiris, but it is emphatically Osiris who dominates – nine references compared to only four for his predecessor god – and only twice does Khentyimentyw occur alone as compared to associated with Osiris. The lintel inscription, which is the largest "type face" of all the subterranean texts, invokes only Osiris: "The prince, count, vizier, governor of Upper Egypt, lector priest, nomarch, sole companion, one revered before Osiris, Iuu." It is evident that by the reign of Pepy I, the ascendancy of Osiris as the primary god of Abydos was well underway.

Throughout the burial chamber inscriptions it is also notable that variations on the wish for a goodly burial occur four times, all but three stressing burial specifically *in Abydos*:

> ... that Osiris-Khentyimentyw gives, that he may be buried in Abydos. ... (Sarcophagus lid)

> A boon that the king gives, and that Anubis and Khentyimentyw Lord of the Desert give, that he be buried in the necropolis.

> A boon that the king gives, and that Osiris and Khentyimentyw give, that he may have a goodly burial in this his tomb of Abydos. (West wall [Figure 4.13])

> A boon that the king gives and that Osiris gives, that he may have a goodly burial in this his tomb of Abydos. (East wall)

Figure 4.13 West Wall of the burial chamber of Iuu. The upper line of inscription reads in part, "May he be buried in this his tomb of Abydos." The middle line reads in part, "May he be buried in the necropolis." Photo: R. James Cook for the Abydos Middle Cemetery Project.

Iuu's tomb therefore broadcast a multidimensional message in this first stage of reworking the low desert landscape. Its superstructure provided a 6th-Dynasty government-sanctioned monumental echo of the Early Dynastic royal monument across the wadi. Its shape and size – square at the base, as pyramids were square, and moreover nearly precisely one third the footprint of Pepy I's pyramid at Saqqara – may have been intended to reinforce the impression of central (=royal) authority it projected. And the inscriptions in Iuu's burial chamber attest both to a new political focus on Abydos, and to the concomitant and accelerating shift to Osiris as lord of the area.

Within one generation, the next stage in the transformation of Abydos into a national ceremonial center had taken place. By the time that Iuu's son Weni constructed his own tomb near his father's burial place, Osiris had gained the explicit epithet "Lord of Abydos," according to the inscriptions in Weni's burial chamber (Richards 2002). There were four references to Osiris distributed among the east, west, and north walls of the chamber. Khentyimentyw, in contrast, was cited once, only in conjunction with Osiris, and only on the west wall of the chamber as part of the sole occurrence of the Abydos burial wish: "… that he be buried in his tomb of the western necropolis, in peace, in peace, before Osiris-Khentyimentyw in Abydos … ." Khentyimentyw's demotion seems therefore to have been accomplished by this time, setting the stage for the development of Abydos into a national ceremonial center for Osiris.

Another component of this second stage was the construction not only of Weni's massive tomb, but also of a vast field of smaller mastabas radiating to its (local) south and north. The extremely orderly pattern of this cemetery-wide development suggests that it took place as part of a unified plan; although only two of these subsidiary mastabas have been excavated (see Figure 4.9) the traces of many more are currently visible on the surface of the cemetery; and the magnetic survey map (Figure 4.14) confirms the existence of several more rows of uniformly sized mastabas. Excavations have revealed that as a first step in this process, Weni's monumental grave – also square in shape – was carefully inserted into the mortuary landscape occupied previously only by his father's tomb. Expertly constructed start to finish (in contrast to the shift in expertise evident in his father's tomb), it was situated precisely just to the south and west of Iuu's tomb. This ensured that the axis to Weni's own eastern chapel was uncluttered even as the visual dominance of his father's monument was preserved, given the position of Weni's tomb behind it and the fact that it was founded one meter lower than Iuu's mastaba. Apparently also as part of this step, corner pillars were added to Iuu's grave depicting Weni offering to his father (Figure 4.15), this architectural detail being repeated on the corners of Weni's tomb (Richards 2007a). Finally, it is possible that as part of this integration of his own tomb into the ritual space of his father's building, the decoration of Iuu's false door was carefully edited through the addition of figures of Weni offering to his father.

The trajectory of Weni's own career is better known to us than that of his father, thanks to the survival of his biography and other tomb equipment, including a second false door excavated in 1999 (Richards 2002). He began his career under Teti, the first king of the 6th Dynasty; continued his rise through governmental ranks under Pepy I; was promoted to the office of Governor of Upper Egypt by

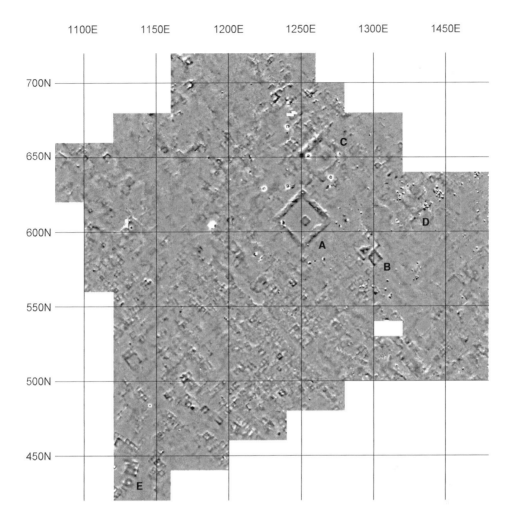

1100E   1150E   1200E   1250E   1300E   1450E

700N

650N

600N

550N

500N

450N

-20   -15   -10   -5   0   5   10   15   20 nT

Figure 4.14 Magnetic survey map of Abydos Middle Cemetery. Note orderly rows of subsidiary mastabas to local south and west of Weni mastaba (A). Iuu mastaba is (C). Idi/Nekhty complex is (B); (D) is an unexcavated complex. Map: T. Herbich for the Abydos Middle Cemetery Project.

(a)

(b)

Figure 4.15 Reinforcing central authority over time: two generations in space and architecture
(a) Pillar of the Vizier Iuu with the Governor of Upper Egypt Weni the Elder offering to his father (discovered in 1999). Photo: Korri Turner for the Abydos Middle Cemetery Project.
(b) View to original context of pillar: niche and limestone footer on southwest corner of Iuu discovered in 2007. Photos: Geoffrey Compton for the Abydos Middle Cemetery Project.

Merenre; and finally attained the rank of Vizier, probably also under Merenre. It is tempting to conjecture that the timing of this comprehensive building project in the Abydos Middle Cemetery was tied to Weni's appointment as Governor of Upper Egypt, a promotion that was emphasized in his biography; and that the goal of this project was to continue the elaboration of the political landscape begun under the previous reign. In this iteration, not only was the diachronic maintenance of central authority reinforced (and in a spatial pattern that is reminiscent of the spatial relationship of Merenre's pyramid to his own father Pepy I's pyramid [see Leclant 1999:10–11 and Lehner 1997:160 on the possibility of a coregency]) but it seems likely that another layer of memory was being evoked. In addition to the architectural echo of 2nd-Dynasty Khasekhemwy's monument at Abydos, the overall visual impact of the newly remodeled Middle Cemetery may have been intended to evoke the visual memory of the 4th-Dynasty Giza pyramids and their setting within orderly fields of officials' mastabas, thereby legitimizing the current regime through a call on motifs of power and permanence from the more recent past. This additional dimension also re-created on the ground at Abydos the same kind of embedded diachronic landscape as that occupied by the 5th- and 6th-Dynasty landscapes in the north.

Conclusions

Smith has argued that "political transformations in early complex polities were predicated on the construction of very specific landscapes" (Smith 2003:24); and it is widely acknowledged that the creation and/or manipulation of landscapes and their symbolic components is especially prominent "in episodes of authority in crisis" (Smith 2003:6). The historical moment of the 5th and 6th Dynasties of the Egyptian Old Kingdom was a time during which the materialization of royal ideology and authority was transformed both thematically and spatially. These transformations were especially pronounced in the 6th Dynasty given the increase in royal activity in the provinces, the rise and spatial distribution of career/commission private biographies, and the growth of politically inspired conceptual landscapes at key provincial sites such as Abydos. Did the Old Kingdom continue much the same as before, following the "break" signaled by the Turin Canon? It seems not; though whether or not Miroslav Bárta is correct in identifying this same time period as that of "the declining Egyptian state" (Bárta 2007:46) remains an open question. What is clear is that by the later Old Kingdom attention was being paid to the legitimation of kingship beyond the political center of Memphis and the social reaches of the high elite, in textual, visual, and spatial terms that foreshadowed elite strategies of the Middle Kingdom.

ACKNOWLEDGMENTS

I am grateful to Willeke Wendrich for her patience and hard work in pulling this volume together; and to Terry Wilfong, for productive discussions regarding the

Turin Canon and the purposes of biography in ancient Egypt. The Abydos Middle Cemetery (AMC) work is possible through the gracious permission of Dr. Zahi Hawass and the Permanent Committee of the Supreme Council of Antiquities, Egypt, and I am grateful also to William Kelly Simpson and David B. O'Connor, co-directors of the Pennsylvania–Yale Institute of Fine Arts/New York University Expedition. I am grateful to the crew members of the AMC Project from 1995 to the present; some of the ideas presented in this essay emerged from discussions with 2007 crew, in particular Geoffrey Compton and Elizabeth Hart. Special thanks are due to the epigraphers of the 2001 and 2007 seasons – Marjorie Fisher, Belgin Elbs, Korri Turner (2001); Heather Tunmore, Lindsay Ambridge, Collin Ganio, Matthew D. Adams, Timothy Sandiford, and Alex Makovics (2007) – without whom the discussion of Iuu's and Weni's inscriptions would not have been possible; to Penny Minturn for expert supervision of the excavation of Iuu's chamber; and to James Cook and Matthew Adams for their excellent photography of same. The AMC Project has been supported by the University of Michigan, the National Geographic Society, Marjorie Fisher, and private donors; research time relating to this chapter was supported by the National Endowment for the Humanities and the American Philosophical Society.

REFERENCES

Adams, M. D. 2005. Community and Society in Egypt in the First Intermediate Period: An Archaeological Investigation of the Abydos Settlement Site. Ph.D. dissertation. Proquest/Ann Arbor.

Allen, J. 2005 The Ancient Egyptian Pyramid Texts. Atlanta: Society for Biblical Literature.

Baines, J. 1995 Kingship, Definition of Culture, and Legitimation. *In* Ancient Egyptian Kingship. D. O'Connor and D. Silverman, eds. Pp. 3–47. Leiden: Brill.

Baines, J. 1997 Kingship before Literature: The World of the King in the Old Kingdom. *In* Selbstverständnis und Realität: Akten des Symposiums zur ägyptischen Königsideologie, Mainz 15–17.6.1995. R. Gundlach and C. Raedler, eds. Pp. 125–74. Ägypten und Altes Testament 36: Beiträge zur Ägyptischen Königsideologie 1. Wiesbaden: Harrassowitz Verlag.

Baines, J. 1999 Forerunners of Narrative Biographies. *In* Studies on Ancient Egypt in Honour of H. S. Smith (Occasional Publications 13). A. Leahy and J. Tait, eds. Pp. 23–37. London: Egypt Exploration Society.

Bárta, M. 2007 The Sixth Dynasty Tombs in Abusir: Tomb Complex of the Vizier Qar and His Family. *In* The Old Kingdom Art and Archaeology. Proceedings of the Conference Prague, May 31–June 4, 2004. M. Bárta, ed. Pp. 45–62. Prague: Publishing House of the Academy of Sciences of the Czech Republic.

Baud, M. 2005 Famille royale et pouvoir sous l'Ancien Empire egyptien. 2nd edition. 2 vols. Cairo: Institut français d'archéologie orientale.

Brovarski, E. 1994a Abydos in the Old Kingdom and First Intermediate Period, Part I. *In* Hommages à Jean Leclant. Vol. 1. C. Berger, G. Clerc and N. Grimal, eds. BdÉ 106/1:99–121. Cairo: Institut français d'archéologie orientale.

Brovarski, E. 1994b Abydos in the Old Kingdom and First Intermediate Period, Part II. *In* For His *Ka*: Essays Offered in Memory of Klaus Baer. D. Silverman, ed. SAOC no. 55:15–44. Chicago: Oriental Institute.

De Marrais, E., L. J. Castillo, and T. Earle 1996 Ideology, materialization, and power strategies. Current Anthropology 37 (1): 15–31.

Dobrev, V. 2007 A New Necropolis from the Old Kingdom at South Saqqara. *In* The Old Kingdom Art and Archaeology. Proceedings of the Conference Prague, May 31–June 4, 2004. M. Bárta, ed. Pp. 127–131. Prague: Publishing House of the Academy of Sciences of the Czech Republic.

Franke, D. 1995 Middle Kingdom in Egypt. *In* The Encyclopaedia of the Ancient Near East, Vol. II. J. Sasson, ed. Pp. 735–747. New York: Charles Scribner's Sons.

Gardiner, A. H. 1959. The Royal Canon of Turin. Oxford: Griffith Institute.

Hawass, Z. 1985. The Khufu Statuette: Is It an Old Kingdom Sculpture? *In* Melanges Gamal Eddin Mokhtar. Pp. 373–395. Cairo: Institut français d'archéologie orientale.

Herbich, T., and J. Richards 2006 The Loss and Rediscovery of the Vizier Iuu at Abydos: Magnetic Survey in the Middle Cemetery. *In* Timelines: Studies in Honour of Manfred Bietak. Vol. 1. E. Czerny, I. Hein, H. Hunger, and D. Melman, eds. Pp. 141–149. Louvain: Peeters.

Hill, M. 1999. Cat. 170. Pepi I Kneeling; and Cat. 171. Sphinx of Merenre I. *In* Egyptian Art in the Time of the Pyramids. D. Arnold and C. Ziegler, eds. Pp. 434–437. New York: Metropolitan Museum of Art.

Kanawati, N. 1992 Akhmim in the Old Kingdom. Part I: Chronology and Administration. Sydney: Australian Centre for Egyptology.

Kanawati, N. 2003 Conspiracies in the Egyptian Palace Unis to Pepy I. London: Routledge.

Kemp, B. 2006 Ancient Egypt: Anatomy of a Civilization. 2nd edition. London: Routledge.

Kloth, N. 2002 Die (auto-) biographischen Inschriften des agyptischen Alten Reiches: Untersuchungen zu Phraseologie und Entwicklung (SAK 8). Hamburg: Buske.

Kozloff, A., and B. Bryan 1992 Egypt's Dazzling Sun. Cleveland: Cleveland Museum of Art.

Krejči, J., and D. Magdolen 2007 Research into Fifth Dynasty Sun Temples – Past, Present and Future. *In* The Old Kingdom Art and Archaeology. Proceedings of the Conference Prague, May 31–June 4, 2004. M. Bárta, ed. Pp. 185–192. Prague: Publishing House of the Academy of Sciences of the Czech Republic.

Leclant, J. 1999. A Brief History of the Old Kingdom. *In* Egyptian Art in the Time of the Pyramids. D. Arnold and C. Ziegler, eds. Pp. 437–439. New York: Metropolitan Museum of Art.

Lehner, M. 1997 The Complete Pyramids. London: Thames and Hudson.

Lichtheim, M. 1975. Ancient Egyptian Literature. Vol. I. Berkeley: University of California Press.

Lilyquist, C. 1999. Cat. 172: Pair Statue of Queen Akh-nes-Meryre II and Her Son Pepi II Seated. *In* Egyptian Art in the Time of the Pyramids. D. Arnold and C. Ziegler, eds. Pp. 437–439. New York: Metropolitan Museum of Art.

Malek, J. 2000. The Old Kingdom (c. 2686–2125 BC). *In* The Oxford History of Ancient Egypt. I. Shaw, ed. Pp. 89–117. Oxford: Oxford University Press.

O'Connor, D. 1999 Abydos, North, *Ka* Chapels and Cenotaphs. *In* An Encyclopaedia of the Archaeology of Ancient Egypt. K. Bard, ed. Pp. 100–103. London: Routledge.

O'Connor, D., and D. Silverman 1995 Introduction. *In* Ancient Egyptian Kingship. D. O'Connor and D. Silverman, eds. Pp. xvii–xxvii. Leiden: Brill.

Parkinson, R. B. 1991 Voices from Ancient Egypt: An Anthology of Middle Kingdom Writings. London: British Museum Press.

Parkinson, R. B. 2002 Poetry and Culture in Middle Kingdom Egypt: A Dark Side to Perfection. London: Continuum.

Petrie, W. M. F. 1902 Abydos I, II. London: Egypt Exploration Fund.

Petrucci, A. 1998 Writing the Dead: Death and Writing Strategies in the Western Tradition. Stanford: Stanford University Press.

Richards, J. 1999 Conceptual Landscapes in the Egyptian Nile Valley. *In* Archaeologies of Landscape. W. Ashmore and B. Knapp, eds. Pp. 83–100. Oxford: Blackwell.

Richards, J. 2000 Modified Order, Responsive Legitimacy, Redistributed Wealth: Egypt, 2260–1650 BCE. *In* Order, Legitimacy, and Wealth in Ancient States. J. Richards and M. Van Buren, eds. Pp. 36–45. Cambridge: Cambridge University Press.

Richards, J. 2002 Text and Context in Late Old Kingdom Egypt: The Aarchaeology and Historiography of Weni the Elder. Journal of the American Research Center in Egypt 39:75–102.

Richards, J. 2007a The Archaeology of Excavations and the Role of Context. *In* The Archaeology and Art of Ancient Egypt: Essays in Honor of David B. O'Connor. Vol. II. Z. Hawass and J. Richards, eds. Pp. 313–319. Cairo: Supreme Council of Antiquities Press.

Richards, J. 2007b "Wonderful things": The 2007 Abydos Middle Cemetery Project. Kelsey Museum Newsletter, Spring:1–4. http://www.lsa.umich.edu/kelsey/research/Publications/spring2007.pdf.

Romano, J. 1998 Sixth Dynasty Royal Sculpture. *In* Les critères de datation stylistiques a l'Ancien Empire. N. Grimal, ed. Pp. 235–303. Cairo: Institut français d'archéologie orientale.

Smith, A. T. 2003. The Political Landscape: Constellations of Authority in Early Complex Polities. Berkeley: University of California Press.

Strudwick, N. C. 2005. Texts from the Pyramid Age. Atlanta: Society of Biblical Literature.

5

Villages and the Old Kingdom

Mark Lehner

Narratives on ancient Egyptian settlements often focus on the New Kingdom, mostly because of two exceptionally well-preserved towns: Deir el-Medina and Amarna. Settlements dating to the Old Kingdom are of great interest too, even though much less is known about them, because the little we know indicates this was a time of early urbanization and increased influence of the central state. There has been an ongoing discussion among Egyptologists on how much the state influenced the daily life of farmers and villagers, and how much villagers organized and governed their own affairs. Until recent decades, some Egyptologists held the view that the Old Kingdom state registered people throughout the land, put bureaucrats in charge of provincial settlements, and replaced villages with strictly controlled estates and new towns (Eyre 1999; Helck 1975:18–44; Malek 2000:102; Malek and Forman 1986:35, 65, 87; Seidlmayer 1996) As Richards (this volume) points out, the gigantic pyramids of the early Old Kingdom suggest an extensive degree of economic and social control. The inference of an invasive state reorganization of the countryside in the early Old Kingdom draws strength from the power of the early gigantic pyramids to impress. Eyre (1999) expressed quite the contrary view and considered Egypt a village society at all periods, with broad continuities throughout history in the way Egyptian villages operated.

We can look at the evidence for ancient Egyptians villages from a global perspective or from a local perspective, two scales that are not mutually exclusive. As in any complex adaptive system, it is the local rules that generate global order. Sometimes central authority designs and imposes order, and sometimes authority is parasitic on organizations that generate and regulate themselves. In pre-modern periods better documented than the Pharaonic millennia, villages were semi-autonomous, and served as the basic fiscal unit of the Egyptian economy. One way of approaching villages, then, is to examine through time, as best the data allows, their role in the larger economic and political network. The other scale, the local perspective, concentrates on the structures of everyday life, the local rules, the algorithms, which generate larger social orders (families, households, nomes, states). The paucity of settlement archaeology and the differences in preservation of the textual and archaeological record give very uneven information for villages and urban centers from different periods and disparate parts of the country. If we want the local, fine-grained perspective, that is, if we want to know the village inhabitants – men, women, children, aged persons, and their animals – and all the variations of individual and social experience, one village from 3000 years of Pharaonic history gives sufficient detail: Deir el-Medina, the community nestled at the foot of the high Theban western desert that housed workers who created pharaohs' tombs during the height of the New Kingdom empire. But we should calibrate our knowledge of Deir el-Medina detailed life against what we know or can reasonably infer about the broader context of settlement and population in Pharaonic Egypt.

Early Egyptian Population and the Village Horizon

The population and area of the larger early Egyptian settlements that functioned as provincial centers, "towns" in our terms, were themselves probably of a scale we would equate with a village. Modern categories, like Roberts' (1996) farmsteads, hamlets, villages, and towns, probably have little to do with the ancient Egyptians' own categories, and neither, probably, do our categories of rural and urban, public and private. The question is whether we could classify, in our terms, almost every early Egyptian settlement as a village or cluster of villages.

In his seminal study on the geography and ecology of early Egypt, Butzer (1976) concluded that population was concentrated in the two places where the Egyptian Nile Valley narrows. The southern concentration was in the Qena Bend, the homeland of pharaohs, roughly between Hierakonpolis and Abydos. Within this latitude, the river valley makes its great eastward bend with Luxor, ancient Thebes, on the south and Qena on the north. The northern concentration was in the stretch of valley between the entrance to the Fayum and the apex of the Delta – the "capital zone."

In the 4th Dynasty, the short period of truly gigantic pyramids, royal family members and high officials built huge mastaba tombs in the court cemeteries near these pyramids, the earliest in a series of pyramids that line the western side of the capital zone.

Old Kingdom texts and relief scenes depict offering bearers bringing produce from villages (*niwt*) and estates (*hwt*), many of which Egyptologists can locate in Middle Egypt, where the cultivated Nile Valley is widest, and in the expansive Delta (Jacquet-Gordon 1962; Kemp 1983:87–92, fig. 2.2). This geographical pattern, along with the title "overseer of new towns" or "villages" (*niwt*) beginning in the 5th Dynasty (Badawy 1967), suggests an active program of internal colonization by the royal house in those areas that were hinterlands, perhaps in part to feed the pyramid projects. Prior to this internal colonization, Upper Egypt might have contained fewer villages than, say, the reported 956 villages in Upper Egypt, and, even more likely, fewer than the reported 1439 villages in the Delta (total 2395) for the period 934–968 CE (Hassan 1995:560, based on Maqrizi). Provincial mastaba tombs, and the first family tombs, appear in the 5th Dynasty. Kemp wrote, "the continued history of Old and Middle Kingdom civilization contained an important element of free wheeling on the apparatus created through the building of the early pyramids" (Kemp 1983:89).

During the Early Dynastic period and Old Kingdom, people built thick enclosures around towns like Elephantine, Kom Ombo, Edfu, El-Kab, and Abydos. These became provincial capitals, and some contained an unusually large residence (Moeller 2004). The disappearance of earlier smaller settlement sites fortifies the idea that people abandoned more numerous villages to reside in walled towns (Jeffreys and Tavares 1994; Kemp 2006:194–201; Seidlmayer 1996). Moeller suggests that, aside from other functions like defense, the walls carried symbolic value, "marking the town as a town" and distinguishing it "from other types of settlement such as villages" (Moeller 2004:265).

Kemp sees a "modest scale of Egyptian society compared with what is normal experience in much of the present world, a scale commensurate with the modest size of the population," which for the Old Kingdom totaled somewhere around 1.2 million compared with 70 million today (Hassan 1995:560; cf. Butzer 1976). "Especially for the Old Kingdom … the valley landscape, richer in wildlife and far more lushly vegetated, would have seemed oddly deserted" (Kemp 2006:200). Taking as an example the settlement at Elephantine/Aswan, Kemp compares the estimated area of the town during the Old Kingdom with the area in 1798 CE. He suggests that the increased size of this settlement parallels similar increases in other towns while the number of settlements remained about the same (Kemp 2006:200). We should note that several times in recent centuries authorities actually counted the number of villages in Egypt. Using counts from the first and second millennia CE, Hassan (1995) estimates just under 3000 villages for all of Pharaonic Egypt.

Following Kemp's examples for archaeological exposures of early settlements, towards the end of the Old Kingdom, Elephantine contained a very large residence, probably of the local governor (Kaiser 1998; Raue 2002, 2005). Archaeologists found another Old Kingdom governor's palace in 'Ayn Asil in the Dakhla Oasis at the heart of a settlement surrounded by a thick wall with semi-rounded towers on one corner and flanking an entrance (Soukiassian et al. 2002). Much of the exposure of Early Dynastic or Old Kingdom settlement at Hierakonpolis belongs to a little-understood palace. In the center of this exposure, a thick, mudbrick, monumental doorway opens into a maze of walls and passages that lead through an indirect route inward to a dais. Behind the platform a ramp rises from large round silos to a platform at the level of the dais (Adams 1995:66–67; Fairservis 1986; Kemp 2006:83, fig. 26, 196–197, fig. 68). We can recognize more developed forms of the features inward from the decorated gate in palaces from later times.

The suggested demographic context of urbanization during the early Old Kingdom is a lower overall density of population for Upper and Lower Egypt, with more people living in the Qena Bend and in the northern narrow valley from the Fayum entrance to the Delta apex, and in both places a move from a wider scatter of smaller villages to those villages that grew into walled towns.

Old Kingdom settlements detected in borings and trenches of the late 1980s and early 1990s for water projects from Giza to Abu Rawash and the area of west Cairo seem to be the archaeological correlate to the art historical and textual record of an expansion of new settlement in the early Old Kingdom (Hawass 1997:57, fig. 1; Jones 1995, 1997; Sanussi and Jones 1997). Old Kingdom settlements at Giza and Abu Roash were newly founded on sand of the low desert or on the interface between the low desert and the banks of a main Nile branch that flowed close to the western edge of the valley (Jeffreys 2008; Lutley and Bunbury 2008). The limited exposures do not allow us to know the form and function of these settlements.

We know little about the smaller settlements lying farther afield in either the northern or southern "capital" zones, much less in the hinterlands of Middle Egypt and the Delta. We might expect to also find evidence of Old Kingdom settlements on virgin ground in the Delta, unless the "new" villages and towns were simply reallocations of existing settlements around old centers like Sais, Buto, Mendes, and Bubastis. While we have textual and pictorial evidence of an internal colonization, we really do not know whether the Old Kingdom state had an interest in urban layout, the footprint and form of settlements in the provinces (Kemp 2006:201).

Central Planning or Self-organizing, Orthogonal and "Organic"

By the Middle Kingdom, settlement planning culminated in what Kemp (2006:211–231) calls model communities. He bases this characterization upon archaeological exposures of Middle Kingdom settlements at Kahun, Dahshur, Abydos South, Tell el-Dabaa, Thebes, and Qasr el-Sagha that display "a grid iron or orthogonal plan." These are for the most part state-planned urban centers, at least in their beginnings. As in Kahun, Kemp notes that the rectangular models fit the bureaucratic and structured character of the Middle Kingdom. But this bureaucratic tendency was already on the rise in the Old Kingdom, when planners laid out the town along the causeway leading to the monumental tomb of Queen Khentkawes in the late 4th Dynasty (Hassan 1943). This settlement is just as rigid and compact as Kahun, albeit on a smaller area, and the same is true for the central Gallery Complex Heit el-Ghurab settlement at Giza (Lehner 2002).

Birds-eye, map views of villages from widely disparate times and regions very often display irregular, so-called "organic" path systems, a self-organized complexity (Schaur 1991; as in the "Islamic city" – see Schloen 2001:108–116; Wirth 1992, 1997; and for one village example in modern Egypt, Berque 1957:48–49). People who live within the intricate order (for it is not chaos) of such ground plans tend to move about topologically, by visual memory. The order is self-organized, with no central authority, and no overarching design. Order of a very complex sort *emerges* in such settlements from inhabitants following local rules (based upon considerations of kinship; path or water proximity; craft specialization; or field access). The resulting order can sometimes tend towards the orthogonal (as in some cellular and crystal structures), but self-organization, which indeed characterizes much of the organic world, is the opposite of design.

Towns and villages in the floodplain were more likely obliged to organize themselves upon limited high ground that the Nile floodwaters surrounded from six to eight weeks every late summer into fall. We might imagine that these villages were not rigorously planned (Vercoutter 1983:136) on the basis of the self-organized character of unplanned settlements and villages of many times and places (Schaur 1991). We have to imagine this feature of ancient Egyptian villages because we have hardly any plans of what might have been this more common village pattern. In fact, Egyptian villages are nearly invisible in the published archaeological record. One finds few plans of wholly excavated villages and only a few excavated parts of settlement that might be classed villages, such as Kom el-Hisn in the western Delta (Cagle 2003; Wenke et al. 1988) or parts of Elephantine at different periods (Kaiser 1998; Ziermann 2003). One reason is the dearth of settlement archaeology in general in Egypt, until recent decades, in favor of monumental temples, tombs, and capital sites. Many of the towns and villages of ancient Egypt probably lie under the towns and villages of modern Egypt, built up over the centuries. In fact, because their non-linear complexity makes such villages hard to "read," and therefore hard to map, one is hard pressed to find maps of unplanned villages from any period, even recent premodern and modern times (Berque 1957:48–49 for an exception).

Core and Province: Material Culture Correlates

Archaeologists found a material culture correlate to the inferred relationship between provincial villages and the state center when they compared material culture from an Old Kingdom settlement in the western Delta with that from an urban center at the foot of the Giza Pyramids Plateau.

Kom el-Hisn, possibly the Pharaonic place named *'Im3w*, occupied an ancient Nile channel that ran through Nome 3 of the western Delta (Figure 5.1 bottom). The Old Kingdom settlement here dates to the 5th and 6th Dynasties, with some settlement continuing into the early Middle Kingdom (Wenke et al. 1988:13), although the Middle Kingdom component is small (Redding, personal communication). Systematic retrieval and analysis of animal bone and plant remains yielded evidence that the inhabitants raised cattle. The carbonized plant remains, recovered through flotation, contained a high percentage of fodder and forage plants such as clover and mustard, which suggests they derive from the use of cattle dung as fuel in hearths. The excavators also found fragments of burnt dung. Grasses would have suggested the cattle grazed in pastures, but the dearth of grasses in the Kom el-Hisn corpus strongly indicates that these were pen-fed or stabled cattle. Moens and Wetterstrom (1988) relate this botanical evidence to historical information. The inhabitants worshipped a cow goddess, Hathor, as a deity. Kom el-Hisn might have been the location for the "Estate of the Cattle" (*ḥwt iḥwt*) attested for the Third Lower Egyptian Nome as early as the 1st Dynasty. At the same time, paradoxically, the investigators found very little cattle bone, and high numbers of pig bone, with a 0.04:1 ratio of cattle to pig (Redding 1992:101). Pig is a village animal, which does not travel well with its short legs. Pigs can be fed waste food products, while providing high-calorie meat (Redding 1991). It appears that in the Old Kingdom, Kom el-Hisn residents raised pen-fattened cattle for export to the ritual and political centers, the temples and pyramid complexes near the apex of the Delta. Redding (1991) predicted that

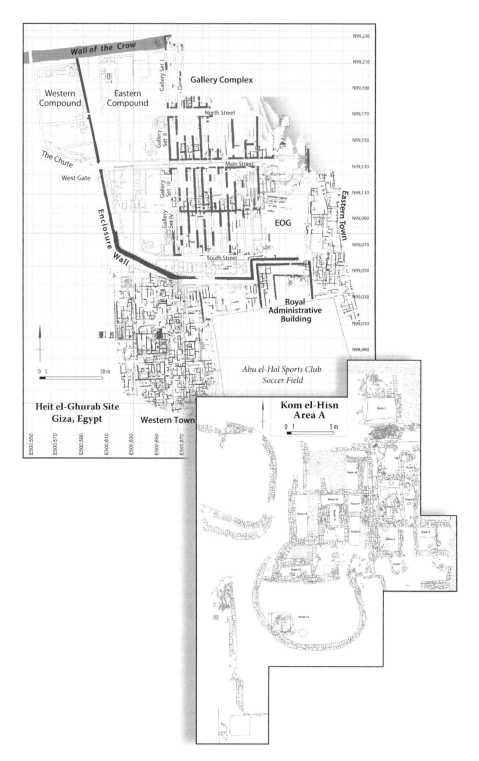

Figure 5.1 Core and periphery: the Heit el-Ghurab settlement at Giza (top), with the village footprint of Kom el-Hisn in the Western Delta (inset, bottom). They represent the very rare information on core and periphery settlements in the Old Kingdom. The Gallery Complex at Heit el-Ghurab expresses an orthogonal layout we might expect as the hallmark of central authority, while villages throughout Egypt like Kom el-Hisn supported the infrastructure, which made it possible for the royal house to build the gigantic pyramids of the early Old Kingdom. This Kom el-Hisn footprint covers about 75 m², while that of Heit el-Ghurab covers approximately 75,000 m² (7.5 ha). Plan of Kom el-Hisn: courtesy of Robert Wenke.

samples of animal bone from settlements in the capital zone, like Giza, would yield reverse patterns from Kom el-Hisn: high ratios of cattle to pig, and high numbers of sheep and goat to pig. The ratio cattle to pig for the entire 4th-Dynasty Heit el-Ghurab settlement is 6 : 1, and for certain areas as high as 16 : 1. We infer that central authorities were provisioning Heit el-Ghurab with prime meat on the hoof, possibly enough to feed 7000 to 10,000 people 200 to 300 g a day, which eleven cattle and thirty sheep or goat could provide (Redding, personal communication). People living in large houses of the area we call the Western Town had preferential access to prime cattle meat (Redding 2007b). People living in the eastern zone of small houses that we call the Eastern Town consumed higher numbers of pig (Redding 2007a:267; in press). The fauna and other material culture, including the objects and flora, from the Eastern Town are more characteristic of material we would expect from a village (Lehner and Tavares forthcoming).

These results correspond to predictions that we can make from a model of the Old Kingdom core and province relationship, where provincial settlements, some newly founded, supply the state provisioning of the center. Or, simply, the results are congruent with Old Kingdom texts and relief scenes that depict offering bearers bringing produce from villages (*niwt*) and estates (*ḥwwt*). However, the Old Kingdom components of Kom el-Hisn (5th–6th Dynasties) are not quite contemporary with the Giza settlements (4th Dynasty). The best we can say is that we expect the patterns we see in Kom el-Hisn assemblages would also obtain in a 4th-Dynasty Delta settlement.

Estates and villages that fed cities (cf. Zeder 1991 for Mesopotamian parallels) or pyramid-building company towns need not have been new settlements whose footprints were laid out by central planners, nor new forms of community organization. The state, which in the early Old Kingdom was basically the royal house (Baud 2005; Strudwick 1985), might have simply expected quotas from designated estates and villages, perhaps a version for its time of the New Kingdom quota system, which had households throughout cities like Amarna supplying linen to temples and palaces (Kemp and Vogelsang-Eastwood 2001:427–434; for a recent premodern parallel, in the reign of Mohamed Ali, see Cuno 1992). In the core–periphery provisioning system, people and households in estates and villages probably functioned like basic constituents of complex organizations in other domains: the elementary parts experienced no major changes despite major changes of phase in an overarching network. Phase transitions between statehood and fragmentation, that is, major change for the "state" of the overarching network, must have sometimes impacted villagers. However, it is possible that sometimes for them the difference was simply what authority, at what level, had a call on their production.

Village Inhabitants in the Center

The Heit el-Ghurab site in Giza (Figure 5.1 top) would seem like the last place to look for evidence of villages in the Old Kingdom, because it was the center of the Egyptian state. Located at the southeastern foot of the Giza Plateau, 400 m south of the Great Sphinx, the Heit el-Ghurab was one district of a larger series of settlement patches strung out north–south along a main Nile channel which ran 200 to 300 m east of the site at Giza (Jeffreys 2008; Lutley and Bunbury 2008; Sanussi and Jones 1997), and so, like Amarna some 1500 years later (Kemp 2008c:34), the 4th-Dynasty Giza settlement was a major inland port at the center of the Egyptian state.

More than twenty years ago, Kemp (1984) drew the disparity between what we know from Deir el-Medina and the workmen's village of Amarna because of the plethora of texts in the former and the paucity in the latter. We are even more textually challenged at Giza. The only texts from over twenty years of excavation (1988–2009) consist of clay sealings. However, just as we know from an abundance of textual culture that the state provisioned the Deir el-Medina workmen's village, we know from an abundance of carefully retrieved and meticulously analyzed material culture that a millennium earlier the state provisioned the Heit el-Ghurab community.

The central feature is the Gallery Complex. State planners assembled large modular units, "galleries," with width to length ratio of 7 : 1, into four great blocks separated by three cross streets. People in gatehouses restricted and controlled access to the streets (Abd al-Aziz 2007a, 2007b; Kemp 2006:188–190; Lehner 2002). A long open colonnade at the front of each gallery could have provided a sleeping area for forty or fifty people. Structures for food production and storage surround the Gallery Complex on the east, west, and south. These include the replication of modular, open-air bakeries with a production capacity beyond the needs of an individual household (Lehner 1992:3–9; 1993:60–67). A large enclosure, the "Royal Administration Building," at the southeastern corner of the settlement features a sunken court of silos, probably for grain storage (Lehner and Sadarangani 2007). In his assessment of the settlement as a work camp, Kemp (2006:189, fig. 66) is missing the Western Town, a maze of walls between the Royal Administrative Building and the escarpment in which we can recognize the thicker walls defining large "elite" houses (Lehner 2007:45–46). This part of the settlement, and certainly the Gallery Complex, display the orthogonal planning that is the signature of top-down design. But the Eastern Town, a series of small chambers and courts, reflects more the self-organization characteristic of villages. Here we find grinding stones for producing flour for the bakeries that surround the Gallery Complex from grain in the central storage of the Royal Administrative Building. In spite of the proximity of state storage and bakeries, we find in the Eastern Town individual hearths and small household storage silos.

At first glance, this urban footprint is so opposite all that a village is thought to represent that we might take it simply as a confirmation of the state overriding of families, households, and villages. The early Old Kingdom state, as in the older view of Egyptology, would have forced service by exactly such a regimented footprint as the Gallery Complex, trying to eradicate the messiness and the illegibility (Scott 1998) of the village and countryside. Gendered spaces, activities, and objects form a major dimension of the "natural" social order. In the Gallery Complex we might expect extreme gender restriction (Wilfong, this volume), on the assumption that barracks would house men, and perhaps only young men at that.

But when we look critically and in more detail, the Heit el-Ghurab site could yield signs that authorities worked with natural social structures, even as they modified them to begin to reach for an economy of scale. For the barracks the planners used the components of a traditional Egyptian house: a relatively open, more public front with columns, smaller back rooms forming a more private domicile, and rear cooking chambers (Lehner 2002). They assembled this catalogue of domestic parts into the Gallery Complex. We might see the galleries as barracks, yes, but also as enlarged houses, where the planners reached for the large scale through the enlargement and reproduction of smaller domestic units.

Groups housed in these units might have come to Giza from specific regions, nomes, communities, or villages. Graffiti on Middle Kingdom pyramids, which Arnold (1990) understood as control notes, indicate that workers served royal duty in home-based fellowships. Scrawled large across explicit written instructions for literate scribes, larger made-up signs like crossed sticks and pitchforks that were not part of the formal repertoire of hieroglyphs may have represented smaller villages for those who could not read formal text. Other marks refer to known towns, "the Memphis team" for example, and some teams may have been named after the owners of large estates. For the Old Kingdom pyramid builders we have to think first of the Egyptian unit of labor organization, *za*, written with the hieroglyph of a rope tied into ten loops – a cattle-hobble. Two millennia later, *za* was translated as the Greek, *phyle* (literally, "tribe"). Eight Heit el-Ghurab galleries could each have housed two gangs of the four *phyles* attested in the 4th Dynasty (Lehner 2004:190–192; Roth 1991). The social basis of the Old Kingdom *phyle* system needs further discussion.

The segregation of people in the Gallery Complex from the rest of the site increased over the time, a segregation marked by a thick enclosure wall (Lehner and Tavares forthcoming). The Gallery Complex may have been "gender-restricted" to only males, but settlement areas outside the Enclosure Wall around the blocks of galleries were probably more gender-balanced. As Wilfong (this volume) points out for Kahun and Deir el-Medina, male workers and administrators probably inhabited the Eastern and Western Towns along with their families, although in the absence of texts other than sealings we must make this inference based upon the house-like patterns and artifacts.

Tavares (2004) identified bone points, bone rods, copper needles, and stone spindle whorls of the sort associated on other sites with weaving, spinning, and sewing. Such objects derive mainly from the Royal Administrative Building and the Western Town. It has been suggested for Egypt and elsewhere in the ancient Near East that weaving and spinning, particularly with the early horizontal loom, were primarily women's actitivites (Barber 1991, 1994). In reviewing this question, Kemp and Vogelsang-Eastwood conclude that "there is in fact no independent way of determining what proportion of men as against women were engaged in the different stages of textile manufacture or whether gender or loom type went together" (Kemp and Vogelsang-Eastwood (2001:436). When people abandoned the Heit el-Ghurab site at the end of the 4th Dynasty they took most objects of value with them. Numerous dolerite stone pounders or fragments of such have been found all across the site. It is commonly assumed that such pounders derive from stone working, and that therefore men primarily used them, but given the wide distribution across the settlement, these objects perhaps had a more general use, and might have been part of the household as well as the mason's toolkit. In spite of abundant evidence of baking in fieldstone extensions flanking the mud-brick Gallery Complex east, south, and west, almost no grinding stones or querns were found in these areas. The Royal Administrative Building yielded several, found around the sunken court of large mudbrick silos – evidently centralized storage – and we found more grinding stones scattered in the Eastern Town. Tomb scenes, limestone models, and later wood models may primarily show women grinding, but we need a more thorough study before deciding grinding was primarily women's work.

The Eastern Town walls conform roughly to the orientation of the planned installations and to the cardinal directions, but this part of the settlement appears to have "self-organized" by incremental additions. Accreted to the grand design of the Gallery Complex, the warren-like character of the Eastern Town layout is similar to non-orthogonal village layouts from widely disparate times and regions. The various kinds of material culture from the Eastern Town – especially the plant remains and animal bone – are also most like samples from village sites than any other part of the site (Lehner and Tavares forthcoming; Redding in press). Indeed, the Heit el-Ghurab site can be seen as a village (the Eastern Town), a town (the Western Town), and a state barracks cobbled together into a larger urban center.

The Exceptional Village of Deir el-Medina

Half a century of archaeology (1905–1951), some eighteen volumes by Bernard Bruyère and others, and an extensive and continuing publication of tombs, chapels, burials, artifacts, and texts, (mostly ostraca – texts written on limestone flakes and pottery vessel fragments) convey to us adjudications, oracles, buying and selling commodities (Janssen 1975), social and sexual relations, laundry lists and love songs (McDowell 1999), and even hints of "village-wide menstrual synchrony" (Wilfong, this volume). Meskell (1998, 1999, 2002) takes Deir el-Medina as a case study in the archaeology of social relations, the archeology of the individual, of gender, of the household, of body and soul. In *Private Life in New Kingdom Egypt*, she begins the section on village life by noting that, "given the paucity of excavated settlement sites, one cannot really discuss rural villages, where most of the farming population would have lived," and that "Egyptologists regard [Deir el-Medina] as so anomalous as to be unrepresentative in terms of daily life" (Meskell 2002:38). She concludes, however, that the Deir el-Medina houses and their fixtures were relatively modest when compared to Amarna, and apparently on this basis suggests that daily life and domestic conditions in the village were similar to many other non-urban sites. In contrast, she states that ultimately Amarna's "unrepresentative character limits fruitful extrapolation to other settlements" (Meskell 2002:33).

In spite of the modest dwellings, Deir el-Medina must have been one of the most unusual villages of its time. At the outset of her book *Village Life in Ancient Egypt*, McDowell (1999) lays this out clearly: "The state supplied its inhabitants with all their needs, not only foodstuffs such as grain, fish, and vegetables (and in good times also pastries), but also fuel, pottery, and laundry service" as well as water. If we understand the Theban east and west banks combined, with their temples connected by processional ways, as one vast urban layout (Kemp 2006:266), Deir el-Medina was in the midst of the prime New Kingdom urban and religious center. The village was close to the Ramesseum, the memorial temple of the 19th-Dynasty king Ramesses II, which became the administrative center for Thebes West, and even closer to the later temple of Ramesses III at Medinet Habu, which overtook the administrative role from the Ramesseum. We get such a fine-grained look at life in this village because of the texts found in its vicinity. Texts are few for the early period (18th Dynasty), more plentiful in the 19th Dynasty, and come with such abundance by the 20th Dynasty that "it is possible to write a day by day account of official activities for much of the period" (McDowell 1999:22). Scholars estimate that 40 percent of the residents were literate and almost every male was taught to read and write. Their buying and selling of everything from bulls (which they must have kept on property elsewhere) to coffins, and their ties to government officials, "puts at least the officials of the gang in the top 2 percent of the population" (McDowell 1999:4–27).

Meskell (1998, 2002) sees textual, architectural, and artifactual evidence for gendered spaces in the Deir el-Medina houses. She associates with women the features of a front room: a low enclosed bed-like structure (the *lit clos*); wall paintings of women breast feeding, grooming, and making music; and figures of the god Bes, a lion-headed dwarf deity associated with sexuality, music, and protective magic. Meskell associates with men the features of a second room: a divan or bench, "cultic cupboards," painted false doors (paneled dummy doors for communication with spirits), and ritual objects. She makes the inference about the second room and men largely on the fact of the divan and its historical and ethnographic parallels in other houses (Meskell 2002:117). At the same time she indicates we cannot assume exclusivity of rooms (Meskell 1998:218). With as many as eight to twelve inhabitants per average house size of $72\,m^2$ (Valbelle 1985:117), people may have slept and probably carried out a variety of activities in these spaces, as well as on the roofs. To a certain extent we can take these findings as a common culture in New Kingdom Egypt. Excavators found divans in many Amarna houses, both in the main city and in the workmen's village. They also found paintings of women, of Bes, and Taweret, the hippopotamus goddess of childbirth, in the front rooms of the workmen's village and other houses at Amarna. One such room contained a bin or altar (Kemp 1979; Meskell 2002:113–114). These parallels suggest that people living at Deir el-Medina and, earlier, at Amarna shared the associations of rooms and gender. On the other hand, for the *lit clos*, "parallels beyond Deir el-Medineh are surprisingly absent" (Meskell 1998:223) and the majority of finds on which Meskell makes her inferences date to occupation during the later Ramesside period. Unfortunately, the Deir el-Medina excavations lack anything approaching stratigraphic control from which we could accurately construe occupation phases. In spite of this, we should not reject the rich Deir el-Medina findings in our attempt to understand village life in ancient Egypt. It is hard to imagine that the villagers of Deir el-Medina developed basic mores, customs, and habits that were radically different from those of other villagers of their time.

Amarna the City of Villages

At Amarna, the short-lived 18th-Dynasty capital of Akhenaten in Middle Egypt, the state stepped down, left its footprint, and walked away in only twenty years. If we assume a rural–urban dichotomy familiar to recent Western culture, Amarna becomes marginal to a study of villages. But was it indeed the case that, "as today, life in larger cities was very different from that experienced by people living in villages and rural settings" (Meskell 2002:17)? If we should not impose our categories, "kitchen, bedroom, foyer" on ancient Egyptian houses (Meskell 1998:218), neither should we impose our rural–urban categories on the entire ancient Egyptian community experience.

The Amarna residential zones, in which houses alone covered approximately 240 hectares (Kemp 2008c:34), flanked a royal center. The suburban dwellers appear to have situated their houses, like people settling in on a beach, free of state planning. Because of its short life, the site is a record of self-organized settlement by colonization (Kemp 2008c:35). Clusters of small houses surround larger villas. As Kemp indicates, the resultant order emerges from many individual choices of larger house owners and their dependents, decisions based on "rules" or preferences, of which we can only guess. To this extent the larger suburban order, though void of town planning, was not chaos. Suburban Amarna was self-organized, characteristic of unplanned settlements (Schaur 1991).

> In El-Amarna, outside the corridor of royal buildings, planning petered out altogether. Instead of a grand unity design we find a few broad but far from straight streets running more or less parallel to the Nile to join the suburbs to the centre, while narrower streets cross at right angles. The overwhelming impression is of a series of joined villages. (Kemp 2006:327)

The major buildings of the royal city center exhibit design and planning (Kemp 2008c:37). But even in the central city, "whilst its regularity of layout and open space set it apart from the housing areas, in its scale and building materials it was a continuation: another piece of mud-brick village standing in stark contrast to a handful of monumental structures" (Kemp 2008c:37).

In the residential zones, house plots of various sizes connect in complex patterns that make distinctive neighborhoods in which, by and large, "rich and poor lived side by side" (Kemp 2006:327; 2008c). The larger houses included kitchens with bread ovens, intramural animal byres, sheds and enclosures that were possibly workshops, gardens, and granaries, shrines for the richest households, and living accommodations, including a porter lodge by the gate, in addition to the private rooms of the main house. In sum, "the larger houses look like little farms" (Kemp 2006:329). The official residents themselves were the farmers. Judging from patterns of land holding documented elsewhere in ancient Egypt, they probably enjoyed produce from plots widely distributed in the floodplain and country. As a conglomerate of "farm centers," the basic building block of hamlets and villages (Roberts 1996:15–18), the suburbs of Amarna offer another glimpse of village life.

Recently, Kemp amplified on the settling into the Amarna suburbs of official residents and their retainers: "The result was a series of tiny, intermingled villages, in which the houses of the officials were, in effect, the houses of the village headmen" (Kemp 2008a:34). The Amarna headmen were priests, administrators, and army men (Kemp 2008c:34) who had strong connections to the countryside where they held land (Kemp 2008b:44), a pattern of "home village'" that persists in Egypt's capital down to the present day. But if administrators at the center would return to social origins in provincial villages, villages also came to the center. The Amarna headmen probably brought dependents from provincial home villages or their urban estates in Thebes or Memphis (Kemp 2008b:44). The High Priest, Panhesy, had his own little village arrayed alongside his enormous urban estate, a bit reminiscent of the Eastern Town alongside the Gallery Complex and Royal Administrative Building in the Heit el-Ghurab site. Panhesy's house was one of the "nuclei around which the bulk of the housing developed," the architectural expression of networks held together by a "common bond of dependency upon an important official" (Kemp 2008c:36–37).

Change and Tradition in Village–State Relations

We know that the Old Kingdom state could intervene and conscript. Weni, who, like his father, rose to the office of Vizier in the 6th Dynasty (Richards, this volume), led a "state" military operation against Asiatic Bedouin at the height of the Old Kingdom. Weni led an army composed of natives of the Delta, five Nubian tribes, Libyans, and

> nobles (h3ty-ꜥ), royal seal bearers, sole companions who were great estate chiefs (hwt-ꜥ3ty), [local] chiefs (hry-tp), and town rulers (hk3 hwt) of Upper and Lower Egypt, companions, overseers of foreigners, chief priests of Upper and Lower Egypt, and chiefs of gs-pr at the head of the troops of Upper and Lower Egypt from the manors (hwwt) and towns (niwt) that they governed (hk3) and from the Nubians of those foreign lands. (Urk I 102-3-8, trans. Eyre 1999:38)

Eyre comments that the levy is territorially based, made up from village or manor: "The military context is one where village identity is revealed strongly" (Eyre 1999:38). A similar kind of village-based levy for pyramid building in the 4th Dynasty might be inferred from the settlement pattern at Giza.

From the archaeological remains we can infer reciprocity between villages and the central government, but not its exact nature and organization. Could officials from the central government have registered and compelled male members of villages, estates, or farmsteads to serve in barracks at Dahshur and Giza for a rotation of duty building the pyramids? More likely the royal house sent an order to provide a quota of labor to local rulers and heads of villages, who would then seek members of the households within their domain to send to the large government projects.

We can relate the question of the degree to which Deir el-Medina people lived exceptional lives to a question about the workers' community at Giza, a thousand years earlier. For building royal tombs in the form of the gigantic Giza pyramids, did the members of the royal house override common social structures of their culture, or work within and through them? The multiplication of households for up-scaling in Heit el-Ghurab to meet the task of building Egypt's largest pyramids is a sign that in the Old Kingdom the household was the most important/fundamental social unit, which could not yet be replaced by a more abstracted compulsory civil service. The very example of Deir el-Medina shows that for even its most exceptional projects, the state allowed the household to function as a basic unit in settlements we would classify as villages or, for larger settlements, a composition of villages.

Most probably ancient Egypt was indeed always a village society (Eyre 1999), not just because most people lived in small settlements and practiced agriculture. Urban living in some vague sense that we have in mind when we assume a distinct life style between "urban" and "rural" hardly existed in Egypt's earliest periods. Even the "towns" were of a scale and composition we might categorize as "village." Unfortunately, factors of preservation and the short history of settlement archaeology in Egypt have not salvaged and recorded many settlements for the early periods. But we sense the presence of the village throughout the early Egyptian social landscape in the textual record, in the few settlements or parts of settlements that archaeologists have exposed, and even in the archaeological record of very exceptional settlements, like Deir el-Medina, Amarna, and the Heit el-Ghurab settlement of the pyramid builders.

REFERENCES

Abd al-Aziz, A. 2007a Gallery III.4 Excavations. *In* Giza Reports: The Giza Plateau Mapping Project. Vol. 1. Project History, Survey, Ceramics and Main Street and Gallery III.4 Operations. M. Lehner and W. Wetterstrom, eds. Pp. 109–140. Boston: Ancient Egypt Research Associates.

Abd al-Aziz, A. 2007b Main Street Excavations. *In* Giza Reports: The Giza Plateau Mapping Project. Vol. 1. Project History, Survey, Ceramics and Main Street and Gallery III.4 Operations. M. Lehner and W. Wetterstrom, eds. Pp. 193–234. Boston: Ancient Egypt Research Associates.

Adams, B. 1995 Ancient Nekhen: Garstang in the City of Hierakonpolis. Whitstable, Kent: SIA Publishing.

Arnold, F. 1990 The Control Notes and Team Marks: The South Cemeteries of Lisht. New York: Metropolitan Museum of Arts.

Badawy, A. 1967 The Civic Sense of Pharaoh and Urban Development in Ancient Egypt. Journal of the American Research Center in Egypt 6:103–109.

Barber, E. J. W. 1991 Prehistoric Textiles: The Development of Cloth in the Neolithic and Bronze Ages with Specific Reference to the Aegean. Princeton: Princeton University Press.

Barber, E. J. W. 1994 Women's Work: The First 20,000 Years. Women, Cloth, and Society in Early Times. New York: Norton.

Baud, M. 2005 Famille royale et pouvoir sous l'Ancien Empire égyptien. Vol. 126. Cairo: Institut français d'archéologie orientale.

Berque, J. 1957 Histoire sociale d'un village égyptien au XXe siècle. Paris: Mouton & Co.

Butzer, K. W. 1976 Early Hydraulic Civilization in Egypt: A Study in Cultural Ecology. Chicago: University of Chicago Press.

Cagle, A. 2003 The Spatial Structure of Kom el-Hisn: An Old Kingdom Town in the Western Nile Delta, Egypt. Oxford: Archaeopress.

Cuno, K. 1992 The Pasha's Peasants: Land, Society, and Economy in Lower Egypt 1740–1858. Cambridge: Cambridge University Press.

Eyre, C. J. 1999 Village Economy in Pharaonic Egypt. *In* Agriculture in Egypt from Pharaonic to Modern Times. A. K. Bowman and E. Rogan, eds. Pp. 33–60. Oxford: Oxford University Press.

Fairservis, W. A. 1986 The Hierakonpolis Project: Season January to May 1981, Excavation on the Kom el-Gemuwia. Poughkeepsie, NY: Vassar College.

Hassan, F. A. 1995 Town and Village in Ancient Egypt: Ecology, Society, and Urbanization. *In* The Archaeology of Africa: Food, Metals, and Towns. T. Shaw, P. Sinclair, B. Andah, and A. Okpoko, eds. Pp. 551–569. London: Routledge.

Hassan, S. 1943 Excavations at Giza, Vol. IV: 1932–33. Cairo: Government Press.

Hawass, Z. 1997 The Discovery of the Harbors of Khufu and Khafre at Giza. *In* Études sur l'Ancien Empire et la nécropole de Saqqara dédiées à Jean-Philippe Lauer. C. Berger and B. Mathieu, eds. Pp. 245–256. Montpellier III: Université Paul Valéry.

Helck, W. 1975 Wirtschaftgeschichte des alten Ägypten im 3. und 2. Jahrtausends vor Chr. Leiden: Brill.

Jacquet-Gordon, H. K. 1962 Les nomes des domains funéraires sous l'ancient empire égyptien. Cairo: Institut français d'archéologie orientale.

Janssen, J. J. 1975 Commodity Prices from the Ramessid Period: An Economic Study of the Village of Necropolis Workmen at Thebes. Leiden: Brill.

Jeffreys, D. 2008 Archaeological Implications of the Moving Nile. Egyptian Archaeology 32:6–7.

Jeffreys, D., and A. Tavares 1994 The Historic Landscape of Early Dynastic Memphis. Mitteilungen des Deutschen Archäologisches Instituts, Abteilung Kairo 50:143–173.

Jones, M. 1995 A New Old Kingdom Settlement near Ausim: Report of the Archaeological Discoveries Made in the Barakat Drain Improvements Project. Mitteilungen des Deutschen Archäologischen Instituts, Abteilung Kairo 51:85–98.

Jones, M. 1997 Archaeological Discoveries in Doqqi and the Course of the Nile at Cairo during the Roman Period. Mitteilungen des Deutschen Archäologischen Instituts, Abteilung Kairo 53:101–111.

Kaiser, W. 1998 Elephantine: The Ancient Town. Cairo: Deutsche Archäologische Institut Abteilung Kairo.

Kemp, B. J. 1979 Wall Paintings from the Workmen's Villa at Amarna. Journal of Egyptian Archaeology 65:47–53.

Kemp, B. J. 1983 Old Kingdom, Middle Kingdom, and Second Intermediate Period. *In* Ancient Egypt: A Social History. B. G. Trigger, B.J. Kemp, D. O'Connor, and A. B. Lloyd. Pp. 71–182. Cambridge: Cambridge University Press.

Kemp, B. J. 1984 In the Shadow of Texts: Archaeology in Egypt. Archaeological Review from Cambridge 3(2):19–28.

Kemp, B. J. 2006 Ancient Egypt, Anatomy of a Civilization. 2nd edition. London, New York: Routledge.

Kemp, B.J. 2008a Amarna's Genesis. Ancient Egypt 8(4):31–36.

Kemp, B, J. 2008b The People of Amarna. Ancient Egypt 8(5):41–46.

Kemp, B. J. 2008c What Kind of City was Amarna? Ancient Egypt 8(6):33–38.

Kemp, B. J., and G. Vogelsang-Eastwood 2001 The Ancient Textile Industry at Amarna. London: Egypt Exploration Society.

Lehner, M. 1992 Giza. *In* The Oriental Institute 1990–1991 Annual Report. G. Gragg, ed. Pp. 19–27. Chicago: The Oriental Institute.

Lehner, M. 1993 Giza. *In* The Oriental Institute 1991–1992 Annual Report. G. Gragg, ed. Pp. 56–67. Chicago: The Oriental Institute.

Lehner, M. 2002 The Pyramid Age Settlement of the Southern Mount at Giza. Journal of the American Research Center in Egypt 39:27–74.

Lehner, M. 2004 Of Gangs and Graffiti: How Ancient Egyptians Organized Their Labor Force. AERAGRAM 7(1):11–15.

Lehner, M. 2007 Introduction. *In* Giza Reports: The Giza Plateau Mapping Project. Vol. 1. Project History, Survey, Ceramics and Main Street and Gallery III.4 Operations. M. Lehner and W. Wetterstrom, eds. Pp. 3–47. Boston: Ancient Egypt Research Associates.

Lehner, M., and F. Sadarangani 2007 Beds for Bowabs in a Pyramid City. *In* The Archaeology and Art of Ancient Egypt: Essays in Honor of David B. O'Connor. Z. Hawass and J. Richards, eds. Pp. 59–82. Cairo: Supreme Council of Antiquities.

Lehner, M., and A. Tavares forthcoming Walls, Ways and Stratigraphy: Signs of Social Control at Giza. *In* Cities and Urbanism in Ancient Egypt. M. Bietak, E. Czerny, and I. Forstner Müller, eds. Papers from a Workshop in November 2006 at the Austrian Academy of Sciences (UZK 35).

Lutley, K., and J. Bunbury 2008 The Nile on the Move. Egyptian Archaeology 32:3–5.

McDowell, A. G. 1999 Village Life in Ancient Egypt: Laundry Lists and Love Songs. Oxford, New York: Oxford University Press.

Malek, J. 2000 The Old Kingdom (c.3200–2160 BC). *In* The Oxford History of Ancient Egypt. I. Shaw, ed. Pp. 89–117. Oxford: Oxford University Press.

Malek, J., and W. Forman 1986 In the Shadow of the Pyramids: Egypt During the Old Kingdom. London: Golden Press.

Meskell, L. 1998 An Archaeology of Social Relations in an Egyptian Village. Journal of Archaeological Method and Theory 5(2):209–243.

Meskell, L. 1999 Archaeologies of Social Life. Age, Sex Class *et cetera* in Ancient Egypt. Oxford, Malden, MA: Blackwell.

Meskell, L. 2002 Private Life in New Kingdom Egypt. Princeton: Princeton University Press.

Moeller, N. 2004 Evidence for Urban Walling in the Third Millennium BC. Cambridge Archaeological Journal 14(2):261–265.

Moens, M.-F., and W. Wetterstrom 1988 The Agricultural Economy of an Old Kingdom Town in Egypt's West Delta: Insights from the Plant Remains. Journal of Near Eastern Studies 47(3):159–173.

Raue, D. 2002 Stadt und Tempel von Elephantine 28./29./30. Grabungsbericht: Der Palast der frühen I. Zwischenzeit: Haus2/Haus150. Mitteilungen des Deutschen Archäologischen Instituts, Abteilung Kairo 58:170–174.

Raue, D. 2005 Stadt und Tempel von Elephantine 31./32. Grabungsbericht: B31 H150/ B24 H154: Der Übergang in die I. Zwischenzeit. Mitteilungen des Deutschen Archäologischen Instituts, Abteilung Kairo 61:29–31.

Redding, R. 1991 The Role of the Pig in the Subsistence System of Ancient Egypt: A Parable on the Potential of Faunal Data. *In* Animal Use and Culture Change. P. J. Crabtree and K. Ryan, eds. Pp. 20–30. MASCA Research Papers in Science and Archaeology. Suppplement to Vol. 8.

Redding, R. 1992 Egyptian Old Kingdom Patterns of Animal Use and the Value of Faunal Data in Modeling Socioeconomic Systems. Paléorient 18:99–107.

Redding, R. 2007a Gallery III.4 Faunal Remains. *In* Giza Reports: Giza Plateau Mapping Project. Vol. 1. Project History, Survey, Ceramics and Main Street and Gallery III.4 Operations. M. Lehner and W. Wetterstrom, eds. Pp. 263–269. Boston: Ancient Egypt Research Associates.

Redding, R. 2007b "Treasures" from a High-Class Dump. AERAGRAM 8(2):6–7.

Redding, R. in press Status and Diet at the Workers' Town, Giza, Egypt. *In* Anthropological Approaches to Zooarchaeology: Colonialism, Complexity, and Transformations. D. Campane, P. Crabtree, S. deFrance, J. Lev-Tov, and A. Choyke, eds. Oxford: Oxbow.

Roberts, B. 1996 Landscapes of Settlements: Prehistory to the Present. London: Routledge.

Roth, A. 1991 Egyptian Phyles in the Old Kingdom (Studies in Ancient Oriental Civilization 48). Chicago: The Oriental Institute.

Sanussi, A. el-, and M. Jones 1997 A Site of Maadi Culture Near the Pyramids. Mitteilungen des Deutschen Archäologischen Instituts, Abteilung Kairo 53:241–253.

Schaur, E. 1991 Non-planned Settlements: Characteristic Features, Path System, Surface Subdivision. Stuttgart: Karl Krämer.

Schloen, D. 2001 The House of the Father as Fact and Symbol. Winona Lake, IN: Eisenbrauns.

Scott, J. C. 1998 Seeing Like a State. New Haven: Yale University Press.

Seidlmayer, S. J. 1996 Town and State in the Early Old Kingdom: A View From Elephantine. *In* Aspects of Early Egypt. J. Spencer, ed. Pp. 108–127. London: British Museum Press.

Soukiassian, G., M. Wuttmann, and L. Pantalacci 2002 Le palais des gouverneurs de l'époque de Pepy II: Les sanctuaries de ka et leurs dependences. Balat IV. Cairo: Institut français d'archéologie orientale.

Strudwick, N. 1985 The Administration of Egypt in the Old Kingdom. London: Taylor and Francis.

Tavares, A. 2004 The Hidden Industry: Weaving at the Workers' Settlement. AERAGRAM 7(2):10–11.

Valbelle, D. 1985 Les ouvriers de la tombe: Deir el-Médineh à l'époque ramesside. Cairo: Institut français d'archéologie orientale.

Vercoutter, J. 1983 Que savons-nous de la ville de la ville égyptienne? *In* La ville dan le proche-orient ancien. F. Brüschweiler, Y. Christe, R. Martin-Achard, B. Urio, and J. Vicari, eds. Pp. 133–136. Leuven: Peeters.

Wenke, R. J., P. E. Buck, H. A. Hamroush, M. Kobusiewicz, K. Kröper, and R. Redding 1988 Kom el-Hisn: Excavation of an Old Kingdom Settlement in the Egyptian Delta. Journal of the American Research Center in Egypt 25:5–34.

Wirth, E. 1992 The Concept of the Islamic City: Privacy in the Islamic East versus Public Life in Western Culture. Applied Geography and Development 40:22–38.

Wirth, E. 1997 Kontinuität und Wandel der orientische Stadt. *In* Die orientalische Stadt: Kontinuität, Wandel, Bruch, CDOG 1. G. Wilhelm, ed. Pp. 1–44. Berlin: Deutsche Orient-Gesellschaft.

Zeder, M. 1991 Feeding Cities. Washingdon, DC: Smithonsian Institution Press.

Ziermann, M. 2003 Elephantine XXVIII: Die Baustrukturen der älteren Stadt (Frühzeit und Altes Reich). Mainz: Philipp von Zabern.

6

Regionality, Cultural and Cultic Landscapes

David Jeffreys

The issue of regional cultural variation has only fairly recently started to exercise social archaeologists and historians of the ancient world and of the Nile Valley, including the Delta. Despite some earlier attempts to trace regional differences (e.g. Kees 1977), we are usually presented with such a monolithic and uniform picture of "ancient Egyptian" or "Pharaonic" civilization (whatever they may be) that considerations of local difference, affinity, and allegiance hardly arise.

The fact that, from at least the Old Kingdom, the logistical catchment area (e.g. for major building works) extended through the entire Nile Valley up to the First Cataract at Aswan, however, means that there must have been considerable mobility among the labor force brought together for such mammoth building programs as the pyramids, and cross-regional awareness is likely to have been enhanced by this. On the other hand the early peopling of the Nile Valley is still poorly understood: models of settlement through climate change leading to desertification and abandonment of the eastern Sahara on both sides of the Nile (Hassan 1986) suggest that populations were established over long periods of time in the late Neolithic, and at different times in different sections of the Nile Valley. Whether this led to very early cultural regional differences is unclear: certainly in a political sense the emergence of dominant regional groups in the Upper Egyptian Nile Valley (Abydos, Naqada, Hierakonpolis) might suggest that a consciousness of independence was still felt at that time (the mid- to late 4th millennium BCE). Whether similar variety existed in Middle Egypt is unknown, due to the lack of archaeologically known settlement or cemetery sites in this area (Butzer 1976).

Few ancient societies can have been as acutely aware of their local landscapes as the inhabitants of the Nile Valley. The fact that the Valley was bounded throughout its length by a constant, immediate horizon to east and west will have made variations in that horizon more conspicuous, while (especially during flood season conditions) the northward and southward visibilities will have concentrated attention on neighboring settlements. The relative homogeneity of western and eastern horizons may have generated an unusual sensitivity to minor changes; in several cases regions of high ground, apparently modest in themselves, clearly acquired some local importance. In the Delta the situation was different in very obvious ways: not only were bounding desert regions out of sight of central regions, but in addition the desert margins themselves were not dramatic frontiers between productive agricultural zones and arid desert, but merged, sometimes imperceptibly, with the floodplain. The Delta did, however, share with the Valley the phenomenon of the annual flood, which had a paradoxical effect: in a physical sense it made mobility and communication between neighboring communities more complicated, but visually it will have made their situation and proximity more conspicuous across the flat calm water of the floodplain.

By contrast the Egyptians' collective awareness of more remote regions, including the desert regions east and west of the Nile, the western oases, the eastern highlands and Red Sea coast, the Sinai peninsula and the cataract regions to the south, may have been extremely hazy. Many of the Egyptian "geographical" identifiers are in effect cultural and ethnic: terms such as Aamu (Levantine/"Asiatic") or Tjehenu and Meshwesh (Libyan) clearly denote different tribe or clan groups, and Egyptian intervention in these areas and in Nubia to the south was almost certainly through or assisted by intermediaries with local knowledge. The very fact that these main groups, as well as others (Hittites, Aegeans, Oasis dwellers of the western desert) are shown in stereotyped form, and are often otherwise unidentified, adds to this impression. The only known functional map from Egypt (although unlikely to have been used *en route*) shows the wadi system linking the Nile Valley at Koptos with the Red Sea, and the mining and quarrying areas in transit, and is almost certainly for the purposes of acquisition rather than more general cartographic information.

It is important to stress the differences between the Egyptian landscape of today and that of antiquity: in modern times the agricultural area of the Delta has been artificially extended to approximately 120 percent of its original size in the Pharaonic period, by a variety of lift, pumped, and center-pivot irrigation techniques. In particular the riverine and marsh environments that are such a prevalent feature in early landscape scenes have now almost entirely disappeared, along with the iconic papyrus plant, which was eradicated from the country in the nineteenth century. One aspect of the floodplain vista which is often overlooked is the fact that, with a lower valley floor in antiquity, landscape features which are inconspicuous or indeed invisible today would have been more pronounced. One important consideration is that many parts of the Valley would have been narrower than they are now, with intrusive features such as islands and desert edge bays being more numerous and more evident.

In view of its unusual, even extraordinary geography (although we have perhaps become over-familiar with it) the Nile Valley presents a series of conundrums when we consider the question of regionality: for example, does the linearity of the society and its landscape work for or against greater assimilation and uniformity? If the evidence for climate change and models of population transfer from the eastern Sahara to the Nile Valley over the fifth and fourth millennia (Hassan 1986) are accepted, then settlement in the Neolithic and Predynastic periods may well have been episodic and individually at a fairly small scale, since we know nothing about competition for space during these periods (besides inferences from later, Dynastic, iconography).

Certainly by Dynastic times the Nile provided a vehicle for mobility of, say, privileged sections of society and (probably) a skilled craft force, carrying style practices from place to place; however, other social groups may have been relatively immobile for at least some of the yearly agricultural cycle. It seems difficult to understand the enormous human effort involved in the construction of major building works such as the Memphite pyramids without the assumption that the workforce was enabled or coerced, at least on a seasonal basis, to converge on the construction site from a wider hinterland. At the time of Menkaure, the penultimate ruler of the 4th Dynasty (c. 2575–2450 BCE), the source pool for materials must have stretched at least to the First Cataract, and therefore the provision of human and livestock resources probably also encompassed the whole country.

Another obvious, fundamental question that arises is how we should define and identify regional diversity in the Nile Valley. One of the standard models of geographical analysis and spatial distribution, that of core and periphery, presents obvious difficulties in this case: with its ribbon-like presentation and the low-density or (supposedly) uninhabited desert regions bounding 90 percent of the high-density inhabited area (the 230 km of deltaic Mediterranean coastline being the 10 percent exception), the "peripheries" are evidently different from those in most other ancient polities, and even the relationships between settlement nodes in the Nile Valley can be expected not to conform to any expectation of a "central-place" norm. Inter-province relations are not well attested in either the documentary or the archaeological record, and, to date, only recent pioneering work between and on the margins of these zones (e.g. Darnell and Darnell 1997) has been able to shed light on the issue. The fact that this information relates specifically to an "Intermediate" period raises the question whether these Intermediate periods (as well as the Pre- and Protodynastic periods) of apparent political dislocation and discontinuity perhaps present the best opportunities to examine the true diversity of Nile Valley society. It is noticeable that divergences from Old Kingdom convention begin to appear at this time, with east bank elite cemeteries proliferating, and even the Memphite pyramid-building pattern failing to conform, perhaps as the capital city began to dissolve.

At present the assessment of regional character is almost entirely on the basis of craftwork, largely from funerary contexts, and funerary representation and sculpture. The term "provincial" as an aesthetic quality judgment is sometimes found applied in assessments of craft proficiency, on the assumption that this describes local variants from the "capital" styles and motifs of Memphis or Thebes. This, however, ignores the fact that even in capital zones, perceived accomplishment may fall short of some modern ideal, and that the mere "provincial" tag hardly gets us much further forward with a proper analysis of regional diversity. Evidently differences in material culture, if sufficiently well represented in the archaeological record, should be an important way in to any identification and evaluation of distinctive local particularities. Ceramic, textile, and other craft production would seem to be an obvious candidate since it would be locally or regionally sourced, while any suspicion of a centralized royal agency would tend to be less informative. Similarly one would accept a genuine, historical regional center such as Hermopolis (Ashmunein) or Herakleopolis (Ihnasya) in preference to the better-known royal foundations such as Thebes, Amarna, or Pi-Ramesse.

Indeed these high-prestige, imposed sites, connected as they almost certainly are with the cult of the person of the ruler and with dynastic integrity, have the shared characteristic that they subscribed increasingly to a royal, ideological form of representation that may have been quite different from any indigenous local tradition.

The perception of these royal cult foundations as being revolutionary and remote "new towns" needs to be treated critically. Akhetaten (Amarna), for example, seems at first sight to be in a remote virgin location, but in fact it occupies the desert edge close to the pre-existing (and subsequent) nome capital of Khmunu (Hermopolis/Ashmunein) and several other satellite settlements. The "boundary stelae" demarcating the perimeter of the lands of the new royal residence in fact describe a segment of the floodplain and its desert extension, carved out from the existing web of property ownerships in existence at the time. We can only speculate on the real politics of such an imposition. Clearly the site was built and intensively occupied, if only for a short period: its abandonment after the death of Akhenaten was more or less complete, although the intention at the time must have been for it to continue, since tombs for the royal family and the elite were begun, and many of them were left completed or in an advanced state. A fascinating glimpse of shifting allegiances and affiliations at this time comes from contemporary tombs at Saqqara decorated partly in the distinctive "Amarna style" and partly in more conventional modes (Zivie 2003). Similarly the new royal city of Pi-Ramesse (Qantir), built for Ramesses II in acknowledgment of his local roots, as well as being a strategic military supply center on the vulnerable northeastern frontier, is in fact not much more than a vast extension to the northeast of the old Middle Kingdom/Second Intermediate Period regional center of Avaris (Pusch 1999), extended again in the port site of Tanis, later to become the royal center and burial site of the Third Intermediate Period. Once again we can do little more than speculate on how such a huge new development, in this case probably itself occupying many hectares of viable agricultural land along the riverbanks, was received locally. Did it bring recognition, prestige, and employment to the area? (Are such terms relevant in the contemporary cultural context?) Or did it deprive existing temple estates of their revenues and force cultivators to migrate further afield? (The term "para-site" might in fact be appropriate for this kind of building phenomenon: a royal development or extension intruded upon an existing community with its own, perhaps long-established, socio-economic equilibrium.)

Differences that leave no physical trace in the archaeological record should also be considered. Are local cult affiliations, for example, mirrored in locally shared experience and values? We have little evidence for the Egyptians' having felt a sense of place, except for rare examples of eulogies for individual towns: such a one is a late New Kingdom composition in praise of Memphis in which, significantly, a listing of the city's leading cults (including some that were not native to Egypt) forms a central part. Equally significant is that (despite modern preoccupations with the funerary sphere) emphasis seems to be on the municipal cults of the city itself. The extent to which landscape played a part in the location of new settlements might also be explored: I have suggested elsewhere that the apparently familiar aspects of the Memphite landscape for incomers from the south (especially Hierakonpolis?) might have been a powerful factor, in addition to the overwhelming logistical argument, in the decision to site the new capital there. Another question: was the use of language locally or regionally distinctive? The nature of monumental hieroglyphic and even cursive hieratic scripts might mask real diversity of dialect and pronunciation – it is perhaps significant that the Coptic (mostly Greek) script, the only one used to write Egyptian that allows for vocalization and a real sense of pronunciation, shows a greater perceived regional variation (Bohairic/northern, Sahidic/southern, Fayumic, Memphitic) than earlier forms in which vowels were not generally written.

As so often happens in the case of Pharaonic Egypt, we are thwarted almost at the outset of any inquiry of this nature by the notorious lack of attention paid to organic settlements in the Nile Valley over the past two hundred years of investigative fieldwork. It could be argued that this is precisely where we would normally expect to find the best evidence of diversity, since goods and tomb decoration produced exclusively for burial are likely to have been influenced by earlier, recognized norms often originating elsewhere (e.g. the so-called "Memphite school," which simply describes the motifs and modes of representation in royal and elite tombs of the later Old Kingdom) and even by nationally held standards of tomb requirements. Avaris is in fact a rare example of a well-recorded local settlement center, where communities of different ethnic backgrounds lived in close proximity. Indeed, given the diversity of the region prior to the New Kingdom, the arrival of Egyptian dynasts in the sixteenth century BCE may seem as much of an intrusion into the existing order as groups such as the Sea Peoples later on.

Egyptian visualizations of landscapes are surprisingly rare and almost always stereotyped: images of terrain are, for example, shown or described as a setting for hunting scenes, or as a context for various deities – Anubis "of the mountain" at Abydos; and Hathor or various other bovid deities identified only as "mistress of the mountain" (Malek 1981:158) at Thebes and Memphis. There is even a suggestion – apparently not widely believed or supported so far – that the natural cliff face at Thebes behind Deir el-Bahri was suggestively shaped and was interpreted in antiquity as an image of Hathor. Certainly funerary depictions show the cow goddess "emerging" from the cliffside and at least one famous tomb features a vaulted chamber housing a full cow statue. At Memphis a convention seems to be the cow deity literally emerging from the rock face, half-cut in the round at the far end of individual tombs, all of the New Kingdom.

One famous tomb scene – in the tomb of the local nomarch Khnumhotep II at Beni Hassan – is distinctive, representing a group of people, evidently not regarded as indigenous or familiar but as Other, and labeled as "Asiatics" (Aamu), in a kind of liminal state between (in the upper registers) the wild and untamed desert environment where animals are hunted, and (below) the ordered world of the agrarian society of the Nile Valley itself (Kamrin 1999:93–96). Here the landscape view is clearly used to situate and categorize the arrival of such incomers and their livestock (a rare occurrence in the social and political backwaters of Middle Egypt?), occupying a halfway territory between "wild" and "safe," as they are led in to be recorded and presented in the same way as other "produce." Similarly, man-made landscape features rarely appear in the normal repertoire: we do not often see pyramids in such representations, beyond the Theban mountain motif with the emerging cow figure and the pyramid-topped tomb chapels in some sections of the Book of the Dead; other funerary documents depict only an idealized landscape of controlled agricultural production, such as the "Fields of Yaru." The one functional map known so far known from Egypt – the Turin papyrus map showing expedition routes through the Wadi Hammamat to the Red Sea coast – is perhaps the only one that really conveys a sense of surroundings and natural environment, although whether the map was really intended to be used *en route* is open to question. Sadly only the wadi sections of the papyrus roll are recorded, showing cultural and natural features as a guide to local landmarks along the way: the Nile Valley and Red Sea areas in the document are either poorly preserved or (if they existed) are missing, and would otherwise have provided a fascinating glimpse of contemporary cartographic attempts at representing such terrains.

Strangely perhaps, one of the most prominent and constant features of the Egyptian landscape – the river Nile – rarely appears in such representations, although the deified version of the flood (Hapi) is a familiar figure. There are also the well-known examples of the "origin of the Nile" motifs or other references in which a number of iconic sites appear: the First Cataract at Aswan (often regarded as the most southerly true Egyptian site), Memphis or Pihapi as the gateway to the Nile Delta (Gardiner 1947:131*–144*), and even Thebes (Gabolde 1995) are regarded respectively as the notional "founts" of the life-giving river. Similarly the symbiosis between the symbolism and the reality of the inundation and the Egyptian temple is in a sense one of paradox: supposedly the standard temple design portrayed a microcosm of the Nile environment, with papyrus- and lotus-columned halls and courtyards providing a simulacrum of Valley conditions, bark shrines and temple axes representing river courses, and perhaps the outer enclosure walls providing an architectural version for the horizons of the valley sides. Yet when temples were actually flooded (recorded examples are fairly rare), the event was clearly regarded as little short of a catastrophe and they required cleansing and purification.

An obvious starting point for considering regional variation would seem to be the nome system – the two collections of local cult and political centers into which the floodplains of the Valley and Delta are divided. While some evidence for organization into local regions dates to the Predynastic period, the recognized organization of nomes is later, and was clearly subject to boundary changes depending on topographical properties such as the course of distributary river networks through the Nile Delta. With one or two exceptions, we have few data to interpret or explain why these individual nomes became associated with certain characteristics (Baines and Malek 1980:14–17; Gauthier 1926). The connection between the Fayum nome and crocodile deities (primarily Sobek) might seem natural enough, although quite when crocodiles disappeared from the Fayum is unknown, but why should Khmunu/Hermopolis, the "Eight" nome of the Ogdoad or group of eight deities, have this particular tag? Why were some nomes, such as the Oxyrhynchite (Ihnasya) and Latopolite (Esna), particularly associated with types of Nile fish, or hare or oryx, when these species were presumably present throughout the length of the river valley? Why do some (Hellenistic) Delta nome names (e.g. Hermopolis) seem to be twinned with those of the Valley nomes, when there seems so little to connect them? Even less well understood is the relevance and significance of the nome emblems that seem to show a parallel set of affiliations. Perhaps significantly, the only nome standard that is not animalistic or totemic is Memphis, the most recently formed, which instead takes an architectural form, that of the "White Walls" – although this designation may itself refer to a landscape feature: the striated limestone cliffs close to the original foundation which formed both the visual backdrop for the town and the location of its earliest elite tomb structures.

Some of these provinces enjoyed certain evident natural advantages that others lacked: for example, Koptos, at the Valley entry point for cross-desert routes (the Wadi Hammamat) to prestige mining areas and the Red Sea coast; the Middle Egypt nomes with unusually broad floodplains; Memphis with its key location at the head of the Delta region. However, there are clear cases where major settlement appears to take place without any of the logistical advantages that we might normally expect. A good example of this is Thebes, which is located in a region that seems to have few natural advantages, and indeed is only a comparatively late and short-lived entry on the local geopolitical map. Previous provincial centers were Armant (Hermonthis) to the south and Quft (Koptos) to the north, which both remained the nome capitals and survived the rise and decline in importance of Thebes. Koptos in particular, benefiting from its access to routes to the Red Sea and the prestigious mining and quarrying sites along those routes, remained the local administrative and power center before and after the local, interim eminence of Thebes. Armant, a shorter distance to the south, may well have closer ties with the new royal foundation: the dominance of its local primary cult of Montu, the nearest to a war deity that Egypt produced, is clear in the preference for dynastic theophoric names (Nesmont, Mentuhotep) adopted at Thebes itself, and in the early cult foundations in the north of the town.

It is therefore worth considering the iconic landscapes of a town and region such as Thebes, which seems to offer little in the way of such natural advantages and whose rise to political prominence seems to be largely or entirely due to promotion by the elite and subsequently by royal patronage (Traunecker 1988), with particular attention to the royal funerary cult. Thebes, and the Protodynastic center of Naqada to the north, are notable for the fact that they are situated on the upstream side of the only conspicuous loop that the Nile makes throughout its entire length in Egypt, allowing a strenuous but short route overland to the northwest that leads to the iconic royal burial site of Abydos – and perhaps more importantly bypasses its immediate neighbor, Koptos/Quft, to the north. It is perhaps no coincidence that the imposing mortuary temple of Ramesses III at Medinet Habu features an added west gate in the enclosure wall that faces the high desert passes behind the temple (Uphill 1972). Indeed a striking feature of the Theban landscape in general is its impressive west bank scenery, due in large part to the fact that a spur of the high desert plateau approaches the west side of the floodplain more closely here than at any other point in the 170-km stretch of the valley between Esna and Farshut. The same phenomenon is evident at Abydos itself, with a cliff line located much closer to the floodplain at Araba el-Madfuna than anywhere else between Farshut and Asyut (166 km). Beyond Egypt, a similar case might be Jebel Barkal, to the south in Sudanese Nubia, whose impressive and unparalleled mountain backdrop was almost certainly deliberately selected for the siting of the Amun temple there (Welsby 1996:115–118, 138–139).

An intriguing paradox of funerary cult landscape orthodoxy surrounds the question of orientation. We are often told (accurately enough) that Egyptians generally associated the west (*imentet*) with death/rebirth and the afterlife, and that the deceased themselves, and deities/cults traditionally associated with funerary custom (Osiris, Anubis), are conventionally thought of as being of the west. However, there are obviously cases where this convention does not apply, notably in Middle Egypt in the First Intermediate Period and early Middle Kingdom. Even before that, at the start of Dynastic history, substantial elite east bank cemeteries are recorded, though often overlooked: we are, for example, familiar enough with the 1st- and 2nd-Dynasty mastaba tombs at Saqqara, but it is often forgotten that an equally prominent necropolis lies across the river, between Maasara and Helwan (Köhler 2004). While the original excavator of this cemetery in the 1940s, Z. Y. Saad, identified this extensive burial ground with the town of Heliopolis, it is quite clear that the Saqqara and Helwan early Dynastic cemeteries should be considered as complementary, and mirror one another in their north–south extent and broad dating. A notable feature of two of the major east bank cemeteries (Helwan and Maadi) is that they occupy the fans of two large wadi systems at the edge of the Valley (the Wadis Hof and Digla respectively): while there is no conclusive proof of this, it might be worth asking if this was entirely a practical location, or somehow connected to a folk memory of water supply and replenishment, and more particularly to the existence of sweet-water and mineral springs in the vicinity. The Helwan cemetery features large tombs with no regular aspect or orientation, which respect the seasonal flash-flood gullies that themselves cut through the fan (Saad 1951:Plans), similar to the arrangement of major monuments of the same period at Abydos. It is only when there is a move to outsized monumental construction (pyramids and mastaba tombs) on the west side of the Valley in the 3rd Dynasty, almost certainly associated with the beginnings of a rise of an overarching solar aspect to the royal cult, that the use of Helwan and the other east bank localities starts to decline.

The same phenomenon of an emphasis on east side locations is, however, most visible in Middle Egypt and, perhaps significantly, during the First Intermediate Period and the early Middle Kingdom. Although the western side of the Valley in this area in earlier periods is one of the least-known parts of the Nile Valley, at present hardly any of the main cemetery sites south to Abydos occupy the west side, and in the best-known cases, such as Deir el-Bersha, Beni Hassan, and Qaw el-Kebir, there is a clear predilection for the east bank. Clearly something other than a simple overriding western-based orthodoxy is operating here, and it is difficult to avoid the suspicion that the explanation is rooted in the landscape in the form of elevation above the floodplain. These key sites share several distinctive features: they are all in a region where an impressive east bank landscape dominates the floodplain; all the elite tombs are situated in a horizontal arrangement well towards the top of the escarpment; and there is a presumption at least that lower-echelon burials occupy the lower slopes of the hillside in each case. At el-Bersha (Willems 2004) and Beni Hassan, the nomarchs' tombs sit just below the visible horizon and are approached by fairly steep and arduous indirect hillside routes, although lower-echelon burials probably occupy the lower slopes; at Qaw the analogy with the Memphite example is perhaps closer, with causeways leading from the Valley edge up to the tombs resembling the approaches to pyramids, though the background landscape and architecture are very different in their details (Sauerbier 2006): instead of a pyramidal shape, the rectangular, slab-like panels, partly built and partly rock-cut, that form the hillside backs of the tombs seem more conditioned by the horizontal backdrop of the cliffscape itself at this point. At Thebes also, the earlier tomb-building pattern seems to reflect a local tradition. The so-called *saff* ("shelf") tombs in the more northerly locations at Tarif (Arnold 1976) are quite different from anything known at Memphis, and even the later 11th-Dynasty tombs (those of the Mentuhoteps Sankhkare and Nebhepetre) do not seem to have the same "Memphite" reference point (the pyramid-shaped *qurn* or peak) as those of the New Kingdom, and show a similar galleried design to the Tarif group, as indeed does the one nonconformist New Kingdom example (the mortuary temple of Hatshepsut, apparently modeled on that of Nebhepetre in its setting and architecture).

In contrast to the Memphite pyramid scenarios, the landscape itself at these Middle and Upper Egyptian sites seems to stand in for a built feature and forms the visual framework for the tombs. At Memphis, the pyramids, when they start to appear, compete with the (equally dominant but impractical) east bank terrain (Gebels Tura and Hof), raising the west bank profile (especially on the western side of the Valley where settlement was concentrated) in a striking way, and would have been especially prominent when seen from the west bank settlement of Memphis. At the same time it is perhaps no coincidence that the fabric for the pyramid casings – the outer, visible parts of the monuments – should be transported from across the Valley at the quarry sites of Tura, Maasara, and Gebel Hof, appropriating the gleaming limestone (the white walls?) for these miniature man-made mountains. At all these sites it may also have been important for the cemeteries to have been viewed from the settlements across the river or some other stretch of water, though the study of ancient fossil courses of the river is still in its infancy.

A particularly interesting case, as in so many ways, is that of Amarna (Kemp and Garfi 1993). The core of the city, with its arterial north–south thoroughfare, temples, palace, and administrative complexes, is situated so as to be equidistant from the eastern cliffs which form a roughly semicircular bay around the eastern side of the plain (but well back from, and higher than, the floodplain itself). Within this orbit there is no particular prominence – the horizon is a general horizontal, broken only by the declivity of the "royal wadi" (Wadi Abu'l Hasah), and it is no accident that the major municipal institutions respect the sightlines to this landscape feature (Figure 6.1). At the same time the distribution of cult, administrative, and residential nuclei (North Town, North Palace, central city, Maruaten, Kom el-Nana, Walled Village, tomb groups) seems almost to duplicate the environmentally imposed patterning of a floodplain settlement complex, even though very different conditions applied.

One recent approach in Egypt to the interrelationship of natural, cultural, and cultic landscapes which addresses such phenomena specifically is to consider issues of intervisibility. Recent local and regional studies at Thebes, Abydos, Hierakonpolis, el-Bersha, and Memphis suggest that this might be a fruitful line of inquiry. The Theban example is well known: the pyramid-shaped hill on the west bank, the "Peak" (Qurnet Murai), forms a focal point for the mortuary

Figure 6.1 Perspective view of Thebes from the east, showing relationship of the "Peak" to funerary structures on the west bank. Adapted from oblique terrain projections from Google Earth.

temples as distinctive as the backdrop of the cliff line at Deir el-Bahri (Figure 6.2). It might repay further investigation to see whether each of those temples were optimally sited to be viewed from specific locations on the east bank. Certain major developments, such as new building under Amenhotep III, mark a shift southwards with a new temple at Luxor, a new palace and harbor(?) complex at Malqata, with the king's mortuary temple alongside, directly across the river. At Abydos (Richards 1999; Wegner 2007), the highly suggestive alignment of Predynastic and early Dynastic funerary sites (Umm el-Gaab, Shunet el-Zebib, and adjacent funerary enclosures) with the major wadi system to the west offers an insight into the way that sightlines from the (presumed) settlement to significant features on the horizon were incorporated into the planning of key funerary monuments on the low desert margin (Figure 6.3). The funerary enclosures and royal tombs also in fact respect an ancient wadi system, as at Helwan, and are built far enough back on its banks to escape damage from flash floods: in a sense the wadi course forms a kind of desert parallel to the Nile in its floodplain. Interestingly the focus at Abydos seems to shift in later Dynastic periods: the late Middle Kingdom and early New Kingdom pyramids and tombs (or cenotaphs?) of Senwosret III and Ahmose respectively are, for example, out of sight of the main wadi; instead they are situated in front of a horizon which assumes a distinctive pyramid shape, but only when viewed from the east (from which they are approached by dedicated causeways).

Figure 6.2 Perspective view of Abydos from the east, showing the changing foci of the late Predynastic and later landscapes. Adapted from oblique terrain projections from Google Earth.

At Memphis a whole series of local landmarks presents itself over the three thousand years of the city's existence. The Old Kingdom Memphite pyramid field, surely one of the most extensive and most human-dominated landscapes of ancient Egypt and indeed of the whole ancient world, consists of built structures that, from the 3rd Dynasty on, imposed a west bank domain on the elite burial pattern of the region (Figure 6.4). While the distribution of pyramids has been discussed, explanations have usually taken a functionalist line and depended on the properties of the bedrock on which they were built in different parts of the 30-km stretch from Abu Rawash to Dahshur (or 80 km to the outlying pyramid of Meidum). This approach does not, however, fully address the apparently random nature of pyramid development, which begins at Saqqara and Zawiyet el-Aryan in the 3rd Dynasty, moves south to Meidum and Dahshur, then leapfrogs north to Giza and Abu Rawash in the 4th, returns to Saqqara (south), then to Abusir and Abu Ghurab, then back to Saqqara at the end of the 5th Dynasty, where it stays until the fall of the Old Kingdom.

In view of the high profile of the Old Kingdom pyramids, a consideration of their visual accessibility seems particularly appropriate. It has been suggested (Jeffreys 1998) that pyramid location might be directly linked to their visibility, either from Heliopolis, the local center of the solar cult that is such a prominent feature of royal ideology from at least the 4th Dynasty, or from Memphis. The most northerly of the pyramids, belonging to Radjedef (Djedefre), the first king to formally affiliate the royal cult to the sun cult, is built where it could clearly be

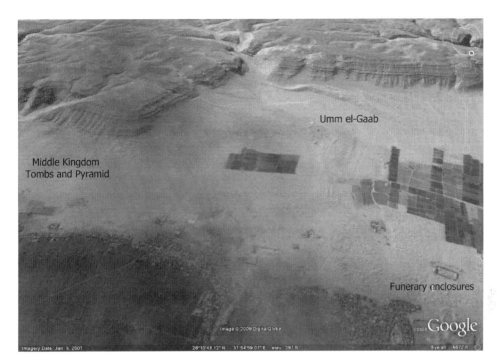

Figure 6.3 Perspective view of the Amarna plain from the west, showing the relationship between the "royal wadi" and the central city. Adapted from oblique terrain projections from Google Earth.

seen from Heliopolis; so are at least one of the sun temples of the 5th Dynasty, although the actual pyramids are not. Significantly, until the 6th Dynasty none of the Saqqara pyramids, or the one non-pyramidal royal tomb (Mastabat el-Faraun), are of kings that acknowledge Ra in their choice of theophoric name, although Userkaf does build a sun temple. Userkaf's sun temple, unlike Niuserre's, seems, however, just not to be in sight of Heliopolis (at least not in sight of the religious focus of the 12th-Dynasty temple and obelisks there), although this may be equally a result of shifts in the location of the "sun city" itself.

Another important aspect of the distribution of pyramids is how they were viewed from Memphis. When we find pyramid clusters (Giza, Abusir), they tend to be aligned in a southwest to northeast configuration. In the case of the Giza group (the only one visible from Heliopolis) this had the effect of appearing as a single structure, since – as was already noted in the nineteenth century – the diagonals of the three pyramids project directly towards the Heliopolis obelisk. (One might even ask whether the Khafra pyramid is deliberately sited on higher ground so as to be visible above the top of the Great Pyramid of Khufu?) However, these arrangements mean that all of the pyramids (except Meidum and possibly Abu Rawash) were individually visible from the core site of Memphis, lying close to the Saqqara escarpment and between the elite Protodynastic cemeteries of Saqqara and Helwan. Perhaps more significantly, the perspective views when seen from Memphis have a curious effect: the pyramids almost all present themselves

Figure 6.4 Perspective view of the Memphite pyramids from Heliopolis. Adapted from oblique terrain projections from Google Earth.

side-on, giving them a more two-dimensional aspect than when seen from the northeast. Although the local series of 3rd-Dynasty step pyramids (Djoser, Sekhemkhet, Gisr el-Mudir?) are clearly close to and highly visible from the settlement core, the largest and earliest true pyramids (Dahshur, Giza, Abu Rawash) are paradoxically also those that are instead furthest from the city center. Subsequent pyramids draw closer to the city and decrease in size, and there is a regular correlation between size and distance from the center. Size constancy scaling, when applied to such distant views, suggests that all eighteen or nineteen completed Old Kingdom true pyramids might have been deliberately designed to appear of uniform size when seen from the capital, implying considerably more competence on the part of the planners than is usually assumed. The broad effect can still be appreciated by viewing the pyramid field from a prominent floodplain elevation such as the remains of the "Apries Palace" (Kom Tuman) at Memphis, but a virtual reconstruction of the ancient landscape (including completed pyramids) is needed to test this idea more fully.

A peculiarity of Memphite landscape is the particular iconology of the sphinx. While various animal-headed (including lion-headed) recumbent lion figures are found throughout Egypt, royal human-headed statues are found in a more restricted range of locales. Images and miniatures of such statuary are known from Amarna and elsewhere, but almost all pristine examples at outsize scales (5 : 1 or larger) are from Memphis or Heliopolis. The most famous of all, the Giza sphinx, is the only rock-cut example at a truly colossal scale, and although the received wisdom is that the final form of it is an image of Khafre/Khephren, various suggestions have been made about the possibility that the outcrop which forms the head of the sphinx was a landscape feature before the 4th Dynasty. However, the above-ground part of the sphinx (essentially the head) assumes no particular prominence viewed from any direction but directly from the east, so any cultic landscape significance would be confined to the Giza plateau and whatever was up on top of it before the pyramids were built. This might suggest that any early Dynastic development on the plateau, possibly including structures superseded by the pyramids themselves, might have been associated with this visible landmark.

Equally important to means of visual access may well be ways in which visibility was deliberately limited or obstructed. A consistent feature of the residential, artisanal annexes at a number of pyramid and other royal-cult sites (Kahun, Amarna, Giza) is the way that any possibility of visibility is (deliberately?) denied. At Illahun/Kahun town there is no access westwards to the pyramid of Senwosret II except through the medium of the "Valley" itself; all other approaches face the Nile Valley. At Amarna the enclosed compound of the Walled Village faces only south-southeast, constraining the view (significantly?) to the Valley and approach road to the travertine quarries of Hatnub. At Giza the "lost city" of laborers, food processors, and administrators (Lehner and Wetterstrom 2007) is specifically restricted in its view of the pyramid temples by the Heit el-Ghurab (wall of the crow), though whether this can have been the main purpose of building such a cyclopean structure is probably doubtful.

It is worth remembering that such landscapes are rarely only static entities, but are also vehicles for mobility. Recent work on the issue of processional activities and pathways within cultic landscapes at, for example, Thebes (O'Connor 1998:154–171), Amarna (Shaw 1994), and Aswan-Elephantine (Seidlmayer 2005) suggests that changing perspectives ought also to be incorporated into the discussion. As in the case of Abydos, the focus could change over time, perhaps in response to changes in the settlement pattern; but even when considered at any given time a plausible itinerary can be identified. Long-term movements should also be considered: climate change and increasing aeolian deposition from the Old Kingdom onwards will have transformed valley-edge landscapes into something like what we see today, and the idea of some unchanging set of vistas of thousands of years should certainly be rejected.

How such a visual range of responses might have applied in the Nile Delta is an interesting question. With no comparable dramatic scenery on its desert borders, and indeed no visibility to the desert regions from its core, a different dynamic has to be imagined. One possibility is that, as in the Valley, settlements themselves provided a visual reference: they would be the only prominences visible during flood conditions, and we must imagine many more of them than today, when many (most?) are covered by the risen floodplain. High points will have been along the riverbanks, and especially where these coincided (in the eastern delta at east) with "turtlebacks" or underlying sand-hill formations of maritime or fluvial origin. The fact that certain Nile island settlements, in the Delta and Memphite areas for instance, were classed and identified with Aegean islands in the Hellenistic period (Braun 1982:47) tends to lend credence to this idea, especially as geoarchaeological survey is beginning to suggest that the appearance of many of the important Nilotic settlements, and especially their cult foci, may have been island or peninsular features (Bietak 2005; Graham and Bunbury 2005; Jeffreys 1996).

One key aspect of the Delta landscape was its Mediterranean coastline. The sea, like the river, is rarely visualized in Egyptian representations, apart from being a vague unspecified context for such episodes as the battle against the Libyan–Sea People coalition under Ramesses III (and that tantalizing possibility of the Red Sea coast being originally shown in the Turin papyrus), and it may be worth asking whether the notion of a defined northern coastline really registered in the Egyptian mentality. The very fact that the identity of the Egyptian term *wadj-wer* ("great green"), and what lay beyond it, are still the subject of such uncertainty and debate may be a reflection of the relative fuzziness of such a concept in the ancient world. Recent restorations of the Delta coast in Pharaonic times (Butzer 2002) convey just how different it was from that of the present day: the physical transition over a small vertical distance from delta to sea must have seemed a very gradual one, from ordered, flood-recession agricultural land crossed by a widespread distributary system, through waterlogged swampland to lagoonal basins to open water.

At the other end of the country, cataract landscapes provide a rather special case. By definition these are environments in which the desert edges approach the floodplain more closely than anywhere else and clearly defined horizons are vividly present.

One theme that seems clear is that, if we are ever even to approach an understanding of broad landscape issues in the Nile Valley, we will need much better-quality information about settlements. Sadly this now seems very unlikely in the short to medium term, with an inexorably rising groundwater table, unprecedented building development in the floodplain, including and sometimes directly affecting settlement sites, and aggressive policies by the archaeological authorities.

REFERENCES

Arnold, D. 1976 Gräber des Alten und Mittleren Reiches in El-Tarif. Mainz am Rhein: von Zabern.

Baines, J., and J. Malek 1980 Atlas of Ancient Egypt. Oxford: Phaidon (later re-issued as Cultural Atlas of Ancient Egypt).

Bietak, M. 2005 The Tuthmoside Stronghold of Perunefer. Egyptian Archaeology 26:13–17.

Braun, T. F. R. G. 1982 The Greeks in Egypt. *In* Cambridge Ancient History. Vol. 3.3. The Expansion of the Greek World, Eighth to Sixth Centuries BC. J. Boardman and N. G. L. Hammond, eds. Pp. 32–56. Cambridge: Cambridge University Press.

Butzer, K. W. 1976 Early Hydraulic Civilization in Egypt: A Study in Cultural Ecology. Chicago: University of Chicago Press.

Butzer, K. W. 2002 Geoarchaeological Implications of Recent Research in the Nile Delta. *In* Egypt and the Levant: Interrelations from the 4th through the Early 3rd Millennium BCE. E. C. M. Van den Brink and T. E. Levy, eds. Pp. 83–97. London: Leicester University Press.

Darnell, J. C., and D. Darnell 1997 New Inscriptions of the Late First Intermediate Period from the Theban Western Desert and the Beginnings of the Northern Expansion of the Eleventh Dynasty. Journal of Near Eastern Studies 56:241–258.

Gardiner, A. H. 1947 Ancient Egyptian Onomastica. Text. Vol. II. Oxford: Oxford University Press.

Gauthier, H. 1925–1931. Dictionnaire des noms géographiques contenus dans les textes hiéroglyphiques. Cairo: L'Imprimerie de l'Institut français d'archéologie orientale pour la Société royale de géographie d'Égypte.

Gabolde, M. 1995 L'inondation sous les pieds d'Amon. Bulletin de l' Institut français d'archéologie orientale 95:235–258.

Graham, A., and J. Bunbury 2005 The Ancient Landscapes and Waterscapes of Memphis. Egyptian Archaeology 27:17–19.

Hassan, F. 1986 Desert Environment and Origins of Agriculture in Egypt. Norwegian Archaeological Review 19:63–76.

Jeffreys, D. G. 1996 House, Palace and Islands at Memphis. In Haus und Palast im alten Ägypten. M. Bietak, ed. Pp. 287–294. Vienna: Verlag der Österreichischen Akademie der Wissenschaften.

Jeffreys, D. G. 1998 The Topography of Heliopolis and Memphis: Some Cognitive Aspects. In Stationen: Beiträge zur Kulturgeschichte Ägyptens: Festschrift für Rainer Stadelmann zur Vollendung des 65. Lebensjahres. H. Guksch and D. Polz, eds. Pp. 63–71. Mainz: Philip von Zabern.

Kamrin, J. 1999 The Cosmos of Khnumhotep II and Beni Hasan. London: Kegan Paul International.

Kees, H. (ed. T. G. H. James) 1977 Ancient Egypt: A Cultural Topography. Chicago, London: University of Chicago Press.

Köhler, E. C. 2004 Seven Years of Excavation at Helwan in Egypt. Bulletin of the Australian Center for Egyptology 15:79–88.

Kemp, B. J., and S. Garfi 1993 A Survey of the Ancient City of El-'Amarna. London: Egypt Exploration Society.

Lehner, M., and W. Wetterstrom, eds 2007 Giza Reports: The Giza Plateau Mapping Project. Vol. 1. Project History, Survey, Ceramics and Main Street and Gallery III.4 Operations. Boston: Ancient Egypt Research Associates.

Malek, J. 1981 Two Problems Connected with New Kingdom Tombs in the Memphite Area. Journal of Egyptian Archaeology 67:156–165.

O'Connor, D. 1998 The City and the World: Worldview and Built Forms in the Reign of Amenhotep III. In Amenhotep III: Perspectives on His Reign. D. O'Connor and E. Cline, eds. Pp. 125–172. Ann Arbor: University of Michigan.

Pusch, E. 1999 Towards a Map of Piramesse. Egyptian Archaeology 14:13–15.

Richards, J. E. 1999 Conceptual Landscapes in the Egyptian Nile Valley. In Archaeologies of Landscape: Contemporary Perspectives. W. Ashmore and B. Knapp, eds. Pp. 83–100. Malden, MA, Oxford: Blackwell.

Saad, Z. Y. 1951 Royal Excavations at Helwan (1945–1947). Cairo: Institut français d'archéologie orientale.

Sauerbier, A. 2006 Die Furstengraber von Qaw el-Kebir. Sokar: die ägyptische Pyramidenzeitalter 13:53–57.

Seidlmayer, S. 1999 New Rock Inscriptions at Elephantine. Egyptian Archaeology 14:41–43.

Seidlmayer, S.J. 2005 Eine Gruppe von Felsinschriften des Alten Reichs. In Dreyer, G. et al., "Stadt und Tempel von Elephantine – 1./ 2. Grabungsbericht", MDAIK 61:5–7.

Shaw, I. 1994 Balustrades, Sairs and Atars in the Cult of the Aten at el-Amarna. Journal of Egyptian Archaeology 80:109–127.

Traunecker, C. 1988 Thèbes–Memphis: quelques observations. *In* Memphis et ses nécropo-
les au nouvel empire: nouvelles données, nouvelles questions. A.-P. Zivie, ed. Pp. 97–
102. Paris: Centre national de la recherche scientifique.

Uphill, E. 1972 The Concept of the Egyptian Palace as a "Ruling Machine". *In* Man,
Settlement and Urbanism. P. J. Ucko, R. Tringham, and G. W. Dimbleby. Pp. 721–734.
London: Duckworth.

Wegner, J. 2007 Reopening the Tomb of Senusret III at Abydos. Egyptian Archaeology
30: 37–40.

Welsby, D. A. 1996 The Kingdom of Kush: The Napatan and Meroitic. London: British
Museum Publications.

Willems, H. 2004 Recent Investigations at Deir el-Barsha. Egyptian Archaeology
25:10–12.

Zivie, A.-P. 2003. Les tombeaux retrouvés de Saqqara. Monaco: Rocher.

7
Tradition and Innovation

The Middle Kingdom

Josef Wegner

In the study of ancient complex societies, considerable attention has been devoted to the processes of primary state formation as well as the factors involved in cases of state disintegration and collapse. No less significant, but certainly less fully investigated as a phenomenon, is the process of *re-formation* whereby state systems are able to re-establish and redefine themselves. Archaeologists in recent years have begun to focus more attention on this issue of "second generation" states, and how societal complexity is reformed in new ways following periods of social fragmentation and decline (Schwartz and Nichols 2006). In the comparative study of state regeneration, the case of ancient Egypt is particularly significant. One of the hallmarks of ancient Egypt is the remarkable longevity of a civilization which managed to adapt itself for the better part of three millennia, surviving significant periods of internal social flux, and in the context of vastly evolving global influences. Popular and scholarly notions of the static, timeless culture of ancient Egypt have long been overturned by richer understandings of the dynamic cultural, social, and political forces that continually acted to reshape Egyptian civilization. Nevertheless, striking in the diachronic study of ancient Egypt is the resilience of its "great tradition": a core political ideology built around the persona of the pharaoh as the divinely sanctioned ruler who was responsible for sustaining Egypt in a state of existence called the *sema-tawy* ("binding together of the Two-Lands"). This was achieved through the king's maintenance of *maat* (divine order) against the continual threat of chaos or *isfet* (see Richards, this volume). These concepts and a rich, embedded system of iconography and religious symbolism formed a civilizational template that became particularly relevant during periods of state reorganization such as the Middle Kingdom (11th–13th Dynasties, c. 2050–1650 BCE), Egypt's first major period of state regeneration which grew out of the political fragmentation of the First Intermediate Period.

As we have seen in earlier chapters in this volume, archaeological and written sources indicate that during the late Old Kingdom and First Intermediate Period significant changes occurred in the nature and expression of political power. During the Old Kingdom, administrative institutions and the language of elite culture had emphasized the pre-eminence of the kingship and royal government. At the end of the Old Kingdom, elite culture underwent a centrifugal process of change. Modes of cultural expression such as burial practices and personal bio-graphical inscriptions reflect an increasing emphasis on provincial authority. The concomitant decentralization of political power culminated in the First Intermediate Period. While there exists evidence for harsh physical realities at that time (such as increased levels of mortality: O'Connor 1972), many scholars have emphasized the degree to which the daily life of the average Egyptian did not change signifi-cantly as a result of the shifting relationship between central and provincial elites. Indeed, as local rulers and their administrative mechanisms stepped into the vacuum left by decreased royal power, the degree of economic prosperity of many provincial centers, particularly the local provincial (nome) capitals, may – in general – have increased (Seidlmayer 2000:119–120). Nevertheless, in terms of its political and socio-economic organization, Egypt was at a crossroads, one that potentially might have replaced the unified state with a form of city-state system familiar from many other ancient civilizations of both the Old and New Worlds. It is of considerable significance in the study of pharaonic civilization that during the Middle Kingdom this latter model was soundly rejected as the centralized state re-emerged with renewed vigor (Morris 2006). The Middle Kingdom rep-resents the first major period of state rebirth in Egypt. Here we will examine some of the key areas of socio-cultural change that define this period of state regeneration.

Inherent in the Egyptian phenomenon of state reformation is the role of his-torical memory and political critique, which can be part of any society, but is particularly prevalent in literate, complex societies that possess a long written tradition and monumental record (Tait 2003). It is perhaps not surprising that Egyptians during the Middle Kingdom looked conspicuously backwards to the Old Kingdom and Early Dynastic Periods as providing a civilizational template to be emulated. Earlier periods of unity and centralized authority emerged during the Middle Kingdom as models for constructing the present. Egypt's Middle Kingdom provides an instructive study of a society engaged in actively constructing its past and reinventing itself. One significant set of information on the historical and political outlook of the Middle Kingdom is provided by its rich literary tradition. These texts include quasi-historical narratives, "tales" set in past ages, *sebayet* or "teachings" which examine the themes of justice and rulership, as well as poems and hymns treating issues of cosmic order. Together they form a high tradition, an elite discourse, which reflects a sophisticated cultural appraisal of society, power, and the role of both the king and the indi-vidual (Parkinson 1991). Whether one interprets the resulting Middle Kingdom as incorporating a new emphasis on social responsibility (Wilson 1956), along with the emergence of a "moral economy" (Richards 2000:43–45), or alterna-tively as an autocratic and "prescriptive society" designed from the top down (Kemp 2006:241–244), it was a period of dynamic change. The modes in which areas of cultural expression as diverse as kingship, literature, and the domestic arts were redefined reflect a period of cultural renaissance mediated by self-awareness, and even purposeful social engineering. To a significant extent, the study of the Middle Kingdom seeks to understand the interwoven influences of tradition and innovation in the crystallization of a distinctive set of cultural forms which define this phase of Egyptian complex society.

The Middle Kingdom arose through a process of military and political expansion initiated by a line of provincial rulers (nomarchs) of the Theban nome of southern Egypt (for a recent overview: Grajetzki 2006:7–75). Following a protracted conflict against a northern political coalition led by kings at Herakleopolis (9th–10th Dynasties), the Theban ruler Nebhepetre Mentuhotep II defeated the Herakleopolitans in c. 2050 BCE and achieved a political reunification of the country (see the map at start of this volume). Symbolically this act of reunification was emphasized as a repetition of Egypt's initial moment of unification; Mentuhotep II declared himself to be the Horus *Sema-Tawy*: the Horus-king who, in accord with past models, had unified Upper and Lower Egypt (Postel 2004). Mentuhotep II and the two kings who succeeded him, Mentuhotep III and IV, belong to the 11th Dynasty, a phase of state reformation that expanded significantly when Amenemhat I, formerly a vizier under Mentuhotep IV, established a new ruling house, the 12th Dynasty. A significant political move at the beginning of the 12th Dynasty was the re-establishment of the royal residence in the Memphite area. After initially returning to Memphis itself, by the end of his reign Amenemhat I had founded a new capital, Amenemhat-Itj-Tawy, "Amenemhat-Seizes-the-Two-Lands" (generally abbreviated to Itj-Tawy), located between Memphis and the entrance to the Fayum region, an area that emerged as a core zone of state-sponsored development during the Middle Kingdom (Arnold 1991; Simpson 1963). The eight kings who comprise the 12th Dynasty ruled for c. 215 years forming a lengthy phase of stable royal reigns. The 12th Dynasty included four kings named Amenemhat (Ammenemes), and three named Senwosret (Sesostris). It ended with the reign of a female pharaoh, Nefrusobek, following whom the ensuing 13th Dynasty displays changes in the expression of political power and patterns of royal succession. A series of some fifty to sixty kings are attested for the 13th Dynasty spanning a period of roughly a century. Some of these kings reigned for as little as a few months, yet there exists no evidence for internal conflict or competition between rival claimants to the throne. Egypt's governmental system continued unabated through this period but at the level of the kingship the traditional pattern of father to son succession appears no longer to have formed the dominant model (Quirke 1991, 2004). At the end of the 13th Dynasty, the Middle Kingdom state retracted back to Thebes, relinquishing its control of the Nile Delta and northern Egypt to other political powers, most prominently the Syro-Palestinian rulers formally known as the Hyksos 15th Dynasty.

Elements of continuity that bind the period c. 2050–1650 BCE include the uninterrupted evolution of the state administrative system, and – after the beginning of the 12th Dynasty – the use of Itj-Tawy as the royal residence city and seat of central authority. Also a prominent feature of the Middle Kingdom is the emergence of a professional military tradition which includes a cadre of career military officials as well as an evolving system for manning the army. The most overt physical expression of the Middle Kingdom military organization is seen in the annexation of Lower Nubia (the area between the First and Second Nile Cataracts) and construction of a permanent fortress system established at the beginning of the 12th Dynasty and maintained through the late 13th Dynasty

(Smith 1995; Trigger 1976). Beyond the dynastic framework of the period, the Middle Kingdom can be discussed effectively in terms of two cultural phases, "early" and "late" Middle Kingdom, based on trends in administration, social organization, funerary traditions, and material culture. The reign of the 12th Dynasty king Senwosret III is a period of rapid socio-cultural changes and a temporal point of transition between these two phases. In broad terms, the early Middle Kingdom (11th Dynasty and first half of 12th Dynasty, c. 2050–1850 BCE) forms a period of consolidation and redefinition of Egypt's state system influenced significantly by the pre-existing social and political order of the First Intermediate Period. The late Middle Kingdom (late 12th Dynasty and 13th Dynasty, c. 1850–1650 BCE) then constitutes the "formal" or "developed" phase of the Middle Kingdom state (Figure 7.1).

In order to investigate processes of change that characterize the Middle Kingdom, and define what makes it distinct from other periods in Egyptian civilization, I propose here to examine two key areas that exemplify its shifting socio-cultural features:

1   changes in religious decorum and allied forms in material culture which illustrate new ways in which Egyptian society constructed the interface between the human and the divine;
2   the construction of authority and administration as expressed in mechanisms of integration between royal/state government and local towns and communities.

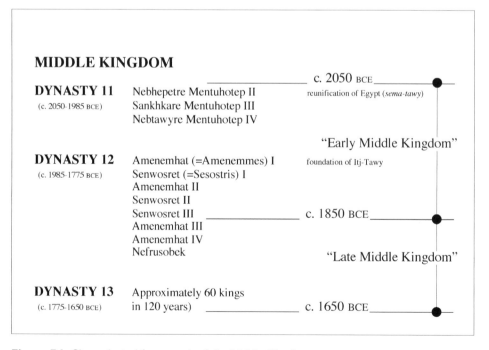

Figure 7.1 Chronological framework of the Middle Kingdom.

For these issues the ongoing contribution of new archaeological evidence serves alongside the rich body of textual evidence to refine our understandings of social and cultural change in the Middle Kingdom. Consequently, we examine these topics through application of an archaeological case study which derives from ongoing archaeological work at the mortuary complex of Senwosret III at South Abydos. The complex of Senwosret III, anciently named Wah-Sut-Khakaure-maa-kheru-em-Abdju ("Enduring-are-the-Places-of-Khakaure-justified-in-Abydos"), is a royal cult foundation built at the height of the 12th Dynasty and maintained until the decline of the Middle Kingdom state at the end of the 13th Dynasty. The site is located 2 km south of the main center of Abydos, cult center of Osiris. As the ancient name indicates, the locale belonged notionally to the greater entity of Abydos. It includes a subterranean royal tomb, an associated mortuary temple, as well as a settlement site that housed a significant population who were involved in the religious and economic maintenance of the Senwosret III mortuary cult. While there exist many potential case studies which would highlight contemporary research in Middle Kingdom archaeology, the value of South Abydos for our present purposes lies in its integrated combination of elements illustrative of various facets of late Middle Kingdom society. South Abydos forms a microcosm of Egypt's late Middle Kingdom, and an opportunity to investigate the changing modes of cultural expression as they emerge during the period c. 1850–1650 BCE. For our case studies, late Middle Kingdom South Abydos therefore constitutes a focus as we turn our archaeological lens on the adaptation of traditional culture and formation of new traditions which define the Middle Kingdom.

Innovations in Religious Decorum and Material Culture

During the Middle Kingdom a significant range of new forms emerge in material culture. Social practice at the time appears to have permitted a widening degree of access to material cultural forms, particularly those incorporating divine symbolism, which formerly had been most closely linked with the elite of the Old Kingdom. A majority of scholars logically anchor a discussion of the Middle Kingdom within the socio-economic and political changes of the First Intermediate Period. It has become a generally accepted tenet that major changes in social organization, cultural forms, and materialization reflect the process of political and economic decentralization of the late Old Kingdom and First Intermediate Period. Provincial elites and other social groups below the levels of royal administration now had access to cultural forms previously defined and controlled by the Old Kingdom elite (see Baines and Yoffee 1998). Formerly royal and elite cultural forms, in this understanding, were co-opted by lower-status social groups. As a result of the better preservation of desert-edge cemeteries, and traditional emphasis on funerary archaeology in the study of ancient Egypt, much discussion has focused on changing features evidenced by mortuary traditions. One of the long-standing formulations in this line of understanding has been the process broadly termed the "democratization" of the afterlife, exemplified by a process of popularization of funerary literature. The fact that royal mortuary literature, the Pyramid Texts, initially limited to royal usage, was adopted by non-royal elites at the end of the Old Kingdom and became part of an evolving non-royal tradition of funerary literature has suggested that we may be witnessing a downward diffusion of formerly "high" cultural forms to lower echelons.

More recently, other scholars have argued in favor of a form of ideological "trickle-down" whereby lower levels of society increasingly adopted and manipulated elite symbols and iconography in the funerary sphere. Access to these elite forms notionally emerges not simply as a wealth indicator but as a form of legitimizing commodity (see Richards 2000, 2005). Funerary traditions become a reflection of changing social organization suggesting ongoing modifications as part of evolving strategies of communication and display. While the outward diffusion of elite prerogatives is certainly *part* of the process, we must question the role of this elite/lower order dichotomy in examining the unique material culture that comes to define the Middle Kingdom (if not also earlier periods: see O'Connor 2000). It is fundamental to recognize that many of the materialized forms that first emerge in the First Intermediate Period – and then culminate during the Middle Kingdom – are not merely transpositions or emulations of high cultural forms. Rather they are drawing from a pre-existing repertoire of cultural expression (*some* elements of which are in origin elite and royal), but rendered in significantly altered modes. Indeed, the cultural repertoire is augmented by a quite dynamic and unique set of forms new to the material tradition, the majority of which have no direct antecedents in elite culture of the Old Kingdom.

One problem frequently encountered in the study of Egyptian material culture is the penchant for modern archaeologists to divide artifacts categorically into those which belong to "daily life" and those classed in the realm of "funerary traditions." While there are objects whose functions and patterns of use placed them discretely into either of these two spheres, the ancient Egyptians did not make such a concrete, bi-partite distinction. Human birth, life, death, and the transition to the afterlife appear to have been conceptualized as a continuum, albeit divided by transitional stages that needed to be navigated, often with divine aid. A wide spectrum of material culture notionally bridged the temporal spheres of life and afterlife. The phenomenon of the "democratization" of the afterlife is, in fact, only one facet of an extensive set of changes in Egyptian society that influenced ideas of access to divinity, and, as a consequence, the material culture of the period. Here we can define this changing pattern of "access to divinity" broadly speaking as an evolving web of cultural values that defined the role of divine models, myths, and religious practices, and the ways in which they impacted, and had relevance to, the experiential world of humankind.

A significant cultural change during the late First Intermediate Period and Middle Kingdom is a marked increase in the use of both two-dimensional and three-dimensional divine imagery which manifests itself in many areas of Egyptian material culture. Magical amulets are one example of a material cultural category where we can see this pattern of changing decorum in the application of divine symbolism. Although amulets had been a component of Egyptian material culture since the Predynastic, their use underwent an exponential increase during the Middle Kingdom. Many of these amulets are structured around the adaptation of divine symbolism, drawn primarily from the fabric of Egyptian myth and tradition. The most popular forms are overtly divine emblems such as the *wadjet* (eye of Horus), *djed* pillar (backbone of Osiris), or *tjet*-knot associated with Isis (Andrews 1994; Pinch 2006). Perhaps the best known and most easily recognizable product of ancient Egyptian material culture is the scarab amulet, an adaptation of the scarab beetle into a stylized three-dimensional object, carved in stone, molded in faience, or made of other materials. This object is fundamentally a creation of the Middle Kingdom and an expression of the unique suite of the cultural and religious changes that effected Egyptian society at that particular stage in its development.

The scarab amulet form initially appeared during the late First Intermediate Period but its use proliferated through the course of the 12th and 13th Dynasties. The scarab beetle is associated with the solar cycle and symbolizes the eternal rebirth of the sun god through the actions of the beetle deity Khepri. It is notionally related also to the idea of physical transformation and change; the word *kheper*, meaning to "become," applied particularly at the religious level to human experiential changes from birth through death and the transition to the afterlife. The adaptation of the scarab beetle as an amulet was a means of magically tying human experience (of the amulet wearer) into the regenerative and transformative cosmic powers of the solar deity.

Of note in the archaeological record is the extensive contextual range of scarab amulets: these artifacts occur in both settlement and cemetery sites, and are associated with all levels of society. Worn as amulets on the body, scarabs were often linked in their early period of development with the burials of young children. Equally, however, during the Middle Kingdom we find them among the personal belongings and burial equipment of the highest-status royal governmental officials. A hallmark of the material culture of the Middle Kingdom is adaptation of the scarab amulet for use as an administrative seal inscribed on its base with the names and titles of officials (Martin 1971), a custom particularly prevalent during the late Middle Kingdom, c. 1850–1650 BCE. In this mode scarabs functioned as part of daily administrative practices (Figure 7.2). Clay impressions produced by personal scarab seals occur in vast quantities in settlement sites of the Middle Kingdom. This single object type adapted a potent divine symbol into a form that applied directly to the transitory phases of human existence. Its use as an administrative tool brilliantly merged popular religious practice with the structured daily activities of the Middle Kingdom bureaucracy. It is a magico-religious object that seamlessly bridges the living world and funerary beliefs and traditions.

Amulets comprise one obvious artifact category which – due to their significant numbers – is symptomatic of the Middle Kingdom penchant for increased use of divine iconography at the level of popular culture. They represent, however, only the proverbial "tip of the iceberg," and many other categories of material culture display the same cultural process at work. The increasing emphasis on religious imagery in Middle Kingdom material culture is vividly illustrated by another type of object: magical wands or "knives" which have been recovered in significant numbers, particularly from tombs of the Middle Kingdom. Carved from hippopotamus ivory, these objects are decorated with complex groupings of divine beings, zoomorphic and anthropomorphic, often with associated hieroglyphic

Figure 7.2 Two late Middle Kingdom scarabs with the names and titles of officials. (From the fortress of Buhen, courtesy of Penn Museum of Archaeology and Anthropology.)

labels (Figure 7.3). Like the scarab amulet, these magical wands show divine powers involved in the mythology of the solar cycle: the cosmic forces which underlie the ability of the sun god to regenerate and survive his daily cycle of birth, death, and rebirth. Analysis of the religious imagery (Altenmüller 1965) suggests the wands were used in apotropaic rituals, most particularly during childbirth and the early life of the newborn baby, but also by extension other moments of physical vulnerability such as sickness. The combination of the divine symbols and the way the wands were used (as part of demonstrative ritual acts with spoken spells) appears to have magically transferred the mythological protection of the young vulnerable sun god to beneficially influence human experience. Again, just as with scarab amulets, these objects derive from both settlement and cemetery contexts. After a period of use, the wands were typically buried in the

Figure 7.3 A Middle Kingdom magical wand. (From Rifeh, 12th Dynasty, courtesy of Penn Museum of Archaeology and Anthropology.)

tomb, along with their principally female owners. Interment extended the apotropaic role of these objects into the funerary sphere, helping to magically ensure the sought-after rebirth in the manner of the sun god. If the Middle Kingdom Egyptians had "democratized" the afterlife, in a much more extensive shift in cultural practices and religious decorum, they had fully integrated divine models into their daily lives in a variety of new ways that generated hitherto unseen forms of material culture.

Case Study 1: The Archaeology of Childbirth in the Late Middle Kingdom

If we look outside of the well-studied evidence of the funerary tradition, can we examine changes in Egyptian customs surrounding access to divinity through actual archaeological evidence? In the archaeology of the household and domestic life during the Middle Kingdom we witness evidence for a rich, evolving magico-religious tradition with a suite of associated material forms. One area which has seen only the most limited analysis in Egyptian archaeology – as indeed in archaeology at large – is the study of childbirth. As an ephemeral stage in human life, childbirth in general tends not to produce extensive, immediately recognizable physical remains in the archaeological record. The archaeology of childbirth, where it is identifiable, however, becomes an extremely informative window into cultural traditions and social practices manifested in association with one of life's critical junctures (Beausang 2000). In Middle Kingdom Egypt there exists evidence for a sophisticated set of magico-religious beliefs and practices as well as an elaborate set of objects and tools. Significantly, as with the similarly liminal moment of death and burial, childbirth offers insight into the evolving rules of decorum which governed access to divinity in Middle Kingdom society.

Excavations at South Abydos since 1994 have been involved in documenting the settlement of Wah-Sut, connected with the mortuary complex of Senwosret III (Wegner 2006, 2007). The major structure currently under study is a palatial-sized (52 × 80 m) residence, "Building A," which functioned as the mayor's home (Wegner 1998, 2001). In 2002, excavations in part of Building A recovered the only known example of an actual ancient Egyptian *meskhenet* or "birth brick," a type of object known to exist from ancient Egyptian written sources, but never identified previously in the archaeological record (Figure 7.4). This object is an unfired mudbrick, 17 cm in width, 35 cm in length, the surface of which is painted

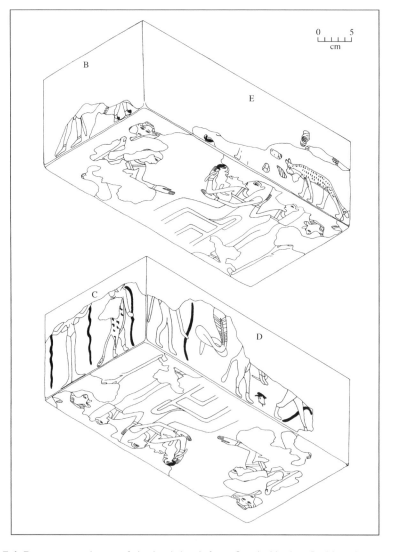

Figure 7.4 Decorative scheme of the birth brick from South Abydos, Building A.

with a complex set of magico-religious imagery explicitly associated with child-birth (Wegner 2002, 2009). One face of the object shows a seated mother holding a newborn baby flanked by two other female figures and framed by standards capped with the head of Hathor, a deity closely associated with fertility and child-birth. The four sides of the brick display a procession of zoomorphic and anthropomorphic deities. These include: the depiction of a striding serval cat, a captive human decapitated by a lion, and a blue-painted goddess grasping snakes and shown nude, standing frontally with splayed feet. The particular context of the birth brick is especially significant since other evidence, including seal impressions and additional small objects, suggest this area of Building A functioned specifically as a female residential unit. I have suggested that this part of the building may have belonged to a wife of one of the six known mayors of South Abydos during the late Middle Kingdom (Wegner 2004, 2009).

Key to the reconstructing of the functions of the Abydos birth brick is the analysis of its magical imagery through comparison with other artifacts that bear parallel iconography. Virtually identical with the imagery on the edges of the birth brick is the decorative scheme used on the above-mentioned magical wands. The iconography of the wands is expressive of the mythology of the cosmic defense of the newborn and vulnerable sun god against hostile forces. The sun god, who can manifest himself in various forms, frequently appears on the wands in the guise of a striding wild cat. Conceptually, the defense of the infant sun god in his period of uncertainty occurs through marshalling the divine allies of the sun god against the agents of *isfet* or chaos. Symbolic destruction of malignant forces is seen frequently through the motif of the decapitation of a foreign human enemy and especially through the imagery of knives brandished by the various benign deities. The images of the striding wild cat on the Abydos birth brick, the enemy decapitation, and other symbolism tie the brick with the apotropaic function of the Middle Kingdom magical wands.

The scene of childbirth on the main preserved face of the brick offers a basis for understanding the mode in which the imagery relates with the practice of childbirth itself. Notably, the human figures in the birth scene are not rendered according to normal artistic conventions. The color chosen for the hair of the mother and two assisting female figures is sky-blue rather than traditional black. Color symbolism here emphasizes the divinity of the three females. Moreover, the mother holding her newborn (male) baby sits not on a normal chair but on a solid-based throne of divinity. Flanked with images of the goddess Hathor, the birth scene is rendered in an artistic mode that emphasizes the idea of a divine trans-figuration of the mother in childbirth. At the moment of delivery the mortal mother is symbolically altered into a manifestation of Hathor herself: her hair becomes a divine blue, her seat is a throne, and she sits protected by Hathor standards. This scene is not simply a depiction of the happy results of delivery, but rather a two-dimensional "visual spell" which invokes the presence of Hathor during childbirth and even magically transforms the human mother into the divine being. Significantly, extant corpora of Egyptian magical spells for mother and child (e.g. Erman 1901) are full of such invocation of divine forces for protection of mother and baby during childbirth. Here we see vividly illustrated the rich application of magico-religious imagery to the experiential world of humankind during the Middle Kingdom. Just as occurs in funerary religion, where Egyptians of the Middle Kingdom are able to associate themselves with Osiris, so too in childbirth divine forces become a magical mechanism for surviving the transitional moments of human experience: a mortal mother is momentarily visited by and symbolically transfigured into the goddess Hathor.

The combination of imagery on the Abydos birth brick contributes to an understanding of the actual mechanics of how the birth brick may have been used. It is known through a variety of textual sources that *meskhenet* bricks were used not singly but in groups of four (Roth and Roehrig 2002). Their mode of use appears likely to have involved the stacking of bricks to compose two parallel supports for the feet and legs of the woman in labor, who would have assumed a squatting position optimal for delivery. Another level of magical symbolism embodied in this tradition of childbirth is witnessed in magical spells that refer to the woman in labor as physically creating a three-dimensional replica of the place of birth of the sun-god: "Open for me. I am the one whose offering is large, the builder who built the pylon for Hathor ... who lifts up in order that she may give birth ..." (Robins 1993). Even more than the invocation of divine transfiguration, the entire physical act of delivery while squatting on stacks of bricks appears magically to transform the human event into a replica of the solar *Akhet* (eastern horizon), and place of eternal rebirth of the young sun god. Cosmological forces are called upon as a divine model for understanding and surviving this challenging human moment.

Closely associated with the evidence for the evocation of divine models in childbirth is a wider repertoire of objects which reflect the growing emphasis on votive worship in second-millennium Egypt. Particularly relevant is a body of magico-religious objects associated with the veneration of Hathor. Fertility figurines, amulets, and images that invoke Hathor in various media (stelae, sistra, masks, plaques) are among a rich repertoire of objects that reflect both individual and community/"corporate" veneration of the fertility goddess (Pinch 1993). Evidence for use of masks and standards depicting the goddess articulates with the Hathor-capped emblems on the Abydos birth brick. These symbols consequently may refer to actual three-dimensional images used as part of birth rituals during the Middle Kingdom.

Combining the evidence of the magical wands, the Abydos birth brick, and other related artifacts provides the basis for a synthetic model of the religious beliefs and techniques of childbirth in the Middle Kingdom (Figure 7.5). Popular religious practices leading up to pregnancy appear to have included use of votive dedications and objects that call upon divine forces to beneficially influence the fertility of the prospective mother. With the inception of pregnancy a specific set of objects appear to have been used. *Meskhenet* bricks seem to have been prepared by qualified artisans and/or magical practioners. An allied object type in the Middle Kingdom are small brick-shaped rods composed of four rectangular segments in faience or steatite with apotropaic imagery that might reflect rituals of preparation in creating the functional *meskhenet* bricks. The ritual preparation of sets of *meskhenet* bricks (which probably would have served only for a single delivery) is likely to have been a pervasive ongoing activity in the daily life of ancient Egyptian communities of all sizes and at all levels of the social spectrum. As we witness in other categories of material culture such as the funerary tradition, the

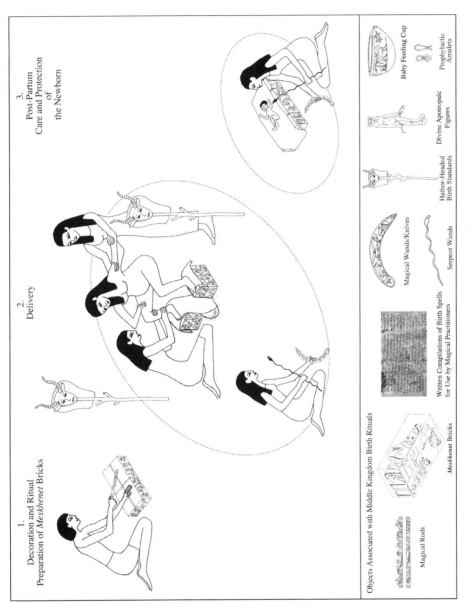

Figure 7.5 Reconstruction of the practice of childbirth during the late Middle Kingdom.

quality and level of artistic investment of birth bricks may have been a function of individual wealth and social status, rather than differing access to the system of religious beliefs and ideology that underlay the practice. The Abydos birth brick is likely to represent the elite end of a much wider practice of decorating and ritually preparing bricks for use in birth procedures. The actual use of the bricks may be closely linked to the magical wands. Commonality of apotropaic imagery suggests that the bricks were stacked to build a birth station (a "pylon for Hathor" in the terminology of the birth spells), which may have been ritually protected by inscribing a protective perimeter using the magical wands. Common evidence of wear patterns on these objects suggests their repeated use in ritual action such as scraping a protective perimeter on the ground.

The birth event would then have occurred within a miniaturized, ritually charged model of the solar *Akhet* in which the birth of the newborn baby draws magically upon the parallels of Egyptian solar mythology to beneficially influence the outcome of labor and delivery. The use of actual Hathor masks placed on standards would create a further layer of access to divinity through which Hathor is invoked not just to protect the birth procedure, but more tangibly to create a divine metastasis whereby the woman in labor becomes a momentary manifestation of the goddess herself. Upon successful delivery, birth bricks may have continued to serve as a protective platform for the newborn in continued apotropaic rituals during this very delicate phase of life. Significant numbers of stillborn and child burials in the settlement of Wah-Sut, as in other ancient Egyptian urban sites, reflect the high degree of infant mortality. This would have been matched by an undoubtedly high mortality rate for women in childbirth. These constitute physical realities that to a large extent help to illuminate the development of these sophisticated magico-religious practices in childbirth during the Middle Kingdom.

The evidence for childbirth beliefs and practices during the late Middle Kingdom at South Abydos provides an archaeological illustration of the fundamental importance of settlement archaeology in deepening our understandings of social developments and cultural practices, particularly where we seek to advance models of cultural change over the *longue durée*. The process of "democratization" of the afterlife which has struck many scholars as a singular phenomenon is definable really as only one facet of a wider complex of cultural changes which characterizes the period. The increasing access to religious imagery in society at large is not constructed just as a way of breaking down the doors to previously royal and elite ideological systems. It is part of a pervasive dynamic adaptation of cultural practices that extend from birth to death in which access to divinity was emphasized. This changing cultural emphasis on depiction of, and "access to," divinity neither started nor ended with the Middle Kingdom, but it is during this period when we see it emerging full-blown as a defining aspect of changes in popular religious practices and material culture.

The Archaeology of Authority and Institutions

Egyptian civilization's periodic cycling between phases of unity/centralization (the Kingdoms) and political fragmentation/decentralization (the Intermediate Periods) has been the basis for many explanations for social, cultural, and technological change. One of the long-engrained assumptions in Egyptological discourse is the notion that the Kingdoms represent periods of state domination – suitably legitimized – where the machinery of government is able to coerce and manipulate lower levels of society. During the Intermediate Periods, the inverse of the situation occurs with the rise of kin-based, local social structures and the loss of the hierarchical, institutional mechanisms of centralized administration, often compounded by foreign intervention. For the study of the period 2050–1650 BCE these issues are significant since the Middle Kingdom state developed one of the most successful and intricate bureaucratic systems in the history of Pharaonic Egypt. How did this system function, particularly as regards the nexus between royal government and the local communities that formed the fabric of society at large?

Textual sources on Middle Kingdom administration include official biographical inscriptions on tombs (primarily from Upper Egyptian centers such as Elephantine, Beni Hasan, Deir el-Bersha, and Asyut) and discrete groups of mortuary stelae (such as the large corpus from the private cenotaph area at Abydos). Actual administrative records include prominently the Lahun papyri (from the late 12th–13th Dynasty from the pyramid complex of Senwosret II: Quirke 1990), a palace accounts papyrus of the 13th Dynasty (Papyrus Boulaq 18), and a 13th-Dynasty administrative document (Papyrus Brooklyn 35.1446: Hayes 1955). Records of specialized administrative activities include the Semna Dispatches (late Middle Kingdom military records from the Second Cataract fortresses: Smither 1945), the Reisner papyri (early 12th-Dynasty accounts papyri including records of the operations of a boatyard at Thinis), and the Hekanakht Letters (a set of correspondence detailing the operations of a small householder of the early 12th Dynasty: Allen 2002).

Despite the limitations inherent in the preserved body of data, a suite of systemic features can be delineated which suggest an evolving organization of authority and administration. A distinction is to be made is between the "early" and "late" Middle Kingdoms administrative systems. Governmental organization in the early Middle Kingdom appears in many respects to represent an outgrowth of First Intermediate Period patterns of administration. Provincial titles continue to be prominent (although for the majority of regions there is no preserved evidence); the system can perhaps be seen as an evolving dialogue at the core of which was a pragmatic and piecemeal integration of existing provincial and nomarchal power structures beneath the umbrella of royal government. Over the course of the 12th Dynasty, however, prominent provincial administrative titles progressively disappear. The important Upper Egyptian hereditary title *hery-tep-aa* ("great overlord"/nomarch) vanishes by the late 12th-Dynasty reign of Senwosret III, a phenomenon that has led many to conclude there was a political program of suppression of the provincial nobility, particularly by this ruler. This notion of an authoritarian elimination of a group of powerful feudal families has largely been discarded (Franke 1991). We do, however, see indications for a process of centralization whereby the vestiges of provincial administrative systems were superseded by a network of royal administrative bureaux and offices that to a significant extent may have streamlined the abilities of the royal government to effect control over local communities.

How was the nexus between royal government and local communities achieved? The interface between central and local authority appears increasingly to have been structured around the system of town and city mayors (*haty-a*) whose authority and activities were directly overseen by the agencies and officials of royal government. Middle Kingdom mayors typically held multiple titles, which included that of *haty-a* (literally "foremost arm") of their local communities and titles which marked their oversight of the economic and administrative aspects of their local temples: "temple overseer," "overseer of temple priests." The mayoral model of local administration may be seen as a mechanism for effectively administering both local communities and their temple institutions via the fewest number of intermediaries. With the decay of "intermediate" provincial power structures that culminates with the reign of Senwosret III, there would have existed in theory only two steps between the households of any local community and the pharaoh himself.

Administrative subdivisions which lay above the level of the town and city mayors are difficult to define in the existing late Middle Kingdom records, though certainly they must have existed. The traditional nome boundaries and names continued to be used, but appear to have served only as geographical and religious designations, no longer serving as functional administrative entities. Some scholars have concluded that communities were grouped into a series of geographically defined administrative districts (*warets*). Problematically, however, the only clear existence of such a super-ordinate district is the entity named *waret tep-res* (the *District of the Head-of-the-South*), which at the time of the 12th Dynasty constituted the area between Elephantine and Asyut in Middle Egypt (traditionally the southern eight nomes), and was administered via a bureau of the vizier at Thebes. The existence of a wider, formalized system of *warets* – however notionally attractive it may be – is more difficult to ascertain. The existing evidence suggests that state administration was effected primarily through two main centers at Itj-Tawy and at Thebes.

The reign of Senwosret III appears to have marked a culmination of this shift towards an enhanced degree of centralization and perhaps a tighter articulation of oversight of local population centers and their temple institutions. As we have seen above, a wider suite of socio-cultural practices suggest a transition at this point between "early" and "late" phases of the Middle Kingdom. The ethos of administration displays an increased degree of precision with the number and functions of individual institutional and official titles being more clearly delineated. Linked to changes in administrative organization during the late Middle Kingdom is a marked increase in use of institutional stamp seals which bear the names of larger administrative entities such as temples, or "departments" such as granaries or storehouses. Paralleling the use of institutional stamps is the dramatic rise in use of scarab seals with personal names and titles as part of daily administrative activities. This practice of sealing, often using a personal name and title seal, forms a valuable window into the mechanics of administration at the height of the Middle Kingdom. Archaeologically, spheres of authority are reflected by the distribution patterns of clay sealings providing the potential for examining the realities of how administration operated on the ground, not merely in accord with a structural framework of institutions and job descriptions (whose functions as elements of a larger system were not necessarily apparent to individual men in various positions of responsibility).

As we trace evidence for changes in governmental organization, the Middle Kingdom emerges as a period of a tightly structured system that underwent modification, perhaps partially unconsciously, but also likely in response to changing priorities and policies emanating from the king and upper tiers of the central administration. For the late Middle Kingdom in particular, impressive is the success of a system of regulation that functioned from its crystallization c. 1850 through the period of decline of the Middle Kingdom state at the end of the 13th Dynasty c. 1650. In essence, an administrative system that evolved through the period of lengthy stable reigns of the 12th Dynasty managed to operate effectively through the entirety of the 13th Dynasty and survive with apparently little difficulty the period of ephemeral kings who comprise that final stage of the Middle Kingdom.

Here I wish to turn to a model recently proposed in examining the organization of power and authority in the ancient Egyptian state. Mark Lehner has advocated application of the "Patrimonial Household Model" as a means of understanding how the Egyptian state operated, in terms of both large-scale (state-level governmental organs) and smaller-scale (local communities) structures bound as a complex adaptive system (Lehner 2000, and see his chapter in this volume). The Patrimonial Household Model – an adaptation of Weber's "patrimonial regime" – proposes a hierarchy of nested households bound by personal ties. The administrative "system" did not function as a rational, impersonal bureaucracy, nor were there definable "public" and "private" sectors of society. The total spectrum of economic and social life according to the Patrimonial Household Model functioned as an extension of the royal household. The Middle Kingdom, with its abundant sources on state administrative systems, provides a valuable period in which to consider the applicability of the Patrimonial Household Model. Here we turn again to look at part of ancient South Abydos. The mayoral residence of the town of Wah-Sut functioned as the house of the town's highest-ranking official, as well as the principal institutional building for this late Middle Kingdom community. Its archaeology reflects the operation of local administrative mechanisms and the nexus between central and local administrative mechanisms through the period of changing patterns of royal power.

Case Study 2: The Mayoral Residence of Wah-Sut

As we have seen above, the major structure examined to date in the town of Wah-Sut is a mayoral residence (*per haty-a*) which was occupied and used by a series of local mayors over a period of some 150 years, from the reign of Senwosret III through to the very end of the 13th Dynasty. The community at Wah-Sut, which may have numbered on the order of several thousand people, represents a state-initiated town. Designed by royal architects under state mandate, it might be suggested that this town is an instance of a special-purpose community that did not function in ways analogous with the main bulk of more "organic" towns and cities. Although it was state-initiated, the urban center established at South

Abydos appears to have replicated a system of settlement organization and administration that is representative of the late Middle Kingdom as a whole.

The mayoral residence is, as mentioned, a 52 × 80 m building, constructed on a low rise on the desert edge (Figure 7.6). Physically and spatially it would have dominated other, smaller households which extended down the desert margin to the edge of the Nile floodplain, as well as a series of other elite households extending in blocks adjacent to the mayoral residence. The building has a complex interior subdivided into a series of separate blocks. The structure as a whole underwent an extensive series of alterations over the 150-year history of its use. The core of the building is comprised by the actual residential unit, fronted by a pillared entry hall and ostentatious columned portico (central courtyard). Room blocks surrounding this area include areas devoted to provisioning of the core residence, as well as – in its original design – a block of chambers used for large-volume grain storage. Notable is the significant remodeling of the building's original design over the course of nearly two centuries of occupation. One major area of transformation is the northwest section, where original granary chambers were remodeled to form a subsidiary residential unit with its own pillared portico. A formal garden with planted trees flanks this area. The birth brick which we have discussed above, and a set of other evidence, suggests this area of Building A may have served as a female residential unit, perhaps occupied by a wife of one of the six known mayors of Wah-Sut.

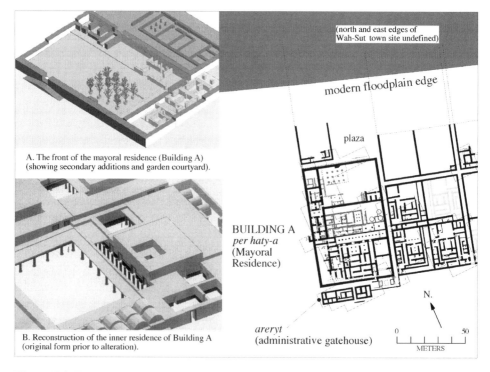

A. The front of the mayoral residence (Building A) (showing secondary additions and garden courtyard).

B. Reconstruction of the inner residence of Building A (original form prior to alteration).

(north and east edges of Wah-Sut town site undefined)

modern floodplain edge

plaza

BUILDING A
per haty-a
(Mayoral Residence)

N.

areryt
(administrative gatehouse)

0   50
METERS

Figure 7.6 The mayoral residence of Wah-Sut, South Abydos.

Important aspects of the functioning of the mayoral residence are reflected in structures associated with the front (Nile-facing) and back (desert-facing) parts of the building. Excavation outside the front of Building A revealed a large, open town square or plaza. A ramp system against the front wall of the mayoral residence leads up to the main doorway, which was raised above the surface level of the plaza. Within the building a series of access corridors and doorways led inwards to reach the main residential unit. The nature of the architecture reflects a tightly controlled mode of access through this main doorway to the person and activities of the mayor.

A separate doorway into Building A appears to have functioned as the primary administrative entrance. Two imposing, multi-roomed brick buildings outside the back doorway have associated deposits of seal impressions which include institutional stamp seals naming the *areryt*, or "administrative gatehouse," of the *per haty-a*. These structures appear to constitute the remains of the actual *areryt*: a facility manned by a staff of officials and scribes who managed inflow and outflow of commodities from the mayoral residence. Based on the seal impressions, activities channeled through the *areryt* included local oversight of the nearby mortuary temple of Senwosret III (of which the mayor was also the titular administrator), as well as extra-local correspondence evidenced by a high volume of seal impressions from papyrus letters. A significant component of the sealing assemblage are impressions of the seals of "royal sealbearers" – the highest tier of royal administrators (Grajetzki 2003) – as well as fragments of papyrus sealings imprinted with royal seals – the mark of operation of central governmental departments.

In a number of respects, the archaeology of the mayoral residence of Wah-Sut fits exceedingly well with predictions of the Patrimonial Household Model. This was a large local household which functioned as a nodal point in economic and social relations for the community at South Abydos. The building, and the person, of the mayor formed a point of convergence in the web of economic and administrative activities that maintained Wah-Sut. Moreover, the presence of extra-local/central state seal impressions reflects a household that was the primary channel of interaction between officials and bureaux of the central government. One can see how the entity of the mayoral residence functions as the key organizational institution of the town and linchpin in the management of the mortuary foundation of Senwosret III at South Abydos. As implied in the original formulations of Weber's patrimonial regime, and more recently by the Patrimonal Household Model, the mayoral household appears to constitute a smaller-scale version of the greater royal household (*per-nesut*). With its dominance over local economic activities, oversight of the nearby temple, and complex system of managing the flow of goods, the *per haty-a* operated in some respects like a royal palace writ small. We see the institution of the *per haty-a* at South Abydos as an organizational vehicle which was established by royal mandate and modeled on the prevailing system of mayoral administration as the administrative nexus between communities and central government in the late Middle Kingdom.

On the other hand, however, the corpus of administrative seal impressions reflects the operations of a tightly regimented, formalized, bureaucratic apparatus (Figure 7.7). Local officials and institutions employed their seals as a mark of the

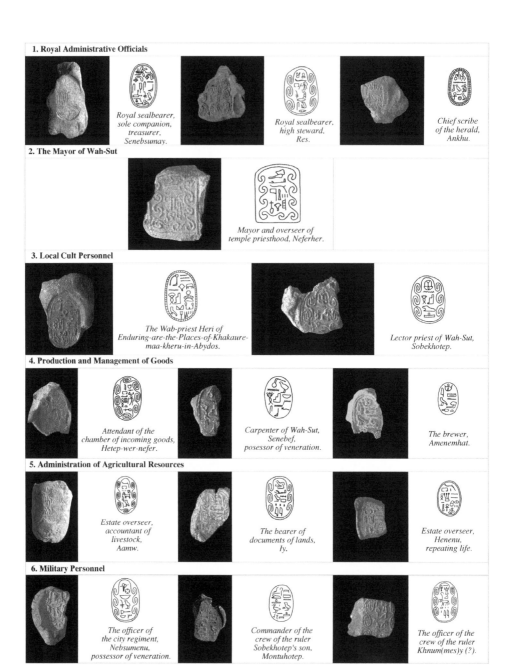

1. Royal Administrative Officials

Royal sealbearer,
sole companion,
treasurer,
Senebsumay.

Royal sealbearer,
high steward,
Res.

Chief scribe
of the herald,
Ankhu.

2. The Mayor of Wah-Sut

Mayor and overseer of
temple priesthood, Neferher.

3. Local Cult Personnel

The Wab-priest Heri of
Enduring-are-the-Places-of-Khakaure-
maa-kheru-in-Abydos.

Lector priest of Wah-Sut,
Sobekhotep.

4. Production and Management of Goods

Attendant of the
chamber of incoming goods,
Hetep-wer-nefer.

Carpenter of Wah-Sut,
Senebef,
possessor of veneration.

The brewer,
Amenemhat.

5. Administration of Agricultural Resources

Estate overseer,
accountant of
livestock,
Aamw.

The bearer of
documents of lands,
Iy.

Estate overseer,
Henenu,
repeating life.

6. Military Personnel

The officer of
the city regiment,
Nebsumenu,
possessor of veneration.

Commander of the
crew of the ruler
Sobekhotep's son,
Montuhotep.

The officer of the
crew of the ruler
Khnum(mes)y (?).

Figure 7.7 A hierarchy of officials: Middle Kingdom administration as represented in the community of Wah-Sut at South Abydos.

fulfillment of responsibilities and accountability in ongoing administrative operations. Seals bearing the name of royal governmental offices and institutions reflect
the presence of a hierarchically organized system by which this one local community was bound to the agencies of central administration. Moreover, although
we are still lacking a large sample of comparable communities for the late Middle
Kingdom, the extant textual data suggest that Wah-Sut did not function in ways
that were appreciably different from elsewhere in Egypt. The governmental titles
as well as range of local institutions seen at Wah-Sut are replicated from the
Mediterranean to Aswan. The degree of standardization of late Middle Kingdom
administration bespeaks a level of governmental "rationalization" that I believe
departs from tenets of the Patrimonial Household Model. I would suggest that
the Patrimonial Household Model has much to offer in understanding the organization of ancient Egyptian society. But, at a certain level, the details do indeed
appear to go out of focus (see Lehner 2000:342). There was a broad, engrained
structure of hierarchical households which indeed was conspicuously manipulated
by the Middle Kingdom state. At the same time, however, there was a level of
"rationalization" to a state system: a web of institutions, offices, and officials which
was not merely a coercive overlay, but one which permeated, manipulated (and
replicated) this system to the benefit of both local communities and the royal
government ("great house") of the pharaoh.

Dwelling exclusively on the household as the only unit of ownership and agency
risks itself becoming as reductionist as archaeological models that create an impersonal, actor-less structure devoid of social relationships and agency. Middle
Kingdom society was not merely a fractal hierarchy of nested households linked
by personal ties. Perhaps we can conclude that a defining feature of Middle
Kingdom society is an ongoing dialogue between the role of patrimonialism and
attempts, perhaps both conscious and unconscious, to enmesh a web of governmental officers and departments with formal oversight of economic and social life.
Viewed within its own terms and conceptual boundaries, Middle Kingdom governmental organization approached a high level of rationalization that permitted
the system to survive even through the period of rapid turnover in the kingship
that defines the 13th Dynasty.

Conclusion

The Middle Kingdom arose, initially on shaky legs, c. 2050, to spark a period of
state regeneration that must be considered to be one of the great periods of
Egyptian civilization. As we have seen, the civilizational template of Egypt's "great
tradition" and a nuanced historical awareness of the past informed the ways in
which the elite and rulers of the Middle Kingdom defined their society. Although
archaism and connections with the past were explicitly manipulated as symbols
of legitimacy, the Middle Kingdom was a period of innovation and social change.
Religious beliefs and practices display a form of symbolic egalitarianism whereby
access to divinity, both in daily life and in funerary traditions, permeated the
bulk of the population. Changes in material cultural forms show that these
new traditions referenced models of the past, but, in the wake of the significant

socio-economic changes of the First Intermediate Period, archaism formed only a limited vehicle in a wider sea of change and innovation. The Middle Kingdom became in many ways a classical phase of Pharaonic civilization. Achievements in high cultural forms of art, architecture, and especially literature were, not surprisingly, again civilizational models as Egyptians of the New Kingdom cast their eyes back to the period of the kings of Itj-Tawy. It is important to recognize that the Middle Kingdom began in Thebes and ended in Thebes. The "southern city" always retained a special administrative status – as the *waret tep-resy* – through the Middle Kingdom. It was there that the final kings of the Middle Kingdom returned as their ability to rule the north disintegrated. Tellingly, one of the major achievements of this time, the highly organized administrative system which reached its formalization in the late Middle Kingdom, survived this period of decline and remained active in Thebes when the leaders of the Theban 17th Dynasty accrued power.

In the study of Egyptian history and archaeology it is important to recognize that the founders of the New Kingdom, c. 1550 BCE, were conscious not so much of their role in founding a "new" kingdom, but of their role in re-establishing the order of the Middle Kingdom. In 2005, work of the Centre Franco-Egyptien d'Étude des Temples de Karnak discovered a striking well-preserved pair-statue of the 13th-Dynasty king Neferhotep I and his queen. This figure once stood inside the Middle Kingdom temple dedicated to the god Amun at Thebes. The statue cannot be removed from the ground as directly atop it sits an obelisk of the 18th-Dynasty female pharaoh Hatshepsut. Forever supporting the obelisk of Hatshepsut above it, these monuments create a striking metaphor for the relationship between the Middle and New Kingdoms. The culture of the early New Kingdom was indelibly tied to the Middle Kingdom, just as the formation of the Middle Kingdom and its period of innovation is linked to the models provided by the Old Kingdom.

REFERENCES

Allen, J. 2002 The Heqanakht Papyri. MMA Egyptian Expedition. Vol. XXVII. New York: Metropolitan Museum of Art.

Altenmüller, H. 1965. Die Apotropaia und die Götter Mittelagyptens: Eine Typologische und religionsgeschichtliche Untersuchung der sog. "Zaubermesser" des Mittleren Reiches, I: text; II: katalog.

Andrews, C. 1994 Amulets of Ancient Egypt. London: British Museum Press.

Arnold, D. 1991 Amenemhat I and the Early Twelfth Dynasty at Thebes. Metropolitan Museum Journal 26:5–48.

Beausang, E. 2000 Childbirth in Prehistory: An Introduction. European Journal of Prehistory 3(1):69–87.

Baines, J., and N. Yoffee 1998 Order, Legitimacy and Wealth in Ancient Egypt and Mesopotamia. *In* The Archaic State: A Comparative Perspective. G. Feiman and J. Marcus, eds. Pp. 199–260. Santa Fe, NM: School of American Research Press.

Erman, A. 1901 Zaubersprüche für Mutter und Kind aus dem Papyrus 3027 des Berliner Museums. Berlin: Akademie der Wissenschaften, Berlin.

Franke, D. 1991 The Career of Khnumhotep III and the So-called "Decline of the Nomarchs." *In* Middle Kingdom Studies. S. Quirke, ed. Pp. 51–67. New Malden, Surrey: SIA Publishing.

Grajetzki, W. 2003 Die Höchsten Beamten der Ägyptischen Zentralverwaltung zur Zeit des Mittleren Reiches: Propographie, Titel, und Titelreihen. Berlin: Achet-Verlag.

Grajetzki, W. 2006 The Middle Kingdom of Ancient Egypt. London: Duckworth.

Hayes, W. C. 1955 A Papyrus of the Late Middle Kingdom in the Brooklyn Museum (Papyrus Brooklyn 35. 1446). New York: The Brooklyn Museum.

Kemp, B. 2006 Ancient Egypt, Anatomy of a Civilization. 2nd edition. London, New York: Routledge.

Lehner, M. 2000 The Fractal House of Pharaoh: Ancient Egypt as a Complex Adaptive System, a Trial Formulation. *In* Dynamics in Human and Primate Societies: Agent-based Modeling of Social and Spatial Processes. T. A. Kohler and G. Gumerman, eds. Pp. 272–353. New York: Santa Fe Institute; Oxford: Oxford University Press.

Martin, G. T. 1971 Egyptian Administrative and Private-name Seals, Principally of the Middle Kingdom and Second Intermediate Period. Oxford: Griffith Institute.

Morris, E. 2006 Lo Nobles Lament, the Poor Rejoice: State Formation in the Wake of Social Flux. *In* After Collapse: The Regeneration of Complex Societies. G. Schwartz and J. Nichols, eds. Pp. 72–84. Tucson: University of Arizona Press.

O'Connor, D. 1972 A Regional Population in Egypt to Circa 600 BC. *In* Population Growth: Anthropological Implications. B. Spooner, ed. Pp. 78–100. Cambridge, MA: MIT Press.

O'Connor, D. 2000 Society and Individual in Early Egypt. *In* Order Legitimacy and Wealth in Ancient States. New Directions in Archaeology. J. Richards and M. Van Buren, eds. Pp. 21–35. Cambridge: Cambridge University Press.

Parkinson, R. 1991 Voices from Ancient Egypt: An Anthology of Middle Kingdom Writings. London: British Museum Press.

Pinch, G. 1993 Votive Offerings to Hathor. Oxford: Griffith Institute.

Pinch, G. 2006 Magic in Ancient Egypt. 2nd edition. London: British Museum Press.

Postel, L. 2004. Protocole de souverains égyptiens et dogme monarchique au début du Moyen Empire. Brepols: Fondation égyptologique de Reine Élisabeth.

Quirke, S. 1990 Administration of Egypt in the Late Middle Kingdom. New Malden, Surrey: SIA Publishing.

Quirke, S. 1991 Royal Power in the Thirteenth Dynasty. *In* Middle Kingdom Studies. S. Quirke, ed. Pp. 123–139. New Malden, Surrey: SIA Publishing.

Quirke, S. 2004 Titles and Bureaux of Egypt 1850–1700 BC. London: Golden House Publications.

Richards, J. 2000 Modified Order, Responsive Legitimacy, Redistributed Wealth: Egypt, 2260-1650 BC. *In* Order Legitimacy and Wealth in Ancient States. New Directions in Archaeology. J. Richards and M. Van Buren, eds. Pp. 36–45. Cambridge: Cambridge University Press.

Richards, J. 2005 Society and Death in Ancient Egypt: Mortuary Landscapes of the Middle Kingdom. Cambridge: Cambridge University Press.

Robins, G. 1993 Women in Ancient Egypt. London: British Museum Press.

Roth, A. M., and C. Roehrig 2002 Magical Bricks and the Bricks of Birth. Journal of Egyptian Archaeology 88:121–139.

Schwartz, G., and J. J. Nichols, eds 2006 After Collapse: The Regeneration of Complex Societies. Tucson: University of Arizona Press.

Seidlmayer, S. 2000 The First Intermediate Period (c. 2160–2055 BC). *In* The Oxford History of Ancient Egypt. I. Shaw. ed. Pp. 118–147. Oxford, New York: Oxford University Press.

Simpson, W. K. 1963 Studies in the Twelfth Egyptian Dynasty I–II. Journal of the American Research Center in Egypt 2:53–63.

Smith, S. T. 1995 Askut in Nubia: The Economics and Ideology of Egyptian Imperialism in the Second Millennium BC. London, New York: Kegan Paul International.

Smither, P. C. 1945 The Semna Despatches. Journal of Egyptian Archaeology 31:3–10.

Tait, J., ed. 2003 "Never Had the Like Occurred": Egypt's View of Its Past. London: UCL Press.

Trigger, B. G. 1976 Nubia under the Pharaohs. London: Thames and Hudson.

Wegner, J. 1988 Excavations at the Town of *Enduring-are-the-Places-of-Khakaure-maa-kheru-in-Abydos*: A Preliminary Report on the 1994 and 1997 Seasons. Journal of the American Research Center in Egypt 35:1–44.

Wegner, J. 2001 The Town of *Wah-Sut* at South Abydos: 1999 Excavations. Mitteilungen des Deutschen Archäologischen Instituts, Abteilung Kairo 57:281–308.

Wegner, J. 2002 A Decorated Birth-Brick from South Abydos. Egyptian Archaeology 21:3–4.

Wegner, J. 2004 Social and Historical Implications of Sealings of the King's Daughter Renisneb and other Women at the Town of Wah-Sut. *In* Scarabs of the Second Millennium BC from Egypt, Nubia, Crete and the Levant: Chronological and Historical Implications, SCIEM 2000 (Denkshriften der Gesamtakademie, Band 35). M. Bietak and E. Czerny, eds. Pp. 221–240. Vienna: Österreichische Akademie der Wissenschaften.

Wegner, J. 2006 Echoes of Power: The Mayor's House of Ancient *Wah-Sut*. Expedition 48(2):31–36.

Wegner, J. 2007 The Mortuary Temple of Senwosret III at Abydos. New Haven, Philadelphia: Publications of the Pennsylvania–Yale Institute of Fine Arts Expedition to Abydos.

Wegner, J. 2009 A Decorated Birth-Brick from South Abydos: New Evidence on Childbirth and Birth Magic in the Middle Kingdom. *In* Archaism and Innovation: Studies in the Culture of Middle Kingdom Egypt. D. Silverman, W. Simpson, and J. Wegner, eds. Pp. 447–496. New Haven: Yale University; Philadelphia: Penn Museum of Archaeology and Anthropology.

Wilson, J. A. 1956 The Culture of Ancient Egypt. Chicago: University of Chicago Press.

8

Foreigners in Egypt

Archaeological Evidence and Cultural Context

Thomas Schneider

The notion of "foreigner" has been used regularly in the study of ancient Egypt, but hardly ever has it been reflected on thoroughly and properly. Modern connotations have frequently been projected and superimposed on the ancient evidence (Schneider 2006). The issue has received more intense attention since the 1980s, fostered by the anthropological debate about the concepts of ethnicity, culture, and territorial identities.

Ethnicity

Egyptology has seen a late reception of the term "ethnicity," and has only rarely applied insights from the anthropological debate with scrutiny to its evidence (cf. Baines 1996; Johnson 1999:211ff.; for an overview with literature cf. Schneider 2003a:316–338; Smith 2003:1–55). The concept of ethnicity has asserted itself since Glazer and Moynihan's study *Ethnicity: Theory and Experience* (1975). As a constituent of social life it denotes the fundamental fact that groups of people are linked together by belief in a common origin, shared features of culture, history, and current experience, and that they possess a sense of identity and belonging together (Heckmann 1992:30, 46, 56). Jenkins has recently upheld the validity of this universal feature of the structuring of human societies by emphasizing that ethnicity is a social construction, rooted in social interaction, with a fluidity linked to culture or social situations, and both collective and individual, "externalized in social interaction and internalized in personal self-identification" (Jenkins 2001:4828).

Ethnicity is not primarily an issue of actual cultural difference but the result of subjective judgments and more fundamental economic conditions, negotiated through social interaction (Alba 2000; Jenkins 2001; Nagel 1994). Very much relevant for the Egyptian evidence is the relation between ethnicity and other principles of social identification. Jenkins (1997, 2001) has proposed to

differentiate between group identification (within ethnic groups) and social cat-
egorization (a group is classified externally by non-members).

Another dichotomy that can be encountered in Egyptological literature is the
one between ethnicity (as a cultural and voluntary classification) and race (a social
classification imposed by compulsion) (van den Berghe 1967; Waters 1990), if it
is not rather assigned to ethnicity as an inherent feature (Alba 2000). Main elements of the concept of ethnicity (Alba 2000; Heckmann 1992) are a common
lineage, shared historical or current experiences (such as the motivation for immigration, the kind of reception by the host society: Lieberson 1961), language,
religion, traditions of food and dress, foklore, music, and other socio-cultural
features, residence and living patterns, an awareness of foreignness and collective
identity (through both internal perception and external attribution), a sense of
solidarity within the ethnic group, group-specific institutions and political aims.
Critical for the development of ethnicity is the state of power the ethnic group is
faced with, inequality and stratification within the ethnic groups, and the avail-
abilty of ethnic resources (Alba 2000).

Acculturation

People of foreign origin who lived in Egypt were subject to an adaptation to the
social and cultural system of their host country. Although this adaptation was
certainly of different intensity, it is crucial to notice that the modern label of
"foreigners" loses its applicability in this setting. With their automatic embedding
in the new society, they no longer formed an inherent part of the world beyond
its boundaries, which was seen as chaotic and potentially threatening, and were
no longer covered by the ethnic stereotypes maintained for the sake of state legitimacy. Entering Egypt meant implicitly taking on a new ideological code, of
the Egyptian (even though of foreign origin) serving the king instead of the
enemy smitten by pharaoh. This is clearly visible in the fact that the Egyptian
comprehensive term *ḫ3s.tjw*, "foreigners," is never used for peoples of foreign
origin in an Egyptian socio-economic context but exclusively reserved for foreigners outside Egypt who are devoid of any opportunity of acculturation. *Absent* vs.
accomplished acculturation is the decisive pair of opposites that served as the
Egyptian criterion for considering an individual a foreigner or an Egyptian
(Schneider 2003a, 2006); a critical issue also with regard to the mimetic portrayal
of foreigners (Smith 2003:175). Ethnonyms like *ʿ3m*, "Asiatic," or *nḥsj*, "Nubian,"
which are used both for *non-acculturated people outside Egypt* and for *adapted
members of the Egyptian social system* convey primarily the notion of foreign origin
but cannot be taken as indicators of a specific degree of ethnicity. The inclusion
of ethnic groups and individuals in the host society entails adaptation processes
of various intensities that can collectively be labeled *acculturation*, although there
is no terminological unanimity (other terms include assimilation, accommodation,
absorption, adaptation, integration, amalgamation: Dupront 1966; Heckmann
1992:167). These stages progress from superficial adaptation that enables survival
in the host society (which can last indefinitely) to more structural changes in social
and professional affiliation, marriage patterns, values, and identity, and ultimately

the stage of complete assimilation to the host society (Alba 2000: 842; Alba and Nee 1997; Gordon 1964:71; Heckmann 1992:176ff.).

A more differentiated view of the degrees of acculturation within the intermediate stage of integration (partial immersion in either cultural system) is essential. Heckmann (1992:167ff.) proposes *accommodation* as a first stage that enables a person to live in the host society but does not embrace the change of basic values or modes of thinking. *Acculturation* is the change of values, the acquisition of linguistic, professional, and cultural knowledge, and the change in behavior and life style fostered by contact with the host society (corresponding to Stephenson's [2000] *integration*). This process still leaves subjects with their separate cultural identity. The third stage of *assimilation* entails the complete reception of the host culture and rejection of the culture of origin. Gordon's path-breaking study of 1964 features the seven-step sequence of *cultural or behavioral assimilation (= acculturation), structural assimilation, marital assimilation (= amalgamation), identificational assimilation, attitude receptional assimilation, behavior receptional assimilation,* and *civic assimilation*. Each of these steps is characterized by an increase in aspects of the host society and a decrease in features of the original ethnic background.

It is critical to distinguish between individual and group acculturation. Factors favoring the fast acculturation of individuals are marked social hierarchies and a strong majority culture, as well as a distinct motivation for assimilation. In the case of group acculturation, crucial requirements are the openness of the group structure, the willingness and ability to acculturate in the minority group, and a majority society disposed favorably towards the group's acculturation (Heckmann 1992:181–207). An important factor both in modern societies and in respect to ancient Egypt is spatial closeness to the host society, residency, or the distribution of settlements that favor spatial assimilation (Alba 2000).

Particularly appropriate for the description of acculturation in ancient Egypt is the socially differentiating concept of *segmented assimilation* (Portes and Zhou 1993). It accounts for the fact that the receiving majority society may be heavily stratified, to the effect that individuals are culturally integrated into specific social strata, for example from low social positions to the lower class of the majority society, without the possibility of social ascent. Two special cases of significance for the Egyptian evidence are that of an ethnic minority (in case of discrimination: Heckmann 1992:55, 59–116) and symbolic ethnicity, when traditions and customs are preserved as relics in the third or fourth generation of immigrants, which is elsewhere completely assimilated to the culture of the majority (Heckmann 1992:32).

To understand the issue of cultural identity correctly, it is also important to note that the focus of personal affiliation was not the state, but one's place of birth, apart from which social position and status generated identity; and that otherness existed within Egyptians as well (Assmann 1996; Moers 2003). Neither from the internal perception of the Egyptian nor from the external perception of the immigrant was non-Egyptian origin seen as a framework of group identity and solidarity. If ethnic identities persevered in Egypt, they defined themselves on a smaller scale.

In this context, it is important to mention the notion of *cultural distance* (cf. Schneider 2003a) – the extent of problems with adaptation as a function of the difference between cultures. Cultural contact was intense and facilitated acculturation. Cultural distance was thus diminished through the appropriation of elements of foreign cultures by the Egyptian elite society – the reception of technological innovation, cultural and religious motifs, language and literature (Schneider 2003b). At the same time, the tenets of Egyptian culture proliferated abroad, not the least in the urban centers of the ancient Near East.

Boundaries

Apart from the parameters of ethnicity and acculturation, the spatial construction of identities has received specific interest over the past two decades. This aspect had always been recognized for settlements and cemeteries of immigrant populations (Pan-grave, C group, Palestinian and Libyan influx in the Delta), but has increased in significance with the new anthropological discourse about borders (cf. Brunet-Jailly 2004; Donnan and Wilson 1994; Lightfoot and Martinez 1995; Newman 2003). In Egyptology, the concept of borders has conventionally relied on the assumption that their essence is to separate the inside/"self" from the outside/"other," and to constitute a barrier against military attack or the influx of people or values. Seeing them as hard territorial lines for the political demarcation of territorial states that have an absolute command of their control function seems at first sight supported by the existence of Egyptian fortifications on the fringes of the Delta and until the Second Cataract in Nubia as the most manifest architectural symbols of a boundary. As tools of military defense and control, and of the exploitation of economic resources and workforce, they substantiate the political and ideological claim to the governance of the territory they are situated in and which they demarcate from external areas. A major shift in the study of boundaries is the adoption of a new perspective that emphasizes the process of bordering, and explores this process on a local level. It perceives borders as institutions that engender a system of communities, affiliations, and identities, imposing on the people living along the border laws of behavior, of exclusion and inclusion, of difference and similarity. Case studies concentrate on the human agency of the people who live and work at these borders, who generate a bottom-up dynamics often in conflict with institutional top-down regulations implemented there. Recent studies have therefore devoted their interest to trans-boundary interaction, integration processes within the borderland, the negotiation of culture, and the development of forms of identity which undermine traditional territorial identity. They emphasize how perceptions of the border constructed from the center of a state which emphasize difference, fear, and threat may conflict with divergent perceptions created in the bordering communities. Instead of applying a core–periphery model where the periphery is seen as passive and depending upon a cultural center, new concepts imagine frontiers as interfaces of culture. Border areas are thus seen as places where new cultural constructs are created, where the creolization of culture takes place. The understanding of local border identities and cultural landscapes that transcend the geopolitical borderline has also been adopted in the study of borders in archaeology (Lightfoot and Martinez 1995).

This is nowhere more visible than at the site of Avaris, which was founded as the first pioneer outpost east of the Pelusiac branch of the Nile in the late 12th Dynasty and has become one of the Egyptological model communities allowing us to observe the merger of cultures, the development of new identities, and the dynamic interplay of different ethnic and religious groups (see case study below). Its successor, Pi-Ramesse, is not only proof of a settlement which, although at the traditional periphery of Egypt, constituted the driving force of Ramesside Egypt. It was also perceived as a community featuring trans-boundary dynamics by the Egyptians themselves, who stated, in praise of the city in pAnastasi IV, that it is situated with all its splendor and degree of achievement "on the boundary between Egypt and Palestine." Similar areas with a high degree of non-Egyptian cultural features behind political boundaries are the first Upper Egyptian nome and the region of Lower Nubia (cf. Smith 2003); the mountainous region of Egypt's eastern border, still populated by Bedja tribes today up to the geographic latitude of Thebes; the Western Nile Delta; and the Egyptian West with a large frontier zone of Egyptian, Libyan, and Nilo-Saharan interchange.

Ideology and Reality

Egyptian ideology adhered to a rigid distinction between Egypt and the outside world, and between inhabitants of Egypt and inhabitants of the chaotic and potentially threatening world beyond its boundaries. As a *topos*, a society's official and normative perception, it has been distinguished from *mimetic* attempts to surmount the prescriptive tenets of tradition – narrative attempts to portray foreigners in a humanistic way as valuable individuals (Loprieno 1988; Smith 2003; cf. critically Buchberger 1989/1990). Loprieno's stimulating approach from the field of literary studies has been projected by Gordon on to the situation of Egyptian society, and taken as a general distinction between (negative) attitudes towards groups and (positive) attitudes towards individuals (Gordon 2001:547), which does not seem to be valid. A valid assessment needs rather to account for the complex cultural situation. The ideological pattern of the *foreigner topos* assigned political and ritual roles on the basis of a strict model of inclusion and exclusion which combined the existence or lack of acculturation with the notion of territorial authority and power hierarchy. Only representatives of peoples outside Egypt who were not part of Egypt's internal cultural system were "outsiders," while foreign mercenaries in the Egyptian army would serve the fight against enemies of Egypt just as much as foreign rulers of Egypt would be portrayed smiting the chaotic world. This principle is still visible in Herodotus' assertion that whoever was nourished by the waters of the Nile was considered an Egyptian.

The positive portrayal of foreign individuals in Egyptian texts (Sinuhe) and of the possibility of living abroad (Doomed Prince) is not just the *mimetic* counterpoint of narrative literature to the stereotypical concepts of ideology but betrays insights into the complex and differentiated system of cultural exchange. Cultural appropriation in the Egyptian elite and the increasing possibility of exhibiting foreignness and ethnicity on the Nile refigured Egypt in the second millennium and changed the receptive framework for immigrants, while simultaneously

Egyptian culture proliferated abroad (Schneider 2006). Beneath the strict demarcations of ideology, the cultural picture exhibits a scenario of great complexity. Large numbers of individuals and groups of foreign descent entered Egyptian society at all times of its history and on all its levels, where they underwent varying degrees of acculturation. Social status and professional affiliation were the principal factors of an individual's orientation, whereas ethnicity as a large-scale factor of identity did not occur before the first millennium BCE. Officials of foreign descent were assimilated into Egyptian elite culture, to the effect that their ethnic origin may have lost all significance to their social career and that political decisions were not dictated by ethnicity, as had been insinuated previously:

> It seems reasonable to assume that they were, indeed, fully accepted within Egyptian society as Egyptians. If this is a correct reading of the situation, then we should not think of these people as foreigners in a modern, nationalistic sense, but rather as Egyptians of foreign origin. ... This point casts a completely different perspective on our perception of the composition of Egyptian society. (Schulman 1986:193 n. 2; cf. Schneider 2003a, 2006)

Evidence and Evaluation

A modern assessment of the issue of foreigners in ancient Egypt is faced with considerable difficulties (Schneider 2003a, 2006):

1   Markers of ethnicity were displayed to a varying, but preponderantly little, degree over the course of Egyptian history, depending on the decorum and the social position of the individual or group. Secondary to features of the dominant society, and not relevant for success in life or afterlife, they will be missing outright, in the majority of cases, from the biographical or archaeological record relating to an individual. Almost all individuals of foreign origin that are preserved in the sources are but one step from losing the last ethnic marker that makes us qualify them as foreigners (an ethnonym or foreign personal name) and do not appear as otherwise (appearance, dress, funerary equipment, etc.) different from "Egyptians" in the evidence. Hardly ever is it possible to assess the importance of an individual's ethnicity of origin in the private domain against the official display of the host society's culture.

2   The evidence for people of foreign origin in the Egyptian material and written record is fragmentary and often ambiguous. The vast majority of written and material remains from Egypt has been lost, and foreigners in lower social strata will have had lesser opportunities to leave traces of their existence than elite officials. Immigration of groups and populations (C-group, Pan-grave, settlement and cemetery patterns) can be observed more unequivocally, although the archaeological evidence for ethnicity is not always unambiguous (Smith 2003).

3   The variety of forms of acculturation over the cultural and social spectrum – from prisoners of war to foreigners turned vizier – is likely to have been very complex. We are lacking the possibility of investigating closer specific milieus

and phenomena of acculturation, with the notable exception of a limited number of case studies.

Foreigners in Egypt: An Overview

Archaic Egypt

Ever since humans settled in the Nile Valley, they will have encountered people of different origin (cf. Raue 2002; Schneider 1998; Wilkinson 2002). Otherness was a feature that persisted even within the boundaries of historical Egypt by way of different appearances, dialects, and traditions (Assmann 1996). Prior to the epoch of a territorial state extending over the whole of Egypt from the Delta to the First Cataract, the demarcation between groups of particular cultural identities followed different parameters, whereas the classic ideological dichotomy between "Egyptians" and "foreigners" and their respective (real or imagined) cultural repertoires was the result of a long political process. Early transfers of people through trade, migration, and nomadism are reflected in the mutual material inventory of settlements (e.g. between Buto-Maadi and South Palestine) and at least indirectly in phenomena of innovation from abroad (pictorial motifs on palettes, mace heads, and knives; recess architecture; the idea of writing). The motif of prisoners is attested as early as Naqada II, as is the depiction of specific cultural markers such as cloak, beard, and conical hat (Schneider 1998). It is doubtful if new evidence from Buto (the cone mosaic or *Stiftmosaik*) can be seen as proof of artistic innovation implemented in Egypt by craftsmen from the Uruk civilization (Wilde and Behnert 2002).

The Old Kingdom and First Intermediate Period

The evidence for foreigners in the Old Kingdom and First Intermediate Period is very limited (cf. for the following in detail Schneider 1998). Reasons for this may be sought in limitations of military activity and the influx of foreign groups or individuals, but may equally lie in the restrictions of decorum, which would not have allowed for the display of ethnicity, in the composition of historical sources. I will outline here the basic thematic issues:

1   *The foreigner topos.* Depictions and sculptures of prisoners form part of the regular ritual and ideological repertoire, from the Djoser complex to the mortuary temples of the 5th and 6th Dynasties. A ritual cage for the possible containment of prisoner figures has been discovered at Giza (Grimm 1987).
2   *Population shifts.* The Old Kingdom attests most probably to the resettlement of C-group Nubians (and perhaps Libyans) to the newly colonialized Nile Delta under Snofru (for Nubians before the New Kingdom, cf. Meurer 1996). Major shifts in the population of Nubia occur towards the end of the 5th Dynasty, when the C-group settles in Lower Nubia and the civilization of Middle Kerma is attested in Upper Nubia. Execration texts are a new type

of ritual evidence attested in the 6th Dynasty. The texts known from the reign of Pepy II mention individually c. 180 "Nubians," bearing preponderantly "Nubian" names and being partly labeled explicitly as *nḥsj*, "Nubian." Since the latter term can denote more particularly members of the Nubian C-group which immigrated into the Lower Nubian Nile Valley during the 6th Dynasty or earlier and constituted a threat to the Egyptian claim to Nubian trade and raw materials, the appearance of execration figures in their names is likely to be seen as a reflection of this shift of population (for the boundary controls, see Meurer 1996:100). The mention of "pacified/settled/acculturated Nubians" (*nḥsjw ḥtpw*) in Pepy I's exemption decree for service extended to the funerary precinct of Snofru at Dahshur seems to relate to integrated C-group Nubians.

3   *Military campaigns and expeditions.* Besides the deliberate resettlement of Nubians under Snofru, expeditions of military purpose for the procurement of raw materials and the pursuit of trade will have entailed regular contacts with foreigners and their capture. The capture of foreigners can be inferred from razzias and expeditions by Sahure, their attachment to work at the royal pyramid sites from a note from Userkaf's reign in the Cairo annal fragment. Depictions of the surrender of Libya from Sahure's reign (with later copies) record enormous figures of prisoners and prey and have been interpreted as testimony to a feudal allegiance of Libya to Egypt (Fecht 1956; Gundlach 1994). Egyptian expeditions far into the plateau of the Sahara under Cheops and Djedefre have only recently come to light (Kuhlmann 2005; Riemer et al. 2005). Razzias to Palestine, the taking of prisoners, and the conquest of a town, respectively, are attested in the biography of Djedkare-Asosi's son Kaemtjenenet and the contemporary (or later, 6th-Dynasty) depictions in the tombs of Kaemheset at Saqqara and the tomb of Inti at Deshasheh. Equally attested are campaigns to Nubia under Pepy II. The Teaching for Merikare, traditionally believed to be set in the First Intermediate Period (cf., however, Gnirs 2006), alludes to incursions of Asiatics in the Eastern Nile Delta. The record of *ʿȝmw*, "Asiatics," in execration texts and of nomadic *ʿȝmw ḥrjw-š*, "Asiatics who are on the sand," indicates a growing concern about the state of affairs to the northeast of Egypt.

4   *Foreigners in Egyptian service.* The alleged reception, in the 4th Dynasty, of "Libyan" and "African" women to the Egyptian elite and the royal harem advocated by early twentieth-century scholars (Junker 1929: 63ff.; Reisner 1947:477) on the basis of depictions and anthropological material (e.g. Queen Hetepheres) cannot be corroborated at present. Foreign individuals employed in private households are attested in the case of Nubian attendants of early 5th-Dynasty officials buried at Giza. Of particular importance are depictions of ocean-going ships from the funerary temple of Sahure and the Unas causeway depicting the employment of Asiatic seafaring specialists on behalf of the Egyptian crown. In these two reigns, additional individuals from Africa (pygmies from Punt, equally under Pepy II) and the Levant are attested in Egypt. A famous scene from the causeway of the pyramid of Unas depicts emaciated bedouins. It is unclear whether the depiction represents actual individuals or the ideological motif which contrasts the chaotic world outside with the affluence of Egypt. Nubians were also recruited for the Egyptian

militia of the 6th Dynasty, serving as auxiliary troops in the campaigns of Uni and Harkhuf and protecting quarry expeditions. The extent of their military use is visible in the considerable number of 6th-Dynasty officials employed in their administration as commanders of Nubian auxiliary troops (*mr j*w: Schneider 1998:22f.).

The First Intermediate Period has preserved depictions of Asiatic prisoners while Nubians appear not only as elite troops, but also as servants on the Cairo sarcophagus of Ashayt (where they are identified as *mdȝy.wt* = Pan-grave Nubians). A Nubian origin has also been proposed for the secondary wives of Mentuhotep buried in shafts of his mortuary temple at Deir el-Bahri, on account of the depicted dark skin and anthropological data (for other cases, cf. Schneider 2003a). The presence of Nubians is most apparent in the case of the Nubian mercenaries of Gebelein, who are portrayed with ethnic markers (Kubisch 2000), depictions in tombs at Gebelein, Moalla, and Aswan, and the wooden model of forty Nubian archers from the tomb of Mesehti at Asyut (either Pan-grave people [Bietak 1985] or Kerma/C-group mercenaries [Meurer 1996]). A Nubian influx is visible in a variety of individuals and artifacts (Meurer 1996:95).

The Middle Kingdom and Second Intermediate Period

The first half of the second millennium is marked by an enormous increase in the evidence for foreigners in ancient Egypt (for a comprehensive presentation and analysis of the material, cf. Schneider 2003a). Whereas individual foreigners show up only exceptionally in the material from the third millennium, c. 800 individuals of probably foreign extraction are still visible in the published documentation from the first half of the second millennium. This is probably due to a more favorable source basis; to the need, possibility, or preparedness to register individuals as foreigners (whereby perception may have been different: contrary to the actual situation, Asiatics are much more frequently noticed than Nubians); and to a greater actual influx of people from Egypt's colonial possessions in Nubia and an intensified foreign policy in the Levant.

Military activity to bolster the Nubian province is attested throughout the Middle Kingdom, while a similarly energetic policy in Syria–Palestine has become fairly plausible due to the fragment of Amenemhat II's annals discovered at Mitrahine (Altenmüller and Moussa 1991; Eder 1995:176–195; Marcus 2007; Obsomer 1995:595–607) and a historical inscription from the Khnumhotep mastaba at Dahshur about an Egyptian involvement in the Levant (Allen 2008). The Amenemhat inscription mentions as one of the aims the capture of a work-force for the king's pyramid city (other Asiatics are given to Egypt as a tribute; their total is c. 2700 people), and the fact that the Egyptian soldiers ate the Asiatic dishes of the prisoners. From the time of Senwosret II comes the depiction of a caravan of "Asiatic" nomads (from the Sinai or Negev) in the tomb of Khnumhotep II at Beni Hassan; possibly mining specialists searching for galena under the protection of the nomarch Hassan (Staubli 1991:30–35). Senwosret III's first boundary stela at Semna prohibits Nubians from south of the Second Cataract to proceed further north; the *Semna Dispatches* from the reign of Amenemhat III register both C-group and Pan-grave Nubians seeking entry to Egypt. In dispatch 5 from Elephantine, Pan-grave people give as a reason for immigration that "the desert is dying of hunger." A delegation of Pan-grave people with their chieftain partakes in the festivities of Sobekhotep II's visit to Thebes (Papyrus Boulaq 18). Glimpses into the raiding of foreign territory for the acquisition of workforce can be gained from the stela of Khusobek (Manchester 3306), and into the use of skilled workers (mainly textile specialists) in a private Theban household from Papyrus Brooklyn 35.1446 from the reign of Sobekhotep III. In the Sinai, the employment of local personnel and South Palestinians in quarrying expeditions is attested under Amenemhat III and IV.

A re-evaluation of the professional affiliations of foreigners and their socio-economic embedding during the Middle Kingdom and the Second Intermediate Period has provided a differentiated picture (Schneider 2003a, as opposed to Helck 1971:77–82). Foreigners are attested across the whole socio-economic spectrum in c. 100 different professions and functions, extending from prisoners of war and compulsory workers to high administrative offices and royalty, including cultic and priestly functions and attesting to the emergence of professional traditions within families. It is interesting to notice that individuals of foreign origin who commissioned for themselves funerary items (e.g. stelae) had themselves not qualified by an ethnonym, which therefore appears to be an external marker applied by Egyptians. A remarkable exception is stela CG 1481 of an African ("Nubian") woman with a clear display of ethnic markers (Schneider 2003a). The scarcity of explicit evidence suggests that exhibiting ethnic difference in the (mostly funerary) sources was not important or viable, while examples of the presence of foreign markers (e.g. names) over several generations of a family indicate the perseverance of traditions of origin at least in a private context. The evidence for marital behavior is often ambiguous. While the adoption of foreigners into existing families by way of marriage is frequent, marriages between foreigners do not occur in the evidence, although they must have been ubiquitous in reality; nor are they often demonstrated in the New Kingdom (Schneider 2006).

Specific attention is deserved for settlements and cemeteries of foreign ethnic groups on Egyptian soil. While Asiatic immigration will be dealt with below, it is instructive to contrast the three Nubian cultures attested in Egypt during this period (Pan-grave, C-group, and Kerma). Pan-grave people ("desert Nubians") were anthropologically different from C-group people ("Nile Valley Nubians"), and they originated very distantly from each other. The Egyptians observed differences in their physique and kept them also terminologically distinct: Pan-grave people were labeled *mḏꜣyw*, whereas C-group Nubians were covered by the term *nḥsjw*. Scattered over Egypt and its Nubian territory from Dahshur until the Second Cataract, the small cemeteries of the nomadic Pan-grave culture (cf. Meurer 1996; Schneider 2003a) were situated on the edge of the desert, while permanent settlements are almost completely absent. Its members represented a Nubian population that attempted to resettle to Egypt between c. 1800 and 1550 BCE, seemingly due to a drought, or intentionally relocated there by the Theban kings of the 17th Dynasty (Beckerath 1964:201f.). Attested through tombs and pottery from Memphis to Elephantine, where they live in small and isolated groups, the Pan-grave people's place of origin seems to have been the Eastern Desert upstream from the Wadi Allaqi.

Thanks to their robust physique, they were deployed as soldiers, a fact corroborated beyond textual evidence by Egyptian weapons retrieved from Pan-grave burials (daggers, axes, bow strings, hand covers) and Pan-grave pottery in the Nubian forts of Buhen and Mirgissa. An acculturation to Egyptian society is clearly visible in the material record (Cohen 1993); anthropological evidence from the group settling at Mostagedda displays distinct signs of a merger with Egyptians. In contrast, the evidence for the Nubian C-group (Meurer 1996; Schneider 2003a) constitutes a model case of an ethnically different frontier community at Egypt's southern border. Attested in Nubia as early as the 6th Dynasty and most probably originating from the Libyan desert and the Southern Nile Valley, the C-group subsisted on agriculture and breeding cattle. Under Egyptian sovereignty in the Middle Kingdom and Second Intermediate Period, their cultural province comprised Lower Nubia and extended until the site of Kubanieh in "the Nubian land," the first Upper Egyptian nome north of the First Cataract. Although a C-group cemetery has been recently uncovered at Hierakonpolis (Friedman 2001), it seems as if large-scale group immigration to Egypt did not take place.

The loss of Egyptian sovereignty over Nubia with the end of the 13th Dynasty enabled the Sudanese Kerma culture to extend its influence to traditional C-group territory. On Egyptian soil, it is represented by individual tombs and groups of two to three tombs each with classical Kerma pottery. The evidence gathered by Bourriau (1981, 1991) comprises the sites of Gurob (late Second Intermediate Period or early 18th Dynasty), Qau (mid- to late Second Intermediate Period), Abydos (late 12th Dynasty and late Second Intermediate Period respectively), Abadiyeh (first half of Second Intermediate Period), and Dra Abu el-Naga (17th Dynasty), with additional evidence from the early 18th Dynasty. Additional Kerma pottery comes from Tell Hebwa, Memphis/Kom Rabi'a, Illahun, Hierakonpolis, and Edfu. The interpretation of the evidence is still in process (cf. Bourriau 1981:36; Meurer 1996:88).

Of particular importance is the evidence for Kerma people unearthed in Ahmose's residence of Ballas, pointing to the existence of Kerma contingents in service of the late 17th Dynasty, and perhaps also in its military. This is further corroborated by Kerma pottery and Nubian arrow heads from Tell el-Dabaa. Although not clearly demonstrable at present, the segregation of groups within urban centers on account of ethnic criteria cannot be excluded. Infrastructures specific to needs of ethnic groups are attested by Syrian sanctuaries at Avaris, and this might have reduced acculturation pressure. In turn, the evidence of Pan-grave burials and Kerma individuals seems to indicate the attractiveness of acculturation, and Avaris itself exhibits not an apartheid of cultures but their amalgamation. It is unclear to what extent clusters of foreigners in private households (e.g. Papyrus Brooklyn 35.1446, stela Moscow Pushkin Museum I.1.a.5349 [4161], stela Marseille 227, naos Vienna ÄS 186 [Schneider 2003:336]) constitute homogeneous ethnic pockets. Ethnic markers can be exhibited by foreigners themselves through their non-Egyptian personal names, the presence of non-Egyptian items in their funerary equipment, and much more rarely by having themselves depicted with non-Egyptian physical features, garments, and headdresses.

Despite the fact that the preserved evidence about foreigners in Middle Kingdom and Second Intermediate Egypt is extremely fragmentary, it still shows an omnipresence of individuals and groups of foreign extraction across the whole social and professional spectrum, and throughout the entire country. Contrary to what has been held until recently, this fact of demographic diversity is by and large comparable to New Kingdom Egypt (cf. Ray 1998:11).

The New Kingdom

Because of the richness of the evidence, the New Kingdom has been paradigmatic for the recent interest in and interpretation of foreigners in ancient Egypt (cf. Bresciani 1990; Panagiotopoulos, 2006; Schneider 2006). While basic parameters about the conditions of their acculturation do not differ markedly from the Middle Kingdom and the Second Intermediate Period, the display and perception of their ethnicity has become more obvious. Religious texts describe foreign people as an inhererent part of the created world (hymns to Amun-Ra in Papyrus Bulaq 17; hymns to the Aten; 4th hour of the Book of Gates). In documents, the use of ethnonyms as applied to individuals diminishes greatly while foreign proper names are preserved far more often (contrast Schneider 1992 and Schneider 2003a). If the display of ethnicity is still rather restricted in the Middle Kingdom, the New Kingdom abounds in the display of accurately observed physical features, headdresses and garments, hairstyles, culture-specific equipment, eating habits, traditions of folklore (dance, music), and foreign language. The fact that the encyclopedic Egyptian knowledge about foreigners that had undoubtedly existed since early times is now rendered in great detail even in the context of temple and tomb depictions can signify a more widespread phenomenon, but is equally proof of a different perception and representability. Increasingly, ethnicity passed for a constituent and increasingly positively viewed factor of human culture, with Libyans, Nubians, Africans, Aegeans, Hittites, Syro-Palestinians, the Sea Peoples, and desert nomads as the typical ethnicities observed.

The military system of the New Kingdom subdued the Levant and Nubia and placed them under a provincial administrative regime; tens of thousands of prisoners and other immigrants entered the Egyptian social system. Partly they constituted mercenary units of the Egyptian army (cf. Cavillier 2005) and the workforce attached to individual temples, where they were assigned to specific settlements (e.g. a "settlement of the Palestinians that his majesty had taken as prey at Gezer" under Thutmosis IV). Concrete acculturation efforts are mentioned with regard to captivated Libyans, whose language Ramesses III is said to have wiped out (stela at the Ptah sanctuary near Deir el-Medina). The resettlement of populations – Palestinians to Nubia, Nubians to Palestine – was employed as a foreign policy device in a deliberate attempt to weaken cultural identity that could threaten Egypt's hegemony; this is known from several New Kingdom documents, most recently one of Akhenaten's letters unearthed at Kumidi/Kamid el-Loz. Foreign mercenaries in the later Ramesside age settled on fiefs of land assigned to them as a remuneration for their service. Foreign specialists in high-grade pyrotechnic industries, for the production of, among other things, weaponry, settled and worked in the respective manufacturing quarters of the great cities (e.g. Pi-Ramesse/Qantir, cf. Pusch 1993). While neither the total number of individually known foreigners in the New Kingdom nor the professional repertoire attested for them exceeds the evidence of the Middle Kingdom, the advantage of the New Kingdom records lies in some well-documented individual cases where personal biographies and cultural attitudes can be studied in more detail. Within the means (and perhaps constrictions) of cultural expression at their disposal, they appear almost completely Egyptianized. In the Book of the Dead papyrus for Maiherpri, who is an exemplary case of a foreigner educated at the court as one of the ḥrd.w. n kȝp, "children of the Kap," and who received the privilege of a burial in the Valley of the Kings, the owner's Nubian background is revealed only in his deliberate choice of depicting him with dark skin (which is confirmed by the preserved mummy of Maiherpri) and minor items from the tomb equipment which would not, however, be conclusive in themselves. The only indication of a foreign descent of the Amarna period vizir Abd'el, whose tomb (with the additional burials of his wife and son) was unearthed at the Bubasteion cliff at Saqqara, is his Semitic name, "Servant of El," whereas tomb architecture and funerary equipment are entirely Egyptian (Zivie 1990). A limited number of around twenty cases allow an insight into the integration history of elite families over several generations, with representatives from the military, state administration, and priesthood (Schneider 2006).

Although the influx of foreigners into state service can be assumed to have been considerable, actual positive evidence is restricted, contrary to what Helck (1971:586; 1986:70f.) has perceived as excessive foreign infiltration of Ramesside state administration (cf. Schneider 2006). Even in cases of a high quota, the impact of acculturation and the predominant importance of profession and status would have meant that ethnicity in itself would not have been a major political factor. The importance of foreigners in New Kingdom Egypt can be indirectly inferred from cases of cultural innovation where the presence of foreigners transferring or implementing cultural knowledge has been suggested. This implies the domains of weaponry and warfare, glass and metal industries, textiles and dyeing, wood working and ship building, but is equally plausible in the case of religious and literary transfers (cf. Schneider 2003b, 2003c). A symbol of the impact of these cultural interactions is the presence of Minoan wall paintings at the site of Tell el-Dabaa which are now dated to the reign of Thutmosis III (Bietak 1999, 2000; Bietak et al. 2007).

The First Millennium BCE

The issue of foreignness has always been at the forefront of Egyptological attention with regard to the first millennium BCE, whose political history was so markedly characterized by foreign dominions (see Vittmann 2003). The visible structural changes of Egyptian statehood and culture raised the question whether it was the foreign rulers who imposed alien structures on Egyptian state and society, or whether the foreign rulers were Egyptianized and changes were contingent on different factors. Egyptological convention has distinguished between two varieties of foreign rule, the Libyan and Kushite rulers (= 21st–25th Dynasties), believed to be thoroughly Egyptianized in contrast to more genuinely "foreign" Persian and Greek rule. The 26th or Saite Dynasty was credited with foreign (Libyan) descent but was never judged to have been a foreign dominion proper. The received assumption of Libyans and Kushites as culturally assimilated ruling elites that did not constitute foreign dominions has, however, been put into doubt since the mid-1980s (Jansen-Winkeln 2000; cf. Jansen-Winkeln 1999, 2002).

The debate can be seen as exemplary for the complexity of culture in the Egyptian Late Period. Arguments in favor of the Libyans and Kushites being Egyptianized point to the fact that they considered Egyptian culture as superior, officially adopting Egyptian religion, and using the Egyptian writing system and language. However, this official display does not need to correspond to their actual ethnicity (e.g. whether they really possessed a knowledge of spoken Egyptian). Arguments adduced in favor of the Libyans' foreignness point to their emphasis of ethnic markers. They adhered to Libyan names; continued to call themselves "chieftains of the Libyans" and "foreigners" (ḫꜣstjw); Libyan local princes were depicted with the Libyan feather on their head, even when acting as Egyptian priests; and titles combined traditional Egyptian and Libyan functions ("high priest and chieftain of the Libyans"). The most obvious characteristic adduced in favor of their rule being foreign is the so-called "Libyan" state structure, the new feudal order of state (Jansen-Winkeln 1999). This order was characterized by a loose federation of separate political entities, defined personally (as depending on a prince and the loyalty towards him) rather than by existing institutions; it was based on a military aristocracy in which the class of warriors was attached to the chieftain in loyalty and fiefs were granted to vassals in return for the loyalty towards the king; the religious domain was incumbent upon the Egyptians. Counterarguments point to the difficulty the assessment of foreignness poses in the first millennium. In the New Kingdom and the Libyan period, ethnicity was a positive marker (Baines 1996) which could be displayed more easily than in earlier times without a loss in prestige. Could the Libyans be no less Egyptian than the Hyksos or Amenemhat I who stemmed from the Nubian frontier, but could show their ethnicity openly whereas earlier it had to be concealed with regard to the prevailing culture? A second argument would point to the more general breakdown of traditional models of statehood all over the Eastern Mediterranean whereby the Libyan period particularism would have been induced by the new economic situation rather than Libyan traditions, a symptom of a larger crisis which would have occurred equally without the Libyans. Numerous changes in the cultural repertoire are ascribed to the Libyans: for example, the fuzzy demarcation between royal and non-royal persons; and new forms of burial (small tombs within the temple precinct; burial of private individuals initially in mass graves or usurped older tombs). These changes can be explained both externally (as derived from Libyan tribal orientations) and internally (as a consequence of Egyptian religious and socio-economic developments) and would offer an alternative to Jansen-Winkeln's assumption of a culture rupture (Jansen-Winkeln 1999, 2000). While the Libyan period has been singled out here as a model case, the complexity of assessing the impact of foreign influence and foreigners in Egypt is equally evident in the Kushite 25th Dynasty and Egypt's increasing Hellenization from the seventh century onwards.

Case Study: Tell el-Dabaa and the Hyksos

Evaluations of the Hyksos have been affected extensively by the state of evidence. The scarcity of source material preserved from the Hyksos themselves and from Lower Egypt in the Second Intermediate Period disprivileged their standing in the debate. The biased view of Egyptian tradition whereby an invasion of Barbarians subjugated Egypt and destroyed its temples has been uncritically followed by Egyptologists who relied heavily on the victorious Theban side. As Kuhrt has put it: "The eventual Egyptian success against them [the Hyksos], which led to the emergence of the New Kingdom, was commemorated by a triumphalist rhetoric that reviled the rule of the Hyksos as irreligious and destructive. ... Serious problems, created by chronological uncertainties and a dearth of contemporary, less emotive sources, beset attempts to gain a more balanced picture of the period" (Kuhrt 1995:173; on modern judgments, cf. Schneider 1998).

New evidence on the cultural background of the Hyksos has come to light mainly from the site of their capital Avaris/Tell el-Dabaa since excavations by the Austrian Archaeological Institute started there in 1966, while other finds have contributed to the increase in evidence. Fragments of what seems to have been the depiction of Ahmose's campaign against the Hyksos were uncovered at the king's Abydos cenotaph in 1993 (Harvey 1994). A text found during Darnell and Darnell's Luxor-Farshut Desert Road Survey (2002:107–119) in the Wadi el-Hol idealizes the military life of a Theban ruler in his struggle against the Asiatics, while a text discovered by Davies (2003) at Elkab speaks about the dramatic invasion of Nubians to the region of Elkab under the 17th Dynasty.

The site of Avaris (for the following cf. Bietak 1996 and bibliography at www. auaris.at/html/bibliographie.html), originally founded by the 12th Dynasty as a pioneer settlement east of the Pelusiac branch of the Nile, has seen a repeated influx of population groups from Palestine (Forstner-Müller and Müller 2006). A massive immigration at the turn of the 12th and 13th Dynasties seems to have consisted of soldiers, sailors, and ships' carpenters working on behalf of the Egyptian state. They used Egyptian-type pottery, while the weapons attested in more than 50 percent of the male burials (battle axes, daggers, javelins) are of a Palestinian–Syrian origin. Levantine traditions were upheld by the settlers both in the domestic architecture (North Syrian central room house or *Mittelsaalhaus*, broadroom house or *Breitraumhaus*) and in funerary beliefs (cemeteries located by the houses; burial of pairs of donkeys by the tombs). A prominent individual of foreign origin is an Asiatic official of the kingdom of Avaris who possessed an Egyptian monumental tomb with chapel and the aforementioned Syrian *Mittelsaalhaus* as his probable residence. The fragments of his limestone statue betray distinct markers of his ethnicity (red mushroom-shaped hair dress, yellow skin color: Schiestl 2006).

A merger of Egyptian and Levantine cultural registers is also visible in the 13th-Dynasty palatial precinct of the following (younger) layer G4. Its garden contained six Egyptian tombs (subterranean burial chamber, chapel as superstructure) which served for the burial of Asiatics, evidenced again by donkey burials and the funerary equipment of tomb m/18 – no. 3 (javelins, Syrian dagger). The latter tomb belonged to an official identified by an amethyst scarab as a "principal of foreign lands and caravan leader" (or "ruler of Palestine": Martin 1998), Sobekemhat, while another tomb owner's titles – seal bearer of the Lower Egyptian king, chief steward – are conventionally Egyptian. Minoan pottery and an Aegean gold pendant indicate relations with the Minoan civilization. The subsequent stratum G testifies to a resettling of the site after the palace had been razed, mainly by woodworkers, because numerous molds for the manufacture of woodworking tools were found. Around 1720/1710 BCE, this settlement with small houses and partly warrior burials comes to an abrupt end due to an epidemic evidenced by emergency burials. Stratum F also features the existence of Palestinian and Egyptian cultural traits side by side: for example, the direct attachment of Houses for the Dead (*Totenhäuser*) to Egyptian residential houses, an increase of Levantine pottery, and the occurrence of tombs with weapons. Fibulae point to Canaanite dresses. A large, typologically Near Eastern temple measuring more than 30 m in length is built in the upper city, which had been abandoned during the epidemic. This sacral precinct was complemented during the time of the following stratum E/3 by a Syrian broadroom temple (*Breithaustempel*) and an Egyptian *ka* house at the beginning of the 14th Dynasty, most probably by King Nehesi, as two door-jambs with his name indicate. Huge offering pits and a renewal of the main temple attest to the fact that there was a continuous cult in this temple until the end of the Hyksos period. Young female servants are buried together with the tomb owners in the cemetery adjacent to the *ka* house. One of the officials of foreign origin buried here is an Asiatic deputy treasurer in front of whose tomb five donkeys were interred.

During the last century of its existence, the city witnessed a significant expansion. This urban background represented the basis from which the Hyksos of the 15th Dynasty extended their kingdom. As can be demonstrated by their names (with the exception of Apopi, which is an Egyptian "babble name" [lallative]), their language of origin was a Canaanite dialect of Northwest Semitic (Schneider 1998). Numerous contemporary rulers of the so-called 14th/16th Dynasties bore equally Northwest Semitic personal names; a possible earlier ruler of Palestinian origin is Chendjer in the 13th Dynasty, although the interpretation of his name remains doubtful (Schneider 2003a). The Hyksos' and other kinglets' ascension to power was an indigenous phenomenon after the collapse of the 13th Dynasty's central authority (for an overview of the literature, see Schneider 1998), occurring in regions of the Delta that incidentally had a population of partly Palestinian origin. Styling it as an invasion by impious foreigners is the product of a later misrepresentation and cannot claim any authenticity. However, the fierceness of the victor's reaction is apparent from two execration pits with killed individuals from Avaris in a stratum dating to the reign of Ahmose. In one of them (locus 1055), three male skulls were found; in the other (locus 1016), two male skeletons lying face down (Fuscaldo 2003).

Scarce though it is, the existing evidence suffices to show that the Hyksos upheld traditions of Egyptian kingship and culture, such as monumental hiero-glyphic epigraphy (door-jamb of Sikru-haddu) or a wider cult policy than ascribed to the Hyksos by the 18th Dynasty, including the worship of Ra and Sobek (Morenz 1996:164) apart from Seth. The most striking monument in this respect is a scribal palette given by the Hyksos Apapi to a scribe Atju on which the king expresses his cultural and royal self-understanding (Goedicke 1988; Morenz

1996:167–170). The Hyksos describes himself as instructed by Thoth and Seshat, as the living portrayal of the sun god (the first attestation), as a ruler who cares for humankind and abides by *maat*. He appears in this document as the most orthodox Egyptian, the very opposite of the Barbarian the Thebans accused him of being. This image of an erudite Egyptian king is further corroborated by papyri of the late Hyksos period (some of those copied at Avaris, such as the mathematical Papyrus Rhind) that testify to the appreciation of literature and of religious and scientific texts in the Hyksos residence (Morenz 1996:159, 163ff.).

The excavation of Avaris has been most influential for our understanding not merely of the history of Egypt between the Middle and the New Kingdom, but of the mechanisms of culture. It has uncovered a model frontier city where a complex cultural interface of Egyptian and Palestinian traditions, created and enacted by a mixed border population, became visible. The 15th-Dynasty Hyksos, as its political exponents who extended their authority towards the traditional center of Egypt from this fringe community, appear to have by and large abided by the traditional tenets of Egyptian kingship. If later traditions of the New Kingdom and the first millennium style them as impious foreign rulers, then this is only by a deliberate alteration of accepted rules of cultural acceptance in the interest of political and religious motives. It bears vivid witness to the tensions between divergent perceptions of foreignness and identity in the mid-second millennium, and reflects a last attempt to maintain the traditional weights of core and periphery. Avaris and the Hyksos anticipated in substance the inversion of core and periphery set into effect by Ramesside and Late Period Egypt. The availability of Egyptian kingship and its cultural authority to borderland representatives set a model realized differently in the Egypt of the first millennium. Moreover, setting Egypt's new core in the former geographical periphery marked a long-lasting structural shift in Egypt's orientation towards the Mediterranean.

REFERENCES

Alba, R. 2000 Ethnicity. *In* Encyclopedia of Sociology. 2nd edition. Vol. 2. E. F. Boretta and R. J. V. Montgomery, eds. Pp. 840–852. New York.

Alba, R., and V. Nee 1997 Rethinking Assimilation for a New Era of Immigration. International Migration Review 31:826–874.

Allen, J. P. 2008 The Historical Inscription of Khnumhotep at Dahshur: A Preliminary Report, Bulletin of the American Schools of Oriental Research 352:29–40.

Altenmüller, H., and A. M. Moussa 1991 Die Inschrift Amenemhets II. aus dem Ptah-Tempel von Memphis. Vorbericht. Studien zur Altägyptischen Kultur 18:1–48.

Assmann, J. 1996 Zum Konzept der Fremdheit im alten Ägypten. *In* Die Begegnung mit dem Fremden. Wertungen und Wirkungen in Hochkulturen vom Altertum bis zur Gegenwart (Colloquium Rauricum 4). M. Schuster, ed. Pp. 77–99. Stuttgart, Leipzig.

Baines, J. 1996 Contextualizing Egyptian Representations of Society and Ethnicity. *In* The Study of the Ancient Near East in the 21st Century. J. S. Cooper and G. M. Schwartz, eds. Pp. 339–384. The William Foxwell Albright Centennial Conference. Winona Lake, IN.

Beckerath, J. von 1964 Untersuchungen zur politischen Geschichte der Zweiten Zwischenzeit in Ägypten (ÄgFo 23). Glückstadt.

Bietak, M. 1985 Zu den nubischen Bogenschützen aus Assiut: Ein Beitrag zur Geschichte der Ersten Zwi-schenzeit. *In* Mélanges Mokhtar I (BdE 97/1-2). Pp. 87–97. Cairo.

Bietak, M. 1996 Avaris, the Capital of the Hyksos: Recent Excavations at Tell el-Dab'a. London.

Bietak, M. 1999 Une citadelle royale à Avaris de la première moitié de la XVIIIe dynastie et ses liens avec le monde minoen. *In* L'acrobate au taureau. A. Caubet, ed. Pp. 29–81. Paris.

Bietak, M. 2000 "Rich beyond the Dreams of Avaris": Tell el-Daba and the Aegean World. A Guide for the Perplexed – A Response to Eric H. Cline. The Annual of the British School at Athens 95:185–205.

Bietak, M., N. Marinatos, and C. Palivou 2007 Taureador Scenes in Tell el-Daba (Avaris) and Knossos. Untersuchungen der Zweigstelle Kairo des Österreichischen Archäologischen Instituts 27. Vienna.

Bourriau, J. 1981 Nubians in Egypt during the Second Intermediate Period: An Interpretation Based on the Egyptian Ceramic Evidence. *In* Studien zur altägyptischen Keramik. D. Arnold, ed. Pp. 25–42. Mainz am Rhein.

Bourriau, J. 1991 Relations between Egypt and Kerma during the Middle and New Kingdoms. *In* Egypt and Africa: Nubia from Prehistory to Islam. W. V. Davies, ed. Pp. 129–144. London.

Bresciani, E. 1990 Lo straniero. *In* L'uomo egiziano. S. Donadoni, ed. Pp. 235–268. Rome, Bari.

Brunet-Jailly, E. 2004 Toward a Model of Border Studies: What Do We Learn from the Study of the Canadian–American Border? Journal of Borderlands Studies 19:1–12.

Buchberger, H. 1989/1990 Zum Ausländer in der altägyptischen Literatur: Eine Kritik. Welt des Orients 20/21:5–34.

Cavillier, G. 2005 Gli Shardana nell'Egitto ramesside (BAR International Series 1438). Oxford.

Cohen, E. S. 1993 Egyptianization and the Acculturation Hypothesis: An Investigation of the Pan-grave, Kerman and C-group Material Cultures in Egypt and the Sudan during the Second Intermediate Period and Eighteenth Dynasty. Ph.D. dissertation. Ann Arbor, MI.

Darnell, J. C., and D. Darnell 2002 Theban Desert Road Survey in the Egyptian Western Desert, vol. 1: Gebel Tjauti Rock Inscriptions 1–45 and Wadi el-Hol Rock Inscriptions 1–45. Oriental Institute Publications, vol. 119. Chicago: The Oriental Institute.

Davies, W. V. 2003 Kush in Egypt: A New Historical Inscription. Sudan & Nubia 7:52–54.

Donnan, H., and T. M. Wilson 1994 An Anthropology of Frontiers. *In* Border Approaches: Anthropological Perspectives on Frontiers. H. Donnan and T. M. Wilson, eds. Pp. 1–14. Lanham. MD, New York, London.

Dupront, A. 1966 L'acculturazione: Storia e scienze umane. Turin.

Eder, C. 1995 Die ägyptischen Motive in der Glyptik des östlichen Mittelmeerraumes zu Anfang des 2. Jts. v.Chr. (OLA 71). Leuven.

Fecht, G 1956 Die ḥꜣtjw-ꜥ in Ṯḥnw, eine ägyptische Völkerschaft in der Westwüste. Zeitschrift der Deutschen Morgenländischen Gesellschaft 106(31): 37–60.

Forstner-Müller, I., and W. Müller 2006 Versuch einer sozioarchäologischen Modellbildung anhand der materiellen Kultur Tell-el Dab'as. *In* Timelines: Studies in Honour of Manfred Bietak. Vol. 1 (OLA 149). E. Czerny, I. Hein, H. Hunger, D. Melman, and A. Schwab, eds. Pp. 93–102. Leuven.

Friedman, R. 2001 Nubians at Hierakonpolis: Excavations in the Nubian Cemeteries. Sudan & Nubia 5:29–38.

Fuscaldo, P. 2003 Tell el-Dab'a: Two Execration Pits and a Foundation Deposit. Egyptology at the Dawn of the Twenty-first Century: Proceedings of the Eighth International Congress of Egyptologists, Cairo 2000. Vol. I. Z. Hawass, ed. Pp. 185-188. New York.

Glazer, N., and D. P. Moynihan 1975 Ethnicity: Theory and Experience. Cambridge, MA: Harvard University Press.

Gnirs, A. M. 2006 Das Motiv des Bürgerkriegs in Merikare und Neferti: Zur Literatur der 18. Dynastie. *In* jn.t d̲r.w – Festschrift für Friedrich Junge. Vol. I. G. Moers, H. Behlmer, K. Demuß, and K. Widmaier, eds. Pp. 207–265. Göttingen.

Goedicke, H. 1988 The Scribal Palette of Athu. Chronique d'Égypte 73:42–56.

Gordon, A. 2001 Art: Foreigners. Oxford Encyclopedia of Ancient Egypt. D. B. Redford, ed. Vol. I. Pp. 544–548. Oxford.

Gordon, M. M. 1964. Assimilation in American Life: The Role of Race, Religion, and National Origin. Oxford.

Grimm, A. 1987 Ein Käfig für einen Gefangen in einem Ritual zur Vernichtung von Feinden. Journal of Egyptian Archaeology 73:202–206.

Gundlach, R. 1994 Die Zwangsumsiedlung auswärtiger Bevölkerung als Mittel ägyptischer Politik bis zum Ende des Mittleren Reiches (Forschungen zur Antiken Sklaverei, Bd. XXVI). Stuttgart.

Harvey, S. 1994 Monuments of Ahmose at Abydos. Egyptian Archaeology 4:3–5.

Heckmann, F. 1992 Ethnische Minderheiten, Volk und Nation: Soziologie interethnischer Beziehungen. Stuttgart.

Helck, W. 1971 Die Beziehungen Ägyptens zu Vorderasien im 3. und 2. Jahrtausend v. Chr. (ÄgAbh 5). 2nd edition. Wiesbaden.

Helck, W. 1986 Politische Gegensätze im alten Ägypten (HÄB 23). Hildesheim.

Jansen-Winkeln, K. 1999 Gab es in der altägyptischen Geschichte eine feudalistische Epoche? Welt des Orients 30:7–20.

Jansen-Winkeln, K. 2000 Die Fremdherrschaften in Ägypten im 1. Jahrtausend v. Chr. Or 69:1–20.

Jansen-Winkeln, K. 2002 Ägyptische Geschichte im Zeitalter der Wanderungen von Seevölkern und Libyern. *In* Die nahöstlichen Kulturen und Griechenland an der Wende vom 2. zum 1. Jahrtausend v. Chr.: Kontinuität und Wandel von Strukturen und Mechanismen kultureller Interaktion. E. A. Braun-Holzinger, ed. Pp. 123–142. Möhnesee.

Jenkins, R. 1997 Rethinking Ethnicity: Arguments and Explorations. London.

Jenkins, R. 2001 Ethnicity: Anthropological Aspects. *In* International Encyclopedia of the Social & Behavioral Sciences. Vol. 7. N. J. Smelser and P. B. Baltes, eds. Pp. 4824–4828. Amsterdam.

Johnson, J. H. 1999 Ethnic Considerations in Persian Period Egypt. *In* Gold of Praise: Studies on Ancient Egypt in Honor of Edward F. Wente (Studies in Ancient Oriental Civilization 58). E. Teeter and J.A. Larson, eds. Pp. 211–222. Chicago.

Junker, H. 1929 Giza I. Vienna, Leipzig.

Kubisch, S. 2000 Die Stelen der I. Zwischenzeit aus Gebelein. Mitteilungen des Deutschen Archäologischen Instituts, Abteilung Kairo 56:239–265.

Kuhlmann, K. P. 2005 Der "Wasserberg des Djedefre" (Chufu 01/1): Ein Lagerplatz mit Expeditionsinschriften der 4. Dynastie im Raum der Oase Dachla. Mitteilungen des Deutschen Archäologischen Instituts, Abteilung Kairo 61:243–289.

Kuhrt, A. 1995 The Ancient Near East: c. 3000–300 BC. Vol. I. London.

Lieberson, S. 1961 A Societal Theory of Race and Ethnic Relations. American Sociological Review 26:902–910.

Lightfoot, K. G., and A. Martinez 1995 Frontiers and Boundaries in Archaeological Perspective. Annual Review of Anthropology 24:471–492.

Loprieno, A. 1988 Topos und Mimesis: Zum Ausländer in der ägyptischen Literatur (ÄgAbh 48). Wiesbaden.

Marcus, E. S. 2007 Amenemhet II and the Sea: Maritime Aspects of the Mit Rahina (Memphis) Inscription. Egypt & the Levant 17:137–190.

Martin, G. T. 1998 The Toponym Retjenu on a Scarab from Tell el-Da'ba. Ägypten und Levante 8:109–112.

Meurer, G. 1996 Nubier in Ägypten bis zum Beginn des Neuen Reiches: Zur Bedeutung der Stele Berlin 14753 (ADAIK, Ägyptologische Reihe, Bd. 13). Berlin.

Moers, G. 2003 "Unter den Sohlen Pharaos": Fremdheit und Alterität im pharaonischen Ägypten. *In* Abgrenzung – Eingrenzung: Komparatistische Studien zur Dialektik kultureller Identitätsbildung (Abhandlungen der Akademie der Wissenschaften in Göttingen, Philologisch-Historische Klasse, Dritte Folge). F. Lauterbach, F. Paul, and U. C. Sander, eds. Pp. 81–160. Göttingen.

Morenz, L. D. 1996 Beiträge zur Schriftlichkeitskultur im Mittleren Reich und in der 2. Zwischenzeit (ÄAT 29). Wiesbaden.

Nagel, J. 1994 Constructing Ethnicity: Creating and Recreating Ethnic Identity and Culture. Social Problems 41:152–176.

Newman, D. 2003 On Borders and Power: A Theoretical Framework. Journal of Borderlands Studies 18(1) (Special Issue: "Communicating Borders"):13–25.

Obsomer, C. 1995 Sésostris Ier: Étude chronologique et historique du règne. Brussels.

Panagiotopoulos, D. 2006 Foreigners in Egypt in the Time of Hatshepsut and Thutmose III. *In* Thutmose III: A New Biography. E. H. Cline, ed. Pp. 370–412. Ann Arbor, MI.

Portes, A., and M. Zhou 1993 The New Second Generation: Segmented Assimilation and Its Variants. The Annals of the American Academy of Political and Social Science 530:74–96.

Pusch, E. B. 1993 "Pi-Ramesse-geliebt-von-Amun, Hauptquartier Deiner Streitwagentruppen": Ägypter und Hethiter in der Delta-Residenz der Ramessiden. Pelizaeus-Museum Hildesheim: Die ägyptische Sammlung (Zaberns Bildbände zur Archäologie 12). Pp. 126–143. Mainz.

Raue, D. 2002 Nubians on Elephantine Island. Sudan & Nubia 6:20–24.

Ray, J. D. 1998 The Marquis, the Urchin, and the Labyrinth: Egyptology and the University of Cambridge: The Steven Glanville Lecture for 1995. *In* Proceedings of the Seventh International Congress of Egyptologists. Cambridge, 3–9 September 1995 (OLA 82). C. J. Eyre, ed. 1–17. Leuven.

Reisner, G. 1947 A History of the Giza Necropolis I. Cambridge.

Riemer, H., F. Förster, S. Hendrickx, S. Nussbaum, B. Eichhorn, N. Pöllath, P. Schönfeld, and G. Wagner 2005 Zwei pharaonische Wüstenstationen südwestlich von Dachla. Mitteilungen des Deutschen Archäologischen Instituts, Abteilung Kairo 61:291–350.

Schiestl, R. 2006 The Statue of an Asiatic Man from Tell el-Daba, Egypt. Egypt & the Levant 16:173–186.

Schneider, T. 1992 Asiatische Personennamen in ägyptischen Quellen des Neuen Reiches (OBO 114). Freiburg, Switzerland, Göttingen.

Schneider, T. 1998 Ausländer in Ägypten während des Mittleren Reiches und der Hyksoszeit (Ägypten und Altes Testamen 42). Teil 1: Die ausländischen Könige. Wiesbaden.

Schneider, T. 2003a Ausländer in Ägypten während des Mittleren Reiches und der Hyksoszeit (Ägypten und Altes Testament 42). Teil 2: Die ausländische Bevölkerung. Wiesbaden.

Schneider, T. 2003b Foreign Egypt: Egyptology and the Concept of Cultural Appropriation. Egypt and the Levant 13:155–161.

Schneider, T. 2003c Texte über den syrischen Wettergott.aus Ägypten. Ugarit Forschungen 35:605–627.

Schneider, T. 2006 Akkulturation – Identität – Elitekultur: Eine Positionsbestimmung zur Frage der Existenz und des Status von Ausländern in der Elite des Neuen Reiches. *In* Der ägyptische Hof des Neuen Reiches: Seine Gesellschaft und Kultur im Spannungsfeld zwischen Innen- und Außenpolitik (Königtum, Staat und Gesellschaft früher Hochkulturen 2). R. Gundlach and A. Klug, eds. Pp. 201–216. Wiesbaden.

Schulman, A. R. 1986 The Royal Butler Ramessessami'on. Chronique d'Égypte 122:187–202.

Smith, S. T. 2003 Wretched Kush: Ethnic Identities and Boundaries in Egypt's Nubian Empire. London.

Staubli, T. 1991 Das Image der Nomaden im Alten Israel und in der Ikonographie seiner sesshaften Nachbarn (OBO 107). Freiburg, Switzerland, Göttingen.

Stephenson, M. 2000 Development and Validation of the Stephenson Multigroup Acculturation Scale (SMAS). Psychological Assessment 128:77–88.

van den Berghe, P. 1967 Race and Racism: A Comparative Perspective. New York.

Vittmann, G. 2003. Ägypten und die Fremden in ersten vorchristlichen Jahrhundert (Kulturgeschichte der antiken Welt 97). Mainz.

Waters, M. 1990 Ethnic Options: Choosing Identities in America. Berkeley.

Wilde, H., and K. Behnert 2002 Salzherstellung im vor- und frühdynastischen Ägypten? Überlegungen zur Funktion der sogenannten Grubenkopfnägel in Buto. Mitteilungen des Deutschen Archäologischen Instituts, Abteilung Kairo 58:447–460.

Wilkinson, T. A. H. 2002 Reality versus Ideology: The Evidence for "Asiatics" in Predynastic and Early Dynastic Egypt. *In* Egypt and the Levant: Interrelations from the 4th through the Early 3rd Millennium BCE. E. C. M. van den Brink, ed. Pp. 514–520. London, New York.

Zivie, A.-P. 1990 Découverte à Saqqarah: Le vizir oublié. Paris.

9

Gender in Ancient Egypt

T. G. Wilfong

The study of gender in ancient Egypt may well be said to have begun with Herodotus, who devotes a few sections of his Book II on Egypt to an examination of gender roles and relations (e.g. II: 35–36, 46, 60, and 64; see Lloyd 1976:146–159, 272–276, 287–291). Like so much of his Book II, Herodotus' notes on gender reflect his basic presentation of Egypt as exotica; he was primarily concerned with showing Egyptian gender roles and relations to be the opposite of those in Greece and thus presented his material in such a way as to make this point. But Herodotus worked in ways not dissimilar to those of modern scholars on gender: he proceeded from the evidence that he had available to make generalizations, and then theorized on the reasons behind what he found in his sources. Moreover, Herodotus' areas of concern – gender in the home, in family relations, in religion, in the marketplace – predict to some extent the preoccupations of modern scholars of gender, and outline some of the areas in which archaeology can use gender to improve our understanding of ancient Egypt.

Gender is, in its most basic sense, the set of social constructions relating to, arising from, and imposed upon biological sex. Although often used as a synonym for biological "sex" or even "women," the category of "gender" goes well beyond either of these (for gender in general, see the survey in Meade and Wiesner-Hanks 2004). Historically, the study of the wider category of gender developed from feminist research devoted to restoring women to a history from which they had often been excluded. Feminist historians came to realize that this was not necessarily enough: women needed to be considered within a larger context of gendered relations and roles, and the basic category of "women" itself could be simplistic and reductive, as its meaning shifted in response to social, cultural, and even biological factors. An important moment in gender studies came with the publication of feminist historian Joan Scott's "Gender: A Useful Category of Historical Analysis" (Scott 1986); the priorities that this essay outlines have proven extremely prescient in terms of the concerns of scholarship on gender today. Gender does not exist in isolation, though, and Scott had already begun to envision gender as part of a larger group of categories (including class or status, race or ethnicity, and age) essential for historians in any field. Although research on gender has gone far beyond the immediate program outlined in Scott's article (note, for example, the problems with the category of gender itself summarized in Meskell 1999:67–77), it remains deeply indebted to its insights and foresights. Scott's area of concern was modern history, but her article can still be read with great profit by those who study in gender in ancient Egypt.

Egyptian evidence for gender is complex and extensive: the Egyptians presented themselves in specifically gendered ways through a complex system of gendered divisions that, for the most part, followed on the divisions of biological sex (Robins 2001). The language of the Egyptians was gendered, and texts provide much of the important evidence for gender, helped by the language and writing systems' gender-specific nature. The visual representations that the Egyptians made of themselves are marked for gender in many ways: physical manifestations of biological sex, cultural gender markers (clothing and accessories, hair, for which see Robins 1999), gendered color code for skin (usually dark reddish brown for men, yellow or light brown for women), and a status-based size and position coding that can reflect gender difference (Robins 1994). The archaeological record reveals complex gendered differences in the material culture – gendered artifacts, practices, and spaces, as well as the physical remains of the ancient Egyptians themselves. This array of evidence for gender in ancient Egypt, though, is frequently ambiguous and often hard to interpret as a whole; it has been more common to focus on a single area of investigation: women. Even the specific study of women in ancient Egypt is a relatively new endeavor, with substantial effort only appearing in the past two decades. The central work in this regard is Gay Robins's *Women in Ancient Egypt* (1993), still an essential reference, and now supplemented by over a decade's worth of more recent scholarship. Certainly, the position of women in Egypt has long been commented on as unusual and different from the situation in other ancient Mediterranean civilizations. Women did occupy a visible and autonomous position in Egypt, and this was considered characteristic of Egypt even in ancient times. As a result, there has tended to be much generalization about and idealization of women's position in ancient Egypt, especially in the more popular literature.

It is important, however, to remember that ancient Egypt was a male-dominated society: women were excluded from administration and rule in all but the most exceptional circumstances. Royal women attained their status by a relationship to a male king, and the few women who managed to rule as king did so as regent to a young son or brother and with the support of senior male officials. The most extensively documented example of a woman who ruled as king is Hatshepsut, the daughter and widow of kings who ruled as regent for her stepson Thutmose III in the 18th Dynasty (Roehrig et al. 2005). Visual and textual representations of Hatshepsut give an idea of the exceptional nature of her position as king: the varying depictions of her with female or male body and attributes and the confused (or deliberately complex) use of male and female referents in her texts attest to the challenges she faced in being a woman occupying a traditionally male position. Royal and elite women often held certain official positions of power, such as the office of God's Wife of Amun, instituted under Ahmose-Nefertari in the early New Kingdom, which gave great resources and influence to its holder and increased in power through the Third Intermediate Period (Graefe 1981). Elite women occupied formal priestly offices in earlier periods, but by the New Kingdom such offices had disappeared, and elite women mainly occupied the positions of "musician" to a particular god or goddess, a trend continuing well into the Late Period (Onstine 2005). The lives and activities of elite women were the best documented of ancient Egypt but were probably the least representative. The majority of women in ancient Egypt at all levels of society had, as primary duties, the administration of a household and the care of children, and women also worked within and outside the home in a variety of capacities, the most common being farming. Whatever their status, women in ancient Egypt shared some common roles and expectations: most ancient Egyptian women were expected to marry and have children. Marriage was a core gendered relationship in the lives of almost all ancient Egyptians; women and men of all levels of Egyptian society were expected to marry. Marriage itself, though, was a relatively informal relationship that was documented mostly by contracts to secure property or ensure support of women (especially in Demotic documents of the later periods) (Johnson 2003). Parents were often involved in initiating and facilitating marriages, which tended to take place within local class and occupational groups, but both men and women could have input in their own choice of partner. Women had a number of property and inheritance rights in the context of marriage (Pestmann 1961). Divorce was, at least in the periods for which we have good documentation, relatively easy and common, and its frequency could lead to a complex of relationships from successive marriages. In spite of the relative informality of marriage and ease of divorce, the married household was a central social unit in ancient Egypt. Within this unit, motherhood was an important role for women, with the precedent and model of the goddess Isis as guide and aid. Much of Egyptian medicine and magic was related, directly or indirectly, to facilitating motherhood in some way (e.g. Nunn 1996:191–197). There were women who lived independently of the expectations of marriage and motherhood, but these were rare, or are at least poorly attested and understood.

The necessary attempts to restore the lives of women to the historical record have left the roles of men in ancient Egypt, and concepts of maleness and masculinity, relatively unexamined, although men are as much a part of the overall concept of gender as women. One could argue that Egyptology in the past was almost entirely a study of ancient Egyptian men and that further work is unnecessary, but the study of "men" as a gendered category important for a wider understanding of Egyptian society needs to be considered. The study of men in the context of gender studies has recently come to prominence, but it initially raised concerns that the rise of "masculinity studies" could become a potential threat to decades of progress in feminist research. However, an emerging body of theoretical literature on men from a gendered perspective addresses these concerns and makes it clear that masculinity studies has great potential (see, e.g., Connell 2005). For ancient Egypt, the topic is very new (though see already Meskell and Joyce 2003:95–127), but, given the predominance of men in much of ancient Egyptian life, masculinity studies have much to offer the study of gender in ancient Egypt (see Wilfong 2007 for a general discussion of masculinity studies and Byzantine Egypt). The category of "man" was largely a normative one in ancient

Egypt and there were privileges and advantages to being a man in Egyptian society. But the men of ancient Egypt were also subject to a range of instabilities and anxieties: economic class, social position, ethnicity, and other factors could affect any man's situation. Social, political, and familial relations between men, as well as relations between men and women, were fraught with potential threats to status and identity. Men lived within gendered constraints and expectations just as complex as those for women: there were things that men did (and did not do) that reflected and affected Egyptian concepts of maleness and masculinity. The gendered expectations for a king (to rule, to father a male heir to succeed him, to play the roles of both Osiris and Horus, etc.) might differ in specifics and scale from those of an official, a scribe, a priest, a soldier, or a farmer, but there were common elements throughout. Men at all economic levels were subject to gendered expectations: to marry, beget children, and support a family; men were expected to fill their male roles and positions in society as their fathers did before them. The potential for failure in any of these male roles and expectations lurks beneath text and image in ancient Egypt, only occasionally manifesting itself in visible anxieties.

Concentration on men and women might suggest that these were the only gender categories that existed in ancient Egypt, but the situation was more complex. Although gender categories often followed along the lines of biological sex (which modern genetics shows is not always so clear-cut itself, cf. Meskell 1999:73–74), there was latitude for movement between gender categories in exceptional circumstances. Men could become "women", as Bata in the New Kingdom Tale of Two Brothers describes himself after cutting off his own penis (Lichtheim 1976:207), while women could take on masculine attributes, such as the occasional images of goddesses with royal beards (e.g. Niwinski 1989:227), representations of the goddess Mut with an erect penis (Leitz 2002:251), or the images of Queen Hatshepsut with a male body (Keller 2005). Ambiguous body types in representational art could also have religious significance, such as the feminized but male "fecundity figures" (Baines 1985b) or the representations of Akhenaten that combine feminine and masculine traits (Montserrat 2000:42–48). But intermediate or "third" gender categories also existed in ancient Egyptian thought: the eunuchs and hermaphrodites known from other Mediterranean cultures (Vittmann 1998; Wilfong 1997:87–89), but also uniquely Egyptian categories that are only now beginning to be understood (DePauw 2003). In looking at evidence for gender in ancient Egypt, it is also easy to miss instances in which gender is ambiguous or absent, yet such cases do occur. Although representations of humans in ancient Egypt are almost always graphically gendered through details of body and costume, there is a subset of material that seems to be deliberately ungendered. The New Kingdom anthropoid "ancestor busts" from Deir el-Medina include good examples, not surprising since they could serve as points of contact for both male and female deceased relatives (Friedman 1994:114–117). Burials of the dead sometimes contain gendered ambiguities or confusions (e.g. mismatched sex of coffins and bodies), while funerary representations of the dead in an idealized state, particularly those of anthropoid coffins, often also show no signs of gender (Wilfong 1997:17–19). The gender of the dead for much of ancient Egyptian history is subject to ambiguities of various kinds: although the dead participate in gendered activities (including sexual intercourse, for which see Willems 1996:311–314), and are shown as gendered in two-dimensional art, the ambiguous three-dimensional figures and the wide reference to all dead (in the Pharaonic period) by way of a male god's name (Osiris) may reflect an ambivalence not yet fully understood.

Much of the foregoing comes to us through textual and representational evidence; the archaeology of gender in ancient Egypt is a relatively new endeavor that is only beginning to yield its results. The potential for archaeological investigation of gender in ancient Egypt is enormous – indeed, archaeological evidence is crucial for an overall understanding of gender in ancient Egypt. Given that the vast majority of Pharaonic period archaeological remains so far found in Egypt are funerary in some way – cemeteries, tombs, individual burials – funerary remains are, for now at least, the most extensive source for the archaeological examination of gender in ancient Egypt. Not only does study of mortuary material get us closest to the physical remains of the ancient Egyptians themselves, but the Egyptians' own emphasis on mortuary practice also guarantees the significance of this material.

In burials, bodies provide the most direct evidence of biological sex. Embalmed bodies are, of course, the most easily sexed, although the sexing of adult skeletons can be done with a high degree of probability in all but the most atypical of cases (Compton 1997). Likewise, embalmed bodies can usually yield the most information about gender issues, through the preservation of skin and other tissues, although again skeletal remains can be impressively informative (e.g. Nunn 1996:64–81). The Egyptians aspired, through most of the Pharaonic period and beyond, to the preservation of the body through mummification, and there are an enormous number of embalmed bodies to survive from ancient Egypt. The investigation of mummies through X-ray, dissection, CT-scans, and other forms of examination reveals a wealth of detail about health and means of death that can have gendered implications. Simple examination can reveal such obviously gendered conditions as circumcision (Nunn 1996:169–171) or recent pregnancy, while more detailed investigation and analysis can reveal a variety of conditions and diseases that are gender-related in some way. Further, the post-mortem treatment of bodies often reveals gendered practices (e.g. the gilding of nipples and genitals in Late Period mummies: Riggs 2005:123–124). In addition to their roles as sources of information on biological sex and gender-related health issues, human remains can also provide a wide range of information on gendered occupations, activities, and traumas as manifested in the body. Such data are only beginning to be the subject of investigation in general, and are relatively under-exploited for the study of gender, but promise to be a significant area for future work. Most occupations involving any kind of repeated physical activity leave traces in the body, and analysis of such traces correlated with gender could prove highly significant. Non-occupational activities and overall life style could likewise manifest themselves in bodies in ways that gender could help illuminate (Nunn 1996:56–57, 171–178). Analysis of injuries found in ancient Egyptian human remains can give a wealth of information about gendered activities and vulnerabilities. Battle-related injuries are perhaps the most widely studied forms of physical injuries from the ancient world; such injuries manifest themselves mostly in male bodies, not surprisingly given the exclusively male make-up of the military in ancient Egypt. Examples such as the mass burial of soldiers of the 11th Dynasty at Thebes (Winlock 1945) show the kinds of pre- and post-mortem injuries that men were subject to as a result of their military activities. Battle-type injuries, however, are not entirely limited to men; one can note the group of bodies from Kerma of Middle Kingdom date examined by Joyce Filer in which men and women in nearly equal numbers exhibit skull injuries of a type consistent with battle wounds (Filer 1997:64). A number of interpretations can be applied to a case of this sort, and other factors (status, occupation, etc.) may be in play as well, but clearly there is much material here for gendered interpretation. Future gendered analysis of injuries in human remains will want to be aware of the possibilities of gendered patterns of abuse. Certain kinds of physical trauma which are associated with spousal abuse in modern populations may well have analogues in ancient remains: forearm breakage, for example, which is noted in the Abydos Middle Cemetery, may have resulted from attempts to ward off blows (Richards 2005:168).

Beyond physical remains, the most common kinds of gendered analysis of mortuary contexts involve the study of grave goods, often done in conjunction with the study of associated human remains. By determining the biological sex of the body, one can make gendered associations based on the contents of individual burials. This can lead to comparison of burials across groups, cemeteries, even different sites involving the interpretation and evaluation of grave goods. In recent years, a number of studies of Predynastic and Early Dynastic burials have begun to look seriously at the implications of gender and grave goods. Given the relative paucity of textual evidence from these periods, such archaeological evidence is often the only source of information on gender. Analysis of early funerary contexts can be done on the level of individual burials (e.g. Burns 1995 for a single grave at Gurob), a cemetery (Savage 2000 for cemetery N7000 at Naga ed-Der), or across a range of cemeteries (as in Hassan and Smith 2002). These examples have the value of including non-elite material, but burials and cemeteries at any status level and of any period in Egyptian history can be studied in this way. One could take, as a nearly random example for analysis, two intact New Kingdom burials from Garstang's excavations at el-Arabeh, E178 and E294 (Garstang 1902:26–27 and pls. 18–20). In E294, a man and woman were found buried together in a stone sarcophagus also containing a number of grave goods (mostly pottery, with a few scarabs and tools); the excavation report notes two potentially significant facts for a gendered analysis – more grave goods are associated with the woman than the man, and one of the pots bears an inscription with a Semitic name. E178 is a group burial, again in a stone sarcophagus, of two women and a man. The contents again are mostly pottery, with the addition of jewelry (including a scarab showing the god Bes) and a pottery vessel in human form. In the absence of a full record or access to the finds themselves, we are left with speculation, but these two burials raise the kinds of questions about gender that archaeologists will want to ask of other finds – what are the reasons for the gendered disparities in grave goods, and what are the gendered relations between the individuals in these burials?

By far the most wide-ranging and sophisticated gendered analysis of non-royal burials in ancient Egypt is to be found in the work of Lynn Meskell on the cemeteries of the New Kingdom workmen's village at Deir el-Medina (Meskell 1999:esp. 136–215, and many other publications). Meskell has performed exhaustive and theoretically informed analyses of individual burials, groups of burials, cemetery areas, and the Deir el-Medina burial ground as a whole, examining them not only for gender, but also for class, ethnicity, and age – indeed one of the most useful contributions of this study is to show how all of these factors are interrelated and need to be studied in connection with each other. Meskell's study showed status variations in different parts of the cemetery, suggestive patterns in child burials, and varying associations of gender and grave goods. One of her objectives is to go beyond generalization about populations to look at the lives of individuals from this evidence, and the examples pursued in detail raise fascinating questions about gender roles and relations at Deir el-Medina.

Elite burials, of course, provide much more information than non-elite burials and can be especially revealing when examined for gender-related issues. Stuart Tyson Smith's exhaustive catalogue of intact elite Theban burials of the 17th–18th Dynasties (1992) shows a significant disparity in the grave goods that can be assigned to men versus those assignable to women. This is precisely what one would expect given the greater status and wealth of men, but the specifics of the gendered property and, perhaps just as significantly, what things were presumably held in common are less predictable and make for interesting investigation. Lynn Meskell (1998) has taken one of these burials, that of Kha and Merit, and subjected it to a much more exhaustive analysis of the gendered and common goods, filtered through her wider study of the Deir el-Medina burials as a whole. Elite burials of the post-New Kingdom era reflect significant gendered changes in practice and also, perhaps, in belief about the afterlife. More and more, women came to be buried independently of men and identified independently of men as well. One finds an increase in funerary papyri specifically for women and grave goods made for women without reference to male relatives. Although issues of decorum had long dictated that women appear alone in funerary monuments of which they were the primary beneficiary (Robins 1993:172), after the New Kingdom there are so many more examples of women appearing alone that there seems to be a wider social tendency at work. Theban elite burials of the Third Intermediate Period illustrate the increasing separation of men and women in the funerary realm. Men still dominated in terms of quality and number of funerary equipment and treatment, but elite women came to have more individual funerary material than before and one finds many more individual burials of women than previously. This trend among elite burials carries on through the Late Period and into the Graeco-Roman period, when burials and funerary equipment reflect a highly gendered transformation of the deceased into the afterlife (Riggs 2005:41–94).

Royal burials followed many of the trends in elite burials, but of course had their own highly distinctive features. The best-preserved royal burial of the Pharaonic period is evidently that of the 18th-Dynasty king Tutankhamun, whose small tomb was packed with a wide variety of material that is relevant for the study of gender (for the tomb of Tutankhamun in general, see Reeves 1990). Tutankhamun's own body was prepared for eternity in a highly gendered way, with his penis bound erect to symbolize his procreative and thus regenerative powers in the afterlife, and the representations of Tutankhamun in the tomb are explictly gendered as well. Tutankhamun's surviving clothing, jewelry, and regalia were all gendered, and specific to his role as king. But the king did not rest alone in his tomb – he was accompanied by two mummified female fetuses or neonates – possibly his own children – and hundreds of images of gods, goddesses, and members of the royal family that are gendered in specific functional ways. Protective goddesses, often winged, surround the king's mummy on all sides in jewelry, coffins, sarcophagus, and shrines, as well as his viscera in an elaborate canopic ensemble where the goddesses are repeated again and again. The protective significance of the goddesses in Tutankhamun's tomb is a highly gendered trait: enclosing protective activity is largely the domain of female deities, and Tutankhamun's tomb reveals a most complex protective system. Conversely, the male gods that accompany the dead king refer to his procreative and regenerative powers, or they offer protection of a more pointed and direct kind, as in the image of the god Anubis guarding the "Treasury." The images of Tutankhamun and his wife Ankhsenamun together, in particular those on the small gold shrine, show the king and his wife enacting gendered roles in a variety of domestic and ritual situations that reflect both real-life relationships and afterlife aspirations. Artifacts relate to the king's relationships with female relatives – the balls of hair and mud that may commemorate the king's marriage and the lock of hair belonging to the king's grandmother Tiye (Fletcher and Montserrat 1997). Other family-related artifacts attest to Tutankhamun's extended family heritage through male and female relatives – personal items of Amarna princesses versus the "official" productions of earlier kings. One could go on with a gendered analysis of Tutankhamun's burial almost indefinitely – it is an extraordinarily rich field.

Burials are not always so easily interpreted in terms of gender. An example of the complexities of gendered archaeological investigation of Egyptian royal burials can be found in the well-known post-Amarna royal burial in KV55. This tomb, discovered by excavator Theodore M. Davis in 1907, might have almost been set up as a cautionary example of the pitfalls of gendered interpretations of burials. Davis found, near the entrance of this tomb, a dismantled gilded shrine belonging to Queen Tiye, and, moving from this fact, he read each successive find in the tomb as further indication of Tiye as the ultimate occupant of the coffin found in the burial chamber. A compliant doctor identified the human remains in the coffin as female, and Davis published the find as *The Tomb of Queen Tîyi* in 1910. Of course, these remains have long since been conclusively identified as male, and the burial as that of Akhenaten (or, less likely, that of his putative successor Smenkhare) with a miscellaneous collection of grave goods salvaged from a variety of male and female Amarna royals. But it is perhaps wrong to fault Davis overmuch, given the atypical nature of his find. The shrines of Queen Tiye (then of a type unparalleled, but subsequently mirrored in the set of shrines in the tomb of Tutankhamun) made his initial assumption that KV55 was the burial-place of Tiye entirely plausible. His interpretation of the burial's vulture necklace as a queen's vulture crown is understandable given this preconception, the frequency with which royal women wore vulture headdresses, and the relative lack of good parallels to this class of artifact prior to the subsequent discovery of Tutankhamun's tomb. The female-headed canopic jars (probably made for Queen Kiya), the other objects inscribed with other names, and the apparent lack of a king's beard on the coffin must have seemed like further confirmation of his identification. The post-Amarna effacement of names and images merely added to the overall confusion of the find. Davis's mistaken identification, which has had wide-reaching repercussions, is a useful cautionary example: the excavator must be sensitive to issues of gender in the course of excavation, but not draw conclusions until all of the evidence is accounted for.

Another royal burial of the 18th Dynasty with strong gendered elements has likewise provoked confusion, as much from modern gendered expectations as from the problems of the find itself, and this is the Theban burial of three foreign wives of Thutmose III (Lilyquist 2003). The problems with this find begin, of course, with the fact that it first came to be known from artifacts that started to appear on the antiquities market in 1916 – what seemed to be a substantial portion of the burial ensembles of three women described as wives of Thutmose III. The bulk of the artifacts were acquired by the Metropolitan Museum of Art in New York and were published by H. E. Winlock as *The Treasure of Three Egyptian Princesses* in 1948. This material inspired speculation and invoked charged narratives of harem life that reflected more twentieth-century gendered expectations than the mundane realities of the lives of royal women in the 18th Dynasty. But the find was not as simple as it initially appeared: nearly a third of the artifacts attributed to this find have turned out to be modern forgeries, and it was only in 1988 that the site of the find itself was properly investigated. Christine Lilyquist's 2003 definitive publication of this material finally places the artifacts in the context of their findspot and also allows a more precise understanding of the women originally buried with this material – neither Egyptian nor "princesses," they were minor wives of Thutmose III with Semitic names. The recent publication of this important find invites a wider gendered analysis of the women, their circumstances, and their time in a way that is only now possible.

Even without grave goods or human remains, mortuary sites can reveal rich gendered analysis, especially the elaborately decorated and programmed tombs of elites and royalty. Such tombs sometimes show an interplay of image and text that reveals the gendered afterlife expectations or aspirations of the tomb owner. David O'Connor (1996) has subjected the Old Kingdom tomb reliefs of Pepyankh/Heny the Black at Meir to a subtle gendered reading, which reveal Pepyankh's expected gendered roles in the afterlife as a husband and procreator and hint at the complexities of the Egyptians' understanding of post-mortem sexuality. In a similar fashion, Heather McCarthy (2002) has "read" the Theban tomb of Queen Nefertari against the representations in the queen's own small temple at Abu Simbel to show her gendered transformation in the tomb – she takes on a male procreative role to identify with Osiris and Ra for a successful afterlife rebirth and transformation. The royal tombs of New Kingdom kings themselves are often filled with images relating to the male kings' rebirth and regeneration in a gendered, procreative role. On a more mundane level, numerous elite tombs show scenes of daily life that reproduce or develop on themes of gendered relations and occupations in the afterlife as a mirror or amplification of such roles and interactions in life. Funerary representations of daily life, of course, cannot always be taken literally, and the gendered aspects of such images are sometimes open to ambiguous interpretation, perhaps none so controversially as the reliefs of the joint Old Kingdom tomb of Niankhkhnum and Khnumhotep. Its largely unparalleled scenes of the two male tomb owners kissing and embracing have led to their identification as brothers (Moussa and Altenmüller 1977), then twins (Baines 1985a), a homosexual couple (Reeder 2000), and the most recent and provocative reading (by David O'Connor: see Wilford 2005) of the two men as a pair of con-joined twins. Even in more traditional representational programs, complex gen-dered relationships can be conveyed by, for example, presence or absence of a spouse (Roth 1999). Tomb decoration is likely to continue to provide a lively area for gendered research for years to come.

For the Egyptians, tombs were "houses for eternity," but the daily life activities of ancient Egyptians and how they related to gender can better be seen in the remains of houses and related structures used by the living. Unfortunately, the archaeological investigation of the houses and, by extension, settlement sites of Pharaonic Egypt has considerably lagged behind investigation of mortuary sites. In large part this is due to nature of the sites themselves – typically under or impinged upon by modern settlements – but it is also the result of the prior emphasis of archaeological research in Egypt on funerary remains. Nonetheless, a small but significant group of settlement sites have been excavated in Egypt and, with a dramatically increased interest in settlement archaeology, this trend is likely to continue and expand. This is certainly welcome for the study of gender in ancient Egypt: many of the gender roles and relations of Egyptian society were enacted within or in connection with settlements. In addition to the houses in which individuals and families lived, worked, and interacted, settlement features such as administrative buildings, royal residences, public spaces, markets, and temples are also areas in which gender was a factor. However, most archaeological investigation and analysis has concentrated so far on houses and domestic struc-tures, and these are the most immediately appealing for the study of gender.

One of the most important excavated settlement sites of Pharaonic Egypt is Tell el-Amarna (ancient Akhetaton), the short-lived capital founded by King Akhenaten. The brief life and subsequent abandonment of the site have provided an extraordinary level of preservation and documentation that allow a wide range of investigations (Montserrat 2000:55–94). For many decades, patient and painstaking excavation has revealed a wealth of archaeological material that will ultimately provide unparalleled insights into the minutiae of daily life in an Egyptian capital city. For the study of gender, most work on the Amarna material has concentrated on houses, particularly the large, elite "villas" of the main city. These houses show considerable consistency in structure that suggests the inter-play between space and gender (Koltsida 2002). Earlier excavators tended to see spaces in the Amarna villas as reflective of a separation of men and women in domestic space roughly parallel to that found in Islamic households of the nine-teenth and twentieth centuries; more recent study, however, suggests a more subtle gendered sharing of spaces within the household (Koltsida 2002:185–188). Such conclusions cannot, of course, be made solely from the remains of the villas on the ground, but must take into consideration contemporary textual and repre-sentational evidence as well. Material culture remains abandoned in the struc-tures, however, do suggest potential gendered space uses that will repay future investigation. Moreover, the site of Amarna is important for the wide range of its domestic spaces – from palaces and the elite villas, to the middle-range and poorer dwellings – and has great potential for the investigation of gendered space across class and status levels. Although Amarna itself is somewhat atypical as a "new" settlement of short duration, its remains may show trends reflected throughout its region or even throughout Egypt as a whole.

Indeed, the majority of settlement sites to survive from Pharaonic Egypt are in some way atypical: in addition to the "planned" town at Amarna, one finds most often purpose-built communities of limited duration, primarily workers' villages. These kinds of settlements tend to survive and be more accessible archaeologically in ways that "regular" towns do not. In layout, however, they may not be typical of towns in Egypt in general: these settlements are usually walled or contained, of regular plan, and their houses tend to exhibit more uniformity of style, size, and plan than those of a town like that at Amarna. Workers' settlements, particularly sites constructed to house the workers constructing royal tombs at Lahun (in the Middle Kingdom) and Deir el-Medina (in the New Kingdom), have proven particularly rich in material culture remains and in surviving architecture, in part because they were relatively short-lived and ultimately abandoned like Amarna. These sites have also yielded a large amount of textual material documenting their daily activities as well as the wider concerns of their inhabitants – an important supplement to the archaeological material, especially as far as the study of gender is concerned.

Workers' settlements like Lahun and Deir el-Medina housed male workers and administrators along with their families; so men and women lived together and interacted in these towns in ways that illustrate gendered roles and relations. The dwellings in both of these towns tended on the whole to be compact and regular in plan; domestic space doubtless had gendered dimensions, but there was less overall space and thus probably less potential for separate gendered areas and greater likelihood of gendered patterns of sharing of space. Food preparation areas tend to have associations with women, while the reception areas near the entrance of the houses are sometimes connected with men, but there was doubtless more mixing of use within the house as a whole. Artifactual material found in context in houses can be helpful but must be read carefully. Do the caches of tools associated with male occupations found at Lahun (groups 7 and 9: Petrie 1891:12–13, 15, and pls. 13–14) suggest a gendered association with their findspots, or do the accompanying artifacts (pottery and a scarab in 7; pottery, a mirror, and jewelry in 9) suggest instead that these were caches of mixed-sex family items, left at the abandonment of the structure against a planned return? Decorated portions of houses or constructions within houses have likewise suggested gendered interpretations, but are ambiguous. The frequent use of decoration in the houses at Deir el-Medina and the not uncommon presence of a decorated feature known as a *lit clos* (Meskell 1999:99–102) almost certainly have significance for gender, but their exact meanings are not always clear and their interpretation often colored by the preconceptions of the investigator. A good example of the pitfalls of interpretation is found in the female figurines that emphasize sexual characteristics earlier known to Egyptologists as "concubines of the dead," in spite of the fact that these are commonly found in domestic contexts and often in association with women and children as well as men (Pinch 1983; Trimble 1995). Indeed, all kinds of male and female figures that emphasize sexual characteristics, usually identified as "fertility figures" and commonly found in domestic as well as temple and funerary contexts, are themselves an important source for gender but are often highly ambiguous in interpretation (Pinch 1993). A good example of the potential problems of such evidence can be found in the identification of structure S. E. VIII at Deir el-Medina as a possible "brothel" primarily on the basis of a wall painting of a dancer in the front room, doubtless also colored by the interpretation of the "Turin Erotic Papyrus" from Deir el-Medina (Omlin 1973) as showing scenes from a brothel. The sources and problems of both of these approaches are dealt with by Janaa Toivari-Viitala (2001:147–152). Often the very ambiguity of the remains seems to encourage such speculations.

Textual evidence will sometimes give clues as to the gendering of space in these workers' settlements that is not immediately apparent from the archaeological record. Thus a text reveals the existence of a gendered space that apparently existed in or outside of Deir el-Medina, and may reflect similar demarcations elsewhere. An ostracon from Deir el-Medina at Chicago refers to a location designated as "the place of women" (Wilfong 2000), apparently beyond the settlement "walls" frequently referred to in Deir el-Medina texts. This ostracon records that eight women visited this location "while they were menstruating," a clear indication of the nature of the "place of women" as a place of menstrual seclusion well attested in other premodern cultures. Absence rosters of the village workers also attest to the times of individual women's menstruation as an excuse for absence from work, presumably because of these trips to the "place of women". (See Toivari-Viitala 2001:162–168 for a comprehensive look at the evidence for menstruation at Deir el-Medina from these documents.) The data in these documents together with the coincidence of the eight women menstruating at the same time in the Chicago ostracon show extraordinary evidence of village-wide menstrual synchrony in the small, close settlement of Deir el-Medina. Although the named "place of women" is attested only at Deir el-Medina in this Chicago ostracon, other instances of menstrual space are attested in Egyptian evidence. In later periods, women's menstrual space is brought inside the house: both Greek and Coptic documents refer to the "space beneath the stairs" as being a women's space associated with menstruation (Wilfong 2002:77), and this may well reflect earlier practice that will warrant future investigation. Otherwise little is known of women's menstrual practices in ancient Egypt, and future investigators of settlement sites in Egypt should be aware of the potentials for archaeological evidence of these practices (e.g. Ehrenberg 1989:35), material that has doubtless been overlooked in the past by excavators unable or unwilling to recognize it. Indeed, it may someday be possible to locate the Deir el-Medina "place of women" in the Theban hills around the site.

Clearly workmen's villages like Lahun and Deir el-Medina provide major sources for the study of gender in ancient Egypt, but their typicality will always remain subject to debate. What seems clear from both the textual and archaeological remains of these sites, though, is that their populations maintained a gender balance comparable to that of the population of Egypt at large and that they provide useful information about gender roles and relations in Egypt in general.

This is probably true of most of the settlement sites known from ancient Egypt, but there are certain kinds of sites that were (or are thought to have been) gender-restricted in some way, and thus provide another angle on the gendered investigation of settlement sites. Military barracks, mining camps, even certain kinds of settlements for temporary workers are often thought to have been single-sex institutions, and the archaeology of such sites may confirm or dispute this idea. One might note, for example, the distinctive "galleries" found in the recent excavations of the 4th-Dynasty settlement at Giza (Lehner 2002), which are convincingly shown to have served as barracks or dormitories for up to 2000 temporary workers. All of the admittedly scant evidence for these workers suggests an all-male workforce, served and provisioned by an all-male or mixed service staff; but the distinctive form of the galleries is dictated by both the single-sex nature of the population living in them and their temporary status (i.e. most of these workers would have rotated off to live with their families). One might look at a very late (Byzantine period) example of a different sort of settlement that is often assumed to be for an all-male population – the gold-mining camp at Bir Umm Fawakhir (Meyer 2001 for the first seasons of excavation). This remote camp is made up of over a hundred small stone structures in a desert wadi off the Wadi Hammamat – in an area mined for gold as early as the New Kingdom. The standing Byzantine camp is a distinctive form of settlement unlike contemporary Nile Valley settlement sites, and some of its features could well have gendered signficance, for again we have a population commonly assumed from the available evidence to have been an all-male community. But other factors certainly contribute to the difference of this settlement: its remote location, its use of stone rather than mudbrick (owing to local availability of materials), its secured nature (with apparent guard huts and controlled access) due to the main activity of the site (mining for gold) and possibly also to the nature of its inhabitants (the miners may have also been prisoners or debtors). Although well past the Pharaonic period, Bir Umm Fawakhir points to potentials of sites of earlier periods, not the least of which being the nearby Wadi Hammamat itself. Although the Wadi Hammamat is primarily studied for the texts of its many graffiti, the presence of these texts *in situ* makes them archaeological artifacts of considerable relevance to the present study. The attestation of an (apparently) all-male desert expedition of the late 11th Dynasty, for example, in the accounts of the expedition to quarry a sarcophagus for Mentuhotep IV has potential for gendered analysis (Wadi Hammamat graffiti 110, 113, 191–192 in de Buck 1948). The striking account of the men of the expedition facing a pregnant gazelle which gives birth on the stone for the king's sarcophagus lid and is then promptly sacrificed gives a vivid vignette of the complex interplay of gender in the context of the desert landscape. Certainly, landscape archaeology in Egypt also has great promise for gender study as well.

The foregoing has been but a small sample of the kinds of gendered analysis and interpretation of archaeological material possible for Pharaonic Egypt. In many ways, this effort is still in its earliest stages – with both the excitement of discovery and the uncertainty of lack of precedent that this implies. Clearly there is much to be done by scholars interested in the archaeological study of gender in ancient Egypt, but even those archaeologists not specifically or solely interested in gender have a part to play in this endeavor. The field archaeologist will need to give greater attention to the recognition and recording of archaeological evidence for gender, while all archaeologists will want to take gender into account as a factor in wider interpretations of their data. Ultimately, gender must be understood, alongside status, class, race, ethnicity, age, and other factors, as a key component of ancient Egyptian life.

REFERENCES

Baines, J. 1985a Egyptian Twins. Orientalia 54: 461–482.

Baines, J. 1985b Fecundity Figures: Egyptian Personification and the Iconology of a Genre. Warminster: Aris & Phillips.

Burns, B. E. 1995 A Grave Group from Gurob. *In* Preserving Eternity: Modern Goals, Ancient Intentions. J. Richards and T. G. Wilfong. Pp. 28–30. Ann Arbor, MI: Kelsey Museum of Archaeology.

Compton, G. F. 1997 Determination of Biological Sex from Human Skeletal Remains. *In* Women and Gender in Ancient Egypt: From Prehistory to Late Antiquity. T. G. Wilfong, ed. Pp. 68–71. Ann Arbor, MI: Kelsey Museum of Archaeology.

Connell, R. W. 2005 Masculinities. 2nd edition. Berkeley: University of California Press.

Davis, T. M. 1910 The Tomb of Queen Tîyi. London: Archibald Constable.

de Buck, A. 1948 Egyptian Readingbook. Leiden: Nederlands Instituut voor het Nabije Oosten.

Depauw, M. 2003 Notes on Transgressing Gender Boundaries in Ancient Egypt. Zeitschrift für Ägyptische Sprache und Altertumskunde 130:49–59.

Ehrenberg, M. 1989 Women in Prehistory. London: British Museum Publications.

Filer, J. M. 1997 Ancient Egypt and Nubia as a Source of Information for Cranial Injuries. *In* Material Harm: Archaeological Studies of War and Violence. J. Carman, ed. Pp. 47–74. Glasgow: Cruithne Press.

Fletcher, J., and D. Montserrat 1997 The Human Hair from the Tomb of Tutankhamun: A Re-evaluation. *In* Proceedings of the Seventh International Congress of Egyptologists. Pp. 403–407. Leuven: Peeters.

Friedman, F. D. 1994 Aspects of Domestic Life and Religion. *In* Pharaoh's Workers: The Villagers of Deir el Medina. L. H. Lesko, ed. Pp. 95–117. Ithaca, NY: Cornell University Press.

Garstang, J. 1902 El Arábah. London: B. Quartich.

Graefe, E. 1981 Untersuchungen zur Verwaltung und Geschichte der Institution der Gottesgemahlin des Amun vom Beginn des Neuen Reiches bis zur Spätzeit. Ägyptologische Abhandlungen 37. Wiesbaden: Harrassowitz.

Hassan, F. A., and S. J. Smith 2002 Soul Birds and Heavenly Cows: Transforming Gender in Predynastic Egypt. *In* In Pursuit of Gender: Worldwide Archaeological Approaches (Gender and Archaeology Series). S. M. Nelson and M. Rosen-Ayalon, eds. Pp. 43–65. Walnut Creek, CA: AltaMira Press.

Johnson, J. H. 2003 Sex and Marriage in Ancient Egypt. *In* Hommages à Fayza Haikal (Bibliothèque d'étude 138). N. Grimal, A. Kamal, and C. May-Sheikholeslami, eds. Pp. 149–159. Cairo: IFAO.

Keller, C. A. 2005 The Statuary of Hatshepsut. *In* Hatshepsut: From Queen to Pharaoh. C. Roehrig, R. Dreyfus, and C. A. Keller. Pp. 158–173. New York: Metropolitan Museum of Art.

Koltsida, A. 2002 Male versus Female Areas in Ancient Egypt: Space and Gender in the Standard Amarna Villa. *In* SOMA 2001: Symposium on Mediterranean Archaeology

(BAR International Series 1040). G. Muskett, A. Koltsida, and M. Georgiadis, eds. Pp. 183–191. Oxford: Archaeopress.

Lehner, M. 2002 The Pyramid Age Settlement of the Southern Mount at Giza. Journal of the American Research Center in Egypt 39:27–74.

Leitz, C. 2002 Lexikon der Ägyptischen Götter und Götterbezeichnungen, Band III: p–nbw. OLA 112. Leuven: Peeters.

Lichtheim, M. 1976 Ancient Egyptian Literature. Vol. II: The New Kingdom. Berkeley: University of California Press.

Lilyquist, C. 2003 The Tomb of Three Foreign Wives of Thutmosis III. New York: Metropolitan Museum of Art.

Lloyd, A. B. 1976 Herodotus: Book II, Commentary 1–98. Leiden: Brill.

McCarthy, H. L. 2002 The Osiris Nefertari: A Case Study of Gender, Decorum and Regeneration. Journal of the American Research Center in Egypt 39:173–195.

Meade, T. A., and M. E. Wiesner-Hanks 2004 A Companion to Gender History. Oxford: Blackwell.

Meskell, L. 1998 Intimate Archaeologies: The Case of Kha and Merit. World Archaeology 29(3):363–379.

Meskell, L. 1999 Archaeologies of Social Life: Age, Sex, Class et cetera in Ancient Egypt. Oxford: Blackwell.

Meskell, L., and R. Joyce 2003 Embodied Lives: Figuring Ancient Maya and Egyptian Experience. London: Routledge.

Meyer, C. 2001 Bir Umm Fawakhir Survey Project 1993: A Byzantine Gold-Mining Town in Egypt (Oriental Institute Communications 28). Chicago: Oriental Institute Press.

Montserrat, D. 2000 Akhenaten: History, Fantasy and Ancient Egypt. London: Routledge.

Moussa, A. M., and H. Altenmüller 1977 Das Grab des Nianchchnum und Chnumhotep. Archäologische Veröffentlichungen (Deutsches Archäologisches Institut Abteilung Kairo) 21. Mainz am Rhein: Philipp von Zabern.

Niwinski, A. 1989 Studies on the Illustrated Theban Funerary Papyri of the 11th and 10th Centuries BC (Orbis Biblicus et Orientalis 86). Freiburg: Universitätsverlag.

Nunn, J. F. 1996 Ancient Egyptian Medicine. London: British Museum.

O'Connor, D. 1996 Sexuality, Statuary and the Afterlife: Scenes in the Tomb-chapel of Pepyankh (Heny the Black) – An Interpretive Essay. In Studies in Honor of William Kelly Simpson. Vol. 2. P. der Manuelian, ed. Pp. 622–633. Boston: Museum of Fine Arts.

Omlin, J. A. 1973 Der Papyrus 55001 und seine satirisch-erotische Zeichnungen und Inschriften. Turin: Museo Egizio.

Onstine, S. L. 2005 The Role of the Chantress in Ancient Egypt (BAR International Series 1401). Oxford: Archaeopress.

Pestmann, P. A. 1961 Marriage and Matrimonial Property in Ancient Egypt (Papyrologica Lugduno-Batava 5). Leiden: Brill.

Petrie, W. M. F. 1891 Illahun, Kahun and Gurob. London: D. Nutt.

Pinch, G. 1983 Childbirth and Female Figurines at Deir el Medina and el-'Amarna. Orientalia 52:405–414.

Pinch, G. 1993 Votive Offerings to Hathor. Oxford: Griffith Institute.

Reeder, G. 2000 Same-sex Desire, Conjugal Constructs and the Tomb of Niankhkhnum and Khnumhotep. World Archaeology 32:193–208.

Reeves, N. 1990 The Complete Tutankhamun London: Thames and Hudson.

Richards, J. 2005 Society and Death in Ancient Egypt. Cambridge: Cambridge University Press.

Riggs, C. 2005 The Beautiful Burial in Roman Egypt: Art, Identity and Funerary Religion. Oxford: Oxford University Press.

Robins, G. 1993 Women in Ancient Egypt. London: British Museum.

Robins, G. 1994 Some Principles of Compositional Domination and Gender Hierarchy in Egyptian Art. Journal of the American Research Center in Egypt 31:33–40.

Robins, G. 1999 Hair and the Construction of Identity in Ancient Egypt, c. 1480–1350 BC. Journal of the American Research Center in Egypt 36:55–69.

Robins, G. 2001 Gender Roles. In The Oxford Encyclopedia of Ancient Egypt. Vol. II. D. Redford, ed. Pp. 12–16. New York: Oxford University Press.

Roehrig, C., R. Dreyfus, and C. A. Keller 2005 Hatshepsut: From Queen to Pharaoh. New York: Metropolitan Museum of Art.

Roth, A. M. 1999 The Absent Spouse: Patterns and Taboos in Egyptian Tomb Decoration. Journal of the American Research Center in Egypt 36:36–53.

Savage, S. H. 2000 The Status of Women in Predynastic Egypt as Revealed through Mortuary Analysis. In Reading the Body: Representations and Remains in the Archaeological Record. A. E. Rautman, ed. Pp. 77–92. Philadelphia: University of Pennsylvania Press.

Scott, J. W. 1986 Gender: A Useful Category of Historical Analysis. American Historical Review 91:1053–1075.

Smith, S. T. 1992 Intact Tombs of the Seventeenth and Eighteenth Dynasties from Thebes and the New Kingdom Burial System. Mitteilungen des Deutschen Archäologischen Instituts, Abteilung Kairo 48:194–231.

Toivari-Viitala, J. 2001 Women at Deir el-Medina (Egyptologische Uitgaven 15). Leiden: Nederlands Instituut voor het Nabije Oosten.

Trimble, J. 1995 A Fertility Statue. In Preserving Eternity: Modern Goals, Ancient Intentions. J. E. Richards and T, G. Wilfong, eds. Pp. 20–21. Ann Arbor, MI: Kelsey Museum of Archaeology.

Vittmann, G. 1998 Der demotische Papyrus Rylands 9 (Ägypten und Altes Testament 38). Wiesbaden: Harrassowitz.

Wilfong, T. G., ed. 1997 Women and Gender in Ancient Egypt: From Prehistory to Late Antiquity. Ann Arbor, MO: Kelsey Museum of Archaeology.

Wilfong, T. G. 2000 Synchronous Menstruation and the "Place of Women" in Ancient Egypt (Hieratic Ostracon Oriental Institute Museum 13512). In Gold of Praise: Studies on Ancient Egypt in Honor of Edward F. Wente (Studies in Ancient Oriental Civilization 58). E. Teeter and J. Larson, eds. Pp. 419–434. Chicago: Oriental Institute Press.

Wilfong, T. G. 2002 Women of Jeme: Lives in a Coptic Town in Late Antique Egypt. New Texts from Ancient Cultures. Ann Arbor, MI: University of Michigan Press.

Wilfong, T. G. 2007 Gender and Society in Byzantine Egypt. In Egypt in the Byzantine World, 300–700. R. S. Bagnall, ed. Pp. 309–327. Cambridge: Cambridge University Press.

Wilford, J. N. 2005 A Mystery, Locked in Timeless Embrace. New York Times, 20 December; electronic version at http://www.nytimes.com/2005/12/20/science/20egyp.html.

Willems, H. 1996 The Coffin of Heqata (Cairo JdE 36418): A Case Study of Egyptian Funerary Culture of the Early Middle Kingdom (OLA 70). Leuven: Peeters.

Winlock, H. E. 1945 The Slain Soldiers of Neb-hepet-Re Montu-hotpe. New York: Metropolitan Museum of Art.

Winlock, H. E. 1948. The Treasure of Three Egyptian Princesses. New York: Metropolitan Museum of Art.

10
Class and Society

Position and Possessions

Wolfram Grajetzki

Describing any society, ancient or modern, there is as yet no agreement on a model which fits all interrelations between people of varied backgrounds, professions, and different sexes. Most societies can be classified as oligarchic in structure, that is, they have a small ruling group of individuals at the top and a high number of people at the base. In modern societies, the ruling group gains its supremacy through economic power, underpinned by an ideology requiring more or less force. In ancient Egypt there was the concept of a divine kingship, according to which the ruler was granted power by the gods. In most periods of human history, the working population has been involved either in food production or in various kinds of material production or crafts. At the bottom or even outside of the society there may have been a stratum of beggars, disabled, or the sick, such as lepers (if they already existed, Störk 1980) and individuals regarded by the majority for different reasons as criminals or outlaws. The relations among the different social groups vary considerably over time and in different societies. In the Indian caste system there is almost no interchange possible between the social groups defined as "castes," at least on a formal level. Other societies claim to have open social barriers, but in each instance the claim must be measured against the evidence for real social mobility.

"Elite," "Class," and "Rank" in Egyptological Literature

Sociologists of various schools divide societies in different ways, the most common being the division into social classes, an expression particularly associated with the political sociology of Karl Marx. The term "class" is frequently used in Egyptology to divide social groups, but often without any further explanation and without providing an ideological framework. However, at least in some more detailed studies, its use is clarified or appears with the qualification that the author will not employ not it in a Marxist way but with "the specific nuances of identity, self-interest and interlevel tension" (Richards 2005:16). Meskell (1999: 139–141) notes the problem with using the term "class" for ancient Egypt to refer to a "mobilized and politicized group," which is not visible in the Egyptian context. She prefers the "expression" rank for Deir el-Medina, regarding the whole population within the village as belonging to some kind of "middle class," while "rank" is a subdivision of "class" (Marshall 2000). In this contribution the term "class" will be used in a wider sense as employed by Richards.

In recent Egyptological literature the term "elite" has become popular (recent examples include Richards 2005; Shaw 2000:495). However, as with "class," this expression is most often not provided with a definition. The word has two basic meanings. In sociology, as in general usage, "elite" denotes a small leading group within a society, enjoying a privileged status, with access to and command of a disproportionate quantity of resources, often supported by individuals of lower social status within the structure of a group. Nevertheless, "elite" can also refer to the "best" in a certain group of people, whether in research, sports, or any other area. A ruling group of people describing itself as "elite" doubtless also tries to imply the meaning of "the best" (Bottomore 1993; Stanworth 2006). In Egyptology the term most often carries the sociological sense of "ruling class," but it is difficult to avoid the impression that many Egyptologists fail to draw a distinction between a "ruling group" and "the best" (in a field). In order to avoid unwanted ambivalence, in this contribution the word "elite" will not be used as a sociological term, but it may occur in translations where an ancient word itself seems ambivalent.

Any investigation of ancient society is in danger of reproducing the particular worldview of the modern writer (cf. also Wendrich, Chapter 11 this volume). The classical example is perhaps the introduction of the "middle class" into the conceptualization of Egyptian society (a critical discussion: Franke 1998; cf. Richards 2005). The term describes best the socio-economic group of people dominating the life style of a large section of society in the Western world. Is the term useful for describing a section of ancient Egyptian society? Such projection of a modern worldview onto ancient sources also appears where Egyptologists divide Egyptian art and religion into "popular" and "official." This model recalls studies by Bourdieu (1979), who was able to show that different tastes and different cultures in Western modern social groups are used for maintaining class boundaries. However, it seems doubtful whether social barriers in ancient Egypt needed to be kept by cultural differences. In the Egyptian ruling class, a strong element of heredity is often visible (Helck 1975). Access to education was certainly only limited to a small number of people. Therefore, it might be questioned whether the difference between "high" and folkloristic or "low" culture is useful for describing ancient Egyptian social and cultural patterns.

Egyptology and Sociology

Egyptology as a discipline is more concerned with art and textual sources than with theory, including social theory. The result is that the subject of "class" and society is often studied in insufficient detail and without a thorough knowledge of sociology. The danger of not providing an ideological framework for history writing and sociological discussion is described by Ste Croix:

... why can't we just go on doing history in the good old way, without bothering about concepts and categories we employ? ... The reply to this ... it is a serious error to suppose that unconsciousness of ideology, or even a complete lack of interest in it, is the same thing as absence of ideology. In reality each of us has an ideological approach to history, resulting in a particular historical methodological and set of general concepts, whether conscious or unconscious. To refuse ... to think about the basic concepts we employ simply results in our taking over without scrutiny, lock, stock and barrel, the prevailing ideology in which we happen to have been brought up. ... (Ste Croix 1981: 33–34)

There are indeed surprisingly few studies on ancient Egyptian society. One of the earliest works on social life in ancient Egypt was written by Petrie (1923). This work is an exception for its time but, with its long generic chapters on daily life, not readily comparable with modern sociological approaches. Helck (1959) discussed in one article the development from Old to New Kingdom society, with more use of categories such as social class. In many, more general books, the form of Egyptian society is briefly considered, but without any explicit theoretical frame; one longer such chapter on Egyptian society is found in Aldred's *The Egyptians* (1998: 184–212); here, different social groups, such as "scribes" and "peasants," are portrayed. A stronger development within the same general approach is taken in Donadoni (1997). In that book, several authors describe their view of important parts of Egyptian society. While each chapter on its own provides significant information, the book does not aim to be a sociological study, and does not provide a detailed study on the links across society and the interaction of the groups presented. Women are confined to a separate chapter. Trigger et al. (1983) call their book *Ancient Egypt: A Social History,* but the content is more a political history of ancient Egypt with a focus on foreign relations, albeit raising general questions on how to approach Egyptian history, with some discussion of social issues. In the *Oxford Encyclopaedia of Ancient Egypt* there appears one entry on "social stratification" providing a general overview of the discussions of recent decades (Wilkinson 2001; cf. Lesko 1999 in the *Encyclopedia of the Archaeology of Ancient Egypt*). Kemp (2006) gives a more expanded account of the whole ancient Egyptian culture, with recurrent emphasis on social issues. He sketches a development from a restricted state in the Old and Middle Kingdom controlling almost all matters of life to a society in the New Kingdom where he sees a relatively free market ("the birth of economic man": Kemp 2006:302–335).

Only two periods have received a greater number of detailed studies on society and social developments. The first is the period of Egyptian state formation, around 3000 BCE, studied in terms of the development of inequality. State formation is connected with the appearance of evidence for distinct social classes in the archaeological record. For this period several investigations on cemeteries set out to trace the development of society (Wilkinson 1996) for a better understanding of this period and better understanding of state formation in general.

Another focal point is the Middle Kingdom, a period for which, already at the beginning of the twentieth century, Egyptologists argued for the existence of some kind of middle class, comprising people with a certain income, but without being part of the ruling class of the formal state administration. This class was first observed from the many Abydos stelae showing people without any titles (the research on the subject is summarized by Richards 2005:7). In recent decades the discussion has been revived, mainly by Egyptologists interested in literature, who postulated a connection between this middle class or a free citizenship and the rise of ancient Egyptian literature. For the late First Intermediate Period and the early Middle Kingdom, Loprieno (1988:86–88) proposed a new group of people responsible for a more critical worldview which is mostly visible in the literature of the Middle Kingdom. However, his approach does not take into account the complete corpus of written sources; the key word in this discussion, *nedjes*, "fellow", is in fact often applied to leading officials in local and national administration (for a detailed discussion, see Franke 1998). Only one detailed study tries to move towards the question from an archaeological source base and incorporates written and other sources into the discussion (Richards 2005).

There are few broader investigations on New Kingdom society in general. Studies often concentrate on the ruling class, well known from their tomb chapels at Thebes, Saqqara, and other places and the rich inscribed material in general. One exception for gaining a wider picture is the village of the workmen at Deir el-Medina, who were responsible for building the royal tombs of the New Kingdom. There are several studies on its people and social relations (e.g. Meskell 1999, 2002). It remains an open question whether this community provides reliable information for the rest of the country. Amarna is another exceptional site, with large parts of a royal city preserved, and here substantial areas of housing have been excavated. The comparison of house sizes has provided a base for studies on the society as a whole (Tietze 1985, 1986).

The Current Dominant Tendency: An Uncritical Use of Literary Sources

As mentioned, Egyptology is still a subject heavily influenced by the written sources. Almost all ancient inscriptions and depictions reflecting interaction between social groups are set up by and for the ruling class. They convey their view and special interest. Egyptologists most often have a similar background to that of the writers of the ancient texts, in the sense that they too belong to a literate, highly educated group, a social environment comparable in ideology. Too often they take ancient Egyptian statements at face value as they hold opinions on social relations similar or even identical to those reflected in the sources (Trigger 2006:19–20). One vivid example is the reception of the so-called "Satire of Trades," probably composed in the Middle Kingdom, but known from the numerous copies made in the New Kingdom, and especially in the Ramesside period. In this composition, different occupations are described in an emphatically negative light, drawing attention to the advantages of being a "scribe." There are, among others, two extreme opinions in Egyptology regarding the message of the text. On one side it is regarded as "satire," as the modern title already announces. Lichtheim states, for example:

> If it were argued that the exaggerations were meant to be taken seriously, we would have to conclude that the scribal profession practiced deliberate depiction out of contempt for manual labor so profound as to be unrelieved by humor. Such a

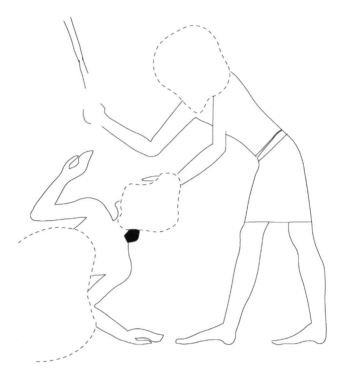

Figure 10.1 Beating of a servant or workman, scene in the tomb of Ineni (early 18th Dynasty).

conclusion is, however, belied by all the literary and pictorial evidence. For tombs
reliefs and texts alike breathe joy and pride in the accomplishment of labor. (Lichtheim
1975:184)

Other commentators just as clearly see the text as revealing the true attitude of a
ruling class towards any manual labor (Burkard and Thissen 2007:172; Loprieno
1997). In this context, it just needs to be mentioned that depictions of beating
workmen are not uncommon in Egyptian tombs (just one example: Shedid 1988:pl.
54, 63; see Figure 10.1). The "joy of labor" is the joy of a ruling class seeing people
working for them and receiving the fruits of other people's labor. Finally, a further
point complicating the picture for understanding the "Satire of Trades" is the
Western view of the Orient, outlined in its many forms by Edward Said in
Orientalism (1978). The cruelty described in this composition of literature can be
seen by a modern Western Egyptologist as being, not socially anchored, but
related to ancient Egypt, as part of the Orient and, therefore, as normal social
behavior there.

Images of Class in Archaeology

In general, for a study on social classes, archaeology seems more helpful than the
written sources, as houses, burials, and objects from many social levels have been

found, presenting the researcher with a much wider range of source material than only texts. The most important archaeological resource for receiving information on social stratification in Egypt is the excavated, well-recorded, and published cemeteries. Multivariate analyses of tomb size, tomb structure, and the number of vessels found in single burials are common methods not only for Egyptian cemeteries (a general overview for Egypt: Richards 2005:69–74). More qualitative approaches take into account the value of objects placed in the tombs, calculated from the value of the material or the time spent on producing objects such as pottery (Hendrickx 1994:217–224; Meskell 1999; Richards 2005).

In relation to this approach, it is important to note that a statistical analysis requires a certain number of tombs, which should represent, ideally, a well-balanced average population. These factors never really apply. In most cemeteries a part of the population seems to be missing, most often the youngest children, or the sex balance does not conform to our expectations (cf. the discussion in Richards 2005:57–58). However, there are many cemeteries of the time of Egyptian state formation, providing at least a rough database, although we should note the methodological problems related to each cemetery. The cemeteries of the First Intermediate Period, for instance the burials in the region of Qau/Matmar (Seidlmayer 1987) and at Sedment (Seidlmayer 1990:247–341), provide another rich data set. For other periods, this enterprise seems more problematic at the moment. Many cemeteries of the classical Old Kingdom, with the exception of those of the capital (Gizeh, Saqqara), have not been located, or have received little attention from excavators. Presumably, archaeologists whose endeavors were financed by museums were under pressure to produce interesting finds, while the burial equipment of lower-class burials was very limited in comparison to both earlier and later periods. There are many cemeteries of the Middle Kingdom known and excavated, but the standard of publication varies, and only a few investigations use the results for gaining information on social history (Richards 2005).

There are also astonishingly few well-excavated burial grounds of the New Kingdom period. The social stratum which we can surmise to have existed under the high state officials is in archaeological terms still inadequately researched. Excavations targeting New Kingdom sites have been mainly focused on temples, royal monuments, and the decorated tomb chapels of the highest officials in Thebes. For the New Kingdom there are almost no cemeteries of a whole population so far excavated and published to a higher standard. The few exceptions include the cemeteries of Gurob (Brunton and Engelbach 1927) and several cemeteries in Lower Nubia, recorded during the Nubian campaign, a large-scale survey and excavation effort to gain knowledge on the archaeology of Lower Nubia before it was flooded. The published results provide an important data set.

Perhaps the most interesting cemetery is Fadrus, excavated by the Scandinavian Joint Expedition. The tombs in the region around Fadrus seem to include all social levels and range from interments without grave goods to decorated tomb chapels. In total, approximately 690 tombs were excavated, recorded, and published. In the excavation report the tombs were arranged into five social groups based on the size and value of the tomb equipment, from burials with no artifacts to those with many high-value objects and an elaborate tomb architecture

(Säve-Söderbergh and Troy 1991:224–225). If we include the decorated rock-cut tombs belonging to the governors of the region, we could distinguish six social levels. Coffins were a common feature of the burials of all levels, but only the three highest social levels had other objects specifically produced for their interment, such as mummy masks, and luxury items, such as metal bowls, razors, and axes. These three highest social levels make up less than 10 percent of the entire population, buried here mainly in the 18th Dynasty. The rest of the population was obviously poorer but still had access to a range of objects. Only about 23 percent of the burials were found without any grave goods, but the conditions for the preservation of organic materials were not very good at Fadrus and possibly matting, baskets, and clothing were included, but have decayed without leaving a trace. In the evaluation of the data it was postulated that the middle of the 18th Dynasty saw an increase in wealth. More objects were placed in the tombs, but it is a matter of debate whether this reflects a change in social structure or a general change in burial customs (Grajetzki 2003:67–76). The ethnic background and occupation of the people buried at Fadrus are not known, but the site represents a rural community far from the centers of power at Thebes and Memphis. How much the location of Fadrus, south of the traditional border of Egypt at the First Cataract, determines the composition of the settlement and the burials is a matter of debate. It has been a long-standing opinion that people at the bottom of the society, such as the farmers, did not leave any traces in the archaeological record (see, e.g., Baines and Lacovara 2002: 12–14; Caminos 1997:1–2). Starting with Emery, as early as 1961 (128–164), this attitude has changed in more recent years. Seidlmayer (2001:210–211) argued especially for the cemeteries in Elephantine and in the Qau/Matmar region that they basically served the farming and working population at these places. He noticed that, were he to assume that these tombs all belonged to some kind of higher social level, we would be faced with problems explaining the social structure of these sites with a very high number of people being part of a ruling class. These cemeteries are placed in a chain along the desert, next to the fertile land and most likely belonging to villages along the Nile (Seidlmayer 1990:206–207). Richards notes the simplicity in technology of digging a surface burial and that it seems unlikely that "most Egyptians did not opt for a formal burial of some kind" (Richards 2005:66).

With these "poorer" equipped tombs and small houses at cities such as Amarna, it seems very likely that the burials and houses of these people have been reached, providing us a direct view on their living conditions.

The workmen's village of Deir el-Medina is the most important other example for a New Kingdom archaeological site presenting information on the social relation of its inhabitants. Here are preserved the houses of the population, their tombs, and exceptional rich written material providing the possibility of in-depth studies of one segment of Egyptian society. From the inscribed material, Janssen divided the people of the village into three groups. There is an upper class consisting of chiefs and scribes, a middle class of the workmen, and some kind of proletariat, consisting of people supplying the workmen with food and water. Janssen (1975:536) argued that the latter group lived outside the village. Meskell (1999) divided the society of Deir el-Medina according to their wealth, clearly visible in the different tomb equipments. She assigned to each object found in a given tomb and belonging to a specific person a price. The ancient prices known from accounts found at the village (Janssen 1975) were the starting point to calculate the ancient value of the items placed in tombs. Meskell observed stark social discrepancies in the 18th Dynasty, while in the Ramesside period these differences seem to be less harsh. However, this might reflect new burial customs which were introduced in all of Egypt in this latter period. Tombs were less often furnished with luxury items, and poor persons were no longer placed in simple individual graves, merely holes in the ground, but were joined with other, perhaps richer members of the community in the same burial chamber, which from this period onwards typically contained multiple burials. The strong contrast between rich and poor individual burials known from the 18th Dynasty seems to disappear (Grajetzki 2003:84–93). The change might reflect a shift in social pattern or new religious beliefs.

A more architectural approach for gaining a picture of the highest state officials at Thebes at the beginning of the New Kingdom comes from Engelmann-von Carnap (1999:78). She arranged the Theban tomb chapels under Hatshepsut/Thutmosis III according to their dimensions into four groups. With her research she just covered the tombs of the highest ruling class in a short period, but her results provide a clear order of the ranks at the royal court. At the top, there are the vizier, high priest of Amun, and mayor of Thebes. In the second group there are the second priest of Amun, the overseer of the granaries of Upper and Lower Egypt, and the treasurer. In the third group she found lower officials, some working for other officials, such as a steward of a vizier. The fourth group comprised the smallest decorated tomb chapels, and here are again lower officials such as an overseer of works or a royal priest.

The most important excavated settlement site of ancient Egypt is Amarna. There are several studies on house sizes for gaining information on the social status of their owner. Tietze (1985) looked at more than 500 houses in this city. He observed that these houses were basically all built along the same lines, reflecting the wish to have a living room in the middle with the other rooms arranged around it. Tietze distinguished three main levels in terms of house size and construction (Figure 10.2). About 55–60 percent of the houses were small and simple and about 50 m² big. The walls were just one half brick thick. These houses were more exposed to the climate than larger houses with thicker walls. About 35 percent of the houses were slightly larger and had some more amenities, such as a courtyard. The walls of these buildings were about one brick thick. Finally, about 10 percent of the houses belonged to the largest and had a whole range of installations. Only for the latter group some inscribed material is known providing evidence that the highest state officials were living here. For the middle group, Tietze identified middle-level officials, and for the group of smallest houses people of a lower class thought to be the personnel of the people living in the larger houses. Of particular interest is the observation that within each group there are a wide variety of arrangements of rooms and building units. Furthermore, the smaller houses tend to cluster around the bigger ones, providing evidence for a wide social mixture of people and for some kind of cliental system, almost as a cluster of villages as outlined by Lehner (this volume).

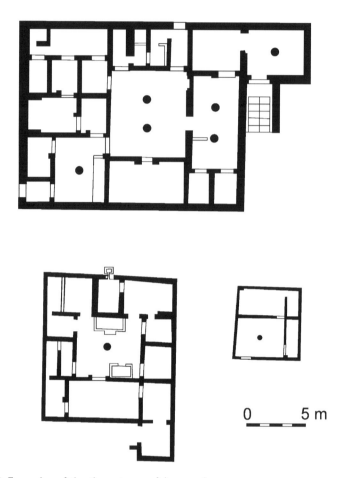

Figure 10.2 Examples of the three types of Amarna houses.

From Pharaoh to Farmer: A Review

Egyptians certainly had their own view of how their society was organized. There are antonymous terms such as *pat*, "elite," and *rekhyt*, "common people." The exact meaning of these words is most often not known. Ancient Egyptians also seem to have divided their society by professions. In the Wilbour Papyrus, a rental record lists high priests, wealthy officials, a larger group of scribes, priests, soldiers, stable masters, citizenesses, and finally cultivators and herdsmen. These people were listed as owning a certain amount of land. Not surprisingly, priests owned in average more land than herdsmen (O'Connor 1983:191–192).

Ancient Egyptian society was in all periods strictly hierarchical (Lesko 1999:745). Social differences and hierarchy were clearly expressed in texts and depictions, but also in placements of houses and tombs. The comparison of the tomb size of kings, as for example the pyramids, and the tombs of common people, most often buried just in the ground, is already striking. Royal officials had certain titles announcing their high rank. In art, important people were shown on a larger scale than less important people. People of lower importance are more often represented in an uncanonical way, while people of higher status are always shown "correctly" (Müller 1997). The tombs of the ruling class were found at one part of cemeteries, burials of less well-to-do people in other parts. In letters, lower officials write long greeting formulae to higher officials, whereas these are omitted when the higher ranked persons write to someone at the lower level (Grajetzki 2006:140–141).

The king was at the top of Egyptian society. He had certainly a special ontological status as a form of the sun god on earth (Assmann 1970). While tombs and houses of rich and poor were often decorated along the same lines, the tomb of the king was different. In the New Kingdom it was decorated with long religious texts, the underworld books, while the burial chambers of private people, whether rich or poor, were most often undecorated. Only the superstructures were equipped with reliefs or paintings. The king had a special titulary, crowns, and attire, and was clearly separated from the rest of the population. Texts and depictions on temple walls are explicit that he received his power directly from the gods. The king's wife and king's mother also had a special status, expressed often in titles such as "mistress of all women." They seem to have had a position between the king and the rest of the population. In the Old and Middle Kingdom they were often buried under a pyramid. In the New Kingdom their tomb decorations included elements of royal and private tombs. Queens had special crowns and were sometimes equipped with divine insignia, not attested for private individuals (Troy 1986).

The relation of the king and the king's family to their subjects changed over time. In the Old Kingdom, there is strong evidence that kings placed their sons in high state positions, while the king's daughters were married to important state officials. In the Middle Kingdom there is little evidence for king's sons in administrative positions or king's daughters married to commoners, even in highest state positions. This changed again in the New Kingdom. There are some king's sons placed as high priests of important temples, but little evidence for king's daughter's married to commoners (Schmitz 1976; for the sons of Ramesses II, see Fisher 2001). The king could marry women from a "common" background. The most famous example is Tiye, wife of Amehotep III. After the Old Kingdom the king's daughters were not married to people of "lower" background. It is not known whether this reflects reality or whether king's daughters just lost their title "king's daughter" when married to a commoner.

Directly under the kings were the highest state officials, such as the "vizier," the "high steward," or the "treasurer." Numerous monographs have been published on New Kingdom titles of officials, some of which provide a general outline (the best overview is found in Helck 1958). Although the group of the men around the king are often called officials, they were in effect the ministers, the men ruling the country for the palace and the king (Drioton and Vandier 1962:305–306). These highest state officials had certain titles announcing their high status, the most important ones in the New Kingdom being "royal scribe" and "fan bearer on the right of the king." These are new titles not attested for the Old or Middle Kingdom, when the classical ranking titles were "member of the elite," "foremost of action," "royal sealer," and "sole friend (of the king)." In periods of strong

Figure 10.3 Egyptian officials, Ramesside relief. Egyptian Museum Berlin. Photo: The author.

central government, the use of these titles was restricted to a very small number of people. Somebody with the title "member of the elite" was almost only second to the king. In older studies, these titles were often given no further attention, and repeatedly just called honorific. In reality, they provide us with a detailed hierarchical order of the men at the royal court. These titles do not, though, provide evidence for any chains of command across the hierarchy.

Offices in ancient Egypt were often inherited. This is best attested at the nome level, where in certain periods local dynasties of nomarchs or governors can be identified. The same is partly visible at the royal court. There are examples that viziers or high priests of Amun followed their father in office (Kees 1964). Family members also often hold other important key positions in the country (Figure 10.3). For example, the vizier Paser, in office under Ramesses II, was the son of the high priest of Amun Nebnetjeru (Raedler 2004:345). In the same reign, the vizier Parahotep was son of the high priest of Ptah at Memphis with the name Pahemnetjer (Figure 10.4). His wife was the daughter of the high priest of Onuris (Raedler 2004:371–372). Evidently, these families formed networks, holding many key positions in the highest administration. Especially in the New Kingdom the administration is highly flexible: military officials were appointed to civil offices or to a temple position such as high priest (Gnirs 1996). There is strong evidence for a broad geographical presence of the high officials. Although viziers had their main office at Thebes, Memphis, or Pi-Ramesse, they appear on monuments in different parts of the country, making it sometimes difficult to identify their base.

The main text sources for information on officials are their biographical inscriptions placed in the tomb chapels or on statues. From these it is clear that they received their legitimation of power directly from the king. Raedler (2006), using the works of Elias (1969) on medieval society, describes the Egyptian court as an example of a "court society." The king is the fixed point in this system. Officials

Figure 10.4 Stela from the tomb of the vizier Parahotep. Behind the vizier are shown lower officials, his clients. Photo: The author.

even identify themselves as body parts of the king: "the mouth of the king" or "the eyes of the king" are common biographical phrases of the New Kingdom for state officials. The king honors his officials and promotes them. Each step in their career is related to the sovereign.

In the inscriptions, officials often praise themselves as coming from a humble background. All success in their careers comes from their own abilities, which were rewarded by the king. However, for good reasons it has been doubted that these inscriptions can be trusted, as most of these officials came certainly from a quite high background of well-educated people (Guksch 1994; Morkot 1990). One particular example of a New Kingdom high state official is Senenmut, high steward under the ruling queen Hatshepsut. The father of Senenmut was an official with the name Ramose married to a woman called Hatnofer. Their intact tomb was found in front of the chapel belonging to their son (Lansing and Hayes 1937). Already the preliminary report inferred from the finds that Ramose must have been a farmer. The difference in size and decoration of the tombs for Senenmut and his father Ramose is indeed striking. Senenmut had a funerary complex consisting of a decorated chapel and, separated from that, an underground burial chamber, also partly decorated. Ramose was just buried in a small chamber in the ground together with his wife and some other unnamed people. On his coffin Ramose bears the simple title *sab*, often translated as "judge," but more likely a generic indication of status. The low social origin of Senenmut remained for a long time a fact in Egyptology, but recent research places his origin in a broader context. Dorman (2003) argued that the burial of Ramose was transferred from another place to be close to the more impressive cult chapel of Senenmut where he was depicted. The tomb chamber of Ramose with the partly gilded coffins and its equipment would correspond in the social stratification of the Fadrus cemetery to the highest social group. Furthermore, new research has clearly shown that before Hatshepsut most Theban officials were buried in chambers under mudbrick chapels (Polz 1995). It is not to be expected that Ramose had a tomb complex comparable to that of his son. From the whole context it seems most likely that Ramose did not belong to the highest state officials, but to a slightly larger group of people having access to several resources such as elaborate coffins and able to provide their children with some manner of better education. He seems to be on the same social level as the people at Fadrus who belonged to a higher social level, having metal objects in their tombs as Ramose had. Furthermore, the title *sab* does not provide any clue as to the social status of Ramose. In the Ramesside period, fathers of high officials, even if they had in life an exalted position, were after their death often just called *sab* (Raedler 2004:308). The rise of Senenmut seems to lie within normal parameters of a quite narrow social mobility strictly within the literate ruling class in the New Kingdom.

A similar picture is gained with the court officials under Akhenaten. They describe in many inscriptions their rise to power, from a position without status to a place beside the king. These inscriptions have often been taken as an indication of a high social mobility under that king. In this view, Akhenaten had chosen people without any links to old families, coming from a humble background (Helck 1958:539). However, the evidence is ambiguous. Some of the people around Akhenaten are already known from the time of Amenhotep III, such as the vizier Aperel, the vizier Ramose, the high steward Ipy, or the artists Men and Bak. The vizier Ramose and the high steward Ipy belonged to the same well-known family of highest state officials, demonstrating that Akhenaten also kept at least some old families in power. For other officials whose family background is not attested in the surviving records, it also seems unlikely that they came from a low background. They needed at least some kind of education which included the knowledge of reading and writing. It seems more likely that they came from the class of well-educated scribes forming the backbone of Egyptian administration (already skeptical, Aldred 1968:104, Morkot 1990; but see Guksch 1994:28–29).

Moving down in the social stratification, there are a high number of lower officials known from their small tombs or stelae, although they do not often appear on many different monuments and they did not often have their own decorated tomb chapels. These are the people often just labeled in groups as "scribes," although the title "scribe" itself is not very common as an individualized marker. As we have seen, there are several cases where such people could reach the highest state positions. Clearly, there was within the literate class a certain social mobility. These lower officials gained their legitimation not directly through the king but via higher officials. There are many stelae showing lower officials with more important ones, where higher officials appear in front of gods, while the lower ones are standing behind their superiors or even in a different register. These stelae make a second network of relations visible from a higher to a lower command level, a network that formed the power base of the highest state officials. Raedler (2004:371–376) describes the case of the priest Nebuhotep. He is depicted on a stela, which also features the vizier Parahotep. The vizier is shown standing in front of Osiris, while Nebuhotep is sitting in a second register. Nebuhotep also left a door-jamb next to the tomb of the vizier at Sedment and may have been buried there.

These stelae and other monuments offer visual evidence for a patron–client system, which is also important for understanding the relation of tombs and the relation of smaller and larger houses at settlement sites. A high official, a person with access to many resources, had several people around him who were dependent. This is already clear in Old Kingdom mastabas, where there are several instances of a steward included in the tomb decoration and buried next to the mastaba of their master (Hassan 1950:67). This system of dependency is also directly depicted on Middle Kingdom stelae where certain lower officials always appear in front of their master (Grajetzki 2001). A well-documented case for adjacent burial of master and client was excavated at Thebes. The high steward of Amun, Amenemope, is mainly known from his monumental and fully decorated rock-cut tomb. Within the burial complex a shaft was found, separated from the main burial apartments, with four coffins, two of them still naming their owners and providing titles (Figure 10.5). These people were not connected by family ties to Amenemope. However, one man, named on a coffin, had the title "head of the workshops." Amenemope was head of the economic division of the Amun temple at Thebes. It seems likely that the people buried in this shaft had a work relation with Amenemope and were dependent (Polz 1991:266–267). The same cliental system is again clearly visible at the houses of Amarna. Many small houses were arranged around the largest ones. About 40 percent of the houses belonging to the highest social level had smaller ones around them. Here the written evidence is missing and therefore it is not so certain whether poorer family members, servants of the household, or people working as subordinates of their master lived here (Tietze 1986).

To this social level of lower officials or clients belongs the best-researched group of New Kingdom people, the so-called "workmen" of Deir el-Medina. Many of them lived in a client relation to the vizier, who was in charge of the workmen's village (Raedler 2004:348–352). As mentioned above, there are different social groups visible within this village, but the people known from their decorated tomb chapels are certainly already on a quite high command level. Most of the decorated chapels belong to the Ramesside period, which seems to be a sign not of increasing wealth, but of changing patterns in burial customs. In the Ramesside period, multiple burials became extremely common. In these circumstances, evidently, a higher number of people contributed to the decoration of a tomb chapel.

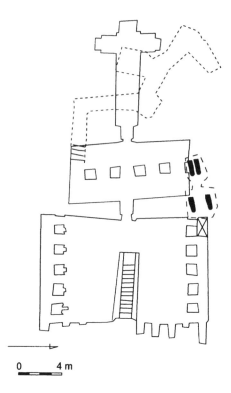

Figure 10.5 Plan of the tomb of Amenemope, the coffins in the subsidiary chamber belonging to clients are marked black.

The same social level of "privileged" workmen is not well attested from other places but some evidence does exist. In Saqqara several small chapels were found belonging to officials who were the heads of certain workshops. Their burial chambers were disturbed, but one, belonging to the "gold washer" and "merchant" Khay, still contained a number of broken objects. There were fragments of coffins, shabtis, and some pottery (shabtis being small statues to assist the dead in the afterlife). Different names survived on these objects, creating the impression that this was a multiple burial in the same style as the one of Sennedjem excavated at Deir el-Medina (Martin 2001:35–36).

Altogether, these people, the king's family, the higher and lower officials, doubtless formed just a small percentage of the entire population. These are the people of the three highest social groups of the tombs at Fadrus, forming less than 10 percent of the population. They would have lived in dwellings the size of the largest Amarna houses. In this context it should be mentioned that there are three times as many Amarna houses belonging to the highest level as there are decorated rock-cut tombs at the site. Many of the owners of the large houses were buried somewhere else and perhaps in tombs which we would assess as small. There must have been smaller chapels and burials, but still quite richly equipped, as for example visible from the high number of finely produced shabtis dating to the Amarna period (Martin 1986).

Under the administrative ruling class, the bulk of the population were involved in food production or to a smaller extent in crafts. There were also other professions such as haircutters, healers, shipmen, and, professionalized to a variable degree in different periods, soldiers. Especially for the farmers, the backbone of Egyptian society, Caminos (1997) and others have drawn a very gloomy picture. They certainly did not have an easy life, but the tomb size statistics in particular illustrate a quite varied social potential, showing a wide range of at least small wealth (Figure 10.6). The distribution of land ownership in the Wilbour Papyrus evidences that the group of landowning people not belonging to the ruling class was quite wide. They could own small plots of land, and a few of them fields of larger size. Assessment of the rural society and economy is complicated by the problem that, in legal terms, the practical and ideal ownership of these fields is still an open question. Were farmers considered to own their fields, or did they just have the right to plough and gain some income from them?

Like the juridical status of the fields, the legal position of the working population remains unknown. For the New Kingdom there are few studies and they are mostly based on philological work (Bogoslovskij 1974, 1981). In general, it is assumed that many lived in some kind of condition similar to medieval serfdom. Berlev (1972) investigated several expressions used in the Middle Kingdom in documents and on monuments, and concluded that the working population of the Middle Kingdom can be divided essentially into two groups. The first comprises those people attached to an office or employed by institutions; the most prominent institutions in the surviving sources are branches of the royal, i.e. national, administration, but others include local administration, temples of kings, and, less prominent than in the Later Period, temples of deities. The Middle Kingdom term for a man in this group was *hem nesut*, "servant of the king," and for a woman, *hemet*, "female servant." The second group comprises people attached to another

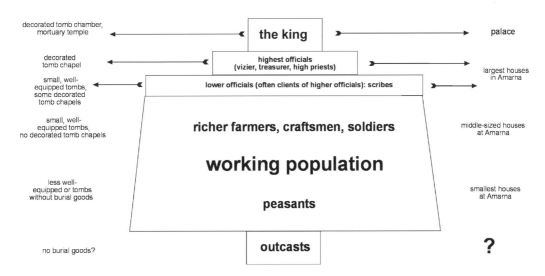

Figure 10.6 Schematic model of Egyptian society in the New Kingdom with reference to tombs and house sizes.

person but not by their office; the Middle Kingdom word for a person in this group was *bak*, "labour-servant." Foreigners in the working population seem to have had their own status, at the level of the *bak*, and were identified by their ethnicity. The only widely attested ethnic name at this period is *aam*, denoting a Semitic-speaking person from the lands neighboring Egypt on the east. The terms *hem* and *bak* have often been translated "slave," leading to the question whether in ancient Egypt there were people enslaved in the manner known from Greek, Roman, medieval, and modern European and American history (Bakir 1952). The opinions vary considerably and the evidence is not always conclusive. The scale and perfection of the largest pyramids of the Old Kingdom have often led to the conclusion that such monumental architecture was only possible under the harshest treatment of the working population. In reaction to this pyramid-slavery thesis, the opposite view that especially the pyramids were built by a free population hoping to gain an afterlife in return has its adherents too. For the latter opinion there is, however, no evidence (for the full discussion: Kemp 2006:179–192).

The study of ancient Egyptian law has shown that the lower classes were treated anything but correctly. Although biographical inscriptions set up for the ruling class always express concern about the weak and poor, the reality, mainly known from a few ostraca, was without doubt very different (Helck 1958:545–546). Without a "patron" coming from a higher social level, a poorer person had little chance of receiving a fair hearing at a court. The known examples demonstrate drastically how the official written sources reflect one view of the world. The truth was different and needs to be searched in archaeology, in the few non-official texts, and by reading between the lines.

REFERENCES

Aldred, C. 1968 Akhenaten, Pharaoh of Egypt: A New Study. London: Thames and Hudson.

Aldred, C. 1998 The Egyptians (rev. and enlarged by A. Dodson) London: Thames and Hudson.

Assmann, J. 1970 Der König als Sonnenpriester (ADAIK 7). Glückstadt: Verlag J. J. Austin.

Baines, J., and P. Lacovara 2002 Burial and the Dead in Ancient Egyptian Society. Journal of Social Archaeology 2:5–36.

Bakir, A. el-M. 1952 Slavery in Pharaonic Egypt. Cairo: Impre. de l'Institut français d'archéologie.

Berlev, O. 1972 Trudovoe naselenie Egipta v epokhu Srednego tsarstva (in English: Study of the Working Population of Egypt in the Middle Kingdom). Moscow: Nauka.

Bogoslovskij, E. S. 1974 Die Wortverbindung sedschemu asch in der ägyptischen Sprache während der 18. Dynastie. Zeitschrift für Ägyptische Sprache und Altertumskunde 101:81–89.

Bogoslovskij, E. S. 1981 On the System of the Ancient Egyptian Society of the Epoch of the New Kingdom: According to Documents from Deir el-Medina. Altorientalische Forschungen 8:5–21.

Bottomore, T. 1993 Elites and Society. 2nd edition. London: Routledge.

Bourdieu, P. 1979 La distinction: critique sociale du jugement. Paris: Éditions de Minuit.

Brunton, G., and R. Engelbach 1927 Gurob (Publications of the Egyptian Research Account and British School of Archaeology in Egypt 41). London: British School of Archaeology in Egypt.

Burkard, G., and H. J. Thissen 2007 Einführung in die Altägyptische Literaturgeschichte I. Altes und Mittleres Reich. Berlin: Lit.

Caminos, R. 1997 Peasants. In The Egyptians. S. Donadoni, ed. Pp. 1–30. Chicago, London: University of Chicago Press.

Donadoni, S., ed. 1997 The Egyptians. Chicago, London: University of Chicago Press.

Dorman, P. F. 2003 Family Burial and Commemoration in the Theban Necropolis. In The Theban Necropolis: Past, Present and Future. N. Strudwick and J. Taylor, eds. Pp. 30–41. London: British Museum Press.

Drioton, É., and J. Vandier 1962 L'Égypte, Clio: Introduction aux études historiques. Les peuples de l'orient méditerranéen, II. 4th edition. Paris: PUF.

Elias, N. 1969 Die höfische Gesellschaft: Untersuchungen zur Soziologie des Königtums und der höfischen Aristokratie. Neuwied: Luchterhand.

Emery, W. B. 1961 Archaic Egypt. Edinburgh: Penguin Books.

Engelmann-von Carnap, B. 1999 Die Struktur des thebanischen Beamtenfriedhofes in der ersten Hälfte der 18. Dynastie. Berlin: Achet Verlag.

Fisher, M. M. 2001 The Sons of Ramesses II (Ägypten und Altes Testament 53). Wiesbaden: Harrassowitz.

Franke, D. 1998 Kleiner Mann (nDs) – was bist Du? Göttinger Miszellen 167:33–48.

Gnirs, A. 1996 Militär und Gesellschaft: ein Beitrag zur Sozialgeschichte des Neuen Reiches, Militär. Heidelberg: Heidelberger Orientverlag.

Grajetzki, W. 2001 Two Treasurers of the Late Middle Kingdom. Oxford: BAR.

Grajetzki, W. 2003 Burial Customs in Ancient Egypt: Life in Death for Rich and Poor. London: Duckworth.

Grajetzki, W. 2006 The Middle Kingdom of Ancient Egypt. London: Duckworth.

Guksch, H. 1994 Zur Selbstdarstellung der Beamten in der 18. Dynastie. Heidelberg: Heidelberger Orientverlag.

Hassan, S. 1950 Excavations at Gîza, Vol. VI, III, 1934–1935. Cairo: Government Press.

Helck, W. 1958 Zur Verwaltung des Mittleren und Neuen Reichs (Probleme der Ägyptologie 3). Leiden: Brill.

Helck, W. 1959 Die soziale Schichtung des ägyptischen Volkes im 3. und 2. Jahrtausend v. Chr. Journal of the Economic and Social History of the Orient 2:1–36.

Helck, W. 1975 Amtserblichkeit, In Lexikon der Ägyptologie 3. W. Helck and O. Otto, eds. Pp. 228–229. Wiesbaden: Harrasowitz.

Hendrickx, S. (with a contribution by V. van Rossum) 1994 Elkab V, The Naqada III Cemetery. Brussels: Musées Royaux d'Art et Histoire.

Janssen, J. J. 1975 Commodity Prices from the Ramessid Period: An Economic Study of the Village of Necropolis Workmen at Thebes. Leiden: Brill.

Kees, H. 1964 Die Hohenpriester des Amun von Karnak von Herihor bis zum Ende der Äthiopenzeit (Probleme der Ägyptologie 4). Leiden: Brill.

Kemp, B. 2006 Ancient Egypt, Anatomy of a Civilization. 2nd edition. London, New York: Routledge.

Lansing. A., and W. C. Hayes 1937 The Museum's Excavations at Thebes 1935–1936. Bulletin of the Metropolitan Museum of Art 52:12–39.

Lesko, B. 1999 Social Organization. In Encyclopedia of the Archaeology of Ancient Egypt. K. A. Bard, ed. Pp. 745–749. London, New York: Routledge.

Lichtheim, M. 1975 Ancient Egyptian Literature I: The Old and Middle Kingdom. Berkeley, Los Angeles, London: University of California Press.

Loprieno, A. 1988 Topos und Mimesis: Zum Ausländer in der ägyptischen Literatur (ÄghAbh 48). Wiesbaden: Harrassowitz.

Loprieno, A. 1997 Slaves. *In* The Egyptians. S. Donadoni, ed. Pp. 185–219. Chicago: University of Chicago Press.

Marshall, T. H. 2000 A Note on "Status." *In* Identity: A Reader. P. du Gay, J. Evans, and P. Redman, eds. Pp. 304–310. London Sage Publications.

Martin, G. T. 1986 Shabtis of Private Persons in the Amarna Period. Mitteilungen des Deutschen Archäologischen Instituts, Abteilung Jairo 42:109–129.

Martin, G. T. (with the collaboration of H. D. Schneider and R. van Walsem) 2001 The Tombs of Three Memphite Officials: Ramose, Khay and Pabes. London: Egypt Exploration Society.

Meskell, L. 1999 Archaeologies of Social Life: Age, Sex, Class *et cetera* in Ancient Egypt. Oxford: Blackwell.

Meskell, L. 2002 Private Life in New Kingdom Egypt. Princeton, Oxford: Princeton University Press.

Morkot, R. G. 1990 Nb-Maat-Ra-United-with-Ptah. Journal of Near Eastern Studies 49:323–337.

Müller, C. 1997 Das Kalksteinfragment E.6783 aus den Musées Royaux d'Art et d'Histoire in Brüssel und verwandte Frontaldarstellungen – eine Analyse. Göttinger Miszellen 160:69–83.

O'Connor, D. 1983 New Kingdom and Third Intermediate Period, 1552–664 BC. *In* Ancient Egypt: A Social History. B. G. Trigger, B. J. Kemp, D. O'Connor, and A.N. Lloyd. Pp. 183–278. Cambridge: Cambridge University Press.

Petrie. W. M. F. 1923 Social Life in Ancient Egypt. London, Bombay, Sydney: Constable & Company Ltd.

Polz, D. 1991 Die Särge aus Schacht II der Grabanlage. *In* Das Grab des Amenemops TT41. J. Assmann, ed. Pp. 244–267. Mainz: Zabern.

Polz, D. 1995 Dra' Abu-el-Naga: Die thebanische Nekropole des frühen Neuen Reiches. *In* Thebanische Beamtennekropolen neue Perspektiven archäologischer Forschung internationales Symposion Heidelberg, 9.–13.6.1993 (Studien zur Archäologie und Geschichte Altägyptens 12). Pp. 25–42. Heidelberg: Heidelberger Orientverlag.

Raedler, C. 2004 Die Wesire Ramses'II.-Netwerke der Macht. *In* Das ägyptische Königtum im Spannungsfeld zwischen Innen- und Außenpolitik im 2. Jahrtausend v. Chr. R. Gundlach and A. Klug, eds. Pp. 277–416. Wiesbaden: Harrassowitz.

Raedler, C. 2006 Zur Struktur der Hofgesellschaft Ramses'II, *In* Der ägyptische Hof des Neuen Reiches, Seine Gesellschaft und Kultur im Spannungsfeld zwischen Innen- und Außenpolitik. R. Gundlach and A. Klug, eds. Pp. 39–87. Wiesbaden: Harrosowitz.

Richards, J. 2005 Society and Death in Ancient Egypt. Cambridge: Cambridge University Press.

Said, E. 1978 Orientalism. New York: Vintage Books.

Ste Croix, G. E. M. de 1981 The Class Struggle in the Ancient Greek World, from the Archaic Age to the Arab Conquests. London: Duckworth.

Säve-Söderbergh, T., and L. Troy 1991 New Kingdom Pharaonic Sites: The Finds and the Sites. The Scandinavian Joint Expedition to Sudanese Nubia 5(2). Uppsala.

Schmitz, B. 1976 Untersuchungen zum Titel S3-NJŚWT "Königssohn." Bonn: Habelt.

Seidlmayer, S. J. 1987 Wirtschaftliche und gesellschaftliche Entwicklung im Übergang vom Alten zum Mittleren Reich: Ein Beitrag zur Archäologie der Gräberfelder der Region Qau-Matmar in der Ersten Zwischenzeit. *In* Problems and Priorities in Egyptian Archaeology. J. Assmann, G. Burkard, and V. Davies. Pp. 175–217. London, New York: Kegan Paul International.

Seidlmayer, S. J. 1990 Gräberfelder aus dem Übergang vom Alten zum Mittleren Reich: Studien zur Archäologie der Ersten Zwischenzeit (Studie zur Archäologie und Geschichte Altägyptens 1). Heidelberg: Heidelberger Orientverlag.

Seidlmayer, S. J. 2001 Ikonographie des Todes, *In* Social Aspects of Funerary Culture in the Egyptian Old and Middle Kingdoms. H. O. Willems, ed. Pp. 205–253. Leuven: Peeters.

Shaw, I. 2000 The Oxford History of Ancient Egypt. Oxford: Oxford University Press.

Shedid, A. G. 1988 Stil der Grabmalereien in der Zeit Amenophis' II. Mainz: Zabern.

Stanworth, P. 2006 Elites. *In* Social Divisions. G. Payne, ed. Pp. 173–193. Houndsmills, New York: Palgrave Macmillan.

Störk, L. 1980 Lepra. *In* Lexikon der Ägyptologie 3. W. Helck and O. Otto. Pp. 1007–1008. Wiesbaden: Harrasowitz.

Tietze, C. 1985 Amarna: Analyse der Wohnhäuser und soziale Struktur der Stadtbewohner (Teil I). Zeitschrift für ägyptische Sprache und Altertumskunde 112:48–84.

Tietze, C. 1986 Amarna: Analyse der Wohnhäuser und soziale Struktur der Stadtbewohner (Teil II). Zeitschrift für ägyptische Sprache und Altertumskunde 113:55–78.

Trigger, B. G. 2006 A History of Archaeological Thought. New York: Cambridge University Press.

Trigger, B. G., B. J. Kemp, D. O'Connor, and A. N. Lloyd 1983 Ancient Egypt, a Social History. Cambridge: Cambridge University Press.

Troy, L. 1986 Patterns of Queenship in Ancient Egyptian Myth and History. Uppsala: Universitetet.

Wilkinson, T. A. H. 1996 State Formation in Egypt: Chronology and Society (Cambridge Monographs in African Archaeology 40). Oxford: Tempus Reparatum.

Wilkinson, T. A. H. 2001 Social Stratification, *In* The Oxford Encyclopaedia of Ancient Egypt. Vol. 3. D. Redford, ed. Pp. 301–305. Oxford: Oxford University Press.

II

Identity and Personhood

Willeke Wendrich

Archaeology and Identity

This chapter seeks to understand in what sense Egyptians considered themselves individuals, how they defined themselves as part of a group, and in what way they projected their identity through their material culture. Defining ourselves as individual unique beings seems to be a typically modern Western concept of identity, while members of ancient societies probably more explicitly comprehended themselves and were defined as part of a group, or groups. At the same time there are indications that in ancient Egypt persons were considered individuals, and understood themselves as such. The concept of personhood, both during life on earth and in the afterlife, was individual, as can be surmised from the fact that for a few generations after their demise the deceased were considered as distinct human beings, known and addressed by name. A person's identity is more than individual traits; it is context-dependent and socially defined through interaction with others, ranging from family relations, a shared history, geographical location, age, gender, profession, ethnicity, to character, health, wealth, and social status. Identity can be embraced, internalized, or forced upon a person or group by external factors (Casella and Fowler 2005; Díaz-Andreu García and Lucy 2005; Insoll 2007; Jones 1997; Robb 2007; Sofaer 2007; Stein 2005; Thomas 1996).

Information on the identity of people in ancient Egypt is not simply accessible, but has to be pieced together from erratically surviving material markers represented in domestic or monumental architecture, decorated tombs, archaeological excavations, scraps of texts, and purposefully composed temple walls. To tease out concepts of identity and personhood from these traces is a difficult task, and we should be well aware that our interpretation likely reflects our own concerns, rather than those of ancient society and individuals. Yet, there are certainly many reasons to attempt a definition and description of the various ways in which persons in ancient Egypt would have defined themselves and others, stood in the world, negotiated social relations, and coped with changing circumstances. The purpose of this chapter is to explore how to define aspects of identity in the material record. These are the material codes for which the persons who interact are on the lookout: are we dealing with a woman or a man; child, adult, or elderly person; belonging to a specific family, rank, or profession; hailing from a particular place? Many of these aspects are perceived through subtle indicators, as part of clothing, food ways, or speech. An important, but problematic issue is regional differences, difficult to demonstrate or define, but their existence can be concluded from the occurrence of several distinct dialects known in Coptic, the latest phase of the ancient Egyptian language, which was written with Greek characters and therefore enables us to understand differences in vocalization and pronunciation (Kaser 1991; Osing 1975:41, 52).

When we speak about identity and personhood in the context of ancient Egypt, we should take into account that the concept of person included a supernatural identity, linked to religious concepts and closely associated with notions of the afterlife. This supernatural identity is a symbolic construction and as much the result of social interaction, ongoing communication, and negotiation with the living and the dead as "personal" or "social" identity (Fowler 2004). Identity before or after the moment of death is thus actively constituted and does not exist outside human communication in the broadest sense, shaped by the interaction of members within a group, or with outsiders. A person is inevitably part of multiple groups, some constituted explicitly, others tacitly considered inherent.

In a volume on historical archaeology, such as this, textual sources are of course taken into consideration. Because they are part of the material culture, their context should be part of the analysis through questions concerning the author, audience, purpose, and occasion, but explicitly also the material, and the archaeological context in which they were found, reflective of where they were functioning, discarded, or lost. Most of the textual sources which give information on personhood belong to the funerary realm. Apart from textual and archaeological information this chapter is also grounded in ethnoarchaeological records, to compare present-day or recent historical aspects of identity, material signifiers, and cultural concepts with ancient Egyptian ones, in order to broaden our perspective, which is inevitably limited by our direct or learnt experience. The concept of what identifies a person varies in different realms, both in the world of the living and in the afterlife. In a society with a rich history of reinventing tradition, changing ideas about society and the individual are presented in familiar traditional terms. This complicates efforts to comprehend how people understood and identified themselves and each other in different periods. Since most of the written sources represent a small layer of literate Egyptians, the results of our analysis are inherently biased.

What our sources clearly show us is that identity is of consequence from the individual to the state level. The characterization, manipulation, and management of individual and group identity are an integral part of Pharaonic rule. Kings demonstrably reinvent their links to the past and their geographical and social embedding in the present as part of a process of legitimation (see also Richards, and Schneider, this volume). The New Kingdom is a particularly good period to focus a study of aspects of person and identity, because of a relative wealth of source material available in comparison to earlier periods. We will, however, also take other eras into account. Dealing with such a wealth of material requires some organization. This complex topic, which intertwines personal, religious, and social concepts, will be considered in three sections, addressing briefly the historical context of the New Kingdom, personal identity and personhood, and material markers of socially negotiated identity.

The New Kingdom Setting: Rulers and Subjects

The golden period of Egyptian history, the New Kingdom (c. 1539–1075) shows interesting shifts in regional emphasis, related to the places of origin of the rulers of the 18th–20th Dynasties. The early 18th-Dynasty rulers claimed victory over the Hyksos, who were characterized as foreign enemies. Thanks to efficient New Kingdom propaganda, Egyptologists have long defined the Hyksos rule as a period of foreign occupation and decline, summarized in the designation "Second Intermediate Period" (Brewer and Teeter 2007:44–46). A more balanced view, based on the careful interpretation of the archaeological remains at Avaris, at one time the Hyksos capital, proposes a gradual growth of influence of first northern, then southern Levantine groups in the Eastern Delta (Bietak 1996, and Schneider, this volume). The conflict between the "Egyptians" and the Hyksos was in fact mostly a conflict between a local Theban faction and the rulers of the Delta, whose sphere of influence included the ancient capital Memphis. During the Middle Kingdom the capital had been moved to Itj-Tawy in Middle Egypt, so Memphis, even if in control of the rulers from the north, did not represent a conquered capital. Thebes, however, was caught in the middle between the powerful Kingdom of Kerma in the south and the northern Hyksos rulers, two powers that were in contact and maintained diplomatic relations, threatening their Theban opponents.

The pharaohs of the 18th Dynasty, directly related to the Theban house of Seqenenre, Ahmose, and Kamose, conquered the Delta and expanded their influence into the Levant. Military campaigns by pharaohs such as Thutmoses I, III, Amenhotep II, and Thutmoses IV resulted in a powerful and wealthy country, united under one ruler. Queen Hatshepsut, daughter of Thutmoses I, wife of her brother Thutmoses II, and ruler for her young cousin Thutmoses III, expanded her economic base by commissioning exploratory expeditions to the land of Punt. These obtained expensive and prestigious commodities such as gold, leopard skins, ivory, ebony, and incense as well as incense trees. In this time of peace, fulminations against the Hyksos were particularly virulent, as part of Hatshepsut's campaign to legitimize her rule as female pharaoh. Thus aspects of identity such as gender, age, and ethnicity were part of a historical definition of what it meant to be "Egyptian" and "King of Egypt."

Part of the legitimation was a close link between the royal house and the priesthood of the god Amun in Thebes. Expansions of the Karnak temple complex, including economically supportive endowments of land, were donated by the king to the priesthood. It has been surmised that the increasing economic and political power of the Amun priesthood was one of the reasons that Amenhotep III initiated religious changes, focusing on the identification between the person of the king and several gods in Egypt, such as the sun disk Aten, the Memphite god Ptah, and the sun god Ra (Johnson 1999). His son and successor Amenhotep IV/ Akhenaten is often considered as the world's first monotheist (see, e.g., Freud 1939 and the inventory by Assmann 1997). This is an unsophisticated description that in the light of a detailed study of the available evidence cannot be upheld. Akhenaten's actions were at least partly political, and directed primarily towards the destruction of the name of the god Amun, while some of the other gods of the pantheon were actively venerated, as illustrated by the names of his younger daughters Neferneferure and Setepenre, which feature the sun god Ra (or Re). A more apt characterization of the theological changes in this period is Assmann's "cognitive revolution" (Assmann 2001b:201–208).

The 18th-Dynasty pharaohs maintained diplomatic contacts with the powers in the Near East, such as Mittanni, the Kassites, and the Hittites, through gift exchange and royal marriages. Even though knowledge and appreciation of what was "foreign" increased dramatically as a result, the ideological depiction of foreigners is traditionally xenophobic. The tomb of Tutankhamun contains many depictions of bound foreigners, representing the three traditional enemies of Egypt, the Asiatics, the Libyans, and the Nubians, or the "9 bows," symbolizing all possible foreigners, depicted on the sandals or foot stool of the pharaoh to be ceremonially trodden upon. The tomb, however, also contained several examples of precious foreign garments, witnessing in the same space a regard for foreign contacts and diplomatic gift exchange (Vogelsang-Eastwood 1999). Tutankhaten, under influence of the high officials Aye and Horemheb, embarked on a restoration of the name and veneration of Amun (which included his own name change). After a brief rule by Aye, the royal succession was taken over by Horemheb, who probably changed his name from Pa-atenemheb, reflecting an identity change from an elite group venerating the Aten to one worshipping the traditional gods, such as Horus. Horemheb was Tutankhamun's general, who dismantled the temples of Akhenaten in Karnak, and inscribed his name over that of Tutankhamun.

Horemheb's vizier, or prime minister, was called Ramesses, and he was the father of the first king of the 19th Dynasty, Sety I. Hailing from the town of Avaris in the Delta, Sety was named after the god Seth, venerated in a temple built by the Hyksos. Seth, in the Heliopolitan tradition the brother and murderer of Osiris, is known as an evil god, but this image is mostly based on much later Greco-Roman sources. The Deltaic Seth was a syncretized form of the Egyptian deity and the Syro-Palestinian god Baal-Reshef (Te Velde 1977). The Eastern Delta, even after the "expulsion" of the Hyksos, continued to be an amalgam of different cultural influences. The grandson of Sety I, Ramesses the Great (Ramesses II), represents the quintessence of "Egyptianness," and yet he moved his capital from Memphis to Pi-Ramesse in the Eastern Delta, just a few kilometers northwest from Avaris. He was succeeded by his son Merenptah, who dismantled the memorial temple of the great king Amenhotep III to build his own monument. A time of dynastic struggle followed and Merenptah was succeeded briefly by Sety II, and his son Siptah, and a sole rule of Sety's widow Twosre after Siptah's death. The role of an official of Syrian descent has raised Egyptological interest: the official Irsu/Bay is depicted in an exceptional position for a commoner, and a foreigner at that, standing behind Siptah's throne. Bay was executed in the fifth year of Siptah's rule (Grandet 2000), and although the exact reason is unknown, it is likely that he had ongoing contacts with Ugarit, and was considered a traitor. The country descended in a period of civil strife, and the pharaohs of the 20th Dynasty were not related to the Ramessides, even though the second king of the dynasty named himself Ramesses III, and styled himself and his building projects after Ramesses II. After his rule there were eight successors who named themselves Ramesses (IV–XI). In the definition of dynasties by the priest Manetho in the third century BCE, the determining factor is not as much the direct family relation between pharaohs, but their regional origin. In a country which exists mainly of a 1000-km-long narrow strip of land, with even the broadening Nile Delta divided by north–south-running river branches, which effectively divided it into a number of parallel strips, and several outlying oases, the country consisted of a number of quite isolated areas. This partitioning of the land, especially apparent in the time of the inundation, related to regional differences which must have been obvious and perhaps resulted in an island mentality that was relevant in Egypt's understanding of the diversity of its population, the strong emphasis on unification and order being a logical compensation.

The monumental inscriptions that relate the fate of the kings, and give us indications of their allegiances, wars, and religious ties, hardly provide information on the population of Egypt in this period. There are, however, a number of excavations that have gained us unsurpassed insights into the daily life of other social layers. The city of Amarna, founded by Akhenaten in his fifth year of rule, was abandoned after approximately thirty years, when Tutankhamun came to the throne. Settlement archaeology concentrating on New Kingdom houses, neighborhoods, villages, and towns is rare, but the excavations at Amarna and a workmen's village located approximately 5 km into the desert give an exceptional insight in what on one level must have been a unique town, built in one grand effort around a ceremonial route, but on another level also was thoroughly traditional (Kemp 2006:284–297). The workmen's village was built in two phases as a walled settlement with standard size houses. Deir el-Medina, the village which housed the workmen and artists who carved out and decorated the royal tombs in the Valley of the Kings on the west bank in Thebes, was in use before and after the Amarna settlement. From the early 18th Dynasty we have several tombs, excavated in the rock around the settlement, which was huddled on the floor of the wadi. The village was reoccupied after the Amarna period. At that time, the inhabitants tried to dig a large well to improve the supply of water, which had to be carried in on donkey back. The result was an enormous hole in the ground, which never yielded a drop of water, but was used as a convenient garbage dump. The inhabitants of Deir el-Medina, which had a percentage of literacy that topped the average by far, threw away their daily notes, practice pieces, laundry lists, which were all written on limestone flakes. Even if Deir el-Medina cannot be considered an average village, its function and location are very specific, and the texts on these ostraca provide a unique insight into daily business and concerns, including information which can be used to tease out aspects of identity (McDowell 1999).

Individuality and Personhood

In our society the one aspect that signifies a person is the name, as means of identification, as opposite of anonymity, which is, very generally speaking, a negative state, associated with loneliness, and being rendered a powerless non-person.

The name conveniently unifies the multiple identities that a person has in different contexts (Bourdieu 2000). The meaning of the name is secondary to the fact that one has a name and is mentioned or referred to by it. In the Western world the first name identifies the person, while the family name (or names of father and grandfather) positions that person in time and space (Bourdieu 2000:302) Thus the family name might express the ethnic background of the father's side of a family (Müller, Sanchez, Yoo), while the first name usually expresses the child's gender, and personal relations or opinions of the parents. In Egypt before and during the Second World War the first name "Hitler" was given to boys in order to express the parents' protest against the British occupation of the country, and it is not an uncommon name among men in their sixties.

Name giving establishes that a person exists, and this was true also in ancient Egypt (Meyer-Dietrich 2006:185). In pre-industrial Egypt this was done on the seventh day after birth with a ritual in which several candles inscribed with different names were lit, and the name on the longest burning candle was given to the child (see also Blackwell 1927:80–81). In the Pharaonic period, name giving seems to have been done at birth, but it is unknown whether a ritual of name giving was performed to assign an identity, similar to the way baptism does in a Christian tradition (Ziff 1960:102–104). The only clearly identifiable moment of name giving was that of the coronation of a pharaoh. The multiple names of the king indicated different aspects of the self, including ritual and official aspects (Quirke 1990:9–27). Ancient Egyptian name giving was clearly important, however. A child would get a name at birth, the *ren a'a*, or great name, but there was limited variety in these names and in order to avoid confusion at some point a person could get a surname, the *ren nefer*, literally the "good" name (Vernus 1986). Through Egyptian history, the father's name was often added, as is customary today in Egypt and the Arab countries, and for the Middle Kingdom it has been attested that the grandfather's name could be added. Girls and young boys could be specified by adding the mother's name (Valbelle 1993). This is concurrent with the visual arts, where, especially in the Old Kingdom period, young boys, identifiable by clearly depicted male sexual organs, were given a dark yellow skin tone, which classified them as perhaps still belonging to the female gender realm. Examples are, for instance, the family statue of the dwarf Seneb from the Egyptian Museum in Cairo (acc.no. JE 51280), or the Pseudo-group statue of Penmeru in the Museum of Fine Arts, Boston (acc. no. 12.1484), both dated to the 5th Dynasty. Gender ambiguity for young children could have been a stage in engendering children (Sofaer 1997), or perhaps it was a means of protection. It had that function, for instance, in premodern rural Egypt, where young boys were dressed as girls to ward off the evil eye.

The meaning of names was part of positioning a child in a social network. From the Deir el-Medina ostraca, which allow the reconstruction of genealogies, it is clear that certain birth names were favored in particular families. Foreign names re-occurred as well, and would often skip generations, linking a foreign-named grandfather and grandson, while the son/father would have an Egyptian name (Ward 1994:63).

It seems that the central government was not concerned with individuals at state level. There was no official documentation of births, marriages, divorces, or deaths. Lists of names are only found for very practical reasons, for instance in the work rosters of Deir el-Medina, in juridical archives to identify buyers and sellers, contractants, or plaintiff and opposite party (Valbelle 1993). Death, in fact, seems to have been a highly individualized occurrence, which concerned the deceased and the family, but not the state.

The name was the identifying element of a person, both before and after death. Representations of persons, ubiquitous in funerary art, do not attempt to portray the individual. Reliefs, paintings, and statues were identified by inscribing the name of the main characters in the scene, such as the deceased and his or her relatives. This is apparent from the early Dynastic period onwards, where, for instance on the Narmer Palette, the name of the king crowns the scene, while the sandal bearer and a priest are indicated by their titles. In Old Kingdom art in which the smaller tombs are provided with stelae for the tomb owner and immediate family, the only names that occur are those of the direct linear family and the gods. Identifying the person whose name is depicted in the large tombs of the officials in Saqqara is enabled by a clear focus on a few persons, depicted much larger than the subsidiary figures, and in proscribed locations in the tomb, near the false door and the offering table. Usurpation of statuary and coffins could be effectuated by simply deleting the old and inscribing the new name, as is amply demonstrated by examples from especially the 21st Dynasty.

Yet there were attempts to produce real likenesses, parallel to the modern concept of a portrait, in which the face is the most identifying part of the body. Most of the evidence dates to the Old Kingdom, for instance the multiple statues of the owner deposited in some of the Giza and Saqqara tombs which occasionally depict different life phases (Robins 1997:76); the occurrence of "reserve heads," which have idiosyncratic features (Aldred 1980:67–70); and textual references to an "image according to life" being commissioned (Bolshakov 1997:234–260).

The importance of the written name is greater after death than in life. The name ensures that the correct person benefits from the provisions in the tomb. The tomb and much of its inventory are identified by name, inscribed on the objects, on funerary cones, and on sealings. But the name also poses a potential threat in a world where magic is a reality. In Egyptian mythology, Isis, through devious tricks, gains knowledge of the name of Ra, and thus gains power over the ancient god. And in the myth she states "a man lives when one recites in his name" (Mc Dowell 1999:118–120). Similarly, a *damnatio memoriae*, a systematic destruction of the name, not only affects a person's memory, but also destroys the individual and the "self" reborn in the afterlife.

In our secularized society, it is difficult to assess how important the ancient Egyptian religious concepts would have been in a person's life and understanding of self (see Kemp 1995). Nevertheless, it is almost inevitable to conclude that the complex of religion, magic, and medicine had a direct, personal corporal reality. A definition of "self" was closely linked to mostly post-mortem aspects: apart from the body and the name, a person also consisted of a *ka*, *ba*, shadow, *akh*, and heart (Assmann 2001a; Loprieno 2003). There have been many attempts to define these aspects of ancient Egyptian personhood. Only a thorough analysis can take into account the gradual changes over time, characterized by developments in thought, regional differences, misunderstandings, and reinterpretations. For the brief outline here, most information is taken from the funerary literature (Pyramid Texts, Coffin Texts, Book of the Dead, the Underworld Books), which gives an implicit outline of the constitution of the self, even though this term in itself is problematic.

The *ka* is often called the "double," because in royal iconography it is created at the same time as the living body, as illustrated by temple reliefs of the divine birth of the king, where the king is followed by a figure with the same appearance, sometimes wearing the hieroglyph for *ka* on its head (Bolshakov 1997). It seems, however, to have a meaning which is closer to "life force," or vital energy, associated through word play with the term for bull, as symbol of ultimate masculine fertility, and the term for sustenance. Commoners are not represented with a second figure, because the depiction in the tomb represents the *ka*, although it could perhaps be maintained that the occurrence of several statues of the deceased in the Old Kingdom tombs of Giza points to the embodiment of the vital force streaming through generations. After death the *ka* is the active self, and part of a network of interactions which unites the generations (Meyer-Dietrich 2006:228). This emphasis on forebears, and the placement of the person in a social network that spans generations, is certainly still of great importance during the New Kingdom. In addition to the so-called *akh-iker-n-Ra* stelae found at Deir el-Medina, and addressed to specific ancestors, nameless and quite featureless human busts have been found, which have been speculated to address ancestors in general. Interestingly, the term *ka* disappears in Demotic, and is replaced by the word *ren*, "name" (Möller 1912:36).

Perhaps the interpretation of the *ka* as "double" is partly inspired by a comparison with the premodern notion of *kareen/kareena*. Winifred Blackman, one of the first women to have a formal academic training in ethnography, published an ethnography of Egyptian farmers in *The Fellahin of Upper Egypt* (1927). In her final chapter she draws many parallels between ancient and modern Egypt in which she sees similarities between the *ka* and the notion in rural Egyptian communities of a "double." The *kareen(a)* is part of personhood, it is born at the same time as a person, it gets married to the spouse's *kareen(a)*, and dies when a person dies. It has an effect on daily life, especially when the double is jealous. It is tantalizing to see the *kareen(a)* as a "survival" of the ancient Egyptian *ka*, but that would be a fallacy. Studying phenomena without reference to the context in which they are embedded leads to supercilious and often simply wrong assumptions and interpretations. Similarly the role of the shadow in early twentieth-century Egypt is important, as is the name of a person. In the Luxor region among the lower class it is very common to have nicknames, which are very different from the "official" name. As seen in Chapter 5, such analogies are tantalizing, but problematic. The context and meaning of the phenomena change, not only between the present and the past, but also during the entire span of Egypt's long history.

In the funerary literature of the Middle Kingdom, the body is in an afterlife state, where death is a period of transition. Terms used, such as *djet*, *hau*, and *khjat*, all indicate the dead body as a corpse. In an excellent analysis of the Middle Kingdom coffin of Senebi, Erika Meyer-Dietrich (2006) proposes that these are different stages, in which the bodily fluids transform post-mortem into the semen of the god Osiris, the life-bringing force. Thus decomposition and transition result in rebirth, and reconstitute the person as self. An important part of the body is the heart, the seat of intelligence and courage, the organ that is weighed against the goddess of truth Maat in the judgment of the dead. It is eaten by the "devourer" Ammut, part lion, part crocodile, part hippopotamus, when the heart is too heavy. In the mummification process the heart is treated separately, and in most periods of Egyptian history it is placed back in the body, rather than in extra-corporal containers, such as canopic jars.

The term *ba* is often translated as "soul," which invokes unsuitable Christian associations, such as an opposition of body and soul. The *ba* is a manifestation of the power of gods, and of the divine king. From the Middle Kingdom onwards the *ba* is part of the living King, while the royal deceased forebears are also *bas* (Žabkar 1975). To non-royal persons the *ba* is considered the free-ranging aspect of the body after death, which has all bodily functions and is, from the New Kingdom onwards, depicted as a bird with a human head. In the Coffin Texts, the *ba* occurs in combination either with the body, the shadow, or sun shade (*shut*) or with the "appearance" or "form" (*iru*). The latter denotes a phase of the reconstitution of the self, while the *ba* and the shadow are the fundamental parts in the development of the *akh* (Meyer-Dietrich 2006). While the body rests in the tomb, the *ba* moves about and unites with the shadow, the visible aspect during the day, depending on the sunlight. We find the same close connection in the eleventh hour of the Amduat (the visualized texts of that-what-is-in-the-Underworld, painted on the tomb walls of the early 18th-Dynasty kings). Here the destruction of the enemies of the sun god Ra is depicted as fire or poison pits in which the bodies, the *ba*s, and the shadows are destroyed (Hornung 1999). Textual evidence thus mostly refers to the *ba*s of commoners in the afterlife, but there are indications that not only the king was considered to have a *ba* during life. As with many religious phenomena, the Middle and New Kingdom periods saw an expansion of funerary rituals of royal origin that became available to an increasingly broader group of persons.

Akh is the term for the privileged deceased, freed from the bonds of the mummified body, and allowed to follow the sun god Ra. It is the self after reconstitution and rebirth, enabled by the rituals of embalmment and mummification. The New Kingdom texts of the *akh-iker-en-Ra* stelae specify that "becoming an *akh*" is the work of the lector-priest, reciting the proper texts, and the embalmer. The good wishes for the deceased are that he may be *akh*, well equipped (*aperu*), and venerable (*shepses*) (Demaree 1983:204). Being well equipped meant owning a tomb with the proper furniture. Although these provisions seem to focus on the individual, the ritual and magical concepts and language were focused on male sexuality, which had to be mediated to be effective for the female deceased (Cooney 2008). Great care was given to provisioning the dead, partly to protect the living from revenge of recently deceased family members, who were known by name. There are several examples of so-called letters to the dead, which plead the good care that the surviving relatives have taken of the deceased (Grieshammer 1975), but tombs were also redistributed. After one or two generations the care-takers of the tomb, be they family, or priests paid for their services, would have died. At that time the individual became part of the more generic forebears, a pool of ancestors not known by name. The living no longer had a personal relation to these deceased, no living memories, because they were generations away. The role of the forebears should not be considered in the sense of lineage, but as real entities, or spirits, that might intervene on behalf of, or against, an individual. There are a few examples of forebears who retained their names and had reached a special status in a community. They would reach a state of divinity, but in a sense these are approachable, accessible gods who understand the living and can mediate. Examples are Imhotep, in Memphis (3rd Dynasty, deified during the New Kingdom), Heqaib, or Pepinakht, in Elephantine (6th Dynasty, deified during the Middle Kingdom), Izi (6th Dynasty, deified during the Middle Kingdom), and Amenhotep son of Hapu (18th dynasty, deified in the Ptolemaic period).

Social Interaction and Identity Markers in Material Culture

Because identity is socially constituted, participation in different groups may result in multiple forms of identity, which, as outlined above, are in a sense united by the personal identification of the name. The term identity has been used for different social phenomena, ranging from specifically and contextually defined roles. These can be listed as opposites or complementary aspects, such as man, woman; father, daughter; employee, employer; blue- or white-collar worker; teacher, student; the sick or the healthy; or as belonging to a group, sometimes ruled by overarching principles such as social status, nationality, and ethnicity. Identity is, however, more than a context-dependent social role. Ultimately it is defined by inclusion or exclusion, belonging or not, the human order of self and other, of signifier and signified (see Thomas 1996:41). Whether formulated as determined by ethnicity, gender, age, profession, social status, or a combination of these, the difference between a social role and social identity can be summarized as temporally versus permanently engrained individual–group relations. This does not exclude multiple identities, but limits these to long-term relations in well-established social contexts.

In spite of the difficulty of trying to understand a mode of communication that is implicit, context-dependent, and often visual, without knowing the signal, the sender or receiver, there are a number of aspects that upon scrutiny give us valuable information. These are evidence for food, dress, domestic architecture, personal belongings in a domestic setting or as part of a tomb inventory, as well as daily and burial customs. Even though it seems relevant to determine whether we are discussing identity as a feature of self-representation or as a definition by others, in practice it is a combination of both. Signifiers are both material and immaterial. Examples of the latter are, for instance, speech and accent and the way one carries oneself. There are some indications of immaterial signifiers in ancient Egypt, mostly accessible through oblique references in textual sources, either as sociolects, speech determined by gender, status, profession, and age, or dialects (Osing 1975). For instance in P. Anastasi 28, 1, a miscommunication is compared to the lack of understanding between inhabitants of the Delta and of Yebu, Elephantine, in the far south (Fischer-Elfert 1986:238).

The subconscious, or tacitly adhered to, classifications of society and individual are best defined through a study of the material culture. Only very few of such detailed studies have been done so far (Meskell 1999, 2002, 2004, 2005; Smith 2003), but this approach is a promising field for further exploration of the topic. The material signifiers can be found in an archaeological context, but that does not make them easily accessible, or comprehensible. As Meskell (1999) concluded, even with the exceptionally good preservation of Egyptian archaeological materials, much still eludes us.

Perhaps the most important material correlate of communicating identity is the body itself. In archaeology the body is evidence of the existence of a person, and by studying the body, particulars such as sex, age, and health can be extrapolated in relation to the archaeological context (Bard 1988). Children have long have been "invisible" in the archaeological record (Lucy 2005) and it has been argued that one of the reasons is the relative small number of children's burials found (Sofaer 1997). In Egypt, child burials and other evidence for children are available, but still the group which is most involved in enculturation, and hence the forming of group identity, is studied rarely (Baxter 2008). The living body is the major identifier of age, an aspect that is often augmented in the living with signifiers such as special tasks, clothing, hair style, or other material signifiers, while the corpse still retains important characteristics and, at least in the higher classes, even gains more of these as part of the burial equipment. A body without a name is, however, not identifiable as a person. Inscribing the name is central in the ancient Egyptian understanding of personhood, and the material culture is geared to this: many of the objects, especially the ones prepared specifically for the grave, have the name of the deceased inscribed; statues have space reserved for the name inscription, for instance on the back pillars, which form the strongest and best-protected part of the object; and tomb reliefs reserve ample space for inscribing the name. The religious identity of a person is closely connected to the name as identifier, and the *ka*, *ba*, the heart, the *iru*, the shadow, and the *akh* are represented mostly by imagery and texts, and in case of the *ka* also by statuary. These are quite deliberate representations of aspects of the person.

The notion that food is closely related to identity "is strongly supported by the claim that sentiments of belonging via food do not only include the act of classification and consumption, but also the preparation, the organization, the taboos, the company, the location, the pleasure, the time, the language, the symbols, the representation, the form the meaning and the art of eating and drinking" (Scholliers 2001:7). In the ancient Egyptian context a study of the depicted contents of offering tables would represent an idealized and standardized food provision for the gods of Egypt, but by proxy also for its inhabitants, while the occurrence of food restrictions, or the naming of populations after food habits, signifies the opposite. We have to be careful to employ the word taboo where the ancient Egyptian language uses *but*, which means "disgust, abomination" and is linked to notions of purity and impurity (Frandsen 1986). From the Late Period there are textual sources which explicitly forbade the use of certain foodstuffs, such as fish, pork, or beans. This was limited to certain regions, and therefore may have been important as a definition of (a part of) a group living within those specific areas. On the other hand the same foodstuffs are known to have been staple foods in other periods and regions, so adherence to these regulations may have been limited to a certain portion of the society (Gamer-Wallert 1970). When the 25th-Dynasty king Piye (c. 750–715) conquered the Delta, he was only prepared to meet with one of the local rulers, stating that the others "could not enter the palace because they were uncircumcised and were eaters of fish, which is an abomination (*but*) to the palace" (translation Lichtheim 1980:80).

In Roman sources inhabitants of the southern Red Sea region were named after what at least in Roman eyes were their specific dietary peculiarities: fish eaters, ostrich eaters, dog eaters, elephant eaters, locusts eaters, and meat eaters (Strabo 16.4.8–13). This is likely a very warped classification of encountered peoples, and a pejorative indication similar to the term Eskimo, from Alqonquian *esquimantsic*, "people who eat their meat raw," as an insulting term for the Inuit (Mintz 2003:24). A detailed study of food remains, either zooarchaeological, archaeobotanical, or through residue analysis of pottery, may provide us with certain trends of the actual use of foodstuffs (Barnard and Eerkens 2007; Cappers 2006; O'Day et al. 2004), and can prevent us from considering populations by only the most obvious or visible aspects of their culture (Edwards 2003). Apart from the food remains themselves there are other material remains closely related to food preparation, serving, and consumption which have served as a signifier (Schärer 1998; Smith 2003). An example is archaeological basketry remains from Middle Egypt and Nubia. Basketry found in the Amarna workmen's village and dating to the New Kingdom period (around 1350 BCE) consisted of flat, undecorated coiled containers made of palm leaf. They were well made, but quite coarse, and most likely used to serve food. The Nubian basketry, excavated in Qasr Ibrim, and dating to a much later period (6th century CE), was made of the same materials, but much finer. More importantly, the Qasr Ibrim baskets were decorated on the outside with colored winders, or patterned stitching. These baskets were used not as containers, but as covers, to protect the contents of cups, or food served on trays. From the decoration and shape it is clear that there was a clear regional difference in ideas of food serving and presentation (Wendrich 1999). In this case, the distinction denotes a spatial difference, traceable over a long period. To simply call this an ethnic difference disregards the growing notion that ethnicity, similar to other forms of identity, is not determined and static, but equally negotiated in social and political settings (Jones 1997).

The study of identity has been separated in the study of ethnicity (Schneider, this volume), gender (Wilfong, this volume), class (Grajetzki, this volume), and age, and is an ongoing process that results in different expressions, depending on the circumstances and the context. The material items which are considered signifiers and are part of self-definition come to the fore when an attempt is made by members of the group to create a common representation, often in times of duress. After the building of the Aswan High Dam in the 1960s, which flooded most of Lower Nubia, several Nubian villages created a space where guests can be received, decorated following traditional concepts. Stimulated by the loss of their village and the distress of the forced resettlement, the villages have created a central place of memory. A similar procedure of self-definition through material culture took place among the Ababda nomads in the southern reaches of the Egyptian Eastern Desert. A sharp increase of tourism and an influx of developers, hotel giants, and tour operators led to the creation of a cultural heritage center (Wendrich 2008). Some of the objects, such as the *djabana*, a globular coffee maker with a wide distribution throughout Eritrea, Ethiopia, Sudan, and Southern Egypt, have grown into very explicit cultural markers, an ethnic symbol of nomadic groups along the Red Sea coast (Figures 11.1 and 11.2).

For the past we often are forced to concentrate on the funerary context, partly because of a bias in the number of cemeteries that have been excavated in comparison to the dearth of settlement archaeology, but also because death requires a definite establishment of identity. This is apparent through the entire depth of Egyptian history (Meskell 1999; Riggs 2005; Wengrow 2006). Explicit presentation of the self in ancient Egypt occurs mostly in textual or visual sources, in many different contexts and for various audiences and purposes. Self-definition was, however, in many cases a luxury. An identity could be forced upon a person by others, and result in the eyes of the "self" in a misrepresentation. On the other hand, enforced stereotypes were sometimes appropriated and re-instituted as part of the "self." In the archaeological record explicit self-representation is very

Figure 11.1 *Djabana* is the term for a hospitality ceremony among several groups where guests are invited to drink three or seven small cups of strong, sweet, ginger-flavored coffee, made from freshly roasted beans crushed and steeped in a globular coffee pot with the same name. Photo: The author.

Figure 11.2 The *djabana* has become a cultural marker for the Beja, a conglomeration of several nomadic groups from the mountainous region along the Red Sea in Egypt, Sudan, Ethiopia, and Somalia. Monument on a street crossing in Suakin, Sudan. Barnard 2007:Fig. 3. Used with permission.

limited. To a certain extent biographies, inscribed in the tomb of high-status officials, can be considered as such. Only certain persons were entitled to use a biographical description, and even then their self-representation was determined by social circumscription. Autobiographies were written as early as the 4th Dynasty, and developed from a simple summing up of rank and titles. They record important functions held during a lifetime, rather than a detailed linear "life history," a "coherent narrative of a significant and directed sequence of events" (Bourdieu 2000:300). The biographies are quite standardized careful compositions, and their purpose was in the first place to convince the reader, members of the family, or priests that the tomb owner was worthy of offerings (*imakh*). Many of the biographies highlight personal relations with the pharaoh, as the main sign of worthiness.

Visual representations, in the form of paintings, reliefs, or statuary, were perhaps another form of self-representation (Stevens 2007), albeit for purposes of sustaining the deceased in the afterlife. Tomb scenes which bridge social signifiers for the dead and the living are the depictions of offering bearers, known from the Old Kingdom onwards. These scenes, which seem to represent the ceremony of carrying the furniture and burial equipment into the tomb, were considered indispensable in Old Kingdom decorated tombs (Walsem 2005:53), and continued throughout the New Kingdom period (Barthelmess 1992). Although clearly an important part of the burial ritual, this type of funerary scene is rarely discussed. It usually occurs near the transportation of the deceased in the coffin on a sledge or carried by bearers on a bier. Settgast (1963) discusses whether all the funerary scenes represent actual performed rituals, or are part of the recitation of remembered and honored traditions, expressed in words rather than deeds. The burial procession is, however, one of the activities that actually did take place. In several scenes the offering bearers are named as sons of the deceased (Barthelmess 1992:71–73). Carrying the carefully prepared and expensive tomb equipment into the tomb would have been a display of wealth and standing and the only time in which the expenditure for the afterlife would be part of an extensive public display in the world of the living. It is perhaps comparable to the display of the trousseau of lower- and middle-class newly weds in present-day Egypt, where the car with the bride and groom is followed by open-bed pick-up trucks with the bedroom furniture, fridge, and television. There are other indications that status played an important part in the burial cortège both for the deceased and for close relatives and colleagues. In high-status burials those who carry the bier are often mentioned by name (e.g. Reeves 1990:72–73). We can speculate that high officials probably fought to be literally in the picture as the one to carry the mummified remains of Pharaoh.

In the manner in which persons, landscape, nature, and objects were depicted, we can perhaps consider changes in style as a reflection of individual agency, of either the producer or the patron who ordered the work. This has been maintained most vocally in relation to Amarna art (e.g. Freed 1999) and Akhenaten's alleged personal intervention, but this then would have been the politically or religiously motivated decision of a small circle only. As outlined above, ancient Egyptian visual representation focused on different aspects than the modern gaze would seek in portraiture.

If we look for the expression of identity in material culture outside the funerary realm, we have to look at settlement archaeology. Domestic architecture communicated identity through the size, amenities, and layout of the dwellings. If we compare Kerma dwellings with the roughly contemporary settlement of Lahun, then the difference is inescapable. The Kerma houses have been constructed from thin mudbrick walls and organic materials: tree trunks and branches, and palm leaf matting. All that remains today are post holes in a marked circular pattern, with wavy wall lines indicating the boundaries of individual compounds (Bonnet 1990, 2004). This forms a stark contrast with the orthogonal layout of several of the settlements to the north, for instance the one at Kahun (Petrie et al. 1891; Quirke 2005). From the few extant examples of settlements dated to different periods – Old Kingdom Giza and Balat; Middle Kingdom Kahun and Karnak, as well as the internal structures of the Nubian forts; New Kingdom Amarna, and to a lesser extent Deir el-Medina – the orthogonal layout clearly is the preferred building style. The rounded Kerma features denote a very different concept, even though Kerma and Egypt were in close contact.

If we concentrate on the New Kingdom period, then we can make an interesting comparison of house styles of two settlements of the same period and the same region, but purportedly inhabited by different classes. The suburbs of the main city at Amarna and the workmen's village (also known as the "Eastern Village") display a marked difference (Kemp 2006; Kemp and Garfi 1993). The layout of the suburbs is characterized by walled compounds, surrounded by smaller housing units, taken to indicate patron–client relations (see Lehner, this volume), while the workmen's village is a walled orthogonally planned settlement in which all house are the same size. For the visitors or inhabitants of Amarna, the occurrence of granaries in the main city house compounds pointed unequivocally at wealth, because they represented land ownership, which required storage of the harvest yield. The number of features a house displayed, such as the number of rooms, use of columns, and bed platforms, were concurrent with the social position of the owner (Tietze 1985, 1986). A comparison of the Amarna main city houses with those from the workmen's village shows that apart from these features, the size of the house, and the space around the dwelling, other aspects communicated a difference that reached beyond wealth or status. In contrast to the standardized New Kingdom temples, in which all gates to the subsequent, more restricted areas lie in a straight line on the axis of the temple, closed off by wooden doors, the entrances of the large Amarna main city estates never lead directly into the main part of the house. One enters the house along a rising path that forms a zig-zag. This seems to be a preferred pattern of Egyptian housing, deeply engrained in domestic architecture of different periods and apparently independent of the size of the house. The modest houses of the Middle Kingdom town of Lahun, for instance, are built along the same principle, even though at first view this does not seem obvious, because there is much variation in building plan. This makes the Amarna workmen's village, where the front rooms open directly onto the street, and the door to the main room is positioned in a straight line behind the entrance, seemingly an anomaly. Pivot holes show that wooden doors would have closed off the house from the street, but the windowless front rooms, in many of which evidence for weaving has been found, would need to get their light from the open door. The entrances of the houses at Deir el-Medina have a comparative layout and in addition many of the front rooms contain a feature which has been characterized as a house shrine or, perhaps, a birthing bed (Meskell 2002). In our perspective both associated activities, worship or breastfeeding, require a private space. The issue of house entrances provokes questions of the right to, or need for, privacy in the domestic sphere. Explicit self-reflection is needed to correct for cultural biases, to avoid, for instance, the interpretation of fourteenth-century BCE culture being railroaded by twenty-first-century prudery or sensibilities.

In detailed comparisons we can begin to tease out aspects of material culture that are used as subconscious markers. It might even be possible to discern at what point, or under which circumstances, individuals or groups purposely advertise themselves as a group, and what the communal factor is that creates or defines a sense of belonging or exclusion. In order to enable a fuller interpretation of issues of identity we can summarize the examples given above in a program of research: a multivariate analysis of a complex multitude of factors is the foundation to decipher elements of identity. By studying the body, adornment and clothing, food ways, architectural styles, and find assemblages, we can define how particular concepts of personhood and identity relate to social factors such as class, rank, age, social status, profession, gender, and ethnicity, as well as "personal" properties such as intelligence, strength, appearance, and health. Our most important task is, however, to address not only how statements of identity were made, but also what individuals or groups were communicating by adhering to particular patterns, or deviating from these.

ACKNOWLEDGMENTS

I would like to thank Jacco Dieleman for commenting on an early draft of this chapter, and for a continuous and inspirational exchange of ideas.

REFERENCES

Aldred, C. 1980 Egyptian Art. New York: Thames and Hudson.

Assmann, J. 1997 Moses the Egyptian: The Memory of Egypt in Western Monotheism. Cambridge, MA: Harvard University Press.

Assmann, J. 2001a Tod und Jenseits im alten Ägypten. Munich: C. H. Beck.

Assmann, J. 2001b The Search for God in Ancient Egypt. Ithaca, NY, London: Cornell University Press.

Bard, K. A. 1988 A Quantitative Analysis of the Predynastic Burials in Armant Cemetery 1400–1500. Journal of Egyptian Archaeology 74:39–55.

Barnard, H. 2007 The Ancient Eastern Desert Dwellers: A Sixth-Century Tribe and Its Pottery, In The Kenena Handbook of Sudan. P. G. Hopkins, ed. Pp. 89–95. London, New York, Bahrain: Kegan Paul.

Barnard, H., and J. W. Eerkens, eds 2007 Theory and Practice of Archaeological Residue Analysis. Oxford: Archeopress.

Barthelmess, P. 1992 Der Übergang ins Jenseits in den thebanischen Beamtengräbern der Ramessidenzeit. Vol. 2. Heidelberg: Heidelberger Orientverlag.

Baxter, J. E. 2008 The Archaeology of Childhood. Annual Anthropological Review 37:159–175.

Bietak, M. 1996 Avaris, the Capital of the Hyksos: Recent Excavations at Tell el-Dabʻa. London: British Museum Press.

Blackman, W. S. 1927 The Fellahin of Upper Egypt. Cairo: The American University in Cairo Press.

Bolshakov, A. O. 1997 Man and His Double in Egytian Ideology of the Old Kingdom. Wiesbaden: Harrassowitz.

Bonnet, C. 1990 Kerma, royaume de Nubie: L'antiquité africaine au temps des pharaons. Geneva: Musée d'art et d'histoire Genève.

Bonnet, C. 2004 Kerma. In Sudan, Ancient Treasures. D. A. Welsby and J. R. Anderson, eds. Pp. 78–82. London: British Museum Publications.

Bourdieu, P. 2000 The Biographical Illusion. In Identity: A Reader. P. du Gay, J. Evans, and P. Redman, eds. Pp. 299–305. London: Sage Publications.

Brewer, D. J., and E. Teeter 2007 Egypt and the Egyptians. Cambridge: Cambridge University Press.

Cappers, R. T. J. 2006 Roman Foodprints at Berenike: Archaeobotanical Evidence of Subsistence and Trade in the Eastern Desert of Egypt. Los Angeles: Cotsen Institute of Archaeology University of California.

Casella, E. C., and C. Fowler 2005 The Archaeology of Plural and Changing Identities beyond Identification. New York: Kluwer Academic/Plenum.

Cooney, K. M. 2008 The Problem of Female Rebirth in New Kingdom Egypt: The Fragmentation of the Female Individual in Her Funerary Equipment. *In* Sex and Gender in Ancient Egypt: "Don Your Wig for a Joyful Hour." C. Graves-Brown, ed. Pp. 1–25. Swansea: Classical Press of Wales.

Demaree, R. 1983 The 3h ikr n Rc-Stelae. On Ancestor Worship in Ancient Egypt. Leiden: Nederlands Instituut voor het Nabije Oosten.

Díaz-Andreu García, M., and S. Lucy 2005 Introduction. *In* The Archaeology of Identity: Approaches to Gender, Age, Status, Ethnicity and Religion. M. Díaz-Andreu García, S. Lucy, S. Babić, and D. N. Edwards, eds. Pp. 1–12. London, New York: Routledge.

Edwards, D. 2003 Ancient Egypt in the Sudanese Middle Nile: A Case of Mistaken Identity. *In* Ancient Egypt in Africa. D. O'Connor and A. Reid, eds. Pp. 137–150. London: University College London Press.

Fischer-Elfert, H.-W. 1986 Die Satirische Streitschrift des Papyrus Anastasi I. Wiesbaden: Harrassowitz.

Fowler, C. 2004 The Archaeology of Personhood, an Anthropological Approach. London, New York: Routledge.

Frandsen, P. J. 1986 Tabu. *In* Lexikon der Ägyptologie. W. Helck and E. Otto, eds. Pp. 135–142. Wiesbaden: Harrassowitz.

Freed, R. E. 1999 Art in the Service of Religion and the State. *In* Pharaohs of the Sun. R. E. Freed, Y. J. Markowitz, and S. H. D'Auria, eds. Pp. 110–129. Boston, New York, London: Museum of Fine Arts, Boston; Bulfinch Press; Little, Brown and Company.

Freud, S. 1939 Moses and Monotheism. New York: Knopf.

Gamer-Wallert, I. 1970 Fische und Fischkulte im alten Ägypten. Wiesbaden: Harrassowitz.

Grandet, P. 2000 L'execution du chancelier Bay O. Institut français d'archéologie orientale 1864. Bulletin de l' Institut français d'archéologie orientale 100:339–356.

Grieshammer, R. 1975 Briefe an Tote. *In* Lexikon der Ägyptologie. W. Helck and E. Otto, eds. Pp. 864–870. Wiesbaden: Harrassowitz.

Hornung, E. 1999 The Ancient Egyptian Books of the Afterlife. D. Lorton, trans. Ithaca, NY, London: Cornell University Press.

Insoll, T., ed. 2007 The Archaeology of Identities: A Reader. London, New York: Routledge.

Johnson, R. 1999 The Setting: History, Religion, and Art. *In* Pharaohs of the Sun. R. E. Freed, Y. J. Markowitz, and S. H. D'Auria, eds. Pp. 38–49. Boston, New York, London: Museum of Fine Arts, Boston; Bulfinch Press; Little, Brown and Company.

Jones, S. 1997 The Archaeology of Ethnicity. London, New York: Routledge.

Kaser, R. 1991 Geography, Dialectical. *In* Coptic Encyclopedia. Vol. 8. A. S. Atiya, ed. Pp. 113b–141a. New York: Macmillan.

Kemp, B. J. 1995 How Religious were the Ancient Egyptians? Cambridge Archaeological Journal 5:25–54.

Kemp, B. J. 2006 Ancient Egypt, Anatomy of a Civilization. 2nd edition. London, New York: Routledge.

Kemp, B. J., and S. Garfi 1993 A Survey of the Ancient City of El-'Amarna. London: Egypt Exploration Society.

Lichtheim, M. 1980 Ancient Egyptian Literature. Vol. III: The Late Period. Berkeley, Los Angeles, London: University of California Press.

Loprieno, A. 2003 Drei Leben nach dem Tod: Wieviele Seelen hatten die alten Ägypter? *In* Grab und Totenkult im Alten Ägypten. H. Guksch, E. Hofmann, and M. Bommas, eds. Pp. 200–225. Munich: C. H. Beck.

Lucy, S. 2005 The Archaeology of Age. *In* The Archaeology of Identity: Approaches to Gender, Age, Status, Ethnicity and Religion. M. Díaz-Andreu García, S. Lucy, S. Babić, and D. N. Edwards, eds. Pp. 43–66. London, New York: Routledge.

McDowell, A. G. 1999 Village Life in Ancient Egypt: Laundry Lists and Love Songs. Oxford: Oxford University Press.

Meskell, L. 1999 Archaeologies of Social Life: Age, Sex, Class *et cetera* in Ancient Egypt. Oxford, Malden, MA: Blackwell.

Meskell, L. 2002 Private Life in New Kingdom Egypt. Princeton: Princeton University Press.

Meskell, L. 2004 Object Worlds in Ancient Egypt. Oxford, New York: Berg.

Meskell, L. 2005 Archaeologies of Materiality. Oxford, Malden, MA: Blackwell.

Meyer-Dietrich, E. 2006 Senebi und Selbst: Personenkonstituenten zur rituellen Wiedergeburt in einem Frauensarg de Mittleren Reiches. Fribourg: Academic Press Fribourg; Göttingen: Vandenhoeck & Ruprecht.

Mintz, S. W. 2003 Eating Communities: The Mixed Appeals of Sodality. *In* Eating Culture: The Poetics and Politics of Food. T. Döring, M. Heide, and S. Mühleisen, eds. Pp. 19–34. Heidelberg: Universitätsverlag Winter.

Möller, G. 1912 Die beiden Totenpayrus Rhind des Museum zu Edinburg. Milan: Cisalpino-Goliardica.

O'Day, S. J., W. Van Neer, and A. Ervynck 2004 Behaviour behind Bones: The Zooarchaeology of Ritual, Religion, Status and Identity: Proceedings of the 9th Conference of the International Council of Aracheozoology, Durham, August 2002. Oxford, Oakville, CT: Oxbow.

Osing, J. 1975 Dialekte. *In* Lexikon der Ägyptologie. W. Helck and E. Otto, eds. Pp. 1074–1075. Wiesbaden: Harrassowitz.

Petrie, W. M. F., A. H. Sayce, and F. L. Griffith 1891 Illahun, Kahun and Gurob: 1889–1890. London: D. Nutt.

Quirke, S. 1990 Who Were the Pharaohs? A History of Their Names with a List of Cartouches. London: British Museum Publications.

Quirke, S. 2005 Lahun: A Town in Egypt 1800 BC, and the History of Its Landscape. London: Golden House Publications.

Reeves, C. N. 1990 The Complete Tutankhamun: The King, the Tomb, the Royal Treasure. London, New York: Thames and Hudson.

Riggs, C. 2005 The Beautiful Burial in Roman Egypt: Art, Identity, and Funerary Religion. Oxford, New York: Oxford University Press.

Robb, J. 2007 Early Mediterranean Village: Agency, Material Culture, and Social Change in Neolithic Italy. Cambridge: Cambridge University Press.

Robins, G. 1997 The Art of Ancient Egypt. Cambridge, MA: Harvard University Press.

Schärer, M. R. 1998 Food and Material Culture – a Museological Approach. *In* Food and Material Culture: Proceedings of the Fourth Symposium of the International Commission for the Research into European Food History. A. Fenton and M. R. Schärer, eds. Pp. 8–25. East Lothian: Tuckwell Press.

Scholliers, P. 2001 Meals, Food Narratives, and Sentiments of Belonging in Past and Present. *In* Food, Drink and Identity: Cooking, Eating and Drinking in Europe since the Middle Ages. P. Scholliers, ed. Pp. 3–22. Oxford, New York: Berg.

Settgast, Jürgen 1963 Untersuchungen zu altägyptischen Bestattungsdarstellungen. Glückstadt, New York: J. J. Augustin.

Smith, S. T. 2003 Wretched Kush: Ethnic Identities and Boundaries in Egypt's Nubian Empire. London, New York: Routledge.

Sofaer, J. R. 1997 Engendering Children, Engendering Archaeology. *In* Invisible People and Processes. J. Moore and E. Scott, eds. Pp. 192–202. Leicester: Leicester University Press.

Sofaer, J. R. 2007 Material Identities. Oxford, Malden, MA: Blackwell.

Stein, G. 2005 The Archaeology of Colonial Encounters: Comparative Perspectives. Santa Fe: School of American Research Press.

Stevens, F. 2007 Identifying the Body: Representing Self. Art, Ornamentation and the Body in Later Prehistoric Europe. *In* Material Identities (New Interventions in Art History). J. R. Sofaer, ed. Pp. 82–98. Oxford, Malden, MA: Blackwell.

Te Velde, H. 1977 Seth, God of Confusion. Leiden: Brill.

Thomas, J. 1996 Time, Culture and Identity: An Interpretive Archaeology. London, New York: Routledge.

Tietze, C. 1985 Amarna: Analyse der Wohnhäuser und soziale Struktur der Stadtbewohner (Teil I). Zeitschrift für ägyptische Sprache und Altertumskunde 112:48–84.

Tietze, C. 1986 Amarna: Analyse der Wohnhäuser und soziale Struktur der Stadtbewohner (Teil II). Zeitschrift für ägyptische Sprache und Altertumskunde 113:55–78.

Valbelle, D. 1993 La notion d'identité dans l'Égypte pharaonique. *In* Atti VI Congresso. Pp. 551–556. Turin: International Association of Egyptologists.

Vernus, P. 1986 Le Surnom au Moyen Empire: Répertoire procédés d'expression et structures de la double identité du début de la XIIe dynastie à la fin de la XVIIe dynastie. Rome: Ponfifical Biblical Institute.

Vogelsang-Eastwood, G. 1999 Tutankhamun's Wardrobe: Garments from the Tomb of Tutankhamun. Rotterdam: Barjesteh and Meeuwes.

Walsem, R. van 2005 Iconography of Old Kindgom Elite Tombs: Analysis and Interpretation, Theoretical and Methodological Aspects. Leiden: Ex Oriente Lux; Leuven: Peeters.

Ward, W. A. 1994 Foreigners Living in the Village. *In* Pharaoh's Workers: The Villagers of Deir el Medina. L.H. Lesko, ed. Pp. 61–85. Ithaca, NY, London: Cornell University Press.

Wendrich, W. 1999 The World According to Basketry: An Ethno-archaeological Interpretation of Basketry Production in Egypt. Leiden: Research School of Asian African and Amerindian Studies (CNWS).

Wendrich, W. 2008 From Object to Agent: The Ababda Nomads and the Interpretation of the Past. *In* The Archaeology of Mobility: Nomads in the Old and in the New World. H. Barnard and W. Wendrich, eds. Pp. 509–542. Los Angeles: Cotsen Institute of Archaeology, University of California.

Wengrow, D. 2006 The Archaeology of Early Egypt: Social Transformations in North-East Africa, 10,000 to 2,650 BC. Cambridge, New York: Cambridge University Press.

Žabkar, L. V. 1975 Ba. *In* Lexikon der Ägyptologie. W. Helck and E. Otto, eds. Pp. 588–590. Wiesbaden: Harrassowitz.

Ziff, P. 1960 Semantic Analysis. Ithaca, NY: Cornell University Press.

12

Changes in the Afterlife

John H. Taylor

Historical Background

Following the death of Ramesses XI, c. 1069 BCE, the 20th Dynasty and the New Kingdom came to an end. For much of the next four centuries Egypt was a politically divided land. In the 21st Dynasty, a line of kings ruled from Tanis in the Delta, while a family of army commanders simultaneously controlled Upper Egypt from Thebes. These southern rulers, who were probably of Libyan ancestry, added religious authority to military supremacy by assuming the title of high priest of Amun. Although nominally under the authority of the Tanite kings, they were in reality virtually independent. This dual rule was interrupted c. 945 BCE when Sheshonq I, founder of the 22nd Dynasty, took the throne. This royal line was also of Libyan descent and Sheshonq and his immediate successors exercised direct control over the whole of Egypt. But after about 850 BCE the political map of the country became increasingly fragmented, as small kingdoms and principalities proliferated (23rd–24th Dynasties). This situation led to tensions, and there was periodic unrest and even internal conflict. In the late eighth century BCE, the 25th Dynasty, a line of rulers from Nubia strongly imbued with Egyptian traditions of religion and kingship, took control of Egypt through a mixture of political maneuvering and military conquest (Török 1997:144–169). Although they acquiesced in the continued government of the principalities by individual dynasts, the Nubians were a cohesive influence, imposing stronger control over Egypt and overseeing a revival in cultural traditions.

The Libyan pharaohs adopted the titles and external trappings of Egyptian kingship, but the nature of their rule differed from that of their New Kingdom predecessors. The kings at Tanis reigned as overlords, tolerating other princes and even "kings" elsewhere in the land (Leahy 1985:58–59). Thus the unique character of the pharaoh, previously a hallmark of the Egyptian state, was no longer maintained, and some of the formal attributes which had previously distinguished the rulers from their subjects ceased to be royal prerogatives (Jansen-Winkeln 2000:7). Below the kings, the chief wielders of power in Egypt now combined the two functions of army commander and high priest, a situation manifested at the major centers of Thebes, Memphis, and Herakleopolis, as well as in important Delta towns such as Mendes. Names and titles on monuments testify to the strong presence of Libyans in positions of influence (Jansen-Winkeln 1994:78, 79–80). Many of these people were the descendants of groups who had moved into Egypt in the later New Kingdom, settling particularly in the Delta and around the mouth of the Fayum region (Jansen-Winkeln 2000: 10; Leahy 1985:55–56). By the 21st Dynasty these Libyans constituted a military aristocracy, controlling most of the army. The priesthood also continued to wield great influence, though here the evidence suggests that families of Egyptian origin maintained the dominant position (Jansen-Winkeln 2000:11).

The period of Libyan domination is characterized by an inward-looking attitude on the part of the rulers, coupled with the establishment of more fortresses and garrisons along the Nile, which has suggested a concern with the forcible control of the Egyptian populace (Jansen-Winkeln 1994:83). The scale of Egypt's foreign contacts appears to have diminished and there are signs that its prestige abroad declined. At home, the economy appears to have been under pressure, as manifested in a reduction in new monumental building projects and the recycling of building stone, sarcophagi, and funerary trappings on a hitherto unprecedented scale (Jansen-Winkeln 1995).

The profile of the population is difficult to assess, but on the basis of textual evidence there appears to have been a preponderance of Libyans in the north and Egyptians in the south (Leahy 1985:56; Taylor 2000:345–346). The possibility of some kind of ethnic division on geographical lines may be reflected also in certain cultural differences – for example the use of different cursive scripts in the north and south of Egypt (Jansen-Winkeln 2000:10, n. 39; Leahy 1985:59). Such phenomena pose questions regarding the extent to which the Libyans were assimilated into Egyptian society and culture, and the degree to which they promoted change (Jansen-Winkeln 2000:4–3; Taylor 2000:346). Throughout this period other changes are manifest in Egyptian society (such as a rise in the status of women: Naguib 1990), in religious practices (the development of mammisiac religion), in craftsmanship (notably advances in the manufacture of faience and metalwork: Bianchi 1990; Hill 2007; Ziegler 1987), and in mortuary practices. It is the last of these areas that forms the subject of this chapter.

Attitudes to Death and Analytical Approaches

The ancient Egyptians' attitude to death and the afterlife is one of the chief defining aspects of their culture. The written sources point to the existence of varied concepts of death itself, ranging from threatening enemy to welcome homecoming (Assmann 2005:23–234). It was regarded not as the end of human existence, but as a transition to a new state of being. Both the living and the dead simultaneously occupied places in the cosmos, as parts of a social framework in which contact remained possible (Assmann 2005:238). Indeed, the parameters of earthly life were transposed to the afterlife, and the living owed a duty of care to the dead (Assmann 2005:339). Basic human needs – food, drink, comforts, sexual pleasures

– still required to be satisfied. Sustenance could be guaranteed by various methods: through the physical supply of food and drink in the grave, by means of a cult which ensured a regular replenishment of offerings, or by the provision of magical substitutes (models and images). Texts also reveal that one's place in the earthly society was to be perpetuated in the next world. Social status, gender, and family or professional affiliations could be defined in the mortuary sphere, primarily by the use of the written word, but also through the spatial arrangement of graves, the structure and materials of which the tomb was made, and the type and quantity of grave goods. As a general principle the community of the dead was physically separated from the dwellings of the living, in a special environment, often – though not invariably – located on the western side of the Nile. Such "mortuary landscapes," which occur throughout Egypt, were often in use for millennia. Excavations and recording of these spots and the complex patterns of use they reveal can provide the basis for analyses of the societies that created them.

The Egyptians' basic approach to the phenomenon of death was not unique to their culture. What distinguished them from other societies was the investment of huge resources in funerary monuments (Assmann 2005:409), a practice which has been termed the "mausoleum culture" (Baines and Lacovara 2002:7). The ideal involved prominent display in the form of substantial and durable mortuary monuments, usually accompanied by extensive use of text and image. The corpse, before it was placed in the tomb, underwent special treatments which transformed it from a corruptible earthly body to a perfect and enduring eternal one, suitable for the next stage of existence. This stage involved a more penetrating integration into the cosmos than was possible during life on earth. Successful attainment of this goal was thought to be greatly facilitated by the performance of mortuary rituals, by enabling the eternal perpetuation of those rituals, and by personally equipping the individual with an armory of written knowledge and objects of magical use (Assmann 2005:237–406). The importance attached to written word and image accounts for the wealth of statuary, body trappings, papyri, and other "grave goods" which distinguished the elite burial.

The same basic notions of life after death pervaded the whole of society, and the variations between the burial practices of elite and non-elite in Egypt do not appear to point to major differences in belief. Rather they reflect differing levels of expenditure on resources. Through the principle of *pars pro toto* a humble person could have a miniaturized version of the grand sepulcher of a high official: "The basic form of a monumental tomb could be reduced to a tiny false door; mortuary offerings to a couple of drops of water and a prayer, embalming and mummification to a few daubs of oil and some cheap bandages" (Assmann 2005:411).

Because of their costliness, the more conspicuous signs of conformity to this ideal were available only to the elite – always a small proportion of the population (Assmann 2005:409–410; Baines and Lacovara 2002:5). Historically, the attention of Egyptologists has focused on these elite remains to a disproportionate extent, at the expense of the more numerous but less visually impressive traces of humbler mortuary practice, a phenomenon which has been properly criticized as the "tomb problem" (Richards 2005:49–52). To arrive at a well-balanced understanding, it is important to examine not just the elite burials but the full range of

mortuary activity within individual sites and throughout Egypt as a whole
(Richards 2005:2, 49). Egyptology as a science has been slow to adopt this
approach, and it is only in quite recent years that the picture has begun to change,
with mortuary evidence being used to elucidate particular periods and sites. This
work involves spatial analyses of cemeteries, plotting the distribution of graves,
and quantitative and qualitative analysis of grave goods – the variability of which
may permit hypotheses about economy, ethnicity, gender, age, and social status
(Bard 1994; Meskell 1999; Richards 2005; Seidlmayer 1990). Such studies have
concentrated notably on the burials of the pre-literate era, the Middle Kingdom
and the New Kingdom (as represented at the craftsmen's community of Deir el-
Medina: Meskell 1999; Smith 1992), since for all of these excavation has been
carried out in a systematic fashion, with recording which at least approaches
adequacy. There is, unfortunately, a lack of this type of analysis for the first millennium BCE (Richards 2005:73), partly because of the plundering of many of the
cemeteries dating to that time and to the often inadequate reporting of such excavation as has been carried out – factors which frustrate attempts to seek potentially
meaningful patterns in the data. The difficulty is compounded by the imbalance
existing in the archaeological record between the Delta and the Nile Valley, a
problem at all periods but a particularly critical one in the Third Intermediate
Period, when many important developments were taking place in the north of
Egypt, little of which can be traced in the mortuary archaeology (Taylor 2000:331).
Apart from the royal necropolis at Tanis, information about burials in the Delta
at this time is limited to rare discoveries such as the elite cemetery at Tell el-
Balamun (Spencer 1999:70–2, 90, pls. 78–80, 104b; 2003:20–30, pls. 18–30),
while the relative abundance of material from Thebes threatens to dominate
studies, exacerbating an already distorted picture. Moreover, the range of questions to which answers can be sought is limited by the fact that grave goods appear
to have been generally less numerous and less variable in the first millennium BCE
than at earlier times (Aston 2003).

For the moment it is most convenient to concentrate on a diachronic approach,
looking at the main changes in burial practice which distinguished the Third
Intermediate Period from earlier eras. This chapter considers four areas in which
change can be observed: royal burials, the use of mortuary landscapes, the treatment of the corpse, and the provision of cult and grave goods.

Royal Burials: Isolation and Integration

In the Old, Middle, and New Kingdoms, royal burials represented the maximum
investment of resources to enable a single individual to enter the afterlife. The
king's burial was monumental, conspicuous, and different from those of his subjects in its architectural form, in the richness of its provisions, and in the religious
texts and images with which the ruler was equipped. These factors reflected the
distinction which existed between ruler and subject in the earthly life, a distinction which was to continue in the next world. At the same time elements of the
royal burial represented an ideal to which others might aspire. Through time there
existed a dynamic relationship between king and subject which found expression

in mortuary practice, non-royal individuals progressively gaining access to elements which had previously been restricted to the king (Forman and Quirke 1996:134). An early manifestation of the trend was the "democratization of the afterlife," which began at the end of the Old Kingdom (Forman and Quirke 1996:65). This involved the non-royal person acquiring the status of "an Osiris" after death and attaining access to certain funerary texts and to kingly attributes which were painted in the object friezes on coffins (Baines and Lacovara 2002:10). The distinctive architectural form of the royal tomb, the pyramid, remained beyond the reach of persons of lower status until the New Kingdom. It was then relinquished by the kings and was taken over by private individuals for their tombs (Baines and Lacovara 2002:10). Despite these "usurpations" of royal prerogatives, the boundary between ruler and subject was maintained. Thus in the New Kingdom, the king's posthumous destiny was to be alone united with the sun god in his journeys, as expressed in the texts and images of the royal Books of the Netherworld, a source not routinely available to his subjects at that time.

During the New Kingdom the body of each pharaoh was buried separately in an elaborate rock-cut tomb in the Valley of the Kings (Hornung 1990). Although the valley formed part of a larger mortuary landscape, the Theban necropolis, access to it was restricted. The royal tombs had no architectural superstructure as had the earlier pyramids, but the mountainous peak of el-Qurn (or Qurnet Murai), which dominated the Valley, may have served as a collective "natural pyramid" (Hornung 1990:26–27). The Books of the Netherworld, which detailed and magically enacted the dead king's participation in the sun god's cyclical journey of rejuvenation, were carved and painted on the tomb walls, on the shrines, and on the sarcophagi inside (Hornung 1999). The cult of the ruler was maintained in a structure called a "Mansion of Millions of Years" (conventionally referred to by Egyptologists as a "mortuary temple") which was physically separate from the burial place, and which had often begun to function during the king's lifetime (Haeny 1997). Queens and royal children were buried in less elaborate tombs (sometimes in collective sepulchers such as tomb 5 in the Valley of the Kings, made for the children of Ramesses II: Weeks 2006) and, exceptionally, in the tomb of the king himself. At this time the elite members of society were accommodated in rock-cut burial shafts with cult chapels above (as at Thebes) or in temple-style tombs (as at Saqqara). The cult place and burial place for the king's subjects were thus united; religious texts and images for the elite were drawn chiefly from the Formulae for Going Out by Day (popularly known today as the "Book of the Dead"), a source not extensively used for kings. Officials might be buried at the place where they had held office, at the royal residence, or in their town of origin. Sub-elites had simple burials without a conspicuous cult setting, at the place of their abode and often in part of the same mortuary landscape as persons of higher status.

Only a few kings' tombs of the Third Intermediate Period are known, but they exemplify a new pattern. The royal necropolis of Tanis, excavated by Pierre Montet, yielded substantial remains of the burials of several pharaohs of the 21st and 22nd Dynasties, together with those of some of their courtiers and relatives (Montet 1947–1960). These tombs and their contents illustrate the key changes which had affected royal burials since the New Kingdom (Lull 2002). The tombs are situated not in a distinct "mortuary landscape," but in the settlement at Tanis, and within the enclosure wall of a major cult temple, that of Amun (the tombs lie in the southwest corner of the precinct, to the right of the entrance to the temple). The tombs were not separate units but formed groups, having been perhaps originally planned as family sepulchers for related rulers. Architecturally they are not distinguished either by massive scale or by monumental form, being much less imposing than previous royal tombs, although a large mudbrick enclosure of undetermined form was built around them in the reign of Sheshonq III (Brissaud 1987:16–18, 25). The only portions of the individual tombs to survive are the subterranean burial chambers, and these were not rock-hewn but built of stone blocks because of the difficulty of reaching workable bedrock in the Delta terrain. The superstructures, now destroyed but probably comprising a pylon gateway with a small courtyard and chapel, appear to have been located directly above the burial chambers. Royal cult place and burial place were thus once more united, as they had been in the pyramid complexes of the Old and Middle Kingdoms, breaking with the tradition of the New Kingdom, in which the cult was maintained in a physically separate temple.

Changes in the siting and architecture of the royal tombs were matched by innovations in the manner of their occupation and provisioning. The king's burial place was now no longer reserved to him alone; the tomb of Psusennes I at Tanis had twin sepulchral chambers, intended for the king and queen (the latter apartment was later occupied by Psusennes' successor, King Amenemope), and high-ranking members of the court were accommodated in adjacent chambers. The mortuary realm thus reflected the contemporary situation in the world of the living, where the distinction between king and subject was diminishing. Changes also affected the religious interpretation of the royal burial place. The extensive passages and chambers of the New Kingdom royal tombs had mirrored the sun's nocturnal journey, culminating in the burial chamber, where the rebirth of the solar deity and the king took place, as indicated in the texts and images on the walls. The comparatively tiny Tanite tombs do not attempt to reproduce this narrative, either in their architectural layout or in the images and texts they contain. Most of the great compositions of the New Kingdom (the books of Gates and Caverns and the Litany of Ra) are absent, though there are extracts from the Amduat and the Book of the Earth. A further departure from precedent is seen in the greater prominence of the Book of the Dead in the royal tombs, a notable innovation being the depiction of the weighing of the heart of the king (from spell 125), a scene usual in non-royal tombs of the New Kingdom but never employed previously in that of a pharaoh (Lull 2002:254–247). Not only are the king's funerary texts a pale reflection of those of the New Kingdom, the extracts which he adopts are also found on the coffins of non-royal persons, as exemplified by the painting of a scene from the Book of the Earth on a priest's cartonnage case (Quibell 1898:pl. 28). It is striking that no new royal mortuary texts are introduced to maintain the distinction of the king from his subjects.

Finally, although the bodies of the 21st- and 22nd-Dynasty kings were mummified and provided with funerary masks, amulets, and jewelry broadly similar to those of the New Kingdom, the range of grave goods placed in the tombs was much reduced. Many items of burial equipment, from stone sarcophagi to small amulets and pectorals, were recycled pieces which had been extracted from earlier burials for reuse. All this suggests not only a shortage of material resources but also a weakening of the ideological basis of the royal burial. The only really striking innovation of the time in this respect is the intensified linking of the dead person with the god Sokar-Osiris, as manifested in the introduction of anthropoid coffins with falcon heads, attested for Sheshonq II and Takelot I at Tanis, and also for the high priest and "king" Harsiese, buried at Medinet Habu (Hölscher 1954:8–10).

Besides the necropolis at Tanis there are few remains of royal burials of the Third Intermediate Period. The only identifiable ones of which physical traces survive are a queen's tomb at Leontopolis, the tomb of "King" Harsiese at Medinet Habu, and the sepulchral chapels of the God's Wives of Amun at the same site (Hölscher 1954:8–10, 17–30; Lull 2002:165–168, 170–173). The Medinet Habu tombs are located within the temple precinct, beside the processional axis, as at Tanis. In the 22nd Dynasty some persons of high status also had burials which reflected the royal model. Sheshonq, son of Osorkon II, and his descendants were buried in stone-built tombs erected close to the enclosure wall of the temple of Ptah at Memphis (Badawi 1957). At Tell el-Balamun, in the Delta, other high-ranking (but not royal) individuals were interred in a group of tombs close to the enclosure wall of the main temple, and two of these were even provided with falcon-headed coffins (Spencer 1999:70–72, 90; 2003: 20–30). Though such instances are rare, they may once have been commoner in the Delta, where preservation of organic remains is poor. Yet even such evidence as we have points clearly towards the blurring of distinction between royal and high elite burials. It would appear, then, that the physical isolation of the royal tomb was counterbalanced by a closer integration of the king's person among his subjects.

Mortuary Landscapes: Continuity, Adaptation, Management

The extent to which non-royal persons trespassed on the funerary prerogatives of the king should not be exaggerated, however. The majority of elite individuals, as well as those of humbler status, found burial in one of the cemeteries, or "mortuary landscapes," which were associated with every major settlement, and also with many minor ones. Since these sites were often in use for millennia, their structures and patterns of use were shaped by a wide range of factors.

The location of burials could reflect the hierarchy of the living: "A necropolis was a community in death, where the distribution and architecture of tombs partially modelled elite organization" (Baines and Lacovara 2002:9). Examples of this concept include the ranks of prefabricated court mastabas in the 4th-Dynasty cemetery beside the Great Pyramid at Giza, and the arrangements in provincial cemeteries such as that at Bersha, where the subordinates of Middle Kingdom governors were interred in subsidiary graves "at the feet of their lord." This "hierarchical" distribution could also be reflected in the allotting of zones of a cemetery to persons of a particular social status, as at Beni Hasan. Sometimes persons who held the same occupation might be buried in a particular place (Baines and Lacovara 2002:9). Arrangements of tombs could also reflect family connections, the grave of one important ancestral figure "attracting" the burials of relatives and descendants. Tombs or shrines of particularly venerated individuals likewise formed foci for burials, as exemplified by the Middle Kingdom shrines close to the cult place of Heqaib at Elephantine (Baines and Lacovara 2002:9). Even more powerful were the influence of temples or the settings for regular religious festivals. Thus mortuary chapels were erected at Abydos close to the Osiris temple, while 18th-Dynasty officials buried at Thebes located their tombs with reference to the mortuary temples of their kings (Helck 1962; Kampp-Seyfried 2003: 2) or to the cult temples of Karnak across the river. At different times, access to certain areas of a necropolis would be restricted (Baines and Lacovara 2002:19–20), helping to concentrate burials elsewhere. With the passage of time there was an ever-increasing need to adapt to the pre-existing landscape and to react to prevailing economic pressures. This led to the frequent reuse of older tombs, either by adding new burial chambers or by taking over looted ones (or both), and the "infilling" of unused space between existing graves or monuments. The development of every cemetery was potentially controlled by some or all of these factors.

For the Third Intermediate Period, the Theban necropolis is the only mortuary landscape for which anything approaching a complete picture exists. Extending along the desert edge for approximately 3 km, it is typical of many burial locations in that different areas were preferred at different periods. Patterns of use at Thebes were rendered more complex than elsewhere because the site incorporated several discrete precincts of royal burials and numerous sites of cult activity. In addition some spots in the necropolis acted as administrative centers. These places served both to attract and to repel burials at different times.

In the Third Intermediate Period, cult places exerted a particularly strong influence on the siting of burials. At Thebes, as at Tanis and Memphis, persons of the highest status were buried within or close to temple complexes. During the first phase of the period, the 21st Dynasty, the most favoured spot was the bay of Deir el-Bahri, in which stood the temples of Nebhepetre Mentuhotep, and Hatshepsut (Niwinski 1988). The importance of the place lay in its being the focus of the cult of Hathor, protectress of the Theban necropolis, and the setting for the key events of the annual Festival of the Valley (Naguib 1990:246). High-status burials were placed in tombs of earlier date or in newly cut but undecorated sepulchers in the cliffs near the temples, though not within the enclosure of that of Hatshepsut (Niwinski 1988:28–29). These included the bodies of many members of the ruling family, including "King" Pinedjem I and his descendants, and numerous other individuals of the Theban clergy. However, the concentration of burials at Deir el-Bahri seems to have occurred mainly in the later years of the 21st Dynasty and to have been related to a reorganization of the Theban necropolis which involved the gathering of mummies of high-status individuals from various other locations (Niwinski 1988:26, 29).

In the 22nd Dynasty, the Ramesseum, the mortuary temple of Ramesses II, became the focal point for high-status burials at Thebes (Nelson 2003; Quibell 1898). Within the enclosure of the temple and in adjacent areas of the necropolis many new tombs were constructed. Unfortunately, robbery and poor preservation have wrought havoc, making it hard to recover details, but it is apparent that the tombs possessed brick-built chapels, some with stone fittings and internal decoration, and beneath, shafts leading to small burial chambers containing usually only two interments (Quibell 1898). It is noteworthy that these tombs did not respect the integrity of the New Kingdom monument which sheltered them; there was substantial remodeling of the temple in order to accommodate the tombs there (Nelson 2003:90–92). During the 22nd Dynasty the temple enclosure of Medinet Habu also came into use as a spot for elite burials. Here were constructed the tombs of Harsiese, the high priest of Amun who adopted kingly status, and others for the God's Wives of Amun, as mentioned above (Hölscher 1954:8–10, 17–30). They were located before the entrance pylon of the main temple, beside the processional way, as had been the royal tombs at Tanis. High-status burials continued to be made at Medinet Habu in the 25th and 26th Dynasties, and during the same period the temple of Hatshepsut at Deir el-Bahri acquired renewed importance as a burial place for the Theban elite (Sheikholeslami 2003).

Throughout the whole of the Third Intermediate Period other persons of official rank were buried in the old rock-cut tombs of the Middle and New Kingdoms in the cliffs facing the river. New shafts were sunk in the courtyards of these tombs and inside the cult chapels; these shafts again led to small chambers accommodating only two or three burials. Above ground there was little visible trace that these tombs were in current occupation. No significant alterations were made to the original wall decoration in the chapels, but sometimes brick structures were added, containing wooden stelae to mark the cult setting for the new occupants (Winlock 1922:32).

Since few tomb superstructures from this period survive at Thebes, the identity of the persons buried is usually only accessible from inscriptions on the coffins or the few other objects placed in the burial chamber. Thanks largely to the uncontrolled exploitation of the necropolis to form collections of antiquities in the early nineteenth century, it is difficult to reconstruct original assemblages and to deduce the principles by which the burials were grouped. Family association is the most clearly demonstrable, with husband and wife seemingly the basic unit, sometimes with children in the same burial place (Carnarvon and Carter 1912:24–26; Habachi 1958:338–345). In some reused tombs, four or more generations of one family were buried successively (Schiaparelli 1924:185–205). In the Deir el-Bahri temple, members of the powerful clans of Montemhat, Besenmut, and related families were interred for many generations, apparently in small groups of three or four, each in separate chambers located beneath the temple floors, as though the monument acted as a gigantic tomb complex (Sheikholeslami 2003:136). This spot, indeed, perhaps succeeded the Ramesseum as the chief focus for burials of the highest elite, since in both places persons related to the royal families of the time were buried.

It is difficult to discover the rationale underlying the location of burials in older tombs. There is no evidence from any New Kingdom tomb at Thebes to indicate that the later occupants were related to the original owners (though this possibility cannot be excluded). In the Late and Ptolemaic periods, access to existing sepulchres was controlled by a necropolis administration, of whom the *wꜣḥ-mw*, or "choachytes," are perhaps the best-documented officials (Strudwick and Strudwick 1999:200–202). Besides caring for the mummies entrusted to them, these officials were responsible for providing tombs, either for building them or for managing the reuse of older sepulchres which had been partitioned among different families. The archaeological finding of family group burials of the fourth to third centuries BCE, reusing tombs such as those of Ankh-hor (TT 414), bears this out (Vleeming 1995:251). Although the archives of the choachytes do not stretch as far back as the Third Intermediate Period, it is a reasonable deduction that a similar organization existed then (Strudwick 2003:185). Substantial family-based burial groups dating to the 25th Dynasty and probably even earlier have been found in older tombs, notably those of two 20th-Dynasty princes in the Valley of the Queens (Schiaparelli 1924:185–205)

Burials did not always remain undisturbed in their tombs. Although an eternal and immutable burial may have been regarded as the ideal, in practice interments were moved from place to place and sometimes gathered into communal tombs (Baines and Lacovara 2002:25). This was probably a regular feature of necropolis management, but it is one which written sources say little about. The placing of large numbers of individuals in particular tombs is often termed "mass burial" and is regarded as characteristic of the Third Intermediate Period (Jansen-Winkeln 2000:9). However, it is important to distinguish the focusing of large numbers of burials in one place over a short period from long-term accumulation over several generations. Many of the group burials of this period were probably assembled gradually (as were those of the Montemhat and Besenmut families at Deir el-Bahri). At Thebes the only convincing cases of real "mass burial" (i.e. the simultaneous interment of large groups) in this period are the caches of the late 21st and early 22nd Dynasties. The "Royal Cache" at Deir el-Bahri seems to be the result of a major reorganization of the Theban necropolis, involving the official dismantling of the royal burials of the New Kingdom and the reinterment of the mummies in a few easily guarded spots – a process which, for once, is backed up by written sources (Jansen-Winkeln 1995; Reeves 1990). Into this cache were also placed the bodies of many members of the Theban ruling elite of the 21st Dynasty, while other members of the Amun clergy were placed in the tomb known as Bab el-Gasus (the "Second Cache"), having perhaps been gathered from various tombs in other parts of the necropolis (Niwinski 1988:28–29). After the beginning of the 22nd Dynasty there is not much evidence at Thebes for the creation of caches in consequence of the clearance of older tombs. There are signs, slight but telling, that many elite burials from the 22nd Dynasty onwards remained undisturbed to the end of the Pharaonic period and even into the early nineteenth century. This suggests that an efficient cemetery organization may have been operating at Thebes throughout much of the Third Intermediate Period.

Largely missing from the picture at Thebes (and most other sites) is knowledge of the burials of non-elite persons. Nineteenth-century accounts mention tombs filled with large numbers of bodies, wrapped but without grave goods, and these possibly represent some of the missing element of the population, but they were not reported in detail and cannot be dated securely. More reliably dated to the Third Intermediate Period are surface burials in the sand which have been found close to foci of higher-status interment, such as the bodies in simple coffins discovered on the terraces at Hatshepsut's temple at Deir el-Bahri (Steindorff 1949).

The Memphite necropolis, which is so rich in burials of the Old Kingdom, New Kingdom, and Late Period, has yielded remarkably little of the Third Intermediate

Period. At Memphis itself is the small group of tombs of very high-status persons, mentioned above, which were built close to the enclosure wall of the great Ptah temple. But it is only at Saqqara that larger numbers of burials have been attributed to this period, and the dating of many even of these is uncertain, on account of the meager grave goods and simple coffins provided for the dead (Raven 1991, 2001:11–12). Clearer evidence of mortuary activity from this period has been found in the region of the Fayum entrance. This area, dominated by the city of Herakleopolis Magna and the frontier town of el-Hiba, was a major military and administrative focus in the Third Intermediate Period. The cemeteries reflect this, and offer instructive parallels to mortuary activity elsewhere. At Herakleopolis itself stone-chambered tombs for elite individuals of the 22nd Dynasty were built within the city (Perez-Die and Vernus 1992:20, 39–77, fig. 11–28, Lam V–VIa, XIII–XXVI). Third Intermediate Period burials have also been found at the neighboring sites of Lahun and Sedment, often reoccupying older tombs (Naville 1894:13–14, pls. VII–IX, XI; Petrie 1890: pls. XXIV–XXVI; 1891: 24–28, pls. XXVIII–XXIX). It is not clear whether the persons buried here lived in Herakleopolis itself or in smaller peripheral settlements. There are signs of similar mortuary activity at el-Hiba, but here only a few Third Intermediate burials have been identified; others perhaps remain to be found or have been destroyed by later reoccupation. At Meidum, north of the Fayum entrance, the Old Kingdom royal monuments which were a conspicuous feature of the cemetery became a magnet for burials of the 22nd Dynasty and later periods, which have been found among the debris of the pyramid face and in the brickwork of the mastaba of Nefermaat (Petrie et al. 1910:22, 37, pl. 28). Other Old Kingdom tombs there were also reused at this time (Petrie et al. 1910:22, 24, 35).

A rare instance of a well-recorded "poor" cemetery of the Third Intermediate Period is that of Matmar, located on the east bank of the Nile south of Asyut (Brunton 1948:73–90). Here a long series of burials from the Predynastic to Coptic eras stretched along the desert edge as far south as Qau. At Matmar itself over five hundred graves of the 22nd–25th Dynasties were closely packed in one spot, and most were found to be undisturbed. The graves were simple pits, the bodies showing few traces of mummification, and grave goods were predominantly beads and amulets. Although these factors suggest that the dead were of relatively low status, it is noticeable that they were buried separately and not in "mass graves."

Treatment of the Body

For millennia the physical body was central to Egyptian concepts of the afterlife. Formal disposal of dead bodies can be traced back in the Nile Valley as far as 55,000 BCE. A diversity of special treatments of the corpse begins to be attested about 3500 BCE and developed over the following millennia. From about 2500 BCE onwards, written sources come to our aid, providing insight into the motivations underlying the formal treatment of the dead. These sources indicate that the individual was conceived of as a composite of different aspects, including the physical body and the non-physical *ka* and *ba*. The connectivity between these aspects was broken at death and had to be restored for existence to continue. Since the human form was the physical base and the focal point for all the aspects of existence, it had to be transformed into a new kind of body in order to continue its role (Assmann 2005).

The preparation of the corpse for this transformation involved a series of operations (Taylor 2001:46–91). First came purification – in practice the purging of the body of corruption products. This required surgical treatment – the opening of the body to extract perishable internal organs – and desiccation to remove all the fluid content and render it sterile, without the possibility of bacterial activity to enable decomposition. After these processes, the corpse consisted of little more than skin, bone, hair, and muscle tissue. Next came a "rebuilding" (Assmann 2005): filling the cavities with linen, sawdust, lichen, or resin, anointing the surface, and performing cosmetic treatments. Some of the materials used were believed to have magical qualities and helped to confer divine status on the deceased. Texts emphasize the divine nature of the bodily members of the individual, and indicate that at the end of the process he had become wholly divine. The only internal organ which was routinely left *in situ* was the heart, regarded as the centre of the individual's being. Liver, lungs, stomach, intestines, and sometimes kidneys were separately preserved and were usually deposited in canopic jars or a chest, placed in the grave near the body. In the final stages of preparation the body was wrapped in layers of linen and carefully fashioned into an eternal image, with an idealized mask covering the head. This form would be reanimated on the day of burial by means of the ritual of "Opening the Mouth"; its appearance was a visible declaration of the divine status which the individual had thereby attained.

The time and resources which were devoted to this treatment varied. At one end of the spectrum was a simple, non-invasive drying and wrapping of the corpse, which probably took only a few days. The more elaborate procedures could occupy seventy days, a canonical time-span which was probably dictated less by practical necessity than by astronomical phenomena which were associated with the notion of rebirth (Hornung 1990:136). It is this process which is now termed "mummification" (a word which is applied loosely to a variety of treatments of the corpse and which does not correspond directly to any ancient Egyptian term). Like the structure of the tomb and its contents, the treatment of the body could be simplified to meet the availability of resources, without apparent detriment to the dead person's posthumous existence. Herodotus' account of mummification, written in the fifth century BCE, indicates that it was chiefly the purification and rebuilding parts of the procedure that were simplified to reduce cost, and archaeological evidence bears this out – many bodies are found not to have been eviscerated and lack oils and resins, yet have usually undergone wrapping and fashioning into the canonical form. At most periods, it seems, the external appearance of the treated body was the most crucial desideratum; as with tomb fittings and grave goods, a simulacrum could be substituted for the real thing.

In the Third Intermediate Period the treatment of elite bodies is distinguished by innovations. Elliot Smith's examination of bodies of the 21st-Dynasty priests of Amun from Thebes revealed a range of new treatments which modified and supplemented the basic process just mentioned (Smith 1906). Packing materials, such as linen, mud, and sand, were inserted beneath the skin through openings to restore substance to the limbs and face (usually shrunken and distorted through the loss of subcutaneous fats during the desiccation process). Elaborate cosmetic treatments were applied to the surface of the body; artificial eyes were inserted into the orbits and the eyelids raised to make the deceased appear alive and conscious; the skin was painted red for men and yellow for women (reflecting iconographic conventions); and the hair was carefully adorned, sometimes with extensions. The organs extracted from the abdomen and thorax were returned to the body cavity in wrapped bundles, usually accompanied by wax figures of protective deities. The wrappings of the body were elaborate but a mask was usually omitted, except in burials of the highest elite.

From these changes it is apparent that restoring the physical integrity of the corpse had assumed a greater importance than before. There was now a more emphatic connection between the actual corpse within the wrappings and the eternal image of the transfigured deceased. The coloring of the skin recalls the painted outer surface of earlier funerary statues (an item now rarely supplied in elite burials). The eternal image was now coincident with the actual surface of the corpse, and the wrappings served to conceal this image, not to act as its outer layer. There is here a change from earlier practice where the iconography of the rejuvenated individual was represented by the body's outer trappings, notably by the mask placed over its head. The function of the mask was not only to effect the divinization of the bodily members, it also enabled the wearer to see (Assmann 2005). It is probably significant that these masks, which were a regular feature of elite burials in the New Kingdom, became a rarity in the Third Intermediate Period, when they were provided chiefly for the kings buried at Tanis and persons of very high status such as the army commander Wendjebauendjed. The ability to see was fulfilled instead by the innovation of placing artificial eyes under the eyelids. These moves, together with the new custom of returning the preserved viscera to the chest cavity, perhaps reflect a desire to place all crucial bodily organs under the direct control of the person. The motivations for these changes are not immediately apparent from written sources, and can only be speculated on. Was the greater self-sufficiency given to the dead a measure of compensation for the decline in the practice of mortuary ritual at the tomb (below)? Was there also a practical reason for the placing of all crucial organs within the body – to prevent their loss in the event of the mummy being transferred from one resting place to another, a phenomenon characteristic of the time?

In the 22nd Dynasty many of the methods just described continued in use for elite burials, but with the passage of time features such as the subcutaneous packing and the coloration of the skin were abandoned. Moreover in the 25th Dynasty the secreting of the organs within the body cavity began to give way to placing them either in canopic jars again or in packages on the thighs, within the wrappings. All of this suggests a return to earlier principles. The idealized image of the resurrected deceased appears to have been transferred once more from the actual surface of the corpse to the external trappings. In the 22nd Dynasty this outer layer of the mummy was often a cartonnage case. Fabricated from sheets of linen impregnated with glue and plaster, this type of case was rather like a mask extended to cover the whole body. It served simultaneously as the inner coffin and the outer surface of the mummy.

In sub-elite burials a much simpler treatment of the body is attested throughout the Third Intermediate Period. Of over five hundred bodies excavated at Matmar only four revealed any traces of mummification, and this was confined to the packing of the thoracic and pelvic cavities (Brunton 1948:80). There were no signs of the more elaborate treatments mentioned above. Bodies of the 22nd–25th Dynasties found by Petrie at Lahun were wrapped but had few trappings, and the bandages contained only "black dust and bones" (Petrie 1891:28), suggesting that no formal preservation had taken place. Low-status bodies of the same general period interred in New Kingdom tombs at Saqqara also appeared to have been merely wrapped without either excerebration or evisceration (Walker in Raven 1991:69–71). In all these instances, the wrappings alone provide any semblance of formal treatment, and in this the lower-status people of the Third Intermediate Period do not differ significantly from their counterparts in other periods. This may suggest that the fluctuating customs of body treatment among the elite did not penetrate to them.

Cult and Grave Goods

The provision for a mortuary cult was at all periods an important aspect of preparations for the afterlife. Food and drink were often placed in the tomb, but these were only tokens and could not supply the deceased in perpetuity. Ideally, a cult place was required – a chapel above the burial chamber or nearby, in which the relatives of the deceased would present offerings to a statue which embodied the ka of the owner. Alternatively the cult could be maintained via the priests of the local temple or at a memorial chapel, separate from the tomb (Baines and Lacovara 2002:8). Before the first millennium BCE, however, the tomb was the principal setting for the cult, and should relatives or priests cease to perform the necessary rituals, the deceased was equipped with the means to perpetuate his own cult through the media of written word, images, and models.

After the New Kingdom, the role of the tomb as the chief focus of the mortuary cult diminished. The tombs themselves were less conspicuous and relatively few possessed a dedicated cult place. Some high-status individuals interred at the Ramesseum in the 22nd Dynasty had chapels with wall decoration and an offering table (Quibell 1898:8), but these were rare. Even rarer were tomb statues to serve as the focus for the mortuary cult, though there is evidence that these were sometimes made of mud and hence may not all have survived (Nelson 2003:91). For most persons of rank who were buried at Thebes at this time the paraphernalia of cult was reduced to a small wooden stela bearing a painted scene. These show the deceased, usually without spouse or other relatives, offering directly to Ra-Horakhty (or, less often, to Osiris), as though to emphasize that the well-being of the dead now depended more on the gods than on the living (Leprohon 1988: 165). In keeping with this, the temples of the gods now assumed a more prominent role as the setting for the cult of the dead, a change that is manifested in the increased number of statues representing non-royal persons that were set up in the temple courtyards from the 22nd Dynasty onwards. As their inscriptions and iconography reveal, these statues were not merely votive in function but were intended to serve as recipients of mortuary offerings.

This shift of emphasis away from the tomb is paralleled in the changing character of the grave goods which were buried with the dead. In earlier periods a wide range of items could be provided. Typical classes of grave goods found in the Old, Middle, and New Kingdoms include coffins, canopic containers, shabtis, papyri, models, amulets, jewelry, clothing, furniture, cosmetic items, professional tools, weapons, games, musical instruments, and food and drink (Smith 1992). Variability in the range of goods that were provided, and in their number and quality, has allowed deductions to be made about the social and economic status of the dead, and can permit investigation of issues such as individual choice in the selection of items for the grave (Meskell 1998: 366). In the Third Intermediate Period the range of grave goods was much reduced, even for the elite. Provisions (food and drink) are rarely found, depriving the archaeologist of the pottery containers which at other periods are such valuable indicators of date and which form the basis for quantitative analyses. Also absent now were domestic and professional goods and most objects of "daily life." The majority of burials contain only those items which were made specifically to be deposited in the grave (Richards 2005:85): coffins, and for the elite, canopic containers, shabtis, an Osirian figure, funerary papyri, and a stela. This contraction of the burial outfit may not necessarily imply economic impoverishment. The images and texts which appear on the funerary objects of the first millennium BCE perhaps to some extent obviated the need for other personal items which had customarily been used to confirm the identity of the deceased and to assist their passage to the afterlife (Pinch 2003:443).

This dramatic simplification of the burial ensemble hampers attempts to trace social patterning through variability. In elite burials little qualitative difference can be observed between the grave goods of men and women, although Quibell commented on an apparent variation in the quality of shabtis in Theban pair burials, with the poorer ones allotted to the wife (Quibell 1898:9–10). Such evidence must be treated with caution; uniformity in the quality of coffins made for men and women has also been observed for the Middle Kingdom (Willems 1988:50–51). Yet when viewed from a diachronic perspective, the Third Intermediate Period does appear to display a more consistent equality of mortuary provisions for males and females. High-status women now had their own stelae and funerary papyri, instead of having to "share" those made for their husbands, as in the New Kingdom (Niwinski 1989:17; Smith 1992:201). Quantitively, the coffins designed for women appear to be no less numerous than those made for men (a contrast to the situation in the Middle Kingdom: Willems 1988:51), and they were also closely similar to those of men in shape, material, and iconography.

If social patterning is difficult to recognize from the available evidence, changes can be observed in the ideological status of the objects which were still provided. As the decoration of tombs became rarer, the coffin came to bear the greatest cargo of religious iconography and texts for the dead (Niwinski 1988:15, 18). Coffins provide an index of change which pervades all levels of society. The silver inner coffin of the 21st-Dynasty king Psusennes I, found at Tanis, resembles that of Tutankhamun in its traditional design, with a human face and feather-patterned body, but that of Sheshonq II, made a hundred years later, looks radically different. The human face of the transfigured king has been replaced by a falcon head, suggesting an identification with Sokar-Osiris, while the feathered design of the body is confined to borders framing figured scenes of the sun god and other deities. The coffins made for the non-royal elite of the early Third Intermediate Period (21st Dynasty) were usually anthropoid in shape, and of wood. Their surfaces were covered, inside and out, with a profusion of small scenes, figures of deities and religious emblems, the principal theme being that of the unity of the gods Ra and Osiris as the key to resurrection (Niwinski 1988: 15). In the arrangement of these images in compartments and long strips, the coffins display an affinity with the tomb chapels and funerary papyri of the late New Kingdom, and the desire to condense a large amount of material into a limited space is also reflected in the complex images used, which frequently convey meaning on several levels. In the 22nd Dynasty, major changes in coffin design are clearly traceable. Solar and Osirian mythology is still alluded to, but the profusion of small images is replaced by simpler designs, and contrasting color schemes play a stronger role than before. The mummy is encased in an envelope of cartonnage, painted and sometimes gilded, which acts as the external surface of the transfigured deceased. The depiction of the maternal sky goddess Nut on the interior surfaces of the wooden coffins which enclosed the mummy emphasized the notion that the coffin projected around the deceased a personal microcosm, in which he played the role of the creator god about to emerge from the womb of the sky goddess. The change of designs from the 21st to the 22nd Dynasty echoes that noted above in the coffins of the kings buried at Tanis, and raises the possibility that new aspects of mortuary practice were developing in the Delta before spreading southwards into Upper Egypt (Taylor 2003:104).

The carefully designed programs of images on coffins find their counterpart in the decline of text in the mortuary world of the Third Intermediate Period. In earlier times the elite burial made prominent use of text, inscribed on the walls of the funerary monument, on stelae, coffins, and grave goods, including papyri. These texts were of two main types, defined by Assmann as mortuary literature and mortuary liturgies, their roles being respectively to equip the tomb owner with knowledge for his personal use, and to perpetuate desired cult acts and destinies through the agency of the written words themselves (Assmann 2005:238). In the mid-eleventh to mid-ninth centuries BCE, elite burials still contained texts on papyri. Two rolls were provided, one containing selections from the Book of the Dead, the other consisting of a varied assemblage of images and texts from different compositions. When compared with the lengthy Books of the Dead of the New Kingdom, many of these texts are brief, and after about 850 BCE the custom of providing them on papyri ended, and would not be resumed until the seventh century. A shadow of the tradition survived through the medium of coffin inscriptions, but even the finest specimens from Thebes carry little beyond repetitive formulae requesting offerings. The few specific spells from the Book of the Dead on coffins are full of errors and omissions. Outside Thebes, access to inscriptional material was apparently even more limited. Coffins from Lahun show well-written inscriptions for elite owners (Petrie 1890:21–23, pl. XXV) but the content of the texts is formulaic and often partially unintelligible (Petrie 1891:26–27). Does this reflect indifference to tradition or a loss of reliable textual source material? The latter is perhaps less likely since a vigorous revival of the funerary text tradition began in the 25th Dynasty.

In view of the fact that many classes of funerary equipment disappeared from use at this period, it is somewhat surprising that canopic jars continued to be provided in many elite burials, particularly since the custom of replacing the embalmed viscera within the body had rendered the jars functionally redundant. Sets of empty jars, or even dummy jars carved of stone and wood, have often been found, inscribed with the owner's name and titles (Taylor 2001:73). The explanation may lie in a perception that four jars of this shape were an essential part of a properly appointed burial and therefore should not be omitted. It is perhaps the only instance in this period of the provision of a magical substitute, and raises the possibility that the dummy jars played a part in the burial ritual of which we have no other record.

Besides coffins and canopic jars, the item of burial equipment which remained most consistently in use at this time was the shabti, but this also underwent changes. In the late New Kingdom, thirty to forty shabtis would have been considered a large supply for one person, but in the 21st Dynasty the standard number increased to 401 (365 "workers" – one for each day in the year – plus thirty-six overseers to control every gang of ten) (Schneider 1977:I, 319–320). To meet this demand the figures were now regularly mass-produced in faience or pottery and the quality of the individual statuettes declined. The figures continued, as before, to bear the name of their possessor, but there was a subtle difference. The inscribed name was now a stamp of ownership, not an indication of identity. Whereas earlier shabtis functioned as substitutes for their owner and in some sense enshrined the being of that individual, like a tomb statue, those of the Third Intermediate Period were "depersonalized," as evidenced by their designation as *hmw*, "servants" or "slaves" (Schneider 1977:I, 319–330). As mere chattels of their master they were no longer eternal images of the deceased in his/her divine state. This repositioning may explain a change in the form of the boxes used to house the shabtis. Those which were used in the later New Kingdom were shaped like shrines, appropriate for images of the transfigured deceased; but in the Third Intermediate Period the tops of the end-boards were often rounded off, the lids were flat instead of bowed, and the sides fixed vertically instead of inclined (Aston 1994:pl. 4 [6], pl. 5 [1, 5], pl. 6 [1–5]). The intention seems to have been to remove the resemblance to a shrine, while remaining functional – as though to deprive the figures inside of divine status, to which they were not now entitled.

The reduction in the range of grave goods is balanced by a growth in the provision of amulets. Until the end of the New Kingdom the range of amulets placed with the body was limited, but in the 21st and 22nd Dynasties there were a greater variety of amulet types and an increased number of specimens per burial. Deity figures became common, and types of amulet previously restricted to royal burials (such as the headrest) were more widely used. This trend continued and blossomed fully in the Late Period. The amulets which appear in burials during this growth-phase include types made specifically for mortuary use, but also several kinds which appear to have been made to be worn in life: faience figurines and pieces of jewelry (plaques, rings, etc.) representing deities such as Bastet and Sekhmet in cat and lion form, the dwarf-like Pataikos, associated with childbirth, and also amuletic strings and cowry shells (Quirke 2005:122–123). These objects are found at settlement sites as well as in graves, perhaps suggesting an increasing closeness between the world of the living and the mortuary realm.

Conclusion

The Third Intermediate Period appears as a phase of minimalization in burial customs. The decline of the elite tomb as the principal focus of the mortuary cult and the reduction in the range of grave goods seem to reflect a change in the significance attached to funerary provision, rather than a simple response to economic pressure. The lack of long-term preparation for death contrasts with the practices of earlier periods when mortuary monuments must have been planned and constructed during the eventual owner's lifetime. It has been suggested that this was related to changes in the profile of the population, and more specifically to the influx of Libyans into Egyptian society. Lacking an ancestral tradition of creating permanent monuments for the dead, the Libyan rulers in Egypt can perhaps be said to have neglected mortuary practice (Leahy 1985). There are certainly no conceptual innovations in burial ritual or provision which could be attributed to them, and the picture which the evidence paints is one of mechanical adherence to concepts which were perhaps not fully understood. The lack of development at royal level perhaps deprived the lower strata of society of the aspirational impetus to imitate, leading to stagnation.

It is only in the final phase of the Third Intermediate Period, the 25th Dynasty, that innovation in the mortuary world appears, and it is innovation which depends heavily on a renewal of past traditions. There was a revival of the pyramid form for the burials of rulers (albeit these were located in their Nubian homeland), and elite persons in Egypt were again able to construct grand monumental tombs. The funerary text tradition was reborn and restructured, with the reintroduction of the Pyramid Texts and a new "edition" of the Book of the Dead. Further development is manifested in a continued closeness of mortuary and temple cult. Private statues continued to be set up in temples, while the role of the coffin as funerary image (and counterpart to the temple statue) evolved. Inner coffins represented the divinized deceased with new elements taken from the canons of sculpture (back pillar and plinth), and this iconography was also adapted for shabtis and Osirian statuettes placed in the tomb. These developments marked the completion of a cycle of cultural change. As happened repeatedly in ancient Egypt, the past provided the seed from which new life would grow.

REFERENCES

Assmann, J. 2005 Death and Salvation in Ancient Egypt. Ithaca, NY, London: Cornell University Press.

Aston, D. A. 1994 The Shabti Box: A Typological Study. Oudheidkundige Mededelingen uit het Rijksmuseum van Oudheden te Leiden 74:21–54.

Aston, D. A. 2003 The Theban West Bank from the Twenty-fifth Dynasty to the Ptolemaic Period. *In* The Theban Necropolis: Past, Present and Future. N. Strudwick and J. H. Taylor, eds. Pp. 138–166. London: British Museum Press.

Badawi, A. 1957 Das Grab des Kronprinzen Scheschonk, Sohnes Osorkon's II und Hohenpriesters von Memphis. Annales du Service des Antiquités de l'Égypte 54: 153–177.

Baines, J., and P. Lacovara 2002 Burial and the Dead in Ancient Egyptian Society: Respect, Formalism, Neglect. Journal of Social Archaeology 2(1):5–36.

Bard, K. A. 1994 From Farmers to Pharaohs: Mortuary Evidence for the Rise of Complex Society in Egypt. Sheffield: Sheffield Academic Press.

Bianchi, R. S. 1990 Egyptian Metal Statuary of the Third Intermediate Period (circa 1070–656 BC), from Its Egyptian Antecedents to Its Samian Examples. *In* Small Bronze Sculpture from the Ancient World. M. True and J. Podany, eds. Pp. 61–84. Malibu: Getty Museum.

Brissaud, P. 1987 Les fouilles dans le secteur de la Necropole Royale (1984–1986). *In* Cahiers de Tanis I. P. Brissaud, ed. 7–43. Paris: Éditions Recherche sur les Civilisations "Memoire" no. 75.

Brunton, G. 1948 Matmar. London: Bernard Quaritch.

Carnarvon, Earl of, and H. Carter 1912 Five Years' Explorations at Thebes: A Record of Work Done 1907–1911. London, New York, Toronto, Melbourne: Henry Frowde, Oxford University Press.

Forman. W., and S. G. J. Quirke 1996 Hieroglyphs and the Afterlife in Ancient Egypt. Norman, OK: University of Oklahoma Press.

Habachi, L. 1958 Clearance of the Tomb of Kheruef at Thebes (1957–1958). Annales du Service des Antiquités de l'Egypte 55:325–350.

Haeny, G. 1997 New Kingdom "Mortuary Temples" and "Mansions of Millions of Years." *In* Temples of Ancient Egypt. B. E. Shafer, ed. Pp. 86–126. London, New York: I.B. Tauris.

Helck, W. 1962 Soziale Stellung und Grablage (Bemerkungen zur Thebanischen Nekropole). Journal of the Economic and Social History of the Orient 5:225–243.

Hill, M. 2007 Heights of Artistry: The Third Intermediate Period (ca. 1070–664 BC). *In* Gifts for the Gods: Images from Egyptian Temples. M. Hill, ed. Pp. 51–63. New Haven, London: Yale University Press.

Hölscher, U. 1954 The Excavation of Medinet Habu, V. Post-Ramessid Remains. Chicago: University of Chicago Press.

Hornung, E. 1990 The Valley of the Kings: Horizon of Eternity. D. Warburton, trans. New York: Timken Publishers.

Hornung, E. 1999 The Ancient Egyptian Books of the Afterlife. D. Lorton, trans. Ithaca, NY, London: Cornell University Press.

Jansen-Winkeln, K. 1994 Der Beginn der Libyschen Herrschaft in Ägypten. Biblische Notizen 71:78–97.

Jansen-Winkeln, K. 1995 Die Plünderung der Königsgräber des Neuen Reiches. Zeitschrift für Ägyptische Sprache und Alterumskunde 122:62–78.

Jansen-Winkeln, K. 2000 Die Fremdherrschaften in Ägypten im 1. Jahrtausend v. Chr. Orientalia 69: 1–20.

Kampp-Seyfried, F. 2003 The Theban Necropolis: An Overview of Topography and Tomb Development from the Middle Kingdom to the Ramesside Period. *In* The Theban Necropolis: Past, Present and Future. N. Strudwick and J. H. Taylor, eds. Pp. 2–10. London: British Museum Press.

Leahy, A. 1985 The Libyan Period in Egypt: An Essay in Interpretation. Libyan Studies 16:51–65.

Leprohon, R. J. 1988 Funerary Stela. *In* Mummies and Magic: The Funerary Arts of Ancient Egypt. S. D'Auria, P. Lacovara, and C. H. Roehrig, eds. Pp. 164–165. Boston: Museum of Fine Arts.

Lull, J. 2002 Las tumbas reales egipcias del Tercer Periodo Intermedio (dinastias XXI–XXV): Tradicion y cambios (BAR International Series 1045). Oxford: Archaeopress.

Meskell, L. 1998 Intimate Archaeologies: The Case of Kha and Merit. World Archaeology 29(3):363–379.

Meskell, L. 1999 Archaeologies of Social Life: Age, Sex, Class *et cetera* in Ancient Egypt. Oxford: Blackwell.

Montet, P. 1947–1960 La necropole royale de Tanis, I–III. Paris.

Naguib, S.-A. 1990 Le clergé féminin d'Amon Thebain à la 21e Dynastie (Orientalia Lovaniensia Analecta 38). Leuven: Peeters.

Naville, E. 1894 Ahnas el Medineh (Heracleopolis Magna). London: Egypt Exploration Fund.

Nelson, M. 2003 The Ramesseum Necropolis. *In* The Theban Necropolis: Past, Present and Future. N. Strudwick and J. H. Taylor, eds. Pp. 88–94. London: British Museum Press.

Niwinski, A. 1988 21st Dynasty Coffins from Thebes: Chronological and Typological Studies. Theben V. Mainz: Zabern.

Niwinski, A. 1989 Studies on the Illustrated Theban Funerary Papyri of the 11th and 10th Centuries BC (Orbis Biblicus et Orientalis 86). Freiburg: Universitätsverlag; Göttingen, Vandenhoeck & Ruprecht.

Perez-Die, M. del C., and P. Vernus 1992 Excavaciones en Ehnasya el Medina (Heracleopolis Magna). Madrid: Ministerio de Cultura.

Petrie, W. M. F. 1890 Kahun, Gurob and Hawara. London: Kegan Paul, Trench, Trübner.

Petrie, W. M. F. 1891 Illahun, Kahun and Gurob 1889–1890. London: David Nutt.

Petrie, W. M. F., E. Mackay, and G. Wainwright 1910 Meydum and Memphis (III). London: British School of Archaeology in Egypt and Egyptian Research Account.

Pinch, G. 2003 Redefining Funerary Objects. *In* Egyptology at the Dawn of the Twenty-first Century. Vol. II. Z. Hawass, ed. Pp. 443–447. Cairo, New York: The American University in Cairo Press.

Quibell, J. E. 1898 The Ramesseum. London: Bernard Quaritch.

Quirke, S. 2005 Lahun: A Town in Egypt 1800 BC, and the History of Its Landscape. London: Golden House Publications.

Raven, M. J. 1991 The Tomb of Iurudef, a Memphite official in the reign of Ramesses II. Leiden: National Museum of Antiquities; London: Egypt Exploration Society.

Raven, M. J. 2001 The Tomb of Maya and Meryt, II: Objects and Skeletal Remains. Leiden: National Museum of Antiquities; London: Egypt Exploration Society.

Reeves, C. N. 1990. Valley of the Kings: The Decline of a Royal Necropolis. London: Kegan Paul International.

Richards, J. 2005 Society and Death in Ancient Egypt: Mortuary Landscapes of the Middle Kingdom. Cambridge: Cambridge University Press.

Schiaparelli, E. 1924 Relazione sui lavori della Missione archeologica italiana in Egitto (1903–1920), I. Turin.

Schneider, H. D. 1977 Shabtis: An Introduction to the History of Ancient Egyptian Funerary Statuettes with a Catalogue of the Collection of Shabtis in the National Museum of Antiquities at Leiden. Leiden: Rijksmuseum van Oudheden.

Seidlmayer, S. J. 1990 Gräberfelder aus dem Übergang vom Alten zum Mittleren Reich: Studien zur Archäologie der Ersten Zwischenzeit (Studien zur Archäologie und Geschichte Altägyptens 1). Heidelberg: Heidelberger Orientverlag.

Sheikholeslami, C. M. 2003 The Burials of Priests of Montu at Deir el-Bahari in the Theban Necropolis. *In* The Theban Necropolis: Past, Present and Future. N. Strudwick and J. H. Taylor, eds. Pp. 131–137. London: British Museum Press.

Smith, G. E. 1906 A Contribution to the Study of Mummification in Egypt. Mémoires présentes à l'Institut Égyptien 5(1). Cairo.

Smith, S. T. 1992 Intact Tombs of the Seventeenth and Eighteenth Dynasties from Thebes and the New Kingdom Burial System. Mitteilungen des Deutschen Archäologischen Instituts Abteilung Kairo 48:193–231.

Spencer, A. J. 1999 Excavations at Tell el-Balamun 1995–1998. London: British Museum Press.

Spencer, A. J. 2003 Excavations at Tell el-Balamun 1999–2001. London: British Museum Press.

Steindorff, G. 1949 The Walters Art Gallery Mummy. Journal of the Walters Art Gallery 12:8–17.

Strudwick, N. 2003 Some Aspects of the Archaeology of the Theban Necropolis in the Ptolemaic and Roman Periods. *In* The Theban Necropolis: Past, Present and Future. N. Strudwick and J. H. Taylor, eds. Pp. 167–188. London: British Museum Press.

Strudwick, N., and H. Strudwick 1999 Thebes in Egypt: A Guide to the Tombs and Temples of Ancient Luxor. London: British Museum Press.

Taylor, J. H. 2000 The Third Intermediate Period (1069–664 BC). *In* The Oxford History of Ancient Egypt. I. Shaw, ed. Pp. 330–368. Oxford: Oxford University Press.

Taylor, J. H. 2001 Death and the Afterlife in Ancient Egypt. London: British Museum Press.

Taylor, J. H. 2003. Theban Coffins from the Twenty-second to the Twenty-sixth Dynasty: Dating and Synthesis of Development. *In* The Theban Necropolis: Past, Present and Future. N. Strudwick and J. H. Taylor, eds. Pp. 95–121. London: British Museum Press.

Török, L. 1997 The Kingdom of Kush. Handbook of the Napatan-Meroitic Civilization. Leiden, New York, Cologne: Brill.

Vleeming, S. 1995 The Office of a Choachyte in the Theban Area. *In* Hundred-Gated Thebes: Acts of a Colloqium on Thebes and the Theban Area in the Graeco-Roman period (Papyrologica Lugduno-Batava 27). S. Vleeming, ed. Pp. 241–255. Leiden: Brill.

Weeks, K. R., ed. 2006 KV5 A Preliminary Report on the Excavation of the Tomb of the Sons of Rameses II in the Valley of the Kings. Revised edition. Cairo, New York: The American University in Cairo Press.

Willems, H. 1988 Chests of Life: A Study of the Typology and Conceptual Development of Middle Kingdom Standard Class Coffins. Leiden: Ex Oriente Lux.

Winlock, H. E. 1922 Excavations at Thebes. Bulletin of the Metropolitan Museum of Art, New York, Part II. December:19–49.

Ziegler, C. 1987 Les arts du metal à la Troisième Periode Intermédiaire. *In* Tanis: L'or des pharaons. Pp. 85–101. Paris: Ministère des Affaires Étrangeres.

13

Consolidation, Innovation, and Renaissance

Penelope Wilson

The Late Period is defined as extending from the end of the Third Intermediate Period around 663 BCE to the "conquest" of Alexander the Great in 332 BCE, comprising Dynasties 26 to 30 and periods of Persian occupation. It is a time seen as the last resurgence of the indigenous rulers of Egypt and of the decline or renaissance of Egyptian culture, depending upon one's perspective. For the first time in Egyptian history there are outside accounts of events in Egypt from Assyria amongst others, and especially in Classical sources. The writings of Herodotus after a visit to Egypt around 450 BCE are extremely influential in creating the effect of a solid "history" of the period (Lloyd 1975, 1976, 1988). His accounts of "events" and personalities can be tied to absolute chronology from cross-reference to other cultures and give a Western slant to understanding the dynamics of the period. The archaeology has tended to be slotted in to this narrative, without being allowed to develop its own framework for the transformations of Egyptian culture at a time of profound changes in a world dominated by the Empires of Assyria, Persia, Babylon, and then Macedon. In the Iron Age global context, Egypt played a key role at times, but remained on the sidelines. Yet the actions of Late Period kings such as Psamtek I Wahibre, Psamtek II Neferibre, Ahmose II, Hakor, Nakhtnebef, and Nakhthorheb, as well as the conquering Persians, Cambyses, and Artaxerxes, suggest a dynamic and thriving sense of the positive integration of ancient ideologies and administrative practices in a new world order, and one that was successful – to an extent (Lloyd 1983, 2000). The key to understanding both Egypt's history and the great amount of archaeology from the Late Period is in how the rulers used and exploited the natural resources of the country, initiated and developed an evolving ideological concept of the rulership of the Two Lands, and reacted to the perceived external threat posed to Egypt. Although such issues were just as real in earlier – and, indeed, later – times (see previous chapters), they continued to pervade many of the ways in which the Egyptian elite defined their ideal virtual world and organized the real world. Issues of "archaism" and "renaissance" are often discussed most with reference to the Late Period, perhaps because it is so far removed in time from the Old and Middle Kingdoms to which reference was made, or to the New Kingdom Empire of almost one thousand years before. It is possible that such a Western sensibility of time arrived in Egypt during the Late Period, but in reality, there was already a well-established model of cyclical time underpinning elite ideology, which made it inevitable that the paradigm of the past served for the present. The fascination is in examining through the archaeological record how the Two Lands were re-established out of chaos in Dynasty 26, and the changes in Egyptian culture as a result.

The scene was set at the beginning of Dynasty 26, with King Psamtek I's greatest ideological and practical achievement being the way that he dealt with Thebes. The "City" was under the control of noble and efficient families, which had welcomed and enabled the Kushite attentions to the sacred site at Karnak. The families of Montemhat, Harwa, and others who were buried in mausoleum-type tombs on the West Bank attest to their devotion to Amun and their custody of the sacred relics and fabric of the buildings. They may have derived their wealth from the dwindling resources of Amun in the immediate vicinity of Thebes. The daughter of Psamtek, a girl of around 10 years old, called Neithikert, was chosen to be adopted by the current God's Wife of Amun, Shepenwepet, as her successor. The Neithikert Stela relates how she sailed from the north to Thebes (Caminos 1964) under the protection of the Prince of Herakleopolis, Sematawytefnakht, who was married into the Saite family. Along the way the Saite procession received, on behalf of her father, the fealty of the nomes and their tribute offerings to take to Amun. The flotilla united the north and south in a manner reminiscent of the great processional festivals of the past. The Neithikert Procession achieved the unification of Egypt on a countrywide level, but in a symbolic and ideological manner, consolidating Psamtek's credentials at the beginning of his reign. The incumbent God's Wives of Amun were of Nubian descent and further joined the Third Land to the Saite king, the line of descent and claim on royal power passing directly from Amun through his "wives" to Psamtek I through his "daughter of the Upper Egypt king" and "daughter of the Lower Egyptian king" (Gozzoli 2006:87–92).

Several aspects of the surviving archaeological material are explored in this chapter to illustrate the strengths of the archaeological data in providing detailed information about the state of Egyptian culture during the Late Period and the themes to which the evidence gives rise.

Militarization

The Assyrian accounts of the defeat of Taharqa and sack and burning of Memphis by Esarhaddon in 671 BCE and then the defeat of Tantamani and the sack of Thebes by Assurbanipal in 664/663 BCE make sobering reading (Pritchard 1969:290–297). The results of the two events suggest that within the world system of the first millennium, Egypt had lost its defensive capability and was reduced to the level of a vassal state, unable to withstand superior military technology. The Late Period revival showed clearly that this was not the case. Part of the response to the Assyrian attack centered on the organization of Egypt as a militarized unit. The earlier "Great Chiefs of the Meshwesh" and the "kings" of Dynasties 21 to 24 are thought to have been descended from military families who acted as feudal warlords in their areas of control (or fiefdoms) (Redford 1992:335–337). They seem to have controlled the resource management of their areas, on a model not unlike that suggested for parts of Egypt in Dynasties 8 and 9, with varying degrees of interaction between regions. At a state level, however, such a fragmentary system in the seventh century within Egypt created the disunited and weak response to the Assyrians. The Dynasty 26 policy of militarization of the borders therefore arose not so much from an ideological as from a problem-solving position to stabilize internal security in order to meet outside threats. Archaeological survey and investigation has been successful in locating Saite military installations in a number of areas. To the northeast of the east Delta, the identification of the "Migdol" fortress 1 km north of Tell el-Herr in Sinai (Oren 1984) has demonstrated the immediate concern in fortifying the border area with Sinai and Palestine. The fort at Tell Defenneh (Leclère 2007; Petrie 1888) and buildings at Tell el-Maskhuta have also been identified as Saite foundations, the latter connected with the canal in Wadi Tumilat linking the Pelusiac Branch of the Nile and the Red Sea (Holladay 1982).

Saite military activity was not restricted to the northeast Delta, and a series of stelae of King Psamtek I from the desert road near Dahshur attest to sorties to control the desert dwellers (Perdu 2002:42–53). Some of the inscriptions imply that trouble was caused by disaffected Delta leaders who had fled to the lands west of Egypt and raised armies there. Psamtek called upon the Egyptian nome leaders to supply troops with which to deal with this force. There may well have been a real threat from the west, but the stelae underline Psamtek's assertion that he was the one who was able to repel invaders, unlike the other Delta princes, who failed to withstand the Assyrians. He showed that he could rally troops from Egypt in a united front, secure the western border for trade, and provide protection for the new inland port at Naukratis. Further military activity in the west is suggested by the recent discovery of the Dynasty 26 fort at Bahariya Oasis (Colin 2004) and the presence of Saite period cemeteries, temples, and settlements in the oases at Dakhla (Dakhleh Oasis Project 2009; Fakhry 1973, 1974) suggest a broader, almost colonial, attitude to the border areas. To the south, expeditions were carried out against the Nubians and were accompanied by the same kind of military building activity, with a fort established at Dorginarti, near the Second Cataract (Heidorn 1991).

Associated with such sites there is a type of construction that has become synonymous with Saite fortifications. It consists of a squareish, mudbrick building with internal compartment walls, filled with rubble and mud debris (Spencer 1999b). The internal arrangements have no linking doorways and no stratified deposits. It appears that the structures are the remains of the foundation platforms upon which a substantial and perhaps tall building was erected. Examples are known from the Egyptian enclosure at Naukratis, Tell Defenneh, Migdol, Tell el-Maskhuta, Mendes (Wilson 1982:41–43), Buto (Hartung 2003), and the corner of the Dynasty 26 enclosure at Tell el-Balamun (Spencer 1996). The latter structure was 61 m by 54 m in size, with an approach ramp intended to enter well above ground level. Spencer considered such a foundation to have supported some kind of secure official structure, perhaps a control point, built to overlook the town and surrounding region and as a defensible building to which to retreat if necessary (Spencer 1999b:299). The Palace of Apries at Memphis (Kemp 1977; Petrie and Walker 1909) may also be part of the same kind of structure, and the discovery of a garment armored with iron scales within the casemate where it had been discarded (Petrie 1888:78) again suggests that it may have had a high-level military purpose. It is not likely that all of the foundations located were for the same type of building, but the technique seems to have ensured that the structures were built above floodwater level, and were fairly tall. One of their primary functions may have been to act as watchtowers over the flat Delta landscape and to act as signaling towers in case of danger or for sending messages over flooded or agricultural terrain.

In addition to the built military installations, military titles from the Third Intermediate Period to the early Ptolemaic period show that the standing armies of the fiefdoms were reorganized, supplemented by mercenary forces and managed more effectively by a high command based at Memphis (Chevereau 1985). Military titles were held in common with civil or priestly titles, so it is not clear whether this was indeed a military elite along the lines of the early Dynasty 18 elite surrounding kings such as Amenhotep II, or whether the titles were given out in much the same way as any other insignia of office. While the degree of actual involvement in military duties is not evident from the titles themselves, they do indicate the command structure, perhaps actually operated by more field-trained soldiers. Such may be the origins of the military family from Sebennytos under Nakhtnebef which founded Dynasty 30. Most striking perhaps are the naval and port authority titles (Chevereau 1985:319–321), which are used by officials from Dynasty 26. These suggest that the marshy areas at the river mouths, the different distributaries of the river, and the routes to the Aegean islands were made into specific areas of control, implying that there was a degree of incoming traffic to be controlled and assessed for duty. At Tell Tibilla the temple town may have been primarily concerned with monitoring and managing sea-borne trade coming into the eastern Delta (Mumford n.d.). It seems most likely that the "navy" was both mercantile and military, with more of a customs and excise duty within Egypt itself (Darnell 1992).

The mapping of the archaeological evidence demonstrates a large Saite military machine and perhaps part of the rationale behind the recruitment of the large numbers of Ionian and Carian mercenaries mentioned in the Classical sources (Herodotus 1966:II, 152, 163). Tangible proof of the presence of foreign mercenaries is surprisingly difficult to find because of the nature of the mercenary soldier as an acultural or assimilated entity, but several cremation burials were fortuitously preserved at Migdol. Egyptian pottery vessels were used to contain the burnt remains of presumably Greeks (i.e. people from the Greek mainland or Aegean islands and coast) buried with Samian wine amphorae as offerings (Oren 1984:30). The practice of cremation was totally alien to Egyptians and its existence stresses the otherness of the foreign forces. Their cultural presence is one of the notable markers of Late Period Egypt.

Foreign Immigrants

There are other positive traces of foreign groups, such as the Carian community buried at Saqqara in the mid-sixth century BCE (Masson 1978) and the cosmopolitan inhabitants of Memphis recorded in documents from the fifth to the fourth century BCE (Smith 1992). At Elephantine from the Persian period onwards there was a Jewish garrison as well as Arameans, Babylonians, Bactrians, Caspians, Medes, and Persians, all of whom are attested in the documents from the site (Porten 1996). Further evidence for the presence of non-Egyptians may come from the East Greek pottery found in Egypt in increasing quantity from the beginning of the Saite period onwards. There are, however, difficulties with the idea of "pots equals people," and the increasing number of contextualized finds of East Greek pottery suggests that each find needs to be assessed more critically (Weber 2001). For example, the wine and oil amphorae from Lesbos, Samos, Clazomenia, Chios, and Milesia found in the Dynasty 27 tombs of Wedjahorresene and Iufaa at Abusir are most likely to have been offerings for the Egyptians buried in the tombs (Smoláriková 2002:106–107). Pottery of a similar date and type from rubbish dumps in one of the Egyptian temple areas at Sais (Figure 13.1; Wilson and Gilbert 2007) as well as fourth-century BCE material from enclosure landfill contexts at Mendes (Redford 2004:137–142) suggest that there was an Egyptian market amongst high officials or temples for the Greek produce. It cannot only be assumed to have been for a "Greek" market. Similarly, increasing numbers of Levantine pottery vessels in Egypt from the Saite period onwards may indicate

Figure 13.1 Fragment of a miniature jar decorated with the face of the god Bes, from a cult area at Sais (Sa el-Hagar), height 5.5 cm. Photo: The author.

increased trade with the Southern Levant as much as the presence of people from that area (Bettles 2003; Maeir 2002).

Ethnicity and acculturation in the Late Period were an increasingly important local issue, especially with the establishment in the Ptolemaic period of the cities of Alexandria, Naukratis, and Ptolemais, whose Greek citizens had certain rights over Egyptians. Ethnic markers such as names can be useful at an individual level to identify non-Egyptians in Egypt and there are some archaeological indicators for larger numbers of non-Egyptian people, particularly at Naukratis.

The full impact of Petrie's rescue excavations at Naukratis is only becoming fully appreciated as the material from the work is published (Villing and Schlotzhauer 2006). Petrie's agenda at the time was to find as much archaic East Greek pottery and sculpture as he could before the local farmers dug away the soil from the site (Petrie 1886). He also recorded buildings and identified their functions, suggesting that some could be associated with Greek religious cults, such as those of Aphrodite, Apollo, and the Dioskourides. There were industrial areas, perhaps including a scarab workshop and faience factory. The huge quantities of East Greek pottery suggested that much of it had been imported for the use of its population, which was therefore predominantly from the Aegean world. They drank wine from decorated *kylix* cups at drinking-symposia and they appreciated the work of painters and potters who signed their cups for votive offerings. Votive statues to Herakles also suggest that there was a military mercenary contingent in the town (U. Höckmann, personal communication, September 2007), and Egyptian structures such as the Enclosure (Helleneion) as well as Nile-silt pottery suggest interaction with Egyptians at some, perhaps an administrative, level.

The great mass of material from the site was not stratified or contextualized well, so that a detailed fine-grained analysis of identity or ethnicity based on specific town quarters or ghettos will be limited. Economic questions, however, such as determining the role of Naukratis as an emporium of Greek port of trade, have been successfully broached (Möller 2000). In this case, the sizable merchant population was involved in the shipping of goods from the Greek world in return for Egyptian luxury products such as linen, papyrus, perfume, and small exotica such as scarabs, but the main export was most likely grain. The settlement history of Naukratis has also been described, with the original part of the city founded in the seventh and sixth centuries BCE in the area of Petrie's excavations, spreading to the north and east in the Ptolemaic period, and then to the west in Roman times (Coulson 1996:11). There are still gaps in the sequence, and detailed mapping of the town may not be possible, unless future systematic geophysical survey could reveal underlying house patterns from the later stages of the city's development. The potential of such archaeological sites extends beyond Egypt as it is just as important for the Aegean too.

Urbanization

The study of continuous settlement patterns is an interesting problem, both at site and regional level, throughout the Late Period. It is difficult to formulate a theoretical framework for understanding the fabric of social life and individual and corporate identity in cities based upon the compressed stratigraphy and mud of town sites in Egypt (Holladay 1982). Egypt was apparently well populated from the end of the Third Intermediate Period through into the Ptolemaic period and with a plethora of cites (Lloyd 1983:299–230, 318–325). The number of sites of importance, especially the nome centers of the Delta with important city mounds dating back at least to the Third Intermediate Period (Leclère 2008), suggests that urbanization was a key feature of Late Period Egypt. The exact form of the process, the organization of "cities," and the basic description of housing units from the Late Period are being addressed by current archaeological work, although with unpredictable results.

The site of the capital city at Sais (Sa el-Hagar) has hardly any archaeological remains surviving (Wilson 2006) to show the development from New Kingdom nome capital to Third Intermediate Period center of the "Kingdom of the West," and then to state capital in Dynasty 26. Small excavations in sensitive areas, however, have shown that there was a settlement in the northern part of the site in the Third Intermediate Period, based upon a differently organized, wealthier Ramesside rural settlement. The small-roomed houses with their internal multiple hearths, indistinct boundaries between house units, and limited small finds, usually consisting of beads, amulets, pottery, and gaming counters, reflect the urban landscape of the Third Intermediate Period and can be detected elsewhere, as, for example, at Hermopolis in Middle Egypt (Spencer 1993). The mixture of well-built walls and smaller, more ephemeral structures suggests that there was an initial "planned" building phase which was then taken over by larger families, dividing up the internal spaces into their own rooms. Houses were also built over or later have built into them cemeteries where the bodies were laid out in a shallow pit, with the minimum of grave offerings and covered with a low mound, or sometimes with a mudbrick surround. In the Saite period, it is assumed that a new citadel was founded at Sais directly upon this earlier town, but the whole of the upper layers and huge mudbrick walls have been removed by *sebakhin*, workers who dug away the rich mudbrick and earth to use as fertilizer on the farm land. In the sacred area of the site, the earlier levels were stripped away by the Saite builders themselves, down to Predynastic layers in the "Great Pit" at Sais (Wilson 2006) and the Early Dynastic administrative layers at Buto (Hartung 2003). It is not clear whether this was a deliberate clearance to the ancient past or simply good construction practice.

If the stratigraphy is complex and the micro-picture is difficult to visualize even at sites such as Tell Nebesheh (Petrie 1888) where there were substantial house remains, the broader picture of city layouts can be re-created more successfully by combining evidence from Sais, Memphis, and Mendes, for example. There seem to have been separate zones in the settlements, and one might expect a typical Late Period city to be multi-nodal, with an administrative quarter, separate cemetery and temple area, harbor and storage facilities, military or police area, and a residential quarter. The inhabitants may have provided the service industries of the city, relying upon family outside the urban area for their agricultural produce, or they may have continued to work outside and used the city as a safer, less exposed place in which to store surpluses and keep their animals. Such is the lack of work so far for this period it has not been possible to include the Saite cities in discussion of the phenomenon at a comparative level (see Yoffee 2005). Analysis of well-recorded material in Egypt will enable the Late Period to make an important contribution to the city-state debate in the future.

There are numerous cemetery sites throughout Egypt dating to the Late Period, but many have not been well recorded. The concentration of elite tombs at Thebes, spanning Dynasty 25 and 26, shows idealizing artistic sensibilities, religious inno-vation, and invention, as well as self-representation on a grand scale (Eigner 1984). Similarly, the elite cemeteries at Saqqara, Giza, and Abusir stress the separateness of the officials and suggest an element of individual choice in the inclusion of specific elements in tomb placement, architecture, and decoration. They include elaborate "sandraulic" systems for closing the sarcophagi (Ikram and Dodson 2008:286–287), Osirian pits (Hawass 2007), solar priest-king hymns (Betrò 1990), as well as promoting individuals as intermediaries between people and the gods. Elsewhere, for example at Quesna (cemetery for Athribis: Rowland and Strutt 2007) and at Kawady (cemetery for Sais: Bakry 1968), the elite were buried in mausoleum-type buildings, with individuals placed in stone sarcophagi within mudbrick, multi-chambered buildings. The Abydos Late Period burials are also suggestive of the importance of local choices in burial, as is likewise seen in the tombs of the governors of Siwa and Bahariya, which include an attenuated set of tomb scenes depicting, for example, the weighing of the heart, funerary provision, and solar procession (Fakhry 1973: 179–206; Hawass 2000:185–195, 203–211). For more ordinary individuals, cartonnage mummies covered in beads and amulets seem to have been the passport to the underworld, buried in mass tombs as at Bahriya Oasis, Saqqara, and Thebes.

Land Ownership

Underpinning the programs of the king and his officials, the exploitation of the land remained paramount. The ownership of land in the Late Period and the nature of the agricultural hinterland supporting cities, temples, and the court seem to be different from the Late New Kingdom. Landholdings of the crown and temple estates may have become less regulated compared to the control implied by Papyrus Wilbour in the reign of Ramesses IV. The surviving land donation stelae from Dynasty 22 onwards perhaps demonstrate the changing economic system relating to land ownership (Meeks 1979), recording royal gifts of various types. These include donations of land, such as the 42 arouras of land bestowed by Sheshonq V upon Bastet at Bubastis (Meeks 1979:670). Other dona-tions were made to maintain some part of a cult, as in a Dynasty 26 offering of land to pay someone to maintain the cult of the lamp of Osiris at Sais (Meeks 1979:647). Some gifts were made as a reward for services rendered, such as the offering of three arouras of land for the revenue of a guardian of pasturage recorded on a stela from year 6 of Osorkon I (Meeks 1979:666). Demotic land leases from Dynasty 25–26 also suggest that there was greater division of lands, possibilities of sale, and private ownership. There may have even been an attempt to reclaim more land to bring it under cultivation and thus extend the agricultural resource base of local ruler and kinglets. Such irrigation practices had been successful in the Assyrian Empire, were part of the Ptolemaic land drive later, and could have been an integral part of the Late Period organization of Egypt.

Some changes may have been enforced. For example the high Nile inundation recorded at Karnak during Dynasty 25 had evidently resulted in bumper crops and destroyed rodents and vermin (Kitchen 1986:388–389). It may also have brought changes to the channels of Nile distributaries, particularly in the Delta, creating new land boundaries and enabling water to reach "new" areas of land for the first time. The knock-on effect in Dynasty 26 may have been that there were increased agricultural tracts in some areas, perhaps even in the hinterland of Sais, and that in the northern and northeastern marshy areas of Buto and Tell el-Balamun it was possible to bring more land under cultivation. The resulting increase in agricultural resources available for taxation benefited the landowners – the king, the temple and some private individuals, such as the soldier and priestly classes. Foreign trade coming into Egypt from the Levant, through the Phoenicians, and the Aegean islands, from the "Greeks," would then have been bankrolled by the export of commodities, such as grain, papyrus, perfumes, and natron, as well as traditional commodities from central Africa, including material coming through the Red Sea by means of the new canal in Wadi Tumilat. Only with exportable commodities could Egypt expect to pay its mercenaries, build its temples, and furnish the elite officials with their pay (Möller 2000). The expansion of the agricultural base could be tested archaeologically by means of the investigation of installations of trade, and investigations into settlement patterns, textually in documentation and geomorphologically by looking at the palaeo-environment around towns.

Kings and Cults

As part of the duties of an Egyptian king, much attention was lavished on the temples at the center of towns and administrative areas. Sais may have been redesigned and remodeled as a northern version of Memphis, with a northern enclosure containing the palace of the kings and a southern enclosure containing the temple of Neith, matching the Memphite northern enclosure with the Palace of Apries and the southern enclosure of Ptah (Wilson 2006:261–266). The successive investment in cult centers elsewhere can be demonstrated, for example, at Mendes (Wilson 1982). Here King Ahmose II established a sanctuary for the god Banebdjed, with four huge stone *naoi* sanctuaries, constructed upon foundations formed from a massive clearance and pulverization of Third Intermediate Period mudbrick buildings and the remains of the tombs of local lords from the end of the Old Kingdom. The late Ramesside enclosure wall of the temple may have been repaired at this time, but it was subsequently rebuilt on the outside by Nakhtnebef I and later again, most likely by Ptolemy II. This pattern was repeated in part at Tell el-Balamun, the stronghold of the northeast shipping routes, where the Dynasty 22–23 local lords had been buried in the Ramesside temple enclosure, like the rulers of Tanis, but with bronze falcon beak fittings rather than the whole silver falcon sarcophagi of the Dynasty 21 kings. In Dynasty 26 Psamtek I built a small temple and enclosure wall within the old Ramesside Amun temple enclosure and then it was reconstructed by Nakhtnebef I (Spencer 1999a). Taken individually, the enclosure wall building suggests royal interest in maintaining key cult centers throughout Egypt, but taken together, the building work implies that there was a statewide building project designed to impose the king's presence on the local populations – especially the elite – and to make the point to the temples that the king was in control.

The new cults and endowments may also imply, however, that temples owned less land than they had under the New Kingdom system, especially from the Persian conquest onwards. Such a loss of income may have meant that there was a relative shortage of temple revenue, resulting in the emergence of a program of income generation. Temples seem to have begun to promote the "sale" of amulets, votive bronzes, ritual objects, parts of the temple, such as powder from the walls, and even the space around the temple that could be used for oracles and incubations (Davies and Smith 2005; Smith et al. 2006a, 2006b). The animal cults of temples may also have furnished a ready "product," with animals being slaughtered, turned into statue-mummies, and sold to devotees to be dedicated to the gods to ensure blessings for the dedicator. The animal necropolis areas throughout Egypt were very busy during the Late Period (Kemp 2006:376), with unprecedented numbers of animals of all kinds being raised and mummified throughout the Late Period. It is possible to take a less cynical view and suggest that the animals cults represented something "Egyptian" in the face of an influx of "foreignness," that is, an assertion of Egyptian national identity (Ikram 2005), or that people living in Egypt felt so insecure that they could only turn to their local gods for the kinds of supernatural protection they desired. The implication may be that the king was no longer thought to have such a divine power as in the past. The phenomenon may have been simply cultural in nature, a fashion trend, trickling down from the royal bull cults, especially the Apis cult, which was an extremely important royal institution (Kessler 1989). Egyptians could also participate in this kind of ritual through different animals, perhaps more suited to individual tastes. There is still much work to be done to understand this phenomenon at a cultural and social level. Most interesting is that there was a "market" for whatever commodities could be offered in the temple and there was a larger group of people who could take part in this process than perhaps had existed before.

The caches of bronzes and animal mummies from Late Period sites provide a strong indication that these were marketable products and that revenues were gained from this practice. By using the threat of Assyrian, Babylonian, and then Persian attacks on Egypt and playing on ever-present fears of low flood and famine as well as individual problems, the temple priests operated a slick system of sale of benefits for payments in kind or metal. The impression given can be one of a general loss of confidence, decline, and decay of Egyptian culture in general. Such an impression should be resisted, however, because comparable data are not available in such quantities from earlier periods or spread across as wide a cross-section of society. It is not known how people obtained amulets in the Old and New Kingdoms, how they obtained votive offerings, or, except for a few cases, how they made them, and the kind of cults operated for people such as Amenhotep son of Hapu imply that there was always a temple fringe of cultic practice. The priesthood also operated a closed system, perhaps to protect their rights and privileges by operating guilds both for priests and for other professions (de Cenival, 1972). By creating exclusive corporations, they maintained their rights, obligations, and social hierarchy within their own networks. This, too, suggests that social organization continued with a formalized system of guilds and obligation systems, establishing a new dynamic within a system of widening elite control.

The presence in Egypt of several important cult centers could have been a source of tension, but it may have created more of a market for those centers, with each one offering specialist shrines or particular festivals. Thebes had been the center of the Late New Kingdom theocracy with Amun-Ra, Lord of the Two Lands, at its head. It seems to have retained its significance through Dynasty 25 and 26, when people from all over Egypt dedicated statues at Karnak – for example, a man and his family from Xois and Petimouthes from Balamun (Guermeur 2004). The cults of the God's Wives of Amun seem to have been responsible for much priestly activity at Medinet Habu as well as for the rejuvenation of various Osiris chapels within the Karnak complex (Coulon and Defernez 2004). Sais itself may have been a key center for pilgrimage in the north. Its temple of Neith, with the twin shrines of the Mehneith and the Resneith, accompanying temples of Atum, Ra, and the special form of Osiris Hemag who was prominent also at Memphis meant that the cosmogony of the creator, in this case the mother of the sun, was covered, as well as the solar cycle (Ra and Atum) and the funerary cults (El-Sayed 1975). At Memphis, the Saqqara temples provided a key focus for visitors to the site and serve to underline the numbers of people who seem to have had some kind of access to the shrines. The movement of people for religious purposes is particularly evident in the Late Period, in terms of both the scale and the numbers of votive objects they left behind. In itself pilgrimage to sacred places was not new, nor was the manifestation of an individual through a statue or stela, but the distances covered by some individuals and the facilities at their disposal, including oracles and all kinds of votive offerings, suggest that it was an important social activity. New cults formed rallying points for certain kings, perhaps endowing lands and elevating the status of certain individuals, while the re-endowment of old cults re-established old families and gods. At Giza, for example, the temple of Isis was re-established and an Inventory Stela written which fictitiously accounted for all of the divine images inside the temple and even provided a pseudo-history of it (Zivie-Coche 1991).

Industrialization

As a result of provision of material for temple and animal cults there may have been what amounts to an industrialization of production of faience and bronze objects in particular at sanctuary sites. It is likely that specialist production was always concentrated around temples or royal centers and that the larger the center the greater was the production capacity. The Dynasty 18 Amarna temple bakeries were organized for the large-scale production of bread, for example, but there was not the step-up to an increased efficiency and scale of production that we would recognize as industrialization. At Pi-Ramesse, the bronze- and glass-working areas of the site may certainly approach this scale for the production of military and royal supplies (Pusch 1990; Pusch and Rehren 1999). The evidence from the Late Period for industrialization of manufacture is not abundant, but may be suggested by a number of developments in technology and recent discoveries. At Saqqara, around the area of the Serapeum, geophysical survey work has detected a large area of temple platforms, with other structures for cultic and domestic use (Leahy and Mathieson 2002). The area discovered appears to be only a part of the complex supplying bronze objects and other services for the myriad cults at Saqqara, and future work may allow an evaluation of the speed and efficiency of the production here. The technological changes in bronze manufacture also indicate an increasing desire for economy and speed of manufacture. Analyses of bronzes and comparison of the results shows that from the Late Period onwards more lead was added to the metal mixture, in some cases up to 25 percent of the content (Ogden 2000). The fluidity of the molten metal was increased and porosity reduced, improving the workability of the metal. Furthermore, in addition to the lost wax technique (Ogden 2000:156–157), not so much copper was required, representing a saving in metal.

There were also developments in the technology of faience manufacture. "Glassy faience" is particularly characteristic of Dynasty 26, although examples from as early as the Middle Kingdom are known (Lilyquist and Brill 1993). It is a near-glass material which contains frit and a high proportion of alkali. The hard, dense, opaque material was colored throughout and had a matte surface. It was particularly suited to sculpting, so that fine detail could be achieved on objects made from it (Friedman 1998:55, 215–216, 267). More work is needed to establish how such a combination of materials had been achieved. Some of the actual innovations may have occurred earlier, but because of the location of production centers near Wadi Natrun, for example, faience-working centers were able to take advantage of the technical knowledge and availability of resources. More curious, perhaps, is the issue of the manufacture of iron products in Egypt. Petrie identified iron-smelting facilities at Tell Defenneh, where aside from the finished tools and weapons there were also crucibles containing "iron" slag (Petrie 1888:77–79; see also Ogden 2000:166–168). Civil and military ironwork was also found at Naukratis and Nebesheh (Petrie 1888:27) as well as a horde of iron tools with an "Assyrian" bronze helmet at Thebes (Petrie 1897:18). Iron working in Egypt is usually associated with East Greek craftsmen and the military because of the provenance of the find. Although there are known to be iron ore sources at Bahariya and in the Western Desert, the material does not seem to have been mined in antiquity. The reason may be that in order to smelt iron on a large scale, a good supply of wood would be needed and Egypt lacked suitable trees. Part of the Egyptian interest in acquiring Cyprus or areas of the Levant may have been driven by the desire for wood for fuel as well as ship-building and for access to ore. It is possible that technological advances in tools used for agriculture may have begun in the Late Period, but such innovations were probably minor and far from universal.

The pottery of the Late Period from around 750 BCE also demonstrates a changing repertoire which may suggest technological as well as functional and ideological purposes (French 1992). For example, there are a group of marl vessels attested in Dynasty 25 in the Theban area, which created a taste for white-slipped, silt vessels, apparently in imitation. It is likely that in the Late Dynastic period new technology in the form of a faster, foot-operated wheel allowed the walls of silt vessels to be made much thinner and also their shapes to become more slender and graceful. Furthermore, it is likely that in order to sustain this technique, the production centers were consolidated, leading to an increasing degree of standardization, especially visible in Lower Egypt.

Distinct types of pottery were introduced in phases throughout the Saite period, attesting to the vitality in the pottery industry. For example, there was a type of thin-walled, silt jar introduced between 570 and 525 BCE which had a long, slender, shaped body, with a rounded base and a long, straight neck decorated with relief bands. The vessels were coated in a thick, red slip or wash and burnished in horizontal lines, sometimes creating a striped effect. It has been suggested that they were in imitation of metal vessels (French 1992:90), such as *situlae* (ritual buckets containing water or milk), but there are other types of vessel made from this fabric such as an almost neckless jar with a large globular body. Vessels made with the features of the god Bes (Figure 13.1) seem to have been introduced in the Third Intermediate Period and flourished in the Saite period, perhaps related to the taking of medicine or other potions (Aston 1996:82). In the oases a special type of keg called a *siga*, with a long neck, barrel-shaped body, and rounded ends, was introduced, perhaps for the transport of water or wine (Hope 2000). Even the characteristic Third Intermediate Period "Fire-dogs" were replaced by horned stands for the heating of large vessels or crucibles. With the continuing study of the pottery forms, their close dating, and the finding of kiln sites and production centers, the functionality of the vessels can be addressed in a more detailed manner, along with the impact on cultural change and social behavior.

"Archaism"

Some of the material culture from Late Period Egypt as well as the daily processes of recording show innovation and a sense of moving away from the past, especially for the larger owner-groups in society. On the other hand, it was important that the Saite kings and the elite used the past to justify the present, mainly through monumental display in temples and tombs. In order to be able to achieve this aim, as much written religious material as possible was codified and listed from earlier periods, then embellished in the Saite period. Certainly the use of the past as a guarantor of authority, representing an accumulation of experience, was already a long-established tradition in Egypt (Baines 1989), but it is intensified in many ways in the Late Period. The funerary texts of Nespasefy seem to have been earlier forms of the Book of the Dead, with later texts apparently added from a papyrus roll found at Tanis (Yoyotte 1977), but in fact the practice went much deeper, eventually creating the so-called "Saite Recension" of the Book of the Dead (Verhoeven 2001: 16–21).

There were many variations in this process by material, place, and period. For example, the copying of art from stone to stone often seems to be occasional rather than continuous copying – a tomb scene from Gebelein was copied at Thebes and the phraseology of royal inscriptions can be shown to have its origins in Classical and Ramesside monumental texts (Der Manuelian 1994). The door-jambs and inner walls of the gate of the Apries Palace at Memphis were decorated with low-relief scenes of rituals carried out by Apries, for example invoking extremely ancient hippopotamus rituals connected specifically with Lower Egypt. Originally the scenes were identified as Middle Kingdom in date by Petrie, but von Bissing (1933–1934) showed that they were Saite imitations of Old Kingdom reliefs and that the Saite artists had shown great interest in the Step Pyramid complex at Saqqara as a model for royal relief scenes. The shaft tombs at Saqqara and Giza may owe their design as much to a desire to copy the deep shafts of the Step Pyramid complex as to security (Eigner 1999). The Pyramid Texts themselves were integrated into temple rituals as well as tomb inscriptions, and the Temple of Hibis, with its multiple and all-embracing forms of Amun, suggests that some form of reassessment and re-imagining of text and ritual had occurred to create something new and multi-layered in meaning. Instead of being preserved merely on papyrus rolls in the Late Period, Books of the Dead and other texts were inscribed on stone sarcophagi. Temples were furnished with great shrines (*naoi*) covered in mythological vignettes and text – at Mendes alone there were four such shrines, there were three at Elephantine, and others are known, for example, from the temple at Saft el-Henneh. Later, in Dynasty 30, magical texts were inscribed all over the stone bodies of statues of semi-deified individuals (Kákosy 1999) and on portable amuletic stelae showing Horus destroying all dangers (Sternberg-el Hotabi 1999). In this way the power was transmitted outwards from the temples to people outside.

The titles of the administrative class also show the preference for imitating the past, but, like some honorific Old Kingdom titles, the exact functions of the posts are not always clear. *ḥrp ḥwwt*, "Director of the Mansions (Estates)," is one of the most prominent titles from the Old Kingdom used in Dynasty 26 and seems to have been used by an official high in the administration. In the Old Kingdom it seems to have been held by the person responsible for the royal regalia and the rituals associated with coronation, but in Dynasty 26 the Estates are often specifically those of Neith at Sais and the title seems to have a priestly and administrative role which fluctuates in importance throughout the Late Period (El-Sayed 1976). The cemeteries of officials from the Memphite necropolis suggest that the administration was a tightly run unit, often with families well established in certain posts and passing on the posts to their sons, forming hereditary dynasties. The occurrence of the king's name in many formal names on sarcophagi and in tombs attests that the earthly allegiance is primary and gives the impression of a bureaucracy formally putting the king first, a symptom of reverence for the Old Kingdom well learned from the Saqqara necropolis. The position of *swnw*, "physician," is prominent in the Saite period, when it seems to have been an elite title, often held by high-ranking individuals with good administrative posts, but it may either have meant that some kind of specialized training was essential amongst the elite or it may have been a means of distinguishing people who had attended an institution of learning, either religious, medical, or administrative – or all three. Wedjahorresenet, the naval commander of Ahmose II and Psamtek III, took up the post of "chief physician" under the Persian king Cambyses, which seems to have been a strange career change. The Egyptian centers of learning were still producing educated officials trained in many fields, as Wedjahorresenet seems to have been.

The elegant reliefs and statues recalling the style of Old and Middle Kingdom precedents may have been intended as a reassuring signal that everything was back to "normal" and that the threat of the foreign invaders had been dissipated by those kings who upheld the ancient values. Psamtek I had successfully regained the ideology of the Two Lands and his successors continued to use it as an over-arching theme with which to sustain Egyptian culture and absorb the effects of the world outside Egypt.

Conclusion

There is no doubt that a distinct flavor of information can be provided from the perspective of the Egyptian archaeology in the Late Period. There is also potential for investigating further the multi-layered social and daily life experiences of individuals and towns at a time of foreign conquest, cultural restabilization, and outside influence. The material from stratified city contexts, from concentrated sets of votive offerings at pilgrimage centers, from technology, from economic data in texts, as well as the subtle hues of nuance from hieroglyphic texts, suggests a rich, vibrant society of the first millennium, still dynamically interwoven with the paradigm of past ideologies.

REFERENCES

Aston, D. 1996 Egyptian Pottery of the Late New Kingdom and Third Intermediate Period (Twelfth to Seventh Centuries BC) (Studien zur Archäologie und Geschichte Altägyptens 13). Heidelberg: Orientverlag.

Baines, J. 1989 Ancient Egyptian Concepts and Uses of the Past, 3rd–2nd millennium BC Evidence. In Who Needs the Past? Indigenous Values and Archaeology. R. Layton, ed. Pp. 179–201. London: One World Archaeology.

Bakry, H. S. K. 1968 A Family from Sais. Mitteilungen des Deutschen Archäologisches Institut Kairo 23:69–74.

Betrò, Maria C. 1990 I testi solari del portale di Pascerientaisu (BN2). Pisa: Giardini.

Bettles, E. A. 2003 Phoenician Amphora Production and Distribution in the Southern Levant (BAR International Series 1183). Oxford: Archaeopress.

Caminos, R. 1964 The Nitocris Adoption Stela. Journal of Egyptian Archaeology 50:71–101.

de Cenival, F. 1972 Les Associations religieuses en Égypte d'après les documents démotiques (BdE 46). Cairo: Institut français d'archéologie orientale.

Chevereau, P.-M. 1985 Prosopographie des cadres militaires égyptiens de la Basse Époque. Paris: Antony.

Colin, F. 2004 Qasr Allam: A Twenty-Sixth Dynasty Settlement. Egyptian Archaeology 24:30–33.

Coulon, L., and C. Defernez 2004 La chapelle d'Osiris Ounnefer Neb-Djefaou à Karnak. Bulletin de l'Institut français d'archéologie orientale 104(1):135–190.

Coulson, W. 1996 Ancient Naukratis, Vol. II: The Survey of Naukratis and Environs. Part I: The Survey at Naukratis (Oxbow Monographs no. 60). Oxford: Oxbow Books.

Dakhleh Oasis Project 2009 http://www.arts.monash.edu.au/archaeology/excavations/ dakhleh/ (accessed July 2009).

Darnell, J. 1992 The *Kbn.wt* Vessels of the Late Period. *In* Life in a Multi-cultural Society: Egypt from Cambyses to Constantine and Beyond (SAOC 51). J. Johnson, ed. Pp. 67–89. Chicago: University of Chicago Press.

Davies, S., and H. S. Smith 2005 The Sacred Animal Necropolis at Saqqara: The Falcon Complex and Catacomb. 73rd Excavation Memoir. London: Egypt Exploration Society.

Der Manuelian, P. 1994 Living in the Past: Studies in Archaism of the Egyptian Twenty-sixth Dynasty. London, New York: Kegan Paul International Ltd.

Eigner, D. 1984 Die monumentalen Grabbauten der Spätzeit in der thebanischen Nekropole. Vienna: Verlag der Österreichischen Akademie der Wissenschaften.

Eigner, D. 1999 Late Period Tombs. *In* Encyclopaedia of the Archaeology of Ancient Egypt. K. Bard, ed. Pp. 432—438. London: Routledge.

El-Sayed, R. 1975. Documents relatifs à Sais et à ses divinités (BdE 69). Cairo: Institut français d'archéologie orientale.

El-Sayed, R. 1976 À propos du titre. *ḥrp-ḥwwt*. Révue d'Égyptologie 28:97–110.Fakhry, A. 1973 The Oases of Egypt. Vol. 1: Siwa Oasis. Cairo: American University in Cairo Press.

Fakhry, A. 1974 The Oases of Egypt. Vol. 2: Bahriyah and Farafra Oasis. Cairo: American University in Cairo Press.

French, P. 1992 A Preliminary Study of Pottery in Lower Egypt in the Late Dynastic and Ptolemaic Periods. Cahiers de la céramique égyptienne 3:83–93.

Friedman, F. D., 1998 Gifts of the Nile: Ancient Egyptian Faience. Rhode Island: Museum of Art RISD.

Gozzoli, R. B. 2006 The Writing of History in Ancient Egypt during the First Millennium BC (ca. 1070–180 BC): Trends and Perspectives. London: Golden House Publications.

Guermeur, I. 2004 Le Groupe familial de Pachéryentaisowy. Bulletin de l'Institut français d'archéologie orientale 104.1:245–90.

Hartung, U. 2003 Tell el-Fara'in-Buto 8. Vorbericht, Mitteilungen des Deutschen Archäologischen Instituts, Abteilung Kairo 59:199–267.

Hawass, Z. 2000 Valley of the Golden Mummies. New York: Harry N. Abrams.

Hawass, Z. 2007 The Discovery of the Osiris Shaft at Giza. In The Archaeology and Art of Ancient Egypt: Essays in Honor of David B. O'Connor. Vol. I. Z. Hawass and J. Richards, eds. Pp. 379–397. Cairo: Supreme Council of Antiquities of Egypt.

Heidorn, L. A. 1991 The Saite and Persian Period Forts at Dorginarti. *In* Egypt and Africa: Nubia from Prehistory to Islam. W. V. Davies, ed. Pp. 205–219. London: British Museum Press.

Herodotus 1966 Herodotus: The Histories. A. D. Godley, trans. The Loeb Classical Library, I–IV. Cambridge, MA: Harvard University Press.

Holladay, J. S. 1982 Cities of the Delta. III: Tell el-Maskhuta. Malibu: Undena.

Ikram, S. 2005 Divine Creatures: Animal Mummies in Ancient Egypt. New York, Cairo: American University in Cairo Press.

Hope, C. A. 2000 Kegs and Flasks from the Dakhla Oasis. Cahiers de la céramique égyptienne 6:189–210.

Ikram, S., and A. Dodson 2008 The Tomb in Ancient Egypt. London: Thames and Hudson.

Kákosy, L. 1999 Egyptian Healing Statues in Three Museums in Italy. Turin: Ministero per i beni e le attività culturali, Soprintendenza al Museo delle antichità egizie.

Kemp, B. J. 1977 The Palace of Apries at Memphis. Mitteilungen des Deutschen Archäologischen Instituts, Abteilung Kairo 33:101–108.

Kemp, B. J. 2006 Ancient Egypt, Anatomy of a Civilization. 2nd edition. Oxford, New York: Routledge.

Kessler, D. 1989 Die heilige Tier und der König. Teil 1. Wiesbaden: Otto Harrassowitz.

Kitchen, K. A., 1986 The Third Intermediate Period in Egypt (110–650 BC). Warminster: Aris and Phillips.

Leahy, A., and I. Mathieson 2002 Late Period Temple Platforms at Saqqara. Egyptian Archaeology 21:14–16.

Leclère, F. 2007 An Egyptian Fort at Tell Dafana. Egyptian Archaeology 30:14–17.

Leclère, F. 2008 Les villes de basse égypte au Ière millenaire av. J.-C.: Analyse archéologique et historique de la topographie urbaine. Cairo: Institut français d'archéologie orientale.

Lilyquist, C., and R. H. Brill 1993 Studien in Early Egyptian Glass. New York: Metropolitan Museum of Art.

Lloyd, A. B. 1975 Herodotus Book II: Introduction (EPRO 43/1). Leiden: E. J. Brill.

Lloyd, A. B. 1976 Herodotus Book II: Commentary 1–98 (EPRO 43/2). Leiden: E. J. Brill.

Lloyd, A. B. 1988 Herodotus Book II: Commentary 99–182 (EPRO 43/3). Leiden, New York, Cologne: E. J. Brill.

Lloyd, A. B. 1983 The Late Period, 664–323 BC. In Ancient Egypt: A Social History. B. G. Trigger, B. J. Kemp, D. O'Connor, and A. B. Lloyd. Pp. 279–348. Cambridge: Cambridge University Press.

Lloyd, A. B. 2000 The Late Period (664–332 BC). In The Oxford History of Ancient Egypt. I. Shaw, ed. Pp. 369–394. Oxford: Oxford University Press.

Maeir, A. M. 2002 The Relations between Egypt and the Southern Levant during the late Iron Age. Ägypten und Levante 12:235–246.

Masson, O. 1978 Carian Inscriptions from North Saqqara and Buhen. London: Egypt Exploration Society.

Meeks, D. 1979 Les donations aux temples dans l'Égypte du Ier millénaire avant J.-C. In State and Temple Economy in the Ancient Near East II (Orientalia Lovaniensia Analecta 6). E. Lipinski, ed. Pp. 605–687. Leuven: Orientaliste.

Möller, A. 2000 Naukratis. Oxford: Oxford University Press.

Mumford, G. n.d. East Delta: Tell Tebilla 10. SEPE website. http://www.deltasinai.com/delta-10.htm (accessed July 2009).

Ogden, J. 2000 Metals. In Ancient Egyptian Materials and Technology. P. Nicholson and I. Shaw, eds. Pp. 148–176. Cambridge: Cambridge University Press.

Oren, E. D. 1984 Migdol: A New Fortress on the Edge of the Eastern Nile Delta. Bulletin of the American Oriental Schools of Oriental Research 256:7–44.

Perdu, O. 2002. Recueil des Inscriptions Royales Saïtes. Vol. I: Psammétique Ier. Paris: Éditions Cybele.

Petrie, W. M. F. 1886 Naukratis, Part I, 1884–5. London: Egypt Exploration Fund.

Petrie, W. M. F. 1888 Tanis, Part II: Nebesheh (Am) and Defenneh (Tahpanhes). London: Egypt Exploration Fund.

Petrie, W. M. F. 1897 Six Temples at Thebes 1896. London: B. Quaritch.

Petrie, W. M. F., and J. H. Walker 1909 The Palace of Apries (Memphis II). London: British School of Archaeology in Egypt.

Porten, B., ed. 1996 The Elephantine Papyri in English. Leiden, New York, Cologne: Brill.

Pritchard, J. B. 1969 Ancient Near Eastern Texts Relating to the Old Testament. Princeton: Princeton University Press.

Pusch, E. B. 1990 Metallverarbeitende werkstätten der frühen Ramessidenzeit in Qantir-Piramesse Nord. Ägypten und Levante 1:75–113.

Pusch, E. B., and T. Rehren 1999 Glass and Glass-making at Qantir-Piramesses and Beyond. Ägypten und Levante 9:171–179.

Redford, D. B. 1992 Egypt, Canaan and Israel in Ancient Times. Cairo: American University in Cairo Press.

Redford, D. B. 2004 Excavations at Mendes. Vol. 1: The Royal Necropolis. Leiden, Boston: Brill.

Rowland, J., and K. Strutt 2007 Minufiyeh: The Geophysical Survey at Quesna. Egyptian Archaeology 30:33–35.

Smith, H. S. 1992 Foreigners in the Documents from the Sacred Animal Necropolis, Saqqara. In Life in a Multi-cultural Society: Egypt from Cambyses to Constantine and Beyond (SAOC 51). J. Johnson, ed. Pp. 295–301. Chicago: University of Chicago Press.

Smith, H. S., S. Davies, and K. J. Frazer 2006a The Sacred Animal Necropolis at Saqqara: The Main Temple Complex. 75th Excavation Memoir. London: Egypt Exploration Society.

Smith, H. S., S. Davies, and K. J. Frazer 2006b The Sacred Animal Necropolis at Saqqara: The Mother of Apis and Baboon Catacombs. 76th Excavation Memoir. London: Egypt Exploration Society.

Smolárikova, K. 2002 Abusir VII Greek Imports in Egypt: Graeco-Egyptian Relations during the First Millennium BC. Prague: Universitas Carolina Pragensis.

Spencer, A. J. 1993 Excavations at El-Ashmunein III: The Town. London: British Museum Press.

Spencer, A. J. 1996 Excavations at Tell el-Balamun 1991–1994. London: British Museum Press.

Spencer, A. J. 1999a Excavations at Tell el-Balamun 1995–1998. London: British Museum Press.

Spencer, A. J. 1999b Casemate Foundations Once Again. In Studies on Ancient Egypt in Honour of H. S. Smith. A. Leahy and J. Tait, eds. Pp. 295–300. London: Egypt Exploration Society.

Sternberg-el Hotabi, H. 1999 Untersuchungen zur Überlieferungsgeschichte der Horusstelen: ein Beitrag zur Religionsgeschichte Ägyptens im 1. Jahrtausend v. Chr (ÄA 62). Wiesbaden: Otto Harrassowitz.

Verhoeven, U. 2001 Untersuchungen zur späthieratischen Buchinschrift. Leuven: Peeters.

Villing, A., and U. Schlotzhauer, eds 2006 Naukratis: Greek Diversity in Egypt. Studies on East Greek Pottery and Exchange in the Eastern Mediterranean (The British Museum Research Publication Number 162). London: The British Museum.

von Bissing, F. 1933–1934 Saitischen Kopien nach Reliefs des Alten Reichs. Archiv für Orientforschung 9:35–40.

Weber, S. 2001. Archaisch ostgriechische Keramik aus Ägypten außerhalb von Naukratis. In Naukratis: Die Beziehungen zu Ostgriechenland, Ägypten und Zypern in archaischer Zeit. U. Höckmann, and D. Kreikenbom, eds. Pp. 127—150. Paderborn: Bibliopolis.

Wilson, K. L. 1982 Cities of the Delta II: Mendes (American Research Center in Egypt Reports, Vol. 5), Malibu: Udena.

Wilson, P. 2006 The Survey of Sais (Sa el-Hagar), 1997–2002. London: Egypt Exploration Society.

Wilson, P., and G. Gilbert 2007 Saïs and Its Trading Relations with the Eastern Mediterranean. In Moving across Borders: Foreign Relations, Religion and Cultural Interactions in the Ancient Mediterranean (Orientalia Lovaniensia Analecta 159). P. Kousoulis and K. Magliveras, eds. Pp. 251–265. Leuven, Paris, Dudley, MA: Peeters.

Yoffee, N. 2005 Myths of the Archaic State: Evolution of the Earliest Cities, States and Civilizations. Cambridge: Cambridge University Press.

Yoyotte, J. 1977 Contribution à l'histoire du chapitre 162 du livre des morts. Révue d'égyptologie 29:194–202.

Zivie-Coche, C. 1991 Giza au premier millenaire. Boston: Museum of Fine Arts.

14

Egypt in the Memory of the World

Fekri A. Hassan

From the earliest known encounters with the various cultures of Western civilizations, ancient Egypt has been a cultural point of reference and an inseparable element of the dynamics by which Europeans and Egyptians have envisioned their own cultures. The viability of Egypt as a historical reference with the power to legitimize and validate "novel" historical religious and cultural paradigms ranging from cultural identity to science is highly remarkable. A number of mechanisms employ certain conceptions and "models" or "schemas" of ancient Egypt within emerging ideologies and cultural "paradigms" to further the claims of a variety of groups and to empower them against their rivals. The result is a multiplicity of interpretations of ancient Egypt: Roman, Christian, Islamic, nationalistic (both foreign and Egyptian), Egyptological, and commercial. By emphasizing different aspects and de-contextualizing these, the various users or consumers of ancient Egypt formulated particular historical narratives, all claiming to be founded on one monolithic tradition. In recent years Egyptologists have realized that even in ancient Egypt a process of legitimation was based on a constant reinterpretation of "ancient" Egypt and a reiterative process of invention of traditions Egypt (see Kemp 2006), and that any study should take into account the past and present social, political, and economic interests.

The Eye of the Beholder: The Classical Discovery of Egypt

We owe most of our views of ancient Egypt to "outsiders" who first came in contact with Egyptians when Egyptian civilization was already more than 3000 years old. Among the Greek intellectuals who flocked to Egypt since the fifth century BCE, it was Herodotus (c. 484–425 BCE) who left one of the most vivid and tantalizing accounts (*Histories*) of ancient Egypt as he presumably experienced it (Lloyd 1988). Less than two centuries later and over the span of the Ptolemaic period (305 BCE–30 BCE), many Greeks resided in Egypt, and one of the key accounts of the Egyptian dynasties was written by Manetho, an Egyptian priest, at the invitation of King Ptolemy Philadelphus (285–246 BCE) to compose a history. Manetho's *Aegyptiaca*, written in Greek (Waddell 1940), revealed the care with which Egyptians maintained historical records in temple archives and libraries that went back in time for more than 3000 years. We only know of this account through excerpts and abbreviated fragments written by the Jewish historian Josephus (b. 37 CE) in the first century CE, by Sextus Julius Africanus about 220 CE, and by Eusebius, Bishop of Caeseria, in 320 CE. The original work by Manetho was abridged to *Epitomes* that boiled down his rich text to a list of pharaohs with a few notes. Sextus Julius Africanus and Eusbius used the abridged version of *Aegyptiaca* in the third and fourth centuries CE, during the formative stage of Christianity, five to six centuries after Manetho completed his original text. Manetho also provided tables revealing the kings of Eastern peoples who were contemporary with the Egyptian kings. This proved to be a bonanza for Christian polemicists, who were preoccupied with comparing the annals of peoples of the ancient world to establish a chronology of the Old Testament.

The Greeks, Ptolemies, and Hellenes selected, emphasized, and glamorized the wisdom of ancient Egypt and developed their own version of Egyptian civilization. In addition to the Greeks who resided in Egypt, there were also many illustrious visitors who came to Egypt for short or long sojourns. For example, Diodorus of Sicily lists among the visitors to Egypt Homer, Lycurgus, Solon, Plato, Pythagoras, Eudoxus, and Democritus. Some of the Greeks were in direct contact with Egyptian priests and were thus able to gain as much first-hand information as the Egyptians were willing to reveal and to the extent that the Greeks were capable of grasping the subtleties of Egyptian thought. A great deal of confusion and misunderstanding was probably also due to the use of Greek language for communication instead of the Egyptian language with its layered philosophical meanings. Notions of ancient Egypt elaborated by Greek scholars were imprinted on the memory of Europeans because Egypt was prominent in the writings of no less than Plato (c. 428–347 BCE), Diodorus (c. 80–20 BCE), and Strabo (c. 64 BCE–21 CE). According to Hornung (2001:23), Osiris and Isis featured prominently in Diodorus' account of Egyptian religion. The views expounded by Diodorus had an extraordinary influence on succeeding periods down to the eighteenth century. Isis, Osiris, and Horus survived in the cultural memory by a process of transfiguration, transmutation, absorption, and amalgamation to fit into the prevailing cultural hegemonic view. The triad first acquired their importance from their association with kingship; they were the gods of kings, royal gods, looming high above all other gods and peoples. Osiris was identified with Sarapis, and with Zeus and Jupiter. Isis also became the "One who is *All*." Her status shifted to the cosmos to become the embodiment of cosmic order, thus circling in the realm of astronomy and astrology independent of her original position as a mother goddess. By the first century CE, she was affiliated with Hermes, who raised her, and was regarded as a co-inventor of writing with him. Her worship spread all over the Mediterranean in the fourth century BCE because she was adopted by sailors as their guardian goddess; her temples were thus founded at ports in many places, including Piraeus, Eretria, Delos, Rhodes, Cos, Samos, Lesbos, and Cyprus, among many others along the Mediterranean coast. Her cult spread afterwards from ports to river valleys along the main trade routes to Germany, Holland, Hungary, and eventually England (Hornung 2001; Takács 1995; Witt 1971).

Ancient Egypt and the Biblical Tradition

Isis, Osiris, and Horus were perpetuated outside Egypt because they were integrated within Greek mythology and biblical traditions. The iconographic and conceptual linkage between Nursing Isis and Nursing Mary is compelling. Mary and Jesus sojourned in Egypt. Mary's sycamore tree at Heliopolis (Mataryia today), where the sacred learned institution once stood, is also a compelling pointer to the identification of Mary both with Isis/Hathor and with the wisdom of ancient Egypt. An old tree is still identified as the Tree of Mary in the middle of the housing projects that have replaced the scared ground of ancient Heliopolis (On). Jesus was identified with Horus. One amulet depicts on one side the head of Christ and scenes from the New Testament and on the other side a winged, young Horus who tames crocodiles and scorpions. The passions of Jesus were mixed with Osirian traditions (Hornung 2001:75). Bes, an Egyptian folk god who protected women during birth, was also identified with Christ.

The biblical account of Moses places him in Egypt and creates an inescapable affiliation between the Hebraic traditions and Egypt. Cyril of Alexandria (d. 444 CE) asserted that Plato and Solon became acquainted with the wisdom of Moses in Egypt. According to Diodorus, Moses appears parallel to Hermes together with Zarathustra in a triad. Clearly, the position of Moses was elevated by this association, gaining legitimacy from the renowned fame of Hermes/Thoth (Hornung 2001). The acclaim to be accorded Moses was within the hegemonic trope of Wisdom, independent of gods and kings. It is that diversion of the intellectual stream of Egyptian thought to the domain of Wisdom that made it possible for one generation after another and in so many different regions to rework Egyptian notions within specific invented traditions and beliefs. Thus ancient Egypt has survived because of its association with Wisdom, as well as with the existential issues of Life and Death, still evident today in the interest in mummies and the ankh amulet (Brier 1994, 2004).

Furthermore, the memory of Egypt has been retained because of the biblical references to Egypt and the mobilization of ancient Egypt in the works of Jewish and Christian Church fathers. Egypt was central to one of the main foundation myths of Jewish identity (Lemche 1998:88–93). According to Lemche,

> being only a handful of persons when they left Canaan, the Israelites came out of Egypt as a mighty nation. In this way Egypt became the cradle of the Israelite people, but would have turned out to be their grave if they had not been liberated from this place in time by the intervention of the God of their fathers, here Abraham, Isaac, and Jacob. (Lemche 1998:89)

Egypt was also central to Christian ideology and theology. The sojourn of the Holy Family in Egypt continues the tradition of placing Egypt within the religious map of the world. Perhaps more important were the contributions by the

Alexandrian Church fathers, including Clement of Alexandria and Origen (Grant 1986). Evidently, the classical and Hellenistic, as well as Jewish, notions of Egyptian wisdom contributed to Wisdom Christology. The title given Christ in Corinthians 1:24 and 30 is "Wisdom" (*sophia*). The influential Jewish philosopher Philo (Modrzejewski 1995) regarded Wisdom as God's daughter, "the first-born mother of all things" (Grant 1986:102). Philo also uses the term *"Episteme"* (Knowledge) when he speaks of a female principle with whom God had intercourse so that she brought forth the only and beloved perceptible son (Grant 1986:100–104).

Contrary to this positive identification with Egypt was the emergence of a tradition that vilified Egypt as a land of paganism. In one of the most perceptive attempts to deal with the *topos* of "Moses the Egyptian," Assmann (1997:217) suggests that the Jews and Christians turned Egypt into a nightmare and a fatal disease. Egypt was the counter-image, a polemical counter-construction created by "normative inversion" – the creation and perpetuation of a binary opposite needed for contradistinctive self-definition. Egypt, rejected and "forgotten," survived as an abomination in biblical accounts (though in cosmotheistic movements such as Neoplatonism, Hermeticism, alchemy, and Deism, the attitude to Egypt was more sympathetic). Assmann assumes this might be explained as a return of the repressed, using an insight from Freud. The struggle between Judaism and Christianity against the prevailing political regimes of the Roman Empire targeted the tangible icons of their world, which included those of ancient Egypt. Egypt, as the foundation of the hegemonic system of the classical world, became the subject of attacks. Only on the ruins of Egyptian temples could churches celebrate and legitimize the new religion that replaced the old. Theophilus, the Archbishop of Alexandria, was adamant, and ultimately successful, in his demand for an imperial edict that would allow him to destroy pagan temples and statues. The early history of the Christian Church as narrated by Theodoret, born 393 CE (cited in Kravachok 2002; Schaff and Wace 1890–1900), includes a graphic description of one of the events during the year 391 CE when Theophilus terrorized pagan philosophers and razed to the ground ancient temples. One of the main targets of destruction was the Sarapeion, the principal temple for the worship of the royal cult of Sarapis founded by Ptolemy III (246–241 BCE). Nothing remains from this temple except one of the columns currently known as the Pompei Pillar.

Backed by royal decrees, the guardians of the new religion were engaged in a political struggle that aimed to dislodge the grip of "pagan" Alexandrian philosophers on intellectual, and hence political, power. For the general public who are not versed in the nuances of theological debates, the use of tangible icons to stand for simplified ideas, regardless of their veracity, has been one of the successful strategies to win mass support. Through misinformation, and disinformation presented with passionate rhetoric and sensational stories and fables, often with fabricated content, popular beliefs were cast. Ancient Egypt was a rich source for stories, and became almost a fairy tale (see Fentress and Wickham 1994:71). The portrayal of ancient Egypt as a pagan culture and the use of the motif of the destruction of idols as a transition from falsehood to truth in early Christianity totally misrepresented Egyptian religion. The stories of Moses and the sorcerers or magicians of Egypt, the golden calf, or the Exodus provided a literary drama with a fascinating imagistic, theatrical aura. In a balanced review of the impact of ancient Egypt on the Old Testament, Currid develops the view that Moses and Aaron's confrontation with the magicians of the Pharaoh (Exodus 7) is a direct polemic against the gods of Egypt and the Pharaoh as a divine figure. The effect of the plagues was to unleash Chaos and upset the "cosmic order," which is the basis for Egyptian cosmogony (Currid 1997:83–120). During the nineteenth century, Currid remarks, scholars preferred to ignore or underestimate the significance of Egypt.

Islam and Cosmic Order

Islam, by embracing the Old and New Testaments as holy books and by continuing to refer to the biblical account of the Exodus, the golden calf, and the encounter between Moses and the Pharaoh, also furthered the memory of Egypt. Both Christianity and Islam spread beyond their place of origin among many groups of people by the emphasis they placed on the social virtues of love, mercy, compassion, charity, and solidarity. In a sense, such notions embodied in the conceptions of the Egyptian goddess Maat were already evident in the Old Testament, again in spite of the condemnation of Egyptian gods. Maat, who ordained the movement of the stars, the succession of seasons, and in general the orderly harmony of the universe, was also the goddess of justice and "truth." Pharaohs, viziers, and high officials abided by Maat and proclaimed that they fed the hungry, provided water for the thirsty, and took care of widows, orphans, and the needy (Assmann 1989). It is indeed logical to envision how such an idea could be used by a people against tyrants and how it would evolve into a universal notion of the fundamental "truth" of the cosmos. In the biblical tradition, Maat appears as the "Justice God," manifest in the "Sedeq" of Yahweh (the word *Sedq* in Arabic means "truth"). In his analysis of power in the biblical tradition, Walsh concludes that "justice is the 'one necessary thing'. The cry of the poor, the need of the other, the claim the powerless make on us is central and non-negotiable. This is what Yahweh, the 'passionate god', takes with absolute seriousness. He wants to feed the hungry, clothe the naked. He wants his banquet hall filled" (Walsh 1987:174–175)

In Islam, the "anti-Egyptian revolution" (Assmann 1998:211) expounded in the book of Exodus (Haarmann 1980:56; Hassan 1998:210; Wood 1998:186) was counterbalanced by a favorable regard for Egypt as a land of virtues (Youssef 1991). From the ninth century and up to the fifteenth century CE, Arab scholars set the foundation for Egyptological learning (El-Daly 2003b).

The Renaissance and Egyptian Wisdom

The admiration of the classical world for Egypt ensured that it met with a similar appreciation in Renaissance European civilization. The "lore" of ancient Egypt became an integral ingredient in the tool-kits of intellectuals; the impact of classical tradition on Western literature is unfathomable (Highet 1976). Classical writers celebrated the wisdom of ancient Egypt and their constructions were appropriated by Renaissance Humanism. The Humanists emphasized intellectual cultivation over spiritual matters, and in their campaign against clerical authorities they fortified their position by the "authority" of the past. According to New (1969), Antiquity legitimated the secular pursuits of the Renaissance. It provided a hitherto underused and seldom appreciated wealth of materials on art, architecture, jurisprudence, philosophy, and the sciences. The great emphasis placed on the works of classical writers led to a surge of interest not only in the texts and antiquities of Rome and Greece, but also in those of Egypt. In Rome, antiquarian surveys and excavations were essential for the birth of a new political philosophy and to the renaissance of art and sciences (Schnapp 1997:2). Classical lore of ancient Egypt became embedded in this crucial episode in the making of European civilization.

The emergence of modern science as exemplified by Isaac Newton also involved references to ancient Egypt. The proponents of the new scientific paradigm were keen on recovering or learning from the "scientific" wisdom of ancient civilizations, among which Egypt was at the forefront, and were sceptical of certain interpretations of the Bible and Church doctrine (Haycock 2003:138). Newton believed that the divine-inspired, true theology was brought to Egypt by Noah's son Ham, who was venerated by the Egyptians as their god "Amon." In 1683–1684, Newton wrote in the first version of his "Philosophical Origins of Gentile Philosophy," "Ye Mosaical religion concerning ye true God contains little else besides what was then in use among the Egyptians" (Haycock 2003:138). The Egyptians passed their knowledge of the true god to Socrates, Confucius, Moses, and Christ. Newton noted that "it's certain that ye old religion of the Egyptians was ye true [Noachian] religion tho corrupted before the age of Moses by the mixture of false Gods with that of ye true one" (Haycock 2003:139). The corruption of true religion also entailed a corruption of scientific knowledge, to which the priests, who were in charge of both scientific, philosophical knowledge and theological teachings, contributed. Newton was concerned with chronology, and, like many others before him, did not believe the biblical account of the age of creation. He became convinced that the Egyptians understood the heliocentric system, though they disseminated their knowledge under the veil of religious rites and hieroglyphic symbols (Haycock 2003:142). Newton's Fellows of the Royal Society of London, founded in 1660, were also interested in hieroglyphs as a possible route to finding a "natural" or "universal" language.

Thus as Europe began to establish the scientific foundations of its modern civilization, the lore of Egypt was in the minds of the great thinkers who were instrumental in shaping the new world order and its paradigmatic outlook. Entrenched in the scientific, humanistic, and theological armature of European civilization, the lore of Egypt was readily accessible to modern minds in all fields of intellectual pursuits. The memory of Egypt thus survived because of the alleged and legendary wisdom of ancient Egypt, which was perpetuated not only in the writings of classical authors and Jewish and Christian philosophers who have never ceased to influence European intellectuals, but also because the "glory" of ancient Egypt was manifest in the magnificence of its pyramids, obelisks, and other monuments that have defied time and resisted decay and destruction. The construction of such eternal edifices was a declaration of the great advances made by Egyptians in masonry, geometry, mathematics, and astronomy. The secrets of this advanced knowledge and wisdom were believed to be encoded in the mysterious hieroglyphic inscriptions. The search to decipher the hieroglyphs was finally crowned by the successful efforts of Jean-François Champollion around 1822, providing for the first time an enviable access to the accounts of Egyptian civilization by the Egyptians themselves.

Egyptology, Colonialism, and Nationalism

The fascination with the Rosetta Stone (Walker 2003) implies an admiration for the triumph of the West in appropriating the civilization of ancient Egypt by deciphering its mysterious text. In the context of colonial rivalry, much has been made of the extent to which Britain and France contributed to the decipherment of hieroglyphs, which was the key to understanding the wisdom of ancient Egypt. Paradoxically, the decipherment of the hieroglyphic signs instigated in the first place by Arab scholars and subsequently Europeans in the eighteenth century (El-Daly 2003a) with the desire to gain knowledge of Egyptian wisdom was achieved at a time when the paradigm of the superiority of "Western" scientific knowledge had displaced sympathetic views of Egyptian know-how.

Ancient Egypt was essential for the new colonial paradigm because by possessing the antiquities of Egypt, the colonial powers inherited the claim to cultural hegemony (Hassan 2003). The French or the British acted as legitimate heirs of the Roman Empire, which manifested its own hegemonic triumph by appropriating Egyptian obelisks to be erected in Rome, which has become known as the "eternal city" on account of its archaeological treasures. Paris, London, and later New York could not have become world cities without Egyptian obelisks (Hassan 2003). In the meantime, ancient Egypt was romanticized as a land of mystery, an exotic destination for the rich, where adventurers could come upon fabulous treasures. The discovery of the treasures of Tukankhamun in 1922 added to the lore of Egypt because it was the subject of sensational newspaper reports.

As an Islamic country, modern Egypt was regarded as a separate entity from Pharaonic Egypt. Most Egyptian intellectuals in modern times have been introduced to ancient Egypt through European scholarship and in the context of the political, military, and intellectual hegemony of the West. Unlike the Europeans, Egyptian intellectuals emphasized the continuity of Egyptian civilization, the survival of many Egyptian conceptions from Pharaonic times to the present, the maintenance of an Egyptian identity (mostly because of the particular Nile setting), the intertwining of Egypt's various cultural strands through its long historical course, the values and virtues of ancient Egypt, and the persistence of the dynamic interplay of ideals, especially between old and new, with an emphasis on the social history of Egypt. Alienated from their own Pharaonic past, Egyptian intellectuals beginning with Rifa'ah Rafi' al-Tahtawi (1801–1873) and well into the 1950s struggled to introduce the Egyptian public to the information they gleaned from European sources (Hassan 1998; Reid 1985, 2002). The politics of "Arabic nationalism" and the economic and ideological troubles and dilemmas of development under neo-colonial regimes were not conducive to the emergence of a viable Egyptian nationalism within a Pharaonic paradigm. This was compounded by the strong affiliation of Egypt with Arabic civilization, the prevalence of religious traditions that denigrate the pharaohs, and the diminution of Arabic scholarly interest in ancient Egypt since the fifteenth century. Moreover, the rhetoric of "nationalism" has now been undermined by globalization.

As movie-making became an attractive medium, the lore of Egypt became one of its favorite subjects. In the 1956 version of *The Ten Commandments*, Cecil B. DeMille, exploited the biblical accounts of the Exodus and Moses to portray Egyptians as villains and Hebrews as heroes (Serafy 2003:84) at a time when Egypt under Gamal Abdel-Nasser had won independence from the British and had vowed not to recognize the state of Israel and to support the rights of the Palestinians for their homeland. In the newer medium of television, a series of documentaries in the 1960s–1990s began to yield to sensational mythologizing of ancient Egypt. One such series, *Pharaohs and Kings* (1995), speculative and biased, conceived and fronted by David Rohl, presented Egypt as a sinister and eerie place (Schadla-Hall and Morris 2003). It also became fashionable in Hollywood movies and on TV to orientalize Egypt in a variety of ways, including the staging of lewd, sensuous women. Cleopatra became an icon of the oriental femme fatale.

Until the 1970s Egyptology maintained a peculiar position in academia, refusing to interact actively with either the social sciences (Weeks 1979) or the physical and natural sciences (Säve-Söderbergh 1976). The Egyptian past has been reduced to the non-contextualized aesthetics of art and architecture and the unending discourse on "peculiar" magic, the cult of the dead, ritual, and religion, with references to pyramids, mummies, tombs, and temples. There is hardly any interest in the scope and perspectives of Egyptian knowledge, technology, and sciences. Also, there is neither a serious attempt to show how Egyptian knowledge has been perpetuated in European civilization nor a keen interest to expound or explore the intricate subject of the relationship of Greek philosophy and Egyptian Wisdom. Having appropriated the decipherment of Egyptian texts as its founding charter, Egyptology has even resisted an integration of archaeology in its paradigmatic scheme (Bietak 1979; O'Connor 1990). Texts are interrogated to contribute to a construction of "cultural history" based on a dynastic sequence of kings and pharaohs, a parochial perspective that has not yielded, except in a few rare exceptions, to an examination of the social dynamics of Egyptian civilization. In the use of archaeological interpretation for nationalistic purposes Egypt is not an exception (Kohl 1998), but Egyptologists have contributed especially to the perpetuation of a mythical discontinuity between ancient Egypt and modern Egypt (El-Daly 2003b:148). Ancient Egypt has thus been encapsulated as an "ahistorical" fossil – the exclusive preserve of Western scholarship to the extent that Egyptians who aspired to become Egyptologists were systematically dissuaded from doing so (Reid 1985, 2002).

The manipulation of national/colonial memories in modern society is most evident in school teaching and in the media (now expanding beyond movies and television to websites). Not unlike professional historians, Egyptologists' function, whether conscious or subconscious, is, more often than they realize, less to analyze the "pastness" of the past than to give an authoritative seal of approval to the preoccupations and self-legitimization of the dominant elite (cf. Fentress and Wickham 1994:127).

Egyptomemes and the West

Egypt remains as mysterious, fascinating, and captivating as ever. I would argue that today we are witnessing another turn in the reformulation of Egypt and the cultural capital that has agglutinated around it over 2000 years. A proliferation of stories, anecdotes, memorabilia, and other material mementos have been integrated in the cultural fabric of European cultures and intellectual epistemes encompassing the full range from rationalism to esotericism. No longer just the subject of scholarly pursuits, *Egyptomemes* (ideas and constellation of ideas related to or affiliated with ancient Egypt) are now marketable items in consumer-oriented societies. The U.S. led the way by using the occasion of erecting an Egyptian obelisk (Needle) in New York to advertise a certain brand of needle and thread (Hassan 2003:64–65, fig. 2.40). The success with which Egyptomemes are propagated and perpetuated by successive generations is not on account of the abstract notions of Egyptian thought or wisdom, but rather by the emotive and affective aspects of the various cultural productions of ancient Egypt. In addition, the complex tapestry of Egyptian civilization, and its rich intellectual and social fabric, its historical transformations and transitions have repeatedly been reduced to a few prominent iconic images, texts, and formulae. The reduced, distorted, and abbreviated versions of ancient Egypt become a historical mask through which the present is viewed and imagined (Anderson 1992).

The ideas and practices of ancient Egypt are psychologically potent and engaging because they deal with anxieties, fears, aspirations, and hopes that cross-cut cultural boundaries and ethnic divides. Such potent, emotionally engaging elements include death, birth, illness, and harm, life after death, control over chaos, mitigation of loss, love, and curiosity. These elements are reinforced by captivating genres of discourse that vary from biblical anecdotes to fantasy fiction, non-fiction, and conspiracy theories (Wynn 2008). The emotional appeal of Egyptian memes is enhanced by practices that range from secret rituals (namely Freemasonry) to theatrical performances, musical scores, and Hollywood movies (Hall 1965; Leadbeater 1986; MacDonald and Rice 2003; Piatigorsky 1999). The association of Egypt with death and immortality leads to the use of Egyptian motifs, such as obelisks, in many cemeteries in Europe and all across the United States (Brier 2004). Mummification has a transcultural appeal because of the primacy of death in human thoughts. However, with a mounting interest in "horror" as a genre of modern European "entertainment," the mummies have become a notorious element of the legacy of ancient Egypt.

Linked cognitively with death are the practices of transcultural social significance such as conception/sterility, healing, and protection from illness and harm. Egyptian wisdom is not just a matter of rarified metaphysical speculation, it is also believed to be of immense utilitarian benefit. Egyptian medicine and magic are means by which people hope to overcome debilitating diseases and undertake actions and gain control over the world. Magic (Pinch 1994) played a prominent role in the medical texts of the New Kingdom (Hornung 2001:56). Magical love charms were also very common in the Greco-Roman world. Isis as a transfiguration of Hathor is the goddess of love, happiness, music, and dance. This association of the Egyptian goddess with the pleasures of life is another hook by which Egypt became entangled in the web of cultures across the ages. Any casual search of the Internet will reveal how the lore of Isis is connected with both wisdom and pleasure. A website under the title "Isisbooks" provides a series of books on love, healing and sexuality, love potions, and love herbs (www.isisbooks.com). Upon placing an order you will be sent a free love spell.

Commercializing Ancient Egypt

The media and the burgeoning tourist industry select and iconicize a few super-kings and -queens (Tutankhamun, Ramesses II, and less so Akhenaten, with Hatshepsut, Nefertiti, and Cleopatra as female celebrities). In addition, a selection of monuments, namely the Pyramids, the Sphinx and Abu Simbel, became the hallmarks of tourist brochures. As Egyptologists and Egypt's Supreme Council of Antiquities appropriate ancient Egypt and leave modern Egypt to its wretched inhabitants, the tourists are encapsulated in a bubble that minimizes their interaction with the natives. This has come to the fore in debates on the recent relocation of the inhabitants of the village of Qurna, and the subsequent destruction of most of the houses built over the Tombs of the Nobles. Addressing the complex problems of tomb robbery, damage by waste water, and aggressive sales methods, considered as harassment by many tourists, the authorities provided a sweeping solution that, however, also destroyed a part of the history and cultural landscape of the West Bank of Luxor, and the informal economy of the local population producing and selling souvenirs (Van der Spek 2008).

Ancient Egypt is fast succumbing to a bizarre parody of its various historical constructions (MacDonald and Rice 2003). In movies, commercials, and tourist brochures, ancient Egypt is trivialized and debased. Tourism and the industry of art and entertainment are robbing this generation as well as future generations of the fruits of knowledge of one of the world's great civilizations. Ramesses, Nefertiti, and Cleopatra are fast becoming "trade-marks" in commercial enterprises (Hassan 1994:664). We have lost sight of Egypt so many times and have cast its character in the theater of history in various roles ranging from Hermes, a champion of wisdom, to Aïda in an opera about love and nationalism, but now we risk reducing Egypt to statuettes of cats and lunatic fabrications to sell books and produce TV "documentaries."

Towards a Theory of Cultural Memory

My own position consists of a nested explanatory strategy that centers upon influential agents (with the potential to command communication and action) in society who are the inheritors of a socially constructed past, and who are dynamically engaged in reworking their social milieu to further their own views, position, or gains. Such agents are the source of "innovations" and the masters of social memory. Although there is most likely an element of repressed personal and social memories in the mind of each person, there seems to be also a dynamic interplay between memory and inputs from encounters with the present. Such encounters entail opportunities, fears, and anxieties that may reshape, delete, or restructure memory. Influential agents in a society may succeed in creating a hegemonic memory by various means of persuasion. They rarely, however, succeed in totally eliminating rival or "neutral" memories. Even if they succeed, there are always other societies where rival memories may thrive or merely persist in the form of secret lore, beliefs held by a marginalized "ethnic" or "occupational" group. At certain points in time, group may come in contact and the memories suppressed or deleted in one society may flow from another society through various mechanisms of cultural transmission.

The written word in books and tomes curated and stored in libraries is one of the great legacies of ancient Egypt. The Egyptians venerated writing and books and regarded them as one of the most fitting legacies of a person. Libraries, from those that were attached to Egyptian temples to the Library of Alexandria, the libraries of Greece, Baghdad, Cairo, and medieval Europe, and our own libraries, hold treasures of past knowledge. However, libraries, as Montaigne remarked, are places of collective forgetfulness; their value lies in the chances they provided for serendipity – the discovery of unsuspected pieces of forgotten knowledge (*Essais*, ii, ix cited in Fentress and Wickam 1994:15). Forgotten or suppressed knowledge may also survive outside libraries and the dominant modes of discourse in oral folk traditions and practices. It is in such traditions that French-educated Germans looked for "memories" to fortify the idea of a German *"Kultur"* and a sense of national identity when they became disenchanted with Napoleon's ideals. Egypt thus survived because it was often referred to in both sacred and profane books.

Introducing the topic of social construction of the past, Bond and Gilliam (1994) posit that there are periods during which the dominant rendering of the past ceases to be efficacious. Other social constructions emerge as contenders for the past with their own interpretations and counter-proposals. The constructions of the past, old and new, are brought into the arenas of politics of knowledge. The past, already socially constructed before any one confronts it, may be re-appropriated, negated, modified, or tweaked to serve individuals and groups in their claims for political power or economic gain. The past may be deployed to assert an identity, legitimize a political agenda, or win support for economic projects.

The potency of the past lies in objects, images, and narrative accounts (oral or textual) that have gained a prominent or sacred status in the social memory as elements of ancient traditions, sacred ritual, or secular practices. Intellectuals play a key role in the construction, appropriation, sanctification, and presentation of the past. My views on this converge with those of Gramsci: "Every social group, coming into existence on the original terrain of an essential function in the world of economic production, creates together with itself, organically one or more strata of intellectuals which give it homogeneity and an awareness of its own function not only in the economic but also in the social and political fields" (Gramsci 1971:5). I would, however, extend Gramsci's notions to those of any major cultural development, whether religious, sectarian, ethnic, or occupational. Religious movements, the "revival" of ethnic identities, or even social movements create (organically) together with their activities intellectuals who give it character, temperament, disposition, and image. Egypt was at the center of the encounter between the intellectuals of Christianity and the "traditional" intellectuals of the classical world (see below). The elaboration of Jewish identity was also inexorably linked by Jewish scholars to a specific social construction of Egypt (Assmann 1997).

Beyond History: Into the Future

Embedded in successive hegemonic cultural paradigms of European civilization from Hellenistic Hermeticism to consumerism, the parodies of Egypt form a genealogical chain of transformations that now structure and inform our own notions of ancient Egypt. They inform a broad spectrum of conceptions that bolster and substantiate a broad range of schemas (a structured configuration of related ideas and practices) that currently contribute to the transformation and re-appropriation of Egyptian texts and icons either for personal satisfaction, academic achievement, or corporate profits. All such schemas, from New Age mysticism (Picknett and Prince 2003) to Egyptology, are embroiled in European hegemonic paradigms.

To counteract the onslaught of "Egyptomania" (Brier 2004), Egyptologists ought to seek a genuine engagement with the public to foster an appreciation of those aspects of Egyptian civilization that may positively contribute to our appreciation of art, politics, and knowledge and to our understanding of ourselves and our place in the world as human beings. The pull of ancient Egypt and its powerful icons is useful for gaining the attention of the public to explore with them the deeper meanings of writing, art, and the rituals of death and resurrection. We may recall that we are still in the grip of "national" memories, which have been tinged with "colonial" memories, and that such memories have been "organically" developed and manipulated in rhetorical discourses directed at internal or external opponents, which is also evident in the nationalistic/colonialist domains of Egyptology within Europe and vis-à-vis Egypt (cf. Hassan 1995; Reid 1997). Accordingly, Egyptologists should begin to critically re-examine the scope and structure of Egyptological discourse and academic curricula and dissertation topics in order to guard against the misuse of Egyptian past for the perpetuation of inequality, injustice, and neo-colonial exploitative strategies.

We have emerged from the twentieth century with serious environmental, economic, and social problems (Ponting 1998). The current situation provides fertile grounds for alternate ideologies that aim to resist the perceived hegemony of the West (Tibi 1998). As long as ancient Egypt is a Western preoccupation and enterprise, many Egyptians will not be able to reconcile their worldview with the Pharaonic past. On the other hand, there is the danger of a naïve call for "Pharaonism," isolating Egypt from its Arabic circle and rich historical involvement in the affairs and civilization of the Arab world. The massacre at Deir el-Bahri in 1997, when a small group of middle-class Egyptian youths gunned down mostly Swiss tourists and Egyptian guards and policemen (Hassan forthcoming), is a ghastly reminder of the dark forces that exploit ignorance and fuel fanaticism (cf. Aziz 1995). The question perhaps is not who owns the past, but how we can make use of the past to redress inequalities and promote peace and prosperity without the blinkers of chauvinistic nationalism or the conceit and arrogance that comes with political power. In Egypt and elsewhere, economic and political forces have rapidly destabilized traditional systems, seriously dislocating and disintegrating the forces that have created the cultural identities of the past (Friedman 1994:249). *Ad hoc* and expedient psychological mechanisms to restore coherence and mental security entail the revival of imagined pasts, violent antagonism with an "Other" to one's acquired identity, affiliation with cults and disciplined groups, and narcissism. The "past" as a source for legitimizing identities may lead to factions within society (e.g. between those who choose a strictly "Coptic" heritage and those who develop a strong, fanatical adherence to an Islamic tradition).

The road ahead must lie in a reconsideration of the information to be gained from a study of ancient Egypt for the benefit of humanity, enriching the human experience by explaining how, barely out of the Stone Age, small communities on the banks of the Nile succeeded in developing a sustainable political system that lasted for more than 3000 years. Egyptologists should aspire to revise their research agenda and teach curricula which focus on the social and cultural dynamics of Egyptian civilization, with an emphasis on an understanding of the social processes by which Egypt was transformed several times throughout its long history from most ancient Egypt to the present. Policy makers and the public need to be informed of the factors that contributed to the special character of Egyptian knowledge and the social context of Egyptian worldview. The philosophical reflections of Egyptians on ethics, good governance, and society surely deserve a prominent place in our map of ancient Egypt. Egyptology needs to become actively engaged not just with current theories in archeology and anthropology, but with the new directions in history, cultural studies, the social sciences, and the humanities.

REFERENCES

Anderson, B. 1992 Imagined Communities. New York: Verso.

Assmann, J. 1989 Mâat: L'Égypte Pharaonique et l'idée de justice sociale. Paris: Julliard.

Assmann, J. 1997 Moses the Egyptian: The Memory of Egypt in Western Monotheism. Cambridge, MA: Harvard University Press.

Aziz, H. 1995 Understanding Attacks on Tourists in Egypt. Tourism Management 16(2):91–95.

Bietak, M. 1979 The Present State of Egyptian Archaeology. Journal of Egyptian Archaeology 65:156–160.

Bond, G. C., and A. Gilliam 1994 Introduction. *In* Social Construction of the Past: Representation of Power. G. C. Bond and A. Gilliam, eds. Pp. 1–22. London: Routledge.

Brier, B. 2004 Egyptomania! Archaeology. January/February:16–22.

Brier, B. 1994 Egyptian Mummies. New York: William Morrow and Co.

Currid, J. D. 1997 Ancient Egypt and the Old Testament. Grand Rapids, MI: Baker Books.

El-Daly, O. 2003a Ancient Egypt in Medieval Arabic Writings. *In* The Wisdom of Egypt: Changing Views through the Ages. P. Ucko and T. Champion, eds. Pp. 39–63. London: UCL Press.

El-Daly, O. 2003b What Do Tourists Learn of Egypt? *In* Consuming Ancient Egypt. S. MacDonald and M. Rice, eds. Pp. 137–150. London: UCL Press.

Fentress, J., and C. Wickham 1994 Social Memory. Oxford: Blackwell.

Friedman, J. 1994 Cultural Identity and Global Process. London: Sage.

Gramsci, A. 1971 Selection from the Prison Notebooks. Q. Hoare and G. Nowell-Smith, trans. and eds. New York: International Publishers.

Grant, R. M. 1986 Gods and the One God. Philadelphia: The Westminster Press.

Haarmann, U. 1980 Regional Sentiment in Medieval Islamic Egypt. Bulletin of the School of Oriental and African Studies 43:55–66.

Hall, M. P. 1965 Freemasonry of the Ancient Egyptians. Los Angeles: Philosophical Research Society.

Hassan, F. A. 1994 Review of Romer, J., and E. (1993), The Rape of Tutankhamun. Antiquity 68(260): 68:663–664.

Hassan, F. A. 1995 African Archaeology: The Call of the Future. African Affairs 98:393–406.

Hassan, F. A. 1998. Memorabilia: Archaeological Materiality and National Identity in Egypt. *In* Archaeology under Fire: Nationalism, Politics and Heritage in the Eastern Mediterranean and the Middle East. L. Meskell, ed. Pp. 200–216. London: Routledge.

Hassan, F. A. 2003 Imperialist Appropriations of Egyptian Obelisks. *In* Views of Ancient Egypt since Napoleon Bonaparte: Imperialism, Colonialism and Modern Appropriations. D. Jeffreys, ed. Pp. 19–68. London: UCL Press.

Hassan, F. A. forthcoming. Terror at the Temple. Unpublished manuscript.

Haycock, D. B. 2003 Ancient Egypt in 17th- and 18th-century England. *In* The Wisdom of Egypt: Changing Views through the Ages. P. Ucko and T. Champion, eds. Pp. 133–160. London: UCL Press.

Highet, G. 1976 The Classical Tradition: Greek and Roman influences on Western Literature. Oxford: Oxford University Press. (Originally 1949.)

Hornung, E. 2001 The Secret Lore of Egypt: Its Impact on the West. Ithaca, NY: Cornell University Press.

Kemp, B. J. 2006 Ancient Egypt: Anatomy of a Civilization. 2nd edition. London, New York: Routledge.

Kohl, P. L. 1998 Nationalism and Archaeology: On the Constructions of Nations and the Reconstructions of the Remote Past. Annual Anthropological Review 27:223–246.

Kravachok, A. 2002. Paganism and Christianity: From Intellectual Struggle to Armed Conflict (in Arabic by K. Lihdo). Damascus: Dar el-Hasad.

Leadbeater, C. W. 1986 Freemasonry and Its Ancient Mystic Rites. New York: Gramercy Books.

Lemche, N. P. 1998 The Israelites in History and Tradition (Library of Ancient Israel). Louisville, KY: Westminster John Knox Press; London: SPCK.

Lloyd, A. B. 1988 Herodotus' Account of Pharaonic History. Historia 37:22–53.

MacDonald, S., and M. Rice, eds 2003 Consuming Ancient Egypt. London: UCL Press.

Modrzejewski, J. M. 1995 The Jews of Egypt from Rameses II to Emperor Hadrian. Edinburgh: T & T. Clark.

Moret, A. 1972 The Nile and Egyptian Civilization. London: Routledge and Kegan Paul. (Originally 1927.)

New, J. F. H. 1969 Renaissance and Reformation: A Short History. New York: Wiley.

O'Connor, D. 1990 Egyptology and Archaeology: An African Perspective. *In* A History of African Archaeology. P. Robertshaw, ed. Pp. 236–251. London: J. Currey.

Piatigorsky, A. 1999 Freemasonry. London: Harvill Press.

Picknett, L., and C. Prince 2003 Alternative Egypts. *In* Consuming Ancient Egypt. S. MacDonald and M. Rice, eds. Pp. 175–193. London: UCL Press.

Pinch, G. 1994. Magic in Ancient Egypt. London: British Museum Press.

Ponting, C. 1998 Progress and Barbarism: The World in the Twentieth Century. London: Chatto & Windus.

Reid, D. M. 1985 Indigenous Egyptology: The Decolonization of a Profession? Journal of the American Oriental Society 105:233–246.

Reid, D. M. 1997 Nationalizing the Pharaonic Past: Egyptology, Imperialism and Egyptian Nationalism, 1922–1952. *In* Rethinking Nationalism in the Arab Middle East. I. Gershoni and J. Jankowski, eds. Pp. 127–149. New York: Columbia University Press.

Reid, D. M. 2002 Whose Pharaohs? Archaeology, Museums, and Egyptian National Identity from Napoleon to World War I. Berkeley: University of California Press.

Säve-Söderbergh, T. 1976 Egyptology. Acta Universitatis Upsaliensis 5:1–11.

Schadla-Hall, T., and G. Morris 2003 Ancient Egypt on the Small Screen – From Fact to Fiction in the UK. *In* Consuming Ancient Egypt. S. MacDonald and M. Rice, eds. Pp. 195–215. London: UCL Press.

Schaff, P., and H. Wace, eds 1890–1900 Select Library of the Nicene and Post-Nicene Fathers. 2nd series. New York: Charles Scribner's Sons (includes the church histories of Eusebius, Socrates, Sozomen, and Theodoret, and selected works of Gregory of Nyssa, Basil, Jerome, Gennadius, and others).

Schnapp, A. 1997 The Discovery of the Past. New York: Abrahams.

Serafy, S. 2003. Egypt in Hollywood: Pharoahs of the Fifties. *In* Consuming Ancient Egypt. S. MacDonald and M. Rice, eds. Pp. 77–86. London: UCL Press.

Takács, S. A. 1995 Isis and Sarapis in the Roman World. Leiden: E. J. Brill.

Tibi, B. 1998 The Challenge of Fundamentalism: Political Islam and the New World Disorder. Berkeley: University of California Press.

Van der Spek, K. 2008 Faked *Antikas* and "Modern Antiques": The Production and Marketing of Tourist Art in the Theban Necropolis. Journal of Social Archaeology 8:163–189.

Waddell, W. G. 1940 Manetho. F. E. Robbins, trans. London: Loeb Classical Library.

Walker, J. 2003 Acquisitions at the British Museum, 1998. *In* Consuming Ancient Egypt. S. MacDonald and M. Rice, eds. Pp. 101–109. London: UCL Press.

Walsh, J. P. M. 1987 The Mighty from Their Thrones. Philadelphia: Fortress Press.

Weeks, K., ed. 1979 Egypt and the Social Sciences: Five Studies. Cairo: American University in Cairo Press.

Witt, R. 1971 Isis in the Ancient World. Baltimore, London: Johns Hopkins University Press.

Wood, M. 1998 The Use of the Pharaonic Past in Modern Egyptian Nationalism. Journal of the American Research Center in Egypt 35:179–196.

Wynn, L. L. 2008 Shape Shifting Lizard People, Israelite Slaves, and Other Theories of Pyramid Building: Notes on Labor, Nationalism, and Archaeology in Egypt. Journal of Social Archaeology 8:272–295.

Youssef, A. 1991 Misr fi Al-Quran wa Al-Sunnah. 3rd revised edition. Cairo: Dar Al-Maʿarif. (Originally 1973.)

15

Epilogue

Eternal Egypt Deconstructed

Willeke Wendrich

History is extremely visible in Egypt, not only in the form of relief-covered temple walls, and impressive engineering feats such as pyramids and monolithic obelisks, but also in artifacts of organic materials startlingly well preserved in the arid desert climate. Eternity and death are closely linked in the accidental or mediated preservation of bodies, while tomb interiors, such as that of Kha, which appear to preserve a complete elite household, including bed sheets, clothing, and food provide a very tangible link to the distant past (Schiaparelli 2008). Temples have been transformed into churches, monasteries, and mosques, forming the religious centers for worship of the gods of ancient Egypt, Christianity, and Islam, creating a sense of continuity in the ever-changing cultural landscape. Egyptians have always expressed awe for their long history and very visible historical remains. Egyptians own their past and consider it to be something distant and wondrous and at the same time very much part of their present. The seeming continuity has led to the myth that Egypt is unchanged and to this day represents an endless, perpetual culture. It is a sentiment typically expressed in grand sweeping statements and overview works. "Eternal Egypt" is an enticing concept that has been selected as the title of a book representing Egyptian history from prehistory to Alexander the Great (Montet 1969), as a catalogue of a selection of objects from the British Museum (Russmann and James 2001), and for an online assortment of information on ancient Egypt created by IBM, the Center for the Documentation of Cultural and Natural Heritage (an Egyptian non-profit organization), and Egypt's Supreme Council of Antiquities.

Especially in popular literature, ancient Egypt is often presented as a monolithic society, without differentiation or change. Statements that "the ancient Egyptians" considered, performed, thought, made, knew, or did certain things are very common. Egyptian history is, however, an amalgamation of 5000 years of development and change, with regional and social variation (Lehner, Grajetzki, this volume), which cannot be compressed into one people ("the Egyptians"), or one era ("ancient Egypt"). Such a wholesale characterization of

Egypt's uniqueness, homogeneity, and continuity is a selective representation of the cultural expressions and the sources from which we attempt to construct these. Considered up close, there are several forms of Eternal Egypt, which partly overlap, but have been devised through a naïve application of Egyptological and ethnoarchaeological approaches stressing a simple form of cultural continuity.

Much of the myth of Eternal Egypt is created by Egyptologists, who have taken ancient Egyptian sources at face value, without critically considering the audience and purpose of texts and visual culture. The statue which graces the cover of this volume is a case in point. It is a Late Period bronze, 26 cm high (British Museum EA 11498), depicting a divine being, one of the Bau of Pe, sporting the body of a youthful man and the head of a falcon. The figure is depicted kneeling, with a clenched fist in the air, and the other one in front of the chest, in the celebratory *henu* position. Together with the jackal-headed Bau of Nekhen, the Bau of Pe are the ancestors of the king and the gesture is used to greet the newborn sun god, or, in mythical parallel, the king at coronation. The statue dates to the Late Period (probably after 600 BCE), but reflects a concept that is known from the Old Kingdom Pyramid Texts (Frankfort 1978:93–95), as well as, for instance, the New Kingdom coronation of Ramesses II (Shorter 1934). As highlighted by Richards and by Wilson (this volume), the emphasis on cultural continuity in Pharaonic Egypt was in many cases closely linked with legitimation. The permanence of power is represented as an inevitable continuity of the same fundamental structures of Egyptian kingship. It brings to the fore that recent developments to incorporate more explicit theory and methods into literary studies is needed to identify an author's objectives and the audience that is addressed (Loprieno 1996). Similarly, the representation of Egypt as surrounded by chaos and potentially adverse powers serves the great emphasis on maintaining order, the ideological foundation of kingship (Schneider, this volume). Most of the textual and visual sources have been created for and were received by a specific social class, involved in the cultural center of the country, and reflect the ideal of durability and permanence of power.

Cultural continuity is also the central consideration in efforts of present-day Egyptians to celebrate their great ancestry. Copts especially have embraced ancient Egypt, as expressed by first names such as Isis, Ramesses, or Nefertiti, and often the not so subtle claim that the Coptic minority represents the true Egyptians, while the Muslim majority derives from the invading, and thus foreign, force. Another often-heard assertion is that the "true" heirs of ancient Egypt are the *fellahin* (famers) of Upper Egypt, witnessed by their physique and their backward way of life. There have been many attempts to trace cultural continuity in present-day Egyptian culture. An early explicit comparison was made by Winifred Blackman (1927) in a chapter following her ethnography of the *fellahin*, in which she systematically compares ancient and modern phenomena, such as those between the concept of *ka* and the *kareen/kareena* mentioned in Chapter 11. The method is problematic, because it compares the ethnographic description with a "flattened history," devoid of any historical development or social variation. At the same time, Blackman stresses the similarities, but is silent about the many differences. More importantly, neither the ancient, nor the modern phenomena are considered in their historical context. Efforts to compare ancient and modern religious phenomena such as the ancient Opet Festival, in which the bark shrines with the gods Amun, Mut, and Khonsu were carried by priests, and the present-day Mulid of the Islamic saint Abu Hagag likewise stress the similarities of the two festivals without regarding their context, the 2000 years of development of the Opet Festival, and the changes within Islam in a period of almost 1400 years. The suggestion of continuity, two religious festivals in the same geographical location both involving the carrying of boats, is not more than that. In an article on ancient Egyptian survivals in Coptic Christianity, Naguib (2008) gives a well-balanced account of the development of the study of "survivals," from tracing formal similarities, to stressing both continuity and change, to considering tradition as fluid, in constant flux and development, in which the meaning changes, even if the form might be the same. Interesting studies, such as those by Haikal (2007) on the survival of ancient Egyptian words or rituals, through Coptic into Arabic, and El-Shohoumi's (2004) comparison of the organization of present-day Islamic cemetery workers with the ancient Egyptian priesthood responsible for treating the dead, gain in value if constructed within a theoretical framework such as offered by Naguib.

The discussions on the use and abuse of ethnoarchaeology equally bear on the image of Eternal Egypt. When applied to a specific research question, the study of modern-day society from an archaeological perspective is extremely useful, but has obtained a negative reputation because of naïve and overly simplistic applications (David and Kramer 2001; Wylie 1985). This is mostly due to either a too formal, or a too simplistic use of analogy, without taking into account the historical and cultural contexts (Wylie 2002). As soon as similarities are considered as static "remnants" of an equally frozen ancient society, the comparison leads us astray, rather than helps our understanding of the variability in ancient, as well as present-day, society. The "direct historical approach" has been used as an excuse to propose that continuity is more prevalent than change, a stance that negates development and denies the inhabitants of both ancient and present-day Egypt the agency for differentiation and transformation.

If we accept that tradition is in constant flux, and is reinterpreted and understood differently depending on the circumstances, then we should interpret our Egyptian sources within their specific contexts and refrain from filling in the gaps with more explicit sources from much later periods. That is what the more recent approaches in Egyptian archaeology do quite explicitly and effectively, as is reflected in the chapters in this volume. The result is, on the one hand, an increase in academic doubt: the oblique references to the Osirian cycle from the Pyramid Texts cannot be interpreted in the light of the lengthy and explicit late New Kingdom narratives of the Contendings of Horus and Seth (Papyrus Chester Beatty I). On the other hand this approach forces us to work in a much more interdisciplinary fashion in which archaeology has its own voice within the different approaches. Rather than being ancillary to historical or textual interpretations (Andrén 1998; Kemp 1984), archaeology has its own narrative, as demonstrated in the previous chapters. Rather than the powerless claim that "archaeology" supports an argument, the authors, who all have extensive experience in interpreting material culture in its context, have shown that the archaeological interpretation regularly is at odds with, and sometimes completely contradicts, other sources of information. These different results are important, because they give us a means to tease out the dynamics of social and intellectual change. Archaeology provides a steady stream of historical modifications, the excavations of the workers' cemeteries at Amarna being a sobering case in point (Rose 2006). In Chapter 1 I outlined that not only ancient Egyptian culture, but also the interpretive layer of our understanding of segments of the society are in constant flux. This depends on the "available" information, and for the larger part on our particular interest and questions. The recent, often grudgingly acknowledged attention to multivocality, which gives voice to non-scholarly debates and the interests of the local population, non-professionals, tourists, and other stake-holders, illustrates vividly that alternative viewpoints are always present, albeit often suppressed. In the case of ancient Egypt, where the percentage of literacy was an estimated 2 percent, archaeology has proven the only means to find traces of villagers, children, women, farmers, and foreigners. In a sense they provide us with a glimpse of ancient multivocality, where most of the textual sources, even those of the privileged villagers of Deir el-Medina, represent a very particular point of view.

REFERENCES

Andrén, A. 1998 Between Artifacts and Texts: Historical Archaeology in Global Perspective. New York: Plenum Press.

Blackman, W. S. 1927 The Fellahin of Upper Egypt. Cairo: The American University in Cairo Press.

David, N., and C. Kramer 2001 Ethnoarchaeology in Action. New York: Cambridge University Press.

El-Shohoumi, N. 2004 Der Tod im Leben: Eine vergleichende Analyse altägyptischer und rezenter ägyptischer Totenbräuche. Vienna: Verlag der Östereichischen Akademie der Wissenschaften.

Frankfort, H. 1978 Kingship and the Gods: A Study of Ancient Near Eastern Religion as the Integration of Society and Nature. Chicago: University of Chicago Press.

Haikal, F. 2007 Spiritualité égyptienne: Transmissions et évolution. Bulletin de la société française d'égyptologie 168:12–48.

Kemp, B. J. 1984 In the Shadow of Texts: Archaeology in Egypt. Archaeological Review from Cambridge 3(2):19–28.

Loprieno, A. 1996 Ancient Egyptian Literature: History and Forms. Leiden, New York: E. J. Brill.

Montet, P. 1969 Eternal Egypt. D. Weightman, trans. New York: Praeger.

Naguib, S.-A. 2008 Survivals of Pharaonic Religious Practices in Contemporary Coptic Christianity. In UCLA Encyclopedia of Egyptology. J. Dieleman and W. Wendrich, eds. Los Angeles: UCLA. http://repositories.cdlib.org/nelc/uee/1008.

Rose, J. C. 2006 Paleopathology of the Commoners at Tell Amarna, Egypt, Akhenaten's Capital City. Memórias do Instituto Oswaldo Cruz, Rio de Janeiro 101(Supll. II):73–76.

Russmann, E. R., and T. G. H. James 2001 Eternal Egypt: Masterworks of Ancient Art from the British Museum. London: British Museum Publications.

Schiaparelli, E. 2008 The Intact Tomb of the Architect Kha in the Necropolis of Thebes. Rome: Adarte. (Originally 1927.)

Shorter, A. W. 1934 Reliefs Showing the Coronation of Ramses II. Journal of Egyptian Archaeology 20:18–19.

Wylie, M. A. 1985 The Reaction against Analogy. Advances in Archaeological Method and Theory 8:63–111.

Wylie, M. A. 2002 Thinking from Things: Essays in the Philosophy of Archaeology. Berkeley: University of California Press.

Index

Page numbers in *italics* denote illustrations.

Printed and bound by CPI Group (UK) Ltd, Croydon, CR0 4YY